Richard Lee Cook

HELL'S HALF ACRE

The True Story from the Fire and Rain Chronicles.

WORKBOOK PRESS LLC
187 E Warm Springs Rd,
Suite B285, Las Vegas, NV 89119, USA

Website:https://workbookpress.com/
Hotline:1-888-818-4856
Email: admin@workbookpress.com

Ordering Information:
Quantity sales. Special discounts are available on quantity purchases by corporations, associations, and others. For details, contact the publisher at the address above.

Library of Congress Control Number:
ISBN-13: 978-1-960752-84-0 (Paperback Version)
978-1-960752-85-7 (Digital Version)

REV. DATE: 04/27/2023

The Horror and Madness Up On
"*Hell's Half Acre*"
A True Story
From The
FIRE and *RAIN*
Chronicles

"Where the souls of the living dead are now nothing more than earth-bound spirits. At the least shadowed memories endlessly wandering in the darkness of despair and hopelessness. Bound by destiny's shackles in an abyss of a blackened pitch. Rarely does a glimmer of light slice through the dense curtain of madness. One survivor still lives. He fought and battled horrors starting at age three. Now he tells the story of an ill-fated family. Telling their life and death moments through poetry, prose, and short stories. Metaphorically laden, the truths lie between and within the battle scars branded in the minds and bodies. Each family member wore a scarlet letter throughout their lives in a small town called Frederick, Maryland. So much history, the home of "Barbara Fritsche." She yelled from her

window on Patrick Street, "Shoot at this old gray head if you must! But spare thy country's flag."

Many truths were tarnished and hidden over the years that became corroded within the consumption of abuse, filth, and vulgarity. Tenderness along with a heartfelt innocence was never experienced in all the days of our lives. Very little love, joy, and or happiness was ever exchanged between the four of us. For the three of us "Fear" was the barrier to normalcy. We were encased within four walls of an abusive fire up on, "Hell's Half Acre." One's memories are tarnished beyond repair. The pain hurt, and regret dulled the shiniest of precious medals. Our lives were like standing in a raging fire under a delude of roaring rain. The rain put the fire out long enough to feel yourself being pulled under the rising waters. You watched your possibilities sink right before your eyes. My mother drowned over and over in a twenty-six-year marriage. My sister met with early death and I was scorned, misread, and bullied to the point of suicide twice in my life, each without success. Yet here I am alone in my later years by choice, I suppose? Who knows, maybe destiny is the real deal.

Since the age of five years old, I have been very aware of several dark "Entities" that have haunted, mocked, and at times drawn me into their darkness. I refer to them as "The Shadows". Still, now at sixty-eight years of age, I often see my "Shadows" always in the distance. I have acknowledged one that has followed me through my life continuously. I have seen and experienced the horrors created by these "Entities" that have shackled themselves to my soul. They have a taunting force that suggests and invite you into their world of dark madness. Whispering lies you long to hear. It makes you weak beyond all measures. Making the "Art of Darkness" seems like "Peace in the Valley". In any case, darkness chained my mother, my sister, and myself as prisoners to the horrors and the madness that consumed us daily and nightly up on "Hell's Half Acre."

I put before you the beginning of what I call, "The Fire and Rain Chronicles." Written about the trials and tribulations that plagued our lives. I am the only living survivor from "Hell's Half Acre." Since 1970, when I made my exit from that hellhole, "The Shadows" that made their presents known to me have followed me ever since. Haunting my every decision, my every movement, and every step that I have taken throughout my life. The horrors and the evil are real. Even after my time is completed here on Mother Earth, I will face the demon shadows that have claimed my soul at a very early age. I have maintained some form of sanity through it all. More than I care to accept. There were those close to my heart that took their own lives. I understand their hearts and minds. Each affected me more than family or friends have ever known. Then there were my own "rationalizations" for the two attempts to take my own life as I walked through my personal "Garden of Good and Evil." **"The Shadows"** that I make mention quite often, are very real. They remind me of the **"Seven Deadly Sins."** Many times, they have altered the paths I chose to travel...

It may be hard for many to accept or even comprehend that the darkness I experienced and still live through to this day is reality. It is more than insanity. It is more than the mind's creative concepts. Unless you have reached into the abyss of true darkness and or lived with an instrument of evil that manifests before your eyes, I can easily believe in your convictions against the idea. Let me ask you a question. Is it impossible to believe or try to believe that it could raise **"Possibilities"?** I tell you, my friends, living in and with the truth, up on "Hell's Half Acre" didn't leave room for any **"Possibilities"** ...

The Prelude

Lee and Bonnie

Upon these pages are the collective chronicles of four family members that once existed and lived in a world of poverty, alcohol, and abuse beyond measure. The abuse, both physical and mental wasn't enough for this perpetrator. He bored his way to the very marrow of our souls. It struck with such force as it clawed at your spirit until it finally absorbed and digested all possibilities. Vanishing in a hideous laugh of mockery with your hopes, dreams, and the belief that things have got to be better somewhere out there. **"RIGHT?"** The deluge of verbal belittling was delivered on 24/7 bases. We believed this man was truly possessed by the evilest of **Hell's "Demons"**. Every other word from this man's mouth was filled with vulgarity so fowl, belittling with raw sexual overtures from his forked tongue of venomous lashings. Each fang of this snake injected a deadly toxin eating its way into your heart and soul. Dissolving what humanity, you may have had. Nearly always backed up with his **"law-of-the-land-Backhands"**. Skillfully administered by an individual that induced **"Fear"** as if it were serendipitously used throughout a twenty-six-year marriage to our mother and our youthful years up on *"Hell's Half Acre"*. He was supposed to be a so-called **"Husband"** and a **"Father."**

I was the firstborn in this second marriage for both my mother and father. The youngest living was my sister Bonnie. There is another sibling, a brother one year younger than I. He was given away at birth to my father's sister and her husband. Therefore, he never got to know or experience the harsh and brutal life we had to endure regularly. This demon/man forced his ways of thinking, his views, and his definitions of self-proclaimed **"LAWS"** throughout the years. This alcoholic-induced Demon constructed a world of dark mental imprisonments, managing us from birth. Developing over time with the charms of **"Sadistic Seductions"** if you will? Don't get me wrong about the brother we never got to know. He was certainly blessed and favored by the Gods as far as we were concerned! The truth was there was never going to be a relationship established *between us and him. There wasn't a bond established with the woman that gave him birth. My sister and I went through our lives void of caring about a sibling that never lived under the same roof. We simply concentrated on living, getting through the next twenty-four hours up on "Hell's Half Acre".*

My brother, how ironic now that I think about it. Even during our elementary school years, our paths never crossed. He and I attended the same junior high school. Seventh through ninth grades and never once had we passed one another through the hallways. Upon my ninth-grade graduation from "West Frederick Junior High School", a brand-new high school was opened in another part of our growing small town of Frederick, Maryland. It was fortunate that I was given the choice of which school to attend. "Frederick High School" or to start my tenth-grade year at "Governor Thomas Johnson High School". I chose the brand-new high school in the hope of a new and fresh start away from the unkind, tormentors and gang of bullies that made it their duty to lessen my worth as a human being. My home, my school, and some neighbors tore my heart apart. I wanted to live a life free of mental and physical abuse. Let's not forget the verbal lashing that belittled me daily, if not by the hour. I created a cage of lead around the only thing left of me. My "Spirit" had never flown with the Eagles. "Why can't I spread my wings? Why can't I fly free?" All I was capable of was running away physically and mentally. To a destination to nowhere...

During the summer of my ninth-grade year, I was thrown into a sinkhole in life. That summer was my "Invitation to Dance." Dad came home from work and was in another drunken rage. It was this night that he took his rage out on me. The reason for this assault was my defying his order for me to quit school. We three knew not to confront him, less one or all three of us would get hurt. Once again, he was destroying a dream of mine. I looked at mom sitting in her chair just feet away. Eye to eye she was signaling me to stand down. Just let it go. There was "NO WAY," I was going to watch him stomp the light out of my one chance to finish school. My eyes reflected on that decision to mom. She stood up moving herself to the edge of the chair. Meanwhile, dad was ranting and raving. Directing every filthy word in my direction. He took several steps toward me. I knew what was about to happen. I jumped up from my seated position on the sofa. My arms were stiff at my side, fists clenched. I yelled at the top of my lungs, "NO!" There before me, he was transforming like a "Jekyll and Hyde." His blood-shot blue eyes changed to a piercing red. There he stood. The demon gritted his teeth. Through those tartare spiked teeth, he growled, "BOY, did you say, "NO!" Once again, he demanded that I was to quit school and go to work with him in construction. I, in my fit of defiance filled with anger, screamed "FUCK YOU!" An Unholy Hell broke loose... With a single backhand swipe, I was slammed up against the wall. Like a "Hen on a June bug," he unleashed several more backhands and slaps to the face and head. Then he grabbed a handful of my blonde hair. Jerking me back and forth like a dog with a ragdoll. I finally conceded through bloody snot and a flood of terrified tears. If only to appease him and hopefully to stop the on-slot beating. I felt as though every inch of flesh on my body ignited in the fire. I could barely see straight. Distraught, weak, and defeated at the age of twelve. Of course, mom jumped up from her chair, screaming, "CHARLES, STOP, STOP!" It was as if he waited for mom to come to my aide. So many times, this scenario played out. Mom would sacrifice herself to defend her children. Once he was spent on energy. His transformation reverted to the slobbering drunk that wouldn't remember a damn thing he did. He'd step over to the door and take a beer-smelling piss. Stagger back through the carnage on his way to bed. Waking at sunrise to go to work as if nothing ever happened...

*That night was the beginning of the end for me. When I fell against the wall, I watched mom pick herself up. Falling back into her chair she started running her fingers through her long hair. With each swipe, she produced a wad of hair. I am watching the woman that put herself in the line of fire once again to divert him from killing Bonnie or me. I picked myself up. Racked with pain. Walked calmly toward the door leading out of that goddamn **"Den of Horrors"**. Each step I took toward freedom had a mounting fear he was behind me. The fear increased with each step. Causing my heart to pound harder. My mind was racing faster than my shoeless feet could pick them up and put them down... I'd had enough of the pain, enough of the building horrors that came out of nowhere. One way or the other I had to escape from "Hell's Half Acre". His drunken rampages weighed heavy on my mind and heart since age five. I staggered to the only place where I felt free with my thoughts and my dreams of a better place for me. I ran across the field of waist-high dry grass as fast as I could. I ran through the rows of the Raspberry Patch. I was running for my life. I had to reach my special place. It's where all was right, all was hidden from the chaos created by a dark, dark place consuming me. Crawling, grabbing clumps of grass to reach the high knob that overlooked three connecting fields of corn, wheat, and rye. This was my alone haven. A space where I'd dream of worlds that must exist out there somewhere. Standing alone staring up at the stars. Silent tears ran down my swollen cheeks. A warm breeze swirled about my bruised and battered body. The summer breeze felt as though a Guardian Angel's arms were gently wrapped around me. If only I had one. So, I wrapped my own bruised arms around myself as another warm summer breeze swirled about my battered body. It felt good! My mind often allowed me to create my special world. Then my emotions surfaced, and I slowly collapsed to the ground. Dawn was approaching and going back to the house would certainly give me pause! Catching my breath through exhausted tears, I muttered to the stars above, **"WHY?"** I turned my head to the right. Before I laid an old Mason Jar half-buried in the dirt. My attention was drawn to the taste of blood on my lips. Caused by the mixture of tears and blood draining into my mouth. The warm blood was flowing from my nose, over my swollen top lip into my mouth. I sat up and held my head back using the sleeves of my torn shirt to wipe the blood from my bruised face. Hell, this was nothing new or even shocking to me. Regardless, damn it, it hurts! However, this beating was a step up from the usual hard slaps and shaking senseless then slammed against a wall or to the floor... I laid back facing up at the summer starlit sky. I was empty, hopeless, unloved, and worthless. Then dad's validation words of my very existence rang loud and clear. **"You're a worthless piece of shit. Better things have run down my leg!"** I broke down once again. He first said that to me when I was five or six years old. I knew exactly the meaning of his words. I received early education and the definitions that go along with sex acts and the reproduction functions of a man and a woman through the acts of animal husbandry. For example, six years old was the first time I watch a stud horse mount a mare. I stood a few feet away as dad guided that monstrous member into a willing mare. Dad narrated from beginning to end. I stood there numb at first. I listened and listened well. I knew sometime in the future he would expect me to do the same procedure.*

*That's when I heard my name being called from a distance. **"LEEeeeeeeee."** I sat up a second time scanning my surroundings through swollen water-soaked eyes. Dear God, that's when I saw the **"Shadow"** that had haunted me since I was five years old. It was floating toward me from across the dirt lane that separated one field from another. With each breeze that blew in my direction, it carried my name hauntingly upon it. The **"Shadow"** now hovered in front of me. Tall, dark, airy mass of undulating smoke. Suspended within were a set of slanted cat-like eerie green* *eyes. Through the years they were soothing at times. Creating a calming hypnotic effect on me. So, soothing like the sound of a purring cat. One that I felt magical even comforting at times. However, "Evil is Evil" and the "Shadow" had scared the hell out of me more times than I care to remember. I felt another breeze circle around me, moving the "Shadow" to the back of me. It whispered suggestions, an evil message that was inviting to the pain I was feeling. I was so tired of the pain and the continuous anguish. I laid back, noticing the Mason Jar once again. I reached my right arm over for the jar. The "Shadow" became an extension of my arm reaching for the glass jar. I heard, "Take it, go ahead and take it!" It was half buried in the ground. I pulled the jar from its resting spot. A whisper from behind told me to smash it against the rock nearby. I did so without reservations. The jar shattered. The voice encouraged me to pick up the largest shard. My mind was spinning. What was I thinking? It didn't matter. Then the "Shadow" moved around to face me. Its eyes had changed from green to a menacing and striking yellow. It encouraged me with a demanding growl to place the shard on my wrist. It whispered **a** sweet haunting melody of "Slice deep into your wrist". That helpless feeling returned. Only this time I felt sick to my stomach as I unbuttoned the cuff. I sled the sleeve up my arm. With my eyes closed, I made a slash down my wrist to my forearm. Quick was the slice. My God! It burnt like hell! I sat there watching the dark red blood flow across my arm and drip off the elbow. The tears flowed down my face as I heard both mom and my sister calling for me. Their calling drew me back to whatever reality there was at that moment. I felt the feeling that I committed a crime. Would I be punished for doing this? Blood wasn't a deterrent in my life. Just the result of compliance, in most cases... Even at an early age, I managed to hide this **intent** from my mother. Slicing my wrist was easily hidden or explained. I realized as the blood slowed and then subsided, that I had not cut deep enough to slice the main vein. After all, that son-of-a-bitch of a so-called father had caused blood to run from my nose, covering my face, neck, and even two black eyes. Time after time, I would run back to the house when I heard them calling my name. For it meant he had passed out. Whereupon my mother would sneak me upstairs and I'd hide under my bed against the wall. Mom and Bonnie would stuff clothes and rags up against me to hide me from sight. That was encased he looked under the bed for me. We all felt some sense of release as he left for work around 5 AM every morning. Monday through Friday, drunk or not he never missed a day of work. This my friends was another day and night in the life of the **Fire and Rain Chronicles** up on "Hell's Half Acre."*

*Back to my estranged brother. He attended **"Old Frederick High School"**. He became a football player, and I became a popular Theatrical Student. Known for the character roles portrayed during my high school years on the stage of **"Governor Thomas Johnson"**. I developed into a dancer, choreographer, and after graduation, a dance instructor for Mrs. Joyce Morrison at the **"Frederick Dance Center"**. Theatre and dance became a vital part of my life in my hometown of Frederick, Maryland. Through the teenage grapevine I was made aware that in the eyes of my estranged brother, I was a real embarrassment. How could I get up on a stage and shake my ass? **"Lee's a Faggot!"** A name that was often thrown in my direction for good measure. Hell, just walking down the street, a catcall or two from a car of rednecks driving by wasn't unexpected. It branded the last of my dignity with a "Scarlet Letter." It hurt like hell at first. It felt as if a hand full of freshly grunted **"Shit"** was thrown and hit its mark, Me! So be it! Did it break my spirit? **"No"** is just the opposite. The name-calling and physical abuse I received came from both male and female **"Bullies."** This was an extension of my cursed life. Every word, every slap, and shove from behind walking down the halls of the school, cut like a knife. Never knowing when it was going to happen. I became a walking sponge. I absorbed it **"ALL"**. Until one day something* exploded inside of me. The bell rang at 3:30 pm. School let out; the multitude would rush to board the buses to go home. I was no exception. There it was! From behind, I received a burning slap to my head. I staggered and slammed against the wall of lockers. Five guys circled me. Their laughing became magnified as they slapped, then kick the books around. The leading attacker, *Tyrone* reached for me. Grabbing my t-shirt, and ripping the thin material from my chest. All this was done in seconds. Those onlookers gasped at first. Then laughed. I wanted to vomit. What I was experiencing created a flashback of my father attacking me. A red veil covered my sight. This bastard in front of me with a handful of my t-shirt became the Demon I was forced to face every single night of my life. The rage exploded and I knocked my attacker to the ground. As he falls to the ground, I jumped on top of him. I grabbed a handful of his hair, slamming his head several times into the floor. The other guys stood there with a look of where in the hell this guy come from. I was always the one who took what they dished out saying nothing I no longer was going to turn the other cheek. It was as if I saw my father attacking me. I had had enough that day. This was the straw that broke the camel's back. There he lay on the floor. The other four attended to their buddy and I gathered my books, papers, and dignity and out the door to board the bus to **"Hell's Half Acre".** I went to the back of the bus and cried a silent rage inside. There I sat wearing my torn *"Red Badge of Courage."* Stop after stop departing students got off the bus. My stop was one of the last. As I exited the bus the driver, was a sweet woman but stern. As I stepped off the bus, she said, **"Cook, it'll get better."** I forced a smile and thanked her. I paused for a minute. Gathered my thoughts, and my strength for what may be waiting before me at the top of the hill. I felt drained and defeated. But today I am a survivor. I walked up the dusty dirt lane to a world of darkness, I know as, *"Hell's Half Acre".*

After my mother's untimely and brutal death, **"04/16/1968"** at the hands of my drunken demonic father over twenty-six years. She was only forty-five years young. The years of mental and physical battering, beatings, and sexual abuse took an unbelievable toll on a once truly beautiful woman inside and out. If I haven't mentioned it or repeated myself, her name was **"Elizabeth Vernus Martinis Wetzel"** was one of Frederick's standout beauties in her late twenties, thirties, and forties. It was a known fact, that **"The Wetzel Sisters"** were beautiful women. There was **"Pearlie"**, **"Cora"**, **"Florence"**, **"Elizabeth"**, **"Edith"** and **"Myra"**. **"The Wetzel Brothers"** were very handsome men, **"Sterling"**, **"Emory"**, **"Charles"** and **"Ralph"**.

"Oh, My God!" The day mom took her very last breath, I watched a veil of sheer darkness cover the world I lived in. I was turning sixteen years old on **April 23.** Just days after holding her pale cold hand in mine. I felt the ebb of death engulfing her body. Her stillness weighed heavy in my hand embrace. At that, very instant a light breeze circled the four walls. Dangling sheets, window curtains, and the papers on a clipboard moved in its swirling direction. Deep in my heart and soul, I believe the circling breeze was her soul/spirit being released. The emotions one feels of loss are staggering on the slot. The personal, Hurt, Pain, Angry, and Sadness. Memories, like flashcards, appear and then catch fire, crumble, and vanish to ashes. After this collage of life's tiny tidbits flooding my mind. I took a deep breath and muttered, **"Mom you are finally free and can rest among the stars."**

Whatever was left of my innocence took wing and vanished at mom's last breath. I knew it was I who had to step up to arrange my mother's funeral. My father wasn't capable, nor could I imagine him arranging a respectable funeral. That was my assessment. Right or wrong I took hold of the reigns. I remember every single passage of time. Each day became longer and more taxing *on the three of us. Even though I existed in a narrow tunnel of light, encircled by the blackest of the pitch. Oh yes! the **"Shadows"** were always hovering in the distance. Like sentinels waiting for the call to arms. For that entire week, I managed to hold my own. All the hurt and pain that needed to be released weren't there. Somehow, I pushed it from being released. The following morning, we were to meet with the Director of the Funeral Home. Decisions were to be made. What was she going to wear? The selection of the Casket. I must say when we entered the room where the Caskets were showcased. I was unnerved by how cold everything thing seemed to me. The polished Caskets lined the walls on both sides. One above the other at a slant. Tiered five high. Walking through the rows of opened caskets displayed the finest of satins and taffeta in an array of blush colors and patterns. The director took us to his office whereupon the final business was handled. The Director quoted the prices of the Coffins. So graceful was his next line, "The selection for the Vault to house your loved one, is for eternity. What flowers for the Casket-Spray were important as a family decision? Bonnie spoke up for the first time since running out of the hospital. Bonnie said, "Mom loved Yellow Roses." Dad and I agreed. Mom's arrangements were finalized with our input. The Funeral Director stood up from behind his huge mahogany desk. Taking his lead, we stood from our seated positions. He walked around the desk and over to us. The Director, his father, and his father before him had prepared and laid to rest nearly every {**Wetzel, Cook, Hoffman,** and **King.**} Generations since the 1700s. It wouldn't be too far into the future that their services would be called upon. He extended his hand and shook each of ours. In a calm and personal voice, he assured us, **"Don't worry about a thing. We will take good care of Elizabeth."** You could tell from his eye-to-eye contact that we had done everything needed from our end. He suggested we go home and rest. Tomorrow evening will be the first viewing. I witnessed my mother taking her last breath on Earth. Bonnie, I, and dad walked out of the funeral home together. We stepped onto the sidewalk. I took a deep breath of fresh air. Dad reached into his back pocket and pulled his wallet out. He handed me a twenty-dollar bill, saying, **"Call a cab and go home. I'll see you later."** We watched him as he walked down the street taking a left onto "Patrick Street". Knew exactly where he was headed. To the nearest beer joint. **"The Hole in The Wall",** then **"The Tick Tock",** ending up at **"The Cozy Corner."** We walked down the same street. Crossing the street and down the alleyway to the cab station. A tiny weather-worn shack. I went up to the window. There sat the woman I had talked to so many times when a cab was needed. **"Need a cab sweetie?"** Smiling, **"Where you are going?"** I answered, **"Up on Route 40 West."** Leaning forward from her chair, **"You're the Cook boy, Lee."** Surprised her knowing me by name. Then she added so sweetly and passionately, **"Sorry to hear you lost your mother. God is merciful. Elizabeth will be missed".** She called out the side door, **"Tony, the Cook kids need to go home".** I already knew what it cost. I took the twenty out of my pocket. She raised her hand, **"No, this ride is on the Company".** Puzzled a bit, I said, **"Thank You very much."** She leaned out the window addressing us both, **"God Bless."** As we walked over toward the cab, I heard her say, **"I guess you know where Charlie Cook is...We'll get a call sooner or later..."** Bonnie and I got in the car. It was a very quiet ride up to "Hell's Half Acre". My sister sat as far away from me as possible. Both of us held our heads out the window. Feeling the air blowing on our troubled minds. The Sun was setting over **"The Braddock Mountains."** The red-orange sky was a sight to behold. Always was. Yet this sunset was coloring my senses from the inside out. Creating warmth where ice had developed nearly all my life. I closed my eyes. The April air was sweet with early blossoms. I rested my head on my arm. Closing my eyes, feeling the air-like fingers through my hair. It was like the romantic touch of a long-lost lover...*

In case you were wondering, dad came home around ten o'clock pm. I was upstairs in my bed, with the lights out. I was listening for the mumbling, cursing, and stumbling over himself to get into the bedroom. This was his first night without his mom lying by his side. What was he feeling? Any blame? Any remorse? How surprised I was, he came home sober... I'll leave it at that!

On the evening of the first viewing. The Director ushered us into the large viewing room. As we stepped through the archway, there were the heavy fragrances of flowers. I remember the floral arrangements lining both sides of the coffin. The flowers were several tiers high against the parlor walls. The fragrances hung in mid-air for the room was cold and all was still. I can only speak for myself when it comes to emotions and thoughts. To gaze down upon a loved one's face with their eyes closed in eternal sleep, created a thousand flashbacks of what she went through. Once, one of Frederick's beauties, as all the **"Wetzel Girls"** were. Her twenty-six-year marriage to Charlie Cook created the woman before me. Forty-five years of age, yet under all that makeup, I can recall every scar, cut, and broken bone she received from Charlie Cook. The makeup created by the Morticians was professionally done. She resembled the photograph we supplied when in her early thirties. However, the "No" amount of powder, pencils, and foundation could hide the physical scarring that that man standing beside me perpetrated on her. I watched him put his hand on hers. My heart was beating like a kettledrum. "Thump, Thump". The thunderous heartfelt hatred I had for my so-called father was being held back with the help of the Almighty above. I wanted to scream at the top of my lungs, **"DON'T YOU FUCKING TOUCH HER!"** Instead, I felt a single tear make its way down my ice-cold cheek. Keeping it together was the hardest thing for me to do. My sister was in her world, and I did not want to cause her to lash out at me. She had her own to deal with. The Director asks if they could open the sliding doors for the lobby was filled with family and friends to pay their respects. We nodded yes...

The first day of viewing into the evening went well. Many of mom's cousins, aunts, uncles, and several brothers and sisters attended the first night. Most were supportive of Bonnie and me, saying; **"If you need anything, we're here for you."** There were many-a-men that over the years had run-ins, let's call it what they were, "Bloody Fights" with Charlie Cook. Always when they were drinking, drunk, and blowing off steam. Which was often. Most were Labors in heavy construction jobs. During the summer season, they would work 12 to 14 hours a day. Most after work would stop downtown in Frederick to have an ice-cold beer or two, or three. You get the picture. Someone would run their mouth about someone's family member and the "shit would hit the fan". Whoever was driving would usher their buddies out of the bar and into the car. As quickly as possible before the police showed up. Quite a few times their asses were hauled off to jail. A few sons-of-bitches would take their frustrations out on their wives, children, and or pets. I can't tell you how many Friday and Saturday nights we would go to the **"Beer Joints"** to meet Dad. I remember so many nights when a fight would break out over someone being nice to mom. Dad would open his fucking-fowl mouth and throw the first fist. If dad didn't start the fight, he certainly joined in where his nose had no business to be a part of.

I can still remember the first fight I witnessed. It was at the age of three. Wherever mom and dad went, I went. It was 1953 on a Saturday night. Friends, family, and co-workers along with the hellraisers and or Rednecks had a favorite watering hole called, *"The Bloody Bucket"*. "TBB" offered live Country Music on Friday and Saturday nights. Great Food, Dancing, and Mixed Drinks. It was just outside Frederick's City limits. There was a local country band playing every *weekend. It was Saturday evening with family and friends getting together for a good Ole time. Usually Uncle Fuzzy, Aunt Myra, and her handsome husband Chaz, a 6'4" Clark Gable look-a-like. Without the mustache. His eyes were the color of a husky dog. That piercing icy blue. His hair was shiny black. Remember it was the 50's and the hair was greased back, hence the shine. When he would lift me into the air with his huge arms, I remember the wonderful scent of the aftershave he wore. He was tattooed from neck to toe. Over the years growing up, dad told me where and what was tattooed below the waist. I mean completely everywhere. The head of his Penis was tattooed with a butterfly. Mom and dad had told me that he had worked in the circus as **"The Tattooed Muscle Man"**. That was during his teenage years. Uncle Chaz would show me how the Eagle across his chest would flap its wings. Each wing was perfectly placed on each massive pec. He had control over making his pecs dance. Therefore, the illusion gave life to the Eagle's wings. I'd squeal gleefully. Whomever the tattoo artist had been, creating realism. Uncle Chaz always wore a tapered white shirt, tuck into his skintight blue jeans. The short sleeves were rolled up above those huge guns. Chaz had to get all his clothes specially made. The first three or four buttons were undone exposing his construction reddish-brown tanned pecs. The last time I ever saw Uncle Chaz was around 1958. Aunt Myra and he got a divorce, and he went back to New Jersey. Well, I was only three years old and to me, Uncle Chaz was "SUPERMAN." I miss him. He was an amazing man in my eyes. Also, Uncle Boots and Aunt Edith were special people. Mom and her sister Edith were singing along with the band or the Jukebox during the band's breaks. This night we sat in one of the corner banquets. Simply having a good old time. A very good-looking man came over to our table and told mom and Aunt Edith they were good singers. Then this well-mannered man created the ultimate sin, he asks my mother for a dance. She was always gracious, telling the nice man, **"I have to decline but thanks for your kind offer"**. Out of nowhere, Dad appeared behind the man like a bird of prey. The next thing I recall was Aunt Edith and Uncle Boots grabbing me, engulfing me as protection. It was like an old western saloon brawl. Glasses, beer bottles, and chairs were hurled by both men and women during the fighting. Women pulling hair, rolling on the floor, and ripping clothes. Mom and Aunt Edith found some humor when two guys fell through the swinging doors leading into the kitchen. You could hear mayhem taking place. Mom and Aunt Edith started singing, **"Get in that kitchen and rattle those pots and pans."** If it weren't so bloody a night, it would have been funny as hell to watch. Oh Yes! The State Troopers and Frederick's State Police were there in no time. Many were arrested, including Charlie Cook and my Uncle Chaz. As Bette Davis once said, **"Fasten your seat belts, it's going to be a bumpy ride"**. After all, had calmed down. Bette would have taken a good look at the aftermath and said, **"What a Dump!"***

*During those three days of mourning my mind was filled with stories that flooded my memories. Each viewing was like a page being written in a book titled. **"In The Center of a Great Lie"**. I remember every one of their faces to this very day. What stood out in my mind were the seated rows of mom's brothers, Sisters, Aunts, and Uncles and their numerous amounts of children. Family members that had faded into the past. A pallet of water-colored memories. Mom's side of the family where most severed themselves from us because of Charlie Cook. That alone became tender tarnished memories. So many cousins I never got to know. I recognized the faces of Bonnie's friends in each room of the funeral home. I believe showing their support for Bonnie. I remember who sat beside whom. I was focusing on my brother Mark and his aunt/Mother. I watched my aunt and brother walk up to the coffin. Paying their respects. I tried my most damn to understand what could have been running through his mind at that moment. Looking into his birth mother's face* *lying in that coffin before him. A woman he never got to know. As a son to her, as a brother to Bonnie and myself. He could have never been so far away from knowing the truth about the life she had lived. Why I cared what he was thinking, or feeling was short-lived as the Reverend led all three rooms into prayer. Meaning, fast as the thoughts ran through my mind, I wondered what was inside his heart when looking down at the woman lying in that coffin. He couldn't possibly imagine the hell she went through all her years on this earth. He had to have had my aunt fill in pieces as he grew up in the Hoffman family. I will leave it at that.*

.

*What flashed through my mind at the most unawkward of times? Where do my sister and myself go from here? We still lived under the same roof up on "Hell's Half Acre." I existed in the world of my creation. My private **"Garden of Good and Evil" What** mattered to me most in this world was my sister. She was four years younger than I was. H was I recall that day when we both were at the hospital holding mom's hand as she was taking her last breaths. We investigated each other eyes. At that very moment, my sister's demeanor toward me changed. I saw it in her tear-soaked eyes. Felt it in the way she pulled her hand out of mine. For whatever reason, it was as if my mom's death became my fault. Now I became the backboard of her woeful anger toward me. I knew why and where most of it was coming from. This wasn't the time nor the place to go down that road. I held mom's hand as her eyes rolled backward. Her last words to me were, **"Get Bonnie and yourself the hell out of that house."** Her words were airy and breathy, but I heard every word. Her cold waxy hand went still. My heart went to my feet in a thunderous thud. The air in the room was being sucked out. My spirit in trials was stretched like rubber bands as I tried to catch up in this world of chaos. I stood in the doorway for what felt like hours. I held onto the frame of the door for some sense of stability. I glanced to my left when I heard my sister crying. Bonnie was sobbing uncontrollably. I grabbed her hand and we hastened down the hall of the hospital ward. Down several stairs and out onto the street in front of the hospital entrance. Bonnie ran across the street. She collapsed to her knees crying. I stood beside her as the world began to spin around us. Echoes of mom's final plea to **"Take Bonnie and get the hell out of that house!"** She fought hard to get that plea out. I saw mom's eyes roll backward all so slowly as she took her last breath. The hospital room started spinning like a demonic carousel. Each horse going up and down had my father in the saddle. I saw the evil, hateful and demonic smile on his face. Then there was my inner voice rising from my gut like an erupting volcano. Shooting boulders into the stratosphere. Only to return like missiles exploding around me. With some sense of reality, **"GET IT TOGETHER!"** Rocketed through my brain. Now to go and tell dad she is gone...*

*On **April 10, 1968**, around 8:30 PM that hell-house claimed another victim. When I say another victim, I mean my mother had the loss of a set of twins and two fetuses that never made it to full term. The loss came with fists to Mom's stomach at five months. Then after Bonnie's birth, mom was pregnant twice again. Lost by beatings and thrown downstairs. A couple of weeks before the 10th of April. Dad transformed into the Beast. I was in the eleventh grade and Bonnie was in the seventh grade. Dad came home from work drunk, angry, and beyond violent. "Hell's Half Acre" was going to claim one of us this night. There was no longer a reason and or a purpose for **"Giving a Good Goddamn".** His anger showed through the gnashing of his heavily cigarette-stained teeth. Mom walked by his chair to go downstairs to the kitchen. He grabbed her skirt. She jerked it out of his grasp. She started down the steps. He snatches a hand full of her hair. Mom screamed, lost her footing, and fell to the bottom when he let go. Dad sat back on his human ashtray. Yelling, **"Lib, fix my supper! you fucking whore."** The following night another fight broke out with him attacking mom. I was upstairs and came running down. I jumped between them.*

*That's what he wanted. He slapped mom sending her into the sofa. I turned to look in her direction. He put both of his dirty hard calloused hands around my throat. Squeezing hard with each breath and movement I tried to make. It was hopeless for his strength equaled his anger. The demon stared into my eyes. I felt as though he was searching for my soul. He drove me back into the wall. His strength was frightening. Lifting me off the floor. The demon pulled me from the wall only to slam me back once again. It was with such force the plasterboard cracked. By this time Mom was up from the sofa yelling, **"Charles let him go!"** She slapped him about the head. No compliance! Mom grabbed him by the crotch. It was easy to do for he always sat around in his boxers. With a hand full of his balls, she **yanks** once, then twice. Slowly bringing him to his knees. Even as he sank to his knee, (which had to be the ultimate pain.) He clamped his two thumbs in the middle of my neck. I blacked out somewhere between the slam into the wall and tried to breathe. I was clawing like a wildcat at his face and eyes. I couldn't breathe and the world went black. While mom was gaining control. I woke up gasping for air where he had let me drop. I tried to swallow but couldn't. I felt a panic never felt. I thrashed on the floor, kicking in the air, and swinging wildly as well. I couldn't see clearly or hear. I remember Mom screaming my name. How I managed to get air flowing was an act of God. Suddenly, a flashing sharp light exploded inside and out of my mouth had risen a grabbled throat scream. Then the house was silent. I stretched out on the floor. From the choking to my stretching out, I had no idea what had happened while I was in a panic. I had suffered a hell' a beating. It took several days to sound like myself. My neck was black-n-blue for weeks. After that night I noticed mom moving slower. Her body was bruised and battered from shoulder to feet. She was silent most of the time. You could tell she had lost the will to fight any longer. No one spoke to dad. Mom, Bonnie, and I simply stopped communicating with one another. That night turned the tide for each of us. The following day I ran down the Hi-way to Hamilton's Restaurant to call an ambulance for mom. By the time I ran back to the house and ran through the door, I saw Bonnie at mom's side sitting on the floor. Mom lay on the sofa gasping for air. In another one of dad's drunken transformations, his fucking rage ravaged the one nearest to him. He was angry with the world. That night we all received some form of his demonic passion. We lost all sense of reasoning. The **"Maybe and Possibilities"** were severed at the neck...No pun intended...*

The old farmhouse we lived in had no modern conveniences. No running water which meant no bathroom. All doors throughout the farmhouse were equipped with latches that moved up or down in which to enter and or exit. That night dad ran mom's forehead into the latch on the door leading to the kitchen downstairs. A gash opened on her forehead about four inches long and opened to the bone as she was thrown to the floor. The blood flowed a deep dark red over her face and into her long black hair. I ran over and cradled her in my arms. Holding her in my arms as the blood flowed over and around the both of us. I remember watching the blood pool on the living room floor. The blood was thick as paint. Looking down at mom's face, the world went silent and in slow motion. Raising my head, out of the corner of my eye, I saw dad standing in the doorway leading outside. He swung the door open. He stepped outside to take a piss. I turned to see Bonnie standing in the corner crying her eyes out. She was traumatized. Watching someone cry in silence is part of a maddening world. If one can blackout and find themself standing to the side watching the scene taking place in front of them, then that is what I have done many times in that house up on "Hell's Half Acre". Darkness and silence surrounded me for a short period. Bonnie was in the corner leading up to the stairs where our bedrooms were. As mom squeezed my hand, a return to living came in full force. Bonnie's crying was magnified two-fold. She was screaming in horror at what had just happened before her twelve-year-old eyes. Although this scenario had been played out many nights in our lives. However, this night was the **"Beginning of the End"** *for each one of us. Hell was unleashed in a chaotic agenda for both Bonnie and me to a greater degree. That bastard suddenly weakened in form and demeanor. The beer and whiskey stopped bubbling through his veins and settled in his brain as he stammered over and into his bedroom. Like so many times after a rage such as this, he fell onto his bed and passed out. As if that was the only purpose a drunk was trying to achieve. Mom was losing so much blood, that she passed out in my arms. By now I am covered in her blood and Bonnie has sunk to the floor. I screamed for Bonnie to get some towels and the washbasin with water. I soaked up the blood that coagulated on our bodies and the floor in a puddle resembling the consistency of Elmer's glue. While I attended to mom, I told Bonnie to run down the highway to Hamilton's Restaurant and call for an ambulance. She stood there in a flood of tears...I yelled in haste,* **"GO NOW!"** *Our mother suffered twenty-six years of physical, mental, and sexual abuse in a marriage that was destined as* **"Doomed"** *from the start. As in many abusive relationships, he was wonderful to her at the beginning of their marriage. She told us so many times that he had months for a date. She finally gave an end. Dad's first marriage was to my mother's first cousin. They had two children, my half-brother Eddie and half-sister Loretta. He and his first wife ended up in divorce. WWII broke out and Charlie Cook served in the Army as a Staff Sargent. He fought in the Philippines. There was "NO" doubt that the war affected the rest of his life. He was shot and stabbed in the shoulder by a Japanese soldier. These were stories that dad told us time after time. After returning home he lived up to his reputation of fighting hellion. The combination of beer, whiskey, and a loudmouth was asking for trouble! Dad then began his pursuit of Elizabeth Wetzel. Mom's first marriage fell apart after the war. She gave birth to her first child, Denny, and then a daughter Pasty with her first husband Dennis. Both died tragically at very young ages. Denny was struck by a dump truck at age six. My mother had witnessed her firstborn child killed right before her eyes. She stood on the corner of the street opposite where Denny was to cross. It was Easter vacation, and the first grader was excited to dye eggs. He stopped and stared at the traffic light turning red. When it changed, he steps off the curb. The driver of a huge dump truck was racing to beat the changing of the light. Disregarding the red light, struck and it threw Denny under the back wheels and crushed his head. As mom told us the story, you could look into her eyes and see it in "real-time". Patsy died at six months old of Pneumonia.*

Mom finally gave in to dad's persistence. Dad became a very jealous and possessive person. It wasn't long before my mother became a battering ram for his threats and beatings. Started with a slap, then became more and more violent. He'd grit his teeth as he barked out, **"YOU EVER THINK OF LEAVING ME AND I WILL KILL YOU!!!"** *I can't begin to tell you how many times in my past growing up we all heard him say those words. The following mornings after beating the hell out of her, then raping her as she lay bloodied and battered, he always told mom,* **"I'm so sorry Lib"** *and* **"It'll never happen again".** *But the following night the drinking would take over and it wasn't long before something would fester in his brain, and we watched the evil manifesting right before our eyes. It would be mom, my sister, or myself that was going to be on the other end of his demonic rage. One of us or all three were going to be sacrificed upon the altar of* "Hell's Half Acre". *We never knew who or when! If he started on one of us kids, mom would jump into the fray to shelter us. Of course, he would beat the hell out of her, as if she were nothing more than a ragdoll or another man. Blood would splash on us and up against the walls. So many times, starting at age five, I would bite and kick that son-of-a-bitch. I would grab hold of his hair and* *yank the hell out of it to get him off mom. Was I stupid for doing so? Maybe?* **"Hell Yes!"**, *I remember being slapped, and backhanded on so many occasions. He would hit me so hard I flew, slamming me into furniture or up against a wall. That living room wall and I often became one. Over the years it was possible to date the impression left behind. My sister was only a year old at the time. However, her crying was proof of how she sensed the horror of violence around her. Even in her first year of life, she felt the doom that lay heavy as the foundation of our futures.*

I must thank the Gods above for the driving force and encouragement of one truly beautiful and inspirational woman. My drama teacher, **Mrs. Anna May Hughes.** *Her belief in my talents empowered my soul with self-worth, laced with the desire to achieve something more than what I was being labeled with and the abusive environment I was raised in all my life. Still, some individuals deemed my sister and me as the product of a* **"no-account drunken son-of-a-bitch"** *like the demon that sired us. We felt the shunning of many a Frederickton-ion. We were considered,* **"Poor White Trash!"** *The "SINS" of the father rained fire over our innocence. We did live in poverty. We were truer than life country folk. Making do with what we had.*

10-27-1977

The date **"10-27-77"**, *was the date my sister Bonnie was killed in a freakish car accident on her way home from her job. Her death brought my life to a sudden stop! As far as I was concerned, Bonnie was the last of any resemblance of the family for me. After the death of my mom's dead mother, father, brother, and guardian. Bonnie soon became self-reliant. It wasn't long before she resented my concerns for her well-being. I was in fear of what dad might be capable of, as Bonnie was. Bonnie was just twenty-two years young at her death. She finally had escaped from* **"Hell's Half Acre"**. *She was living on her own. Creating her world with a man she had fallen in love with. The strange thing surrounding her death that night, was that two hours later her boyfriend's way home to meet Bonnie, Chris crashed into the same tree that Bonnie had hit earlier. He knew nothing of her death. The wreckage had been cleared from the spot. Chris told me that he swerved off the road to keep from hitting Bonnie who was standing in the middle of the road. She was frantically waving him to get out of the way. He didn't remember much after that until he woke up in the hospital days later. He never got to see her or attend the funeral. Chris also nearly lost his life on that November night...*

"The following are the newspaper accounts of that night.
On his way home to meet Bonnie,
he didn't know she
was killed two hours earlier at that very same spot-on Ball Road"

He Didn't Know She Was Dead When He

By Allan Frank
Washington Star Staff Writer

When Christopher A. King drove away from Pete and Benny's Lounge in Frederick, Md., and headed home, he had no idea that his fiance, Bonnie Lou Cook, had been killed in an automobile accident about two hours earlier.

For the two had been playing pool together at the lounge until Bonnie Lou had left, about 10:30 p.m. Thursday.

So King drove his 1969 Pontiac along in the rain on the same road that Bonnie Lou had taken toward the apartment they shared.

Several miles down the road,

King's car went off the shoulder on Ball Road near Maryland Route 355 and struck a locust tree, seriously injuring him.

Incredibly, the tree was the very same locust into which Bonnie Lou Cook's 1967 Chevrolet had crashed two hours and 15 minutes earlier, killing her.

King did not find out that his fiancee was dead until he awoke Friday in the Washington County Hospital in Hagerstown in fair condition with head injuries.

YESTERDAY, feeling "very terrible and groggy" from the concussion he had suffered, King, 29, was unable

Then he crashed into the same tree she had hit

to talk for more than a few moments and had trouble maintaining his train of thought.

He said he "had no idea" that his 22-year-old financee had died when he left the bar. "I finished shooting a game of pool before I went home.

She went home about two, or 2½ hours before I did. The wreckage had been cleared. I was not aware of her accident. . . ."

About Bonnie's death, King could say only that he had "a breakdown" and was "really upset."

Bonnie Lou was remembered yesterday by others who loved her.

Her brother remembered her laughter. When she laughed, he said, "It was like sunshine," Richard Lee Cook said.

Bonnie Lou was known to everyone at Pete and Benny's Lounge, where she worked as a bartender.

Tired from a full day's work, Cook left the club before King, who was finishing a pool game, and began driving in a nighttime rain storm toward the couple's apartment about four miles away.

Set Off to Meet Her

Two hours and 15 minutes later, King was seriously injured when his car rammed into the same tree, which earlier Thursday had been hit by yet another car, in which the occupants suffered no injuries.

To several of Cook's relatives, the free-spirited sensitive woman had found a fine, equally sensitive man in King, an employe at the Maryland School for the Deaf in Frederick whom she had lived with for nearly two years. Although Bonnie Lou Cook was a "free spirit," her brothers and co-workers believed she probably would have married King.

"THEY WERE VERY much in love with each other," Richard Lee

Cook said. "I visited him in the hospital and we're still trying to find out what happened. He just found out that she was dead."

"They were real close," Susie Stanley, a bartender at Pete and Benny's said yesterday. "They got along real good. She got off work at 6 p.m. but stayed around and he came over to meet her here. They played pool together. She was a real good pool player, for a girl she couldn't be beat. And she beat a lot of the guys too."

Bonnie Lou most often felt free when she was working with horses, her brother and Susie Stanley said. "She was crazy about horses," Stan-
See ACCIDENT, E-5

ACCIDENT

Continued From E-1

ley said. "She started working here about four months and at first she was working two jobs, here and training horses or something at Bowie Race Course."

Richard Lee Cook said his sister was "an extremely earthy person. She had high ideals, enjoyed life and was very independent. She enjoyed different things and different people. She always took the underdog under her wing; she would pick the ugliest dog or the runt of the litter.

"She was a blue jean kid all the way. She loved the outdoors and animals," he said. "Something beautiful to her, that was art to her, was watching her Appaloosa, Apache, run free through the fields, mane flying in the wind."

AT THE FREDERICK COUNTY Fairgrounds, at Orren Stein's Stand-

ardbred farm in Walkersville, at Bowie and at horse farms in Puerto Rico, Bonnie Lou Cook worked with animals, exercising them, training them and riding them in championship shows.

Bonnie Lou and Richard Lee Cook suffered through a great deal together, two of their other brothers said. Bonnie Lou and Richard Lee dropped out of school for a year in 1965 to stay at home after their mother died following an operation.

Richard Lee Cook said they became closer than ever during that time and had remained best friends. "She expressed herself in art and so do I," he remembered. "She did mostly pencil drawings, mostly of horses. I have several of them," he said falteringly. "And I know she loved me."

He couldn't talk much more.

The funeral is to be tomorrow at 10:30 a.m. at the Smith, Fadeley, Keeney and Basford Funeral Home in Frederick, with burial in the Lutheran Cemetery in Jefferson, Md.

ROMANCE ENDS TRAGICALLY WITH 2 CRASHES AT SAME SPOT

By Earl Byrd
and Charles A. McAleer

Washington Star Staff Writers

They were young lovers holding hands over a drink in Pete and Benny's Lounge, laughing and making plans and dreaming dreams that would never be.

And, when the Frederick couple parted shortly before midnight Thursday, there was no thought that it would be the last time they would see each other alive.

Bonnie Lou Cook, 22, left her 29-year-old boyfriend, Christopher A. King, sitting in the popular lounge about one mile south of Ball Road. She entered her 1967 Chevrolet and drove off into the foggy and rainy night.

She had driven about a mile along Ball Road heading for home when, according to Cpl. Millard Mastrino of the Maryland State Police at Frederick, her Chevy swerved out of control at high speed, crossed the center line and slammed into a locust tree.

The Chevrolet crumpled and Bonnie Lou Cook died instantly, the dreams of young love ending on a curve in the road about 11:15 p.m. She was pronounced dead of head and internal injuries.

The rain had not let up and it was still foggy when Christoper King rushed from the lounge and entered his 1969 Pontiac about two hours later. Police are not certain how he found out about the tragedy but Sgt. Robert Storer believes he had been notified of his girlfriend's death.

Roaring off into the night, his windshield wipers beating a frantic tempo against the rain, King accelerated to a "high rate of speed," police said, and dashed along the same road his lover had taken.

Then, suddenly, he was at the same curve where Bonnie Cook had lost control.

It was not considered a hazardous curve but Christoper King's car began to skid, sliding, swerving out of control and slamming into the same locust tree.

The rain was still falling and it was 1:25 a.m.

King's car, like his girlfriend's, was demolished. He was slumped behind the wheel, unconscious, suffering from facial and head injuries, but alive.

As the flashing red lights of an ambulance taking King to the Washington County Hospital in Hagerstown disappeared into the night, Cpl. Mastrino stood in the rain and shook his head, searching his memory, trying to recall anything as tragic and ironic that had happened during his 15 years on the force.

He could not.

The accident: it was just that

By CAROL NIEDERHAUSER

FREDERICK, Md. — A man injured in a car accident at the same place where his girlfriend was killed in another crash two hours earlier said Sunday he had "absolutely" no knowledge of her death before his accident.

Christopher A. King said it wasn't until the next day that he found out about the death of Bonnie Lou Cook.

Miss Cook, 22, was killed late Thursday night when her car struck a large tree along a wet and foggy Ball Road. Two hours later King, 29, struck the same tree in his car.

Both cars were traveling at a high rate of speed, State Police said.

The two had been together at Pete and Benny's tavern where Miss Cook worked Thursday evening. They left at different times, but both apparently were headed for the home they shared in Frederick.

"She left about two hours before I did," King said Sunday night. He said he had stayed behind to finish a game of pool.

King is now in Frederick Memorial Hospital recovering from a concussion and facial cuts.

King's mother said she and her husband told him of Miss Cook's death on Friday.

"He asked me how Bonnie was and how she was taking the accident," Sarah Cook said. After they told him what happened, she said, he "broke down."

"It was just a bizarre incident that happened. It just doesn't seem possible, but it happened," Mrs. King said Sunday.

King talked over the weekend with State Police, who were investigating rumors that King attempted suicide after hearing of Miss Cook's death.

After talking to King and others who were at the tavern, Sgt. Victor Wolfe said he found no truth to the stories.

Police said there was a sharp curve in the road where the accidents took place, but that it was not considered especially hazardous.

ashes Into Same Tree His Girlfriend Was Killed at–2 Hours Earlier

was raining and foggy ight 22-year-old Bonnie Cook spun off a country in her '67 Chevy, hit e and died.

o hours and 15 minutes, her lover, unaware of his theart's accident, spun off the same road and hit the same tree.

"I didn't know about her death until I woke up in the hospital. The police told me they had just finished clearing away the wreckage of her car when they got the call to come out . . . that someone else had hit the same tree," said Christopher King, 20, who is recovering from severe head injuries.

The bizarre, carbon-copy accidents occurred the night of October 27, just outside Frederick, Md.

Earlier that evening, the couple had been together at a lounge where Bonnie worked. She left to go home about 10:30, and Chris, who had been playing pool, promised to follow her when he finished.

"We were so deeply in love. What happened is like a foggy dream that doesn't come clear," he said. "I don't know how the accidents happened. There were no skidmarks in either one."

Chris said that Bonnie had predicted her own death. On October 10, she had visited a cemetery to put flowers on her mother's grave.

"When she returned, she was terribly upset," Chris recalled. "She told me she would never see the age of 23. She said there was another plot next to her mother's grave that was meant for her.

"She told me she was afraid to die, but she truly believed it was going to happen."

It did.

— STEVE ROTHMAN

Praise, like gold and diamonds, owes its value to its scarcity.

— Samuel Johnson

DEATH CAR: Impact of crash tore off half the roof of Bonnie Lou Cook's car — killing the 22-year-old girl.

XED SPOT: The two

ers — driving their own s — crashed into this e in separate accidents hours apart.

of Children in U.S. Are Adopted

e United States has over illion adoptees under the ural parents' rights and responsibilities.

Freak accidents kill woman, injure friend

A Frederick woman was killed in an automobile mishap late Thursday night and a local man described as her boyfriend was seriously injured about two hours later in another auto accident at the same location.

The woman, identified as Miss Bonnie Lou Cook, 22, of 1005 Motter Ave., died from massive head and internal injuries after her car ran off Ball Road about four miles south of Frederick and struck a tree.

About two and a half hours later, Christopher Allen King, 29, also of 1005 Motter Ave., suffered severe head and face lacerations and a cerebral concussion when his car smashed into the same tree.

Police said both accidents occurred on Ball Road just west of Reels Mill Road under foggy and rainy weather conditions.

They said Miss Cook was operating her car eastbound on Ball Road at a speed too fast for road and weather conditions when the car crossed the center line and ran off the left side of the road, traveling about 25 feet before striking a tree. The accident occurred at about 11:10 p.m.

Speed and driver error were listed as contributing causes of the accident.

Miss Cook was pronounced dead by Medical Examiner Dr. Robert J. Thomas.

A little over two hours later, at about 1:25 a.m., King was injured when his car operated in the same direction on Ball Road, struck the same tree.

Driver error and speed were again listed as contributing factors.

King was transported to Frederick Memorial Hospital, and later transferred to Washington County Hospital, where he was reported in fair condition Friday morning.

State police described King as the boyfriend of Miss Cook.

They said the investigation of the accidents is continuing. Troopers C. R. Shlum and K. C. Anders investigated the accidents.

Police said a third accident, apparently unrelated, occurred at the same location Thursday night before the Cook mishap, when an eastbound pickup truck crossed the center line and knocked down a mailbox. No injuries were reported in that accident, police said.

The Cook car was described as a total loss.

Hell's Half Acre
by Richard Lee Cook

What you are about to read contains true moments in my life. I use poetry, prose, and short stories to tell what it was like to live up on "Hell's Half Acre" in the early fifties. Each poem in this collection tells the story of my memories of growing up in the backwoods of Frederick, Maryland. Each prose digs deep into the heart of emotions, that forced a young boy to grow up much sooner than expected. Secrets that were locked in a family that most considered from the wrong side of the tracks. Alcohol, verbal abuse, and physical abuse were regularly. I spent nearly eighteen years of my life in a rundown shack, with no running water or bathroom. I might add a very early education in the world of sex as well.

My name is Richard Lee Cook, always known as Lee. I was born and raised in Frederick, Maryland. I was born on April 23, 1951, at the foothills of Braddock Mountain. My grandmother on my father's side named me Richard after Richard Burton, the famous actor that was in his heyday at the time. As a child, I had sandy blonde hair and cinnamon-brown hazel eyes with freckles across my nose. Hello! I resembled "Howdy Dowdy"!

However, this book is also about my sister, Bonnie Lou Cook. Bonnie was born on February 26, 1955. She was named after a nurse that dad had at the hospital during WWII. At the age of twenty-two, she was killed in a car accident on her way home from her job. It was a foggy, wet evening on Ball Road. After years of growing up in a family that had nothing, was nothing, she was finally headed on the right track in her life. But the hand of fake, that we all knew so well in life, had to step in and destroy the dreams of one so beautiful. God-damned unfair! I'm still to this. day, so damn angry for the powers to be, to take someone so young in their life before they had a chance to taste the wonders of life before them. I had a brother that was killed at age six. His name was Denny, mom's firstborn. Also, mom's second-born, Patsy was her name. She passed away at six months of age. What a kick in the ass to have been born, then die tragically before they were given the chance to exist!

My mother was born in 1922, in the Union Bridge area of Maryland. She was one of nine children. Around the age of fourteen or so, her mother was struck by a car and killed while walking along a highway. Soon thereafter, the children under eighteen were put into foster homes. When each sibling grew to the age of eighteen, it was, "See you later". During her youth and before she married my father, she was considered one of Frederick's most beautiful young women in the forties and fifties. As we're all Wetzel women. Her sisters were Pearlie, Florence, Edith, Myra, and Esther. Her brothers were very handsome men, Sterling, Charles, and Emory.

My father was born in Jefferson, Maryland on February 10, 1917. It was well-known who Charles Lee Cook was. He was always proving he was king of the hill. His nickname was "CAT". Always fighting like an alley cat about or over something just for fun. So, I heard. He started smoking cigars and then cigarettes around the age of thirteen. Quit school before the seventh grade and worked in construction until the day he died. Got married at an early age and had two children with his first wife "Evelyn", my mother's first cousin. They got divorced after he returned home from WWII and married my mother "Elizabeth". Mom had ten children during their twenty-six years of marriage. Only three of us lived, Lee, Mark, and Bonnie. I'll tell the story of each of those that never got to breathe air. Charlie Cook served in the Army overseas in the Philippines during World War II. Shot, stabbed, decorated, and discharged at the end of the war in 1945. Came home and married my mother and that was where all her troubles began.

The years of wasted lives, untapped talents, and dreams were destroyed at a time when America herself was trying to heal from the long hard years of war. At a time when young men and women got married and started a family, owning their first car, white picket fences surrounded their first home with a dog in the yard. Well, quite a few came back with nothing to their names. No matter what I may say about my drunken-ass dad, he never missed one day of work in his life and that's the only credit he will get from me.

To tell the stories, I will pick them at random. Vignettes in the styles of Poetry, Prose, and Short Stories. They are filled with my thoughts, created thoughts foretold, thoughts to come true, and those that have not. Thoughts, no dark memories of what and who am I. Emotions were frayed beyond the separation of one end to the other. Emotions that governed my every move through life. Many are severed, quite a few murdered by others as if slicing my throat. But it is I who have struck the match that lights the fuse of my own destiny...

A FAMILY TORN APART

*Let me begin by telling you how my heart was beaten, bruised, and ripped from my chest. On April 16th, 1968, seven days before my sixteenth birthday, this would be the last time I would see my mother alive. It was a horrific nightmare that I have never awakened from. That moment will be forever imprinted in my mind, heart, and soul. As far back as I can remember, my mother lived and suffered nothing less than, **"The Death of a Rag-Doll".** I learned at an early age that reality is a dark and cruel bastard!*

*So is the day when we took the first steps leading up to the funeral home. Up to our final goodbye. At my side was my younger sister, Bonnie. I took each step as if oblivion was my destiny. A few steps behind us were the **"Son-of-a-Bitch"** that gave this day its purpose. Our father, our mother's husband of twenty-six years. Twenty-six years of anger, jealousy, and unspeakable physical and mental abuse. On this day, there wasn't one person paying their respects that didn't know that as a bald-faced fact. Everyone in the funeral home knew of the turbulent and violent marriage between "Lib and Charlie". Hell, nearly every adult at the funeral home had had some type of altercation with our father through the years. As a kid, teen, and serviceman, he was given the nickname, **"CAT".** Because he fought like a wildcat, with one goal to achieve. **Never let your man get back up!** For some dark purpose, he would look for reasons to start a fistfight. When someone had the nerve enough to challenge him, he would grit his teeth and taunt his foe with; his motto of choice, **"There are only two things in this God-damn world I love to do. That's a fuck'in and a fight'en! I'm up for both. Choice one or the other!"** Then he would kiss his right thumb and the proverbial, **"Shit would hit the fan."** I can't begin to tell you how many times we were covered in blood and beer as we witnessed his bloody and drunken brawls. Whether at home or downtown in the **"Beer-Joints"** it didn't matter. Bonnie and I huddled beside mom as we watched the old western salons come to life. Tables were overturned; chairs were thrown at each other. Beer bottles are being thrown at one another. Bottles were broken and smashed against the floor and the walls. We witnessed many a beer bottle smashed on someone's head. Shattered glass rained throughout the cigarette-smoked-filled beer joints. Sometimes the huge glass plate windows at the front facing the street would have a person rocketed through them. Picture an old-time western salon where the fight within flowed over and out onto the street. Mom shielded us by taking us to the back of the bar. Until some woman or woman would call mom a **"Fucking Whore"** or a **"Cunt."** Well, that was all it took for mom to slap the hell out of a bitch or two. Hair is being pulled out by the roots. Scream after scream of **"LET GO BITCH!!"** We watched men and women beating the shit out of each other. Our hometown in the 50s and 60s was a small one but growing each year in leaps and bounds. My sister and I spent quite a few late nights in the jailhouse after mom and dad were locked up for fighting and the destruction of property. The fights started inside but landed out on the sidewalks and into the street. We were witnesses to dad's bloody and drunken rampages and charged with **"Disorderly Conduct".** Usually, the charges placed upon mom were dropped, in order to take Bonnie and me home...*

The three large rooms in the funeral home were filled with family and friends. People I never *met and or relatives I didn't know. It didn't matter anyway. The state I was in on that third and final viewing left me filled with anger, hate, and loathing toward quite a few fake and phony sons-of-bitches having the nerve to show up to pay their last respects. I was feeling so many different emotions inside my mind and body. All were evil and dark. It felt like a thousand tiny beings were racing through my veins. Each one scrapping and scratching along the way. I wanted to reach out and let my hidden evil do their bidding. I took several very deep breaths during that week... The three of us sat in the front row facing the coffin. There were flowers surrounding the coffin and the air was filled with that cold aroma of flora. Once you have experienced that smell, it's something you never forget. Seated directly behind us were mom's sisters and brothers, along with their wives, children, and or husbands. Behind them were nieces, nephews, and a multitude of first and second cousins on my mother's side of the family. Our Native American Blackfoot Heritage could be seen etched on each one of their faces. You could nearly hear their collective heartbeats as their Indian blood was surging through the veins like a single drum beat of one heart. It looked like a **"War Council"** was about to take place. During that horrific week, it was I who had to make all the arrangements for mom's funeral. At sixteen years of age, my mother died in my arms. I was worried about my twelve-year-old sister. I heard my mother's final words echo through my mind as if in a barrel. Her last words, **"Lee, take Bonnie and yourself and get the hell out of that house. Far away from your father!"***

    *I maintained my emotions keeping everything intact. All the while the anger was becoming darker and darker inside. Building up in a ball of confusion encircled by dark grief and an evil rage. However, when back at the house it was a different story together. Inside my mind was an explosive bomb that was about to go off. But the other part of me stayed in control of my sanity. Several dark and evil emotions were weighing heavy on the not so evil of part me. The good, mild and meek portion, if you will? All my life I have had **"Dark Shadows"** that followed me. Feeding my emotions and thoughts. There were two that were very dark in nature. Encouraging the feeling that, **"I wanted to kill my dad!!!!"** Every night from age five the shadows were urging me to just go and slice his fucking throat? Even then a voice softly spoke to me saying, **"In due time my friend, in due time."** On the night of her final beating that brought about her death. Why didn't I take that goddamn shotgun off the wall, load it and blow that motherfucker's head completely off his shoulders? Why? Why? **WHY DID I NOT JUST DO IT?** At that very moment when I was about to take a step further into the darkness...*

    *The Preacher began to deliver his words of wisdom and comfort. Whatever was being said to the three rooms filled with friends and family by the Preacher, went in and out on deaf ears. I remember glancing to my right for a second. They're sat dad, two chairs from me. Stone-faced, staring at mom in the casket. Leaves me wondering if he felt any remorse. I prayed that he'd relive every second of those twenty-six years! I want him to remember every one of his fists that struck her, the slaps leading up to beat her like a dog. I wondered, **"Was he feeling anything at all? Was he waiting or wishing to get this whole damn thing over with, so he could get another drink of whiskey?"** I pray that he feels every blow he placed upon her body over those years. I reached over to lay my hand on Bonnie's tightly clasped hands resting in her lap. She was silently mourning. She also was filled with rage. There were tears slowly running down her high cheeks. I watched several drips off her chin and onto my hand covering hers. To my confusion and shock, she slowly rejected the touch of my hand upon hers. She seemed repulsed by my touch. No expression except for that shocking body language. Leaving me in the wake of her icy cold vibes of repulsive anger. My heart froze at that instant, cold as the repulsion I just experienced. I withdrew my hand in* *heartbroken disbelief. "**WHY?**" I told myself, "**Not now Lee, give my sister her space**". We both were having our private moments of personal thoughts, rage, the confusion that brought us to this point in our lives.*

*I felt a pulling, a need to turn my head to the left. I slowly raised my head and made eye contact with my estranged younger brother. He was sitting beside my father's older sister. She was his aunt, but she also became his mother shortly after his birth. Seated to their left were my aunt's daughter, sons, and their wives and children. Each showing as much respect as they could mustard-up out of respect, I suppose. On the right side, the same row was my half-brother from my father's first marriage, and his wife and their three children. They were the only relatives on my father's side of the family that had anything to do with me or Bonnie. I kept in touch with them during my teen years. Little did I know at the time, (up to my half-brother's death) just what my two nephews and niece really thought of me. I was never told of my half-brother's death. Nearly a year later I received a phone call from one of the nephews. It was after a Christmas card I sent to my half-brother and family. Long story short! The youngest nephew was somehow in charge of the funeral arrangements. I was informed, that he refused to have me attend his father's funeral. I would be an embarrassment! Not one family member ever tried to contact me about my brother's death. I still have not to this day ever confronted the youngest of my nephews about keeping me from the funeral. "**What goes around, Comes around.**"*

*Then there sat my "**half-sister Loretta**" and two of her girls. She seated herself far in the back. Whatever... another estranged "relative" that decided to disown me. A shunning of sorts. What in the hell did I ever do to give these "**two astute human beings**" to warrant their contempt towards me? Who in the hell do they think they are? I don't, didn't, and certainly will not waste any more of my precious time in giving a damn to either one of them! Why should I give a "**Fiddler's Fuck**" about either one of them! Another colorful saying my father instilled in me, and I will have to admit, it's one phrasing that is filled with a strong sentiment like, "**Do unto others as they would do unto you!**" It expresses one's true gut feeling and tastes as sweet as honey as it rolls off the tongue, "**I don't give a Fiddler's Fuck!**" What I've learned during my years of observing my fellow men and women, is through their **body language**. Or even how one "**cocks-their-eyes**" in your direction or away from you. Living my youthful years in our small town of Frederick, Maryland, the "**Social Grapevine**" was either **sweet** or **bitterly sour**. It's created by, let's say a "neighbor". Whispering on the hush-hush to other individuals that is so God-damn bored within their own life, that they don't have a god-damn thing to do but create a scandal and or a damaging rumor. Hell, I have witnessed this firsthand. It was started by a neighbor chatting across their fence to one another as they are hanging their laundry out to dry. Even the guys as they're working on their cars. The guys are worse than the women. Exchanging stories about their conquests being achieved in the backseats, in the barns, or in the woods. Once their own laundry is hung out to dry in front of their buddies they can't wait to pass on the "hush-hush information". Each asks the other not to say a word. "**Just keep it to yourself, because we are the best of buddies**". I quote, "**WHAT A PIECE OF WORK IS MAN. HOW NOBLE IN REASON!**" ... They are so "**coy**" in hiding their own dark secrets. Believing they have a perfect unstained life. Each is the master of concealing their very own treachery. Yet there's the need to "**create artful diversions**" from the obvious stains upon their own sheets. Not even a gallon of "**Clorox Bleach**" could ever disinfect or wash away their own imperfections and dirty deeds. Our mother's funeral is taking place and there sit my father's family members. Seated with glass eyes that reflect the light of darkness and the evil that consumes their petty lives. A black canvas painted with* contentment that is their true nature. They never liked my father's first wife either. She just happened to be my mother's first cousin. I bet you could hear dad's family voicing their disapproval, saying **"My God, he went and married another one of those "Wetzel" women!"** One thing I will praise dad's first wife for, Alease had the sense to leave and divorce Charlie Cook. It's all so very, very ironic! Let me put this out on the table for you to taste its flavors.

{Could it truly be that we, by the association are from the wrong side of the tracks? Could it be because of the poverty lifestyle that haunts our families from birth? Is it the alcohol, the sexual and physical, as well as the horrific mental abuse running rampant within our own families throughout each generation? Was it that I put myself on the "world stage" for display, allowing myself to be judged? Was it that by allowing myself to be studied under a microscope of sorts, it would be discovered there is a gay person among our family trees? Was it because I loved being damned by the <u>"Holier Than Thou?"</u> Maybe the world will find out something a bit more damning on my father's side of the family. Something that could upset all their apple carts within their perfect family values. A dirty secret that was handed down to me when I was in my single-digit age...I have never spoken a word of it to a living soul.} "Oh, the webs we <u>Spiders</u> weave!"}

*Jesus Christ people, if only you could imagine what the three of us went through daily. The number of times that this child was beaten for trying to protect his mother. A fight between mom and dad was nearly every night situation. Something would cause him to go off! Always when he was "Two Sheets to the Wind." Starting at age of three or four, when it was just mom and myself. On February 26th, 1955, my sister Bonnie Lou was born. Most of my young childhood was getting yelled at in profanities aided by slaps, whipped with my dad's leather belt, and or thrown against walls for coming to the aid of my mother. Or simply not being fast enough to his beck-and-call. When you are **"young and carefully taught"** by a demonic teacher, one learns your lessons well. Simply life's techniques in survival. You tend not to do stupid things without thinking about the consequences first. Like when he'd hit me so God-damn hard against my head, it was like being struck by an enormously charged bolt of lightning that flashes across the pitch-black night sky. **"Fighting back was futile and dangerously stupid."** The worst part was pretending to be knocked out and staying still. The horror would be mounting inside, along with the pain. In your mind, you prayed he was finished or was he going to attack you while lying there motionless? There were times when that bastard would come over and give you a pluralizing kick to see if I was faking. All the time say to yourself, **"STAY STILL!"***

*I can easily recall that first horrendous night when I faced evil, eye to eye. Dad violently grabbed me around the throat, picking me up off the floor. Slamming my entire body up against the wall. I remember falling in slow motion down the wall once he had released his hand from around my throat. There was no air to breathe. I sat on the floor facing him attacking mom as she fought him with all her might. His fist struck mom in the face, knocking her to the floor. I have lived that one single night over and over all my life. I became frightened of **"life"** itself that very night. I'm not saying I didn't come to her aide ever again. My life and way of thinking immensely changed. I swore I would never become anything like him! **I would kill myself without any reservations!** Here is what happened that night...*

Fear of being strangled again made me a part of the wall that night. I couldn't move. I was screaming inside but not a goddamn sound came out. I remembered that I stopped fighting for air to breathe. I looked into his eyes and saw the monster inside. I heard hundreds of high-pitched Violins reaching a high-pitch climax. Then I was propelled across the room and slammed into the wall. I slid to the floor. I scrambled to the corner of the meeting walls. In pain, in terror, my eyes watched this hideous monster standing in the center of the floor over mom. I was being forced to watch *"A Drunken, Demonic Maniac"* who had just beaten my mother unconscious. Seeing her fall to the floor bloody, bruised and with her face swelling, took me to a dark place. I would often slip into and out of the darkness to escape the terrors and horrors I felt. A chosen world where I was biding my time. I was curled up into a ball in a state of confused terror for the first time. I was being given an impromptu education in the world of *"Human Copulation"* ... What I was witnessing was an act of a demonic sexed-crazed rapist! He dropped to his knees and threw mom's dress up and ripped her underwear off. Violently spreading her limp legs. I watched him pull his pants down to his knees. There before me was his teeth-grinding animal that turned his head in my direction. What I saw before me wasn't my father!

This creature had yellow-green eyes like a snake. He had spiky needled teeth contained within a hideous grin. His mouth was drooling with saliva and blood. I no longer was screaming in total horror. My bruised body was tightening from head to toe. I think I was trying to shrink and disappear. Everything had gone black... I do remember the silence, a loud humming static that hurt my head as it grew in volume. Coming into focus was a dark tunnel. Leading to a vignette of light around the scene that was taking place before me. Then I heard the *"demonic voice"* screaming my name! *"LEE!!!!!!! OPEN YOUR FUCKING EYES!!!"* I was ordered to watch, as he proceeded his vicious on-slot, telling me that this is what, ***"Being A Man Is!!!, This Is How You Fuck a Woman!"*** I watched him thrust and thrust violently between mom's spread legs. Mom was slowly coming back to reality and began to fight with what strength she could muster up at that moment. Suddenly she realized that I was a witness to this act of sexual depravity. I was trying to focus on my mother screaming through her desperation and pleading tears, ***"Not in Front of The Boy!!!!"*** I remember locking onto the words, ***"LEE! TURN YOUR HEAD, DON'T LOOK!!!!"*** Listening to my father grunting and growling as he thrust into her with an animalistic glee. Both were yelling at me, at the same time. It was far too late; I was frozen in a dark place encircled by madness and terror! In my world of fear, I heard his angry voice, ***"BOY!!! YOU BETTER FUCK'IN WATCH ME!!! IF YOU KNOW WHAT IN THE HELL IS GOOD FOR YOU!*** *GODDAMN IT LEE... OPEN YOUR FUCKING EYES!!!!!!!"* I had no choice but to watch. My eyes were locked at the end of this tunnel. The fear in me was so overpowering. My heart swelled as my eyes exploded like a silent dam bursting. Four years old to adulthood in a blinding flash. ***"GONE, WAS MY CHILDHOOD INNOCENCE..."*** After all, I was only four years old... That night I met a boy my age in that tunnel. His name is Chance. The two of us became friends, and we held onto each other many times after that night. A split image, one of the dark and the other of light. I can recall the many times I blacked out by closing my eyes and holding my breath. I felt myself slowly falling into a world of slow motion. I would open my eyes and I was running through tall fields of wheat. Yelling out into this world for my twin. CHANCE! CHANCE! There on the outskirts of the darkness, he stood. Calling my name, LEE! We run toward one another, throwing our arms around each other. That feeling was one escape. I never strayed too long. Chance urged me to go back. Why? I always returned. Back to Hell's Half Acre.

I am glancing over at my brother, I'm thinking, "Welcome to my world. To the rundown shanty *in the middle of nowhere. No running water. Which meant no indoor toilet. Dad had christened the tiny farm, "**HELL'S HALF ACRE!**" Try to conceive a story that you'll never know. What in the hell was going on in a four-year-old child's mind? My brother would have been three years old at that time. The emotional toll in coping and surviving day to day in situations such as the above fore mentioned. Coping with these situations became the norm. It was impossible to think too far ahead. It got to a point where you believed it was a matter of time before one of us would be killed. Right or wrong, the fact of having a life of sanity vanished in the thickening haze over the years. Here I sit staring at my brother. If my brother would pass away, I would never be informed of his death! I know he is married and has children, that much I know through the town's grapevine. Good for him and his family. The fact is, I made a promise to God and myself at an early age, that I would **NEVER, NEVER** bring a child into a fucked-up world like this one! The idea, the possibility my seed could be handed over to a world of terror and horrors. **Never!** It would be a crime for me to do so. What I lived and had witnessed could possibly be an inherited trait and repeated, "**HELL NOOOOOOOOOOO!**" I glance back to my right towards my father. Shaking my head with the thoughts of those seated in this funeral home judging us, myself. Why is it, that my blood brother has never wanted to have anything to do with us? His birth mother, his sister, or me? As far as for myself, I can't help but believe it's because he knows I'm gay? Well, rumors and accusations do run rampant through a small town. You are judged by what one hears or conceives of you. Hell, the stories that I could pass along about personal trysts, would curl quite a few people's hairs. These individuals allowed their curiosity to find the right time to approach me. Several high school football personalities and a couple of town officials had become, let's just say, profound acquaintances. My radar was always in operation. I never flaunted my bisexuality. These guys had everything to lose if found out. Not one of them would ever have to worry about me ever telling a soul. As fearful as I was of the tryst. I was a teenager, a young man that craved affection. These guys were handsome, built, and far from being the bullies that threaten me so many times. I will say to you, that their passion was beautiful, raw, caring, and given freely. Each still holds a special place in my heart.*

*I can close my eyes at any point in my life and see mom lying in that casket before me. My mother was only forty-five years old. A loveless marriage of twenty-six years filled with outrageous abuse and the numberless beatings added to her untimely death. At age twenty-two, my sister Bonnie was killed in a freak car accident on her way home from her place of work. My father lived and died a lonely existence along with all the memories that that bastard created over his lifetime. Their physical bodies have turned to dust. I, alone hold the memories of "**A FAMILY TORN APART.**" I will keep the memory of each one alive in my heart and mind. For that is all I possess in this life until I am no longer on this plane of existence. Through me, their lives will be captured in my writings of Poems, Prose, and Short Stories. They are remembered in my dreams and in the reoccurring nightmares. The "**Shadows**" that have always walked beside me, have cursed me with so many details as they guide me through the most painful moments. I have excepted my world of darkness, filled with the "**Shadows**" that haunt and sometimes govern me. I relive the tragedies of all our lives like the flickering reels of film on an old-time movie projector. Each frame flickers a portrayal of light in the darkness of my life I refer to as "**The Me Nobody Knows.**" I reached out into the light for help, and it was my own shadow that embraced me.*

My God, I just realized that this is the longest amount of time, I have ever spent with my estranged brother in my sixty-eight years. We've never talked to one another. In sixty-four years, I may have conversed on the phone for a minute or two, reaching out and trying. It was as if I were a plaque. We never bonded as blood brothers. My brother made the choice to disown or disregard the idea I was ever his brother at all. That's a fact and that is fine, truly it is! It's really a shame that he never got to know his year older blood brother. In the year 2019, it is a fucking crime that he developed the inherited trait of narrow-minded thinkers! **"For Christ's Sake, So I'm a man that enjoys the company of both Men and Women!"** *I hope you know it's not a choice one decides to suddenly make or a disease. Brother Dearest, friends, and relatives; It's decided at conception! It's nature that makes the selection by "The Father of All Things." It is* **HE**, *God himself that makes that decision! Who are we to question his wisdom? The truth to be known, there are quite a few gay men and Lesbians within our immediate families. Look within your own adopted lineage,* **"SURPRISE!"** *There are quite a few of our relatives that just happen to switch hits for the other team. It's 2019 and the world will turn with or without you...Your choice is heard and felt clear.*

My brother and I went to the same elementary school and junior high school in Frederick, Maryland. Not once in all those **years** *did, we pass one another in the hallways, why was that? Dearest brother, maybe it was for the best, all the way around for the two of us. There is one singular question I have had in my heart and soul I would love to know. I would love to know, during the six days that our mother lay in the Frederick Memorial Hospital, did you visit her even once? I would like to believe you did. Mom was only forty-five years old at her untimely death. When she was young, she was considered one of the most beautiful women in Frederick. At her death, from all the years of turmoil and beatings that she went through for twenty-six years.* **You didn't live through any of the scars, cuts, broken jaws, broken ribs, punctured lungs, blackened eyes, and her teeth knocked out and wired shut**. *They "ALL" took their toll on her beauty, body, and spirit. She was pregnant a total of* **ten times**, *giving* **life to five** *children. She had five terminated by fists thrust into her belly, or she was knocked down or thrown downstairs. I witnessed three bloody miscarriages firsthand. At an early age, I was well educated in the facts of life and death. I helped my mother wipe up and clean up the blood many times. I helped to bury three* **fetuses** *back into the woods of,* **"Hell's Half Acre."** *For as long as I live and beyond, I will never forget the nights I witnessed her pain and agony and how much each lost pregnancy affected my outlook on life in general,* **NEVER! will I ever be able to Forget, Never-Ever!** *I've been saddled with this alone.*

Mom left dad once for two weeks. He hounded her to come back, yet in her mind, she knew better. But it was the heart that betrayed her. She couldn't leave her children in that goddamn house of horrors, Warden-ed by a demonic force. We begged her not to come back! No such reasoning. When she returned everything was fine until he came home from work drunk one evening. He had his usual pint of "Club Four Hundred Whiskey" and a six-pack of beer. We all set down in front of the television to watch "Rawhide." They shared the whiskey back and forth and popped open a couple of cans of beer a piece. He started to get loud and cuss at mom. He wanted to know who in fuck was she fuck'in for those two weeks? That's when we all knew he was going to create a blood bath. He jumped up from his filthy chair and grabbed mom by her hair. **"All Hell Broke Loose!"** *He yanks the hell out of her hair. Slinging her like a rag doll around the room. Mom, Bonnie, and I were begging him to stop. The more we begged the nastier he got. Mom was fighting back but couldn't get him to let go of her hair. I jumped up and slapped him with all my might across his goddamn head and face. Finally, I kicked him in the nuts as hard as I could. He let go of her hair* *and she reached for a glass ashtray on the stand beside her chair. She slammed the ashtray up against his head. It shattered into a multitude of pieces. Dad turned his head in my direction saying,* **"Little man, I'll deal with you in a little bit."** *Somehow, he managed to grab mom's hair again. That's when I jumped into the hole again. I grabbed a hold of his hair with both hands and yanked his head backward with all my might. I screamed in his fucking ear as I held his head backward.* **"LET HER THE FUCK GO!!!!! NOW!!!!"** *With each increasing jerk of his hair, I repeated,* **"NOW! NOW! GODDAMN YOU, LET HER THE FUCK GO!!! NOW!!!!!!!!!!!!!!!!!!!!!!!!!!!!!!!!!!!!!"** *He finally let his grasp go and she fell to the floor. Of course, his rage turned to me. Somehow that infamous backhand struck me across the face, causing me to fly across the room up against the wall. I was spitting blood and my face was on fire. Mom jumped up covered in blood, attacking the son-of-a-bitch like a crazed animal. That was the night she had had enough and fought back with her own rage. It wasn't the first time, nor the last. The evil take she alone contained was unleashed that night. Mom was no longer the woman I knew as my mother. Emerging from within her was a dark force that change her demeanor toward Bonnie and me. She had gotten a few good licks into him. Causing the drunken fucker to lose his footing and fall to the floor. He lay exhausted where he fell. I looked down at him. Dad had a handful of mom's long black hair. I looked down at my clenched fists. Between the fingers was his hair. It took a while for me to regain some sense of it all. Once again, the room looked like a bloodbath had taken place. Mom collapsed on the sofa trying to calm my sister down. Another night of being traumatized by that son-of-a-bitch! Even Bonnie had droplets of blood in her blonde hair. The bastard slowly got to his feet and staggered over to the door. He opened the door and pulled out his dick and took a piss like he often had done. Three or four times a night. When he finished, he went into his bedroom and fall asleep. Leaving the door wide open. During the summer we got quite a few mountain breezes encircling the small farmhouse. My point is, that when the breezes blew through the house, the hot summer air enhanced the urine odor. After so many years of repeated pissing in the same spot, it had developed a very strong pungent urine smell. Such was the way up on Blueberry Hill at* **"Hell's Half Acre!"**

Mom was born in Union Bridge, Maryland on October 18, 1922. She was the youngest of nine siblings. A family that struggled to make ends meet daily. I can't recall the date of my grandmother's death; I know mom told me she was struck and killed by a car while walking along the highway. Mom was placed in a home shortly after her mother's death. She told us it wasn't a very pleasant place, the girls worked hard until they turned eighteen. Mom never spoke much about the people in charge of her schooling. I know she married a handsome Puerto Rican named Dennis Lema. In their first year of marriage, she gave birth to her first child, a son named after his father. A year or two afterward, she gave birth to a beautiful baby girl, named Pasty. Pasty died six months later from Phenomena. A year later she and her husband Dennis got divorced. So, it was just her and my half-brother Denny. It was long after that she was being pursued by my father. After saying no several times, she finally gave in and said yes to a date. Mom knew he had a "Bad boy" image but was very kind to her and Denny. He just got over a divorce from his wife, my mother's first cousin. They had two children that were being kept by my dad's mother. Then mom's entire world fell apart right before her eyes. At age six, Denny was coming home from school for Easter vacation. Mom always went to meet him to watch him cross the one busy street running through town. At that time there were no crossing guards on the corners to watch the children. Denny was struck and killed by a huge dump truck running the red light. She watches helplessly as the truck struck him out of the blue as stepped off the curb. Throwing him under the back wheels, crushing his head. This horror was right before my mother's eyes. She relived that moment over and over for the rest of her life.

In a few more hours mom would be buried and locked in the memories of those who cared. Dear God, I hope she finally received the peace she so well deserved. Peace should be the only thing for her now. Most of us are still living some form of "Hell on Earth" No bullshit! Simply the facts." Those who have great faith, are destined to reach heaven. For me and countless others will simply be "Dust in the Wind."

Behind the three of us were seated mom's close relatives There were so many seated or standing throughout the joining rooms. In our hometown of Frederick, no matter where we lived. We were considered trash from the wrong side of the tracks. One thing the founding fathers could never take from us was the fact, that the Wetzel women and men were damn good-looking. Misfortune and the battle to stay alive seemed to be our curse on this earth. In my frozen trance from the icy stares aimed in my direction, I felt a hand touch my shoulder and the distinct voice of my cousin Betty-Lou. Apparently, she homed in on the fact that I wasn't alone in what I was feeling. My mom and most of the Wetzel members had a keen sense of dread. Betty whispered in my ear, "Lee, you're not alone. Family is right behind you. Hell, I'm here! Hang in there!" Betty-Lou brought me back from somewhere dark, a place I had known all too well. The touch of her strong hand on my shoulder and her words eased my mind. It wouldn't have taken very much for me to do something I would have regretted for the rest of my life. For I was cornered and had nowhere else to go that day. It wasn't so much those that were doing the same thing they had done all my life growing up. I would not have been able to control my emotions at that moment in time. Christ Almighty, I was overwhelmed, defeated, lost, hurt, and in pain, and never felt so alone in my life. Even now that moment echoes in my heart of hearts. Just as strong as it did sit there in that funeral home. Plus, my sister, the one person I loved more than life itself, just rejected the touch of my hand. She must have been embarrassed, ribbed, and called names for having a labeled brother. To top it all off, being a seventh grader is hard enough. If that wasn't hard enough, she managed to steer herself in the direction of drugs. Who was I after mom's death to tell her what is right and wrong? But I did and she resented me for doing so. I did my best to guard her against dad. I stepped in as a father, mother, brother, and caretaker. After all, we lived through every unsavory action and savage thought that that "Mother-fucker" acted on. We grew up fast and beyond our years. The truth, we couldn't imagine what he would or might do in the future. Bonnie came to me after mom's burial begging me to make her a promise. Not to ever leave her alone in that house with him!

I had a hard time keeping my eyes off my younger brother sitting among the glass eyes. He seemed to be going through the motions of the day. What could he have been thinking, what was really going on in that mind? Let me explain the story behind my brother as his birth mother told me. My brother was born eleven months after me, "Premature." He weighed two and a half pounds and was put in an incubator for weeks. Mom was very weak and remained ill for a period. It was very clear that dad certainly couldn't take care of a newborn. Dad, during two marriages, had never changed a diaper in his life or even fed a baby. While mom and my brother were healing in the hospital, dad's older sister and husband met with mom and dad to discuss what would be best for my brother. They wanted to adopt my brother as their own. An agreement was reached between them; however, his name would remain as given, including the last name. It was discovered later that his last name was changed to my dad's sister's married name Hoffman. That promise not to change his last was broken. It's my understanding, through nights of heavy drinking and arguing. Discord and resentment went haywire between dad and his sister for some time... Over the years the brother that was no longer. He never was fortunate enough to experience the magnificent world of, **"HELL'S HALF ACRE!"** *His world was many miles from the alcohol, fighting, and brutal beatings. The mental and physical abuse that his birth mother, sister, and older brother endured. How lucky not to be a part of this fucked-up family! My brother never had to experience the life of poverty that we had always lived in. No running water, and no indoor bathroom. He would never experience taking a bath in a creek each day during the summer months. With no inside plumbing, we used an old outhouse, named "Bessie-May." She didn't smell that good during the sizzling summer temperatures in July and August. She was portable, we would pick her up and set her over a freshly dug hole when the current hole filled up. Often, we had to fight wasps, snakes, and those damn spiders. When winter approached, we used "Piss-Pots" referred to as a "Bed Pan." During the winter months, we would huddle around the oil stove to stay warm during blizzards. It got quite cold back in the woods in that small farmhouse. When it snowed, it snowed! An expression supplied by daddy dearest,* **"Asshole deep to a twelve-foot Indian."** *During the lean years and there were many, we lived on one meal a day. Snacking on fried dough with jelly. I wonder if my little brother ever felt a leather belt sting across his body. How many backhands across the head and face did he ever receive? Just because you happen to be in the line of fire. It's truly amazing the damage a drunk can in-flick on his surroundings. Most mornings he drew a blank it had ever happened. My brother couldn't possibly conceive the life contained in this world of chaotic anger, hatred, brutality, and fear.*

Do I resent my brother? Yes and No... First, how can I do so if I don't know him? Yes, for never trying to communicate with his blood. Actions speak louder than words and in saying so, distance is framed within the heart and mind. Our lives up on Blueberry Hill were a living hell. Just a little understanding and compassion would have been something we could have excepted. After mom's death, we had reason to escape our warden of terror, hate, pain, and mental anguish. We flew the coop, so to speak, and went on with our lives. Taking steps to live better, more of normal environment. Even then, I was continuously taunted by the rednecks. Still, by the grace of God, I'm still here and happy with what I accomplished in my life. Putting myself through college, attending the "American Academy of Dramatic Arts in New York City. The nation's number school for theater arts. I pursued my dream and by God, I was accepted for **ME!** *Though I carry the horror and terror of my youth with me for all the days of my life, I have survived an abusive demon that tore a family apart!*

ELIZABETH WAS HER NAME

"This is a true story, a story that I live over and over...
But a story that's needed to be told!"

    I am often reminded to leave the past where it is, so I say sorry in advance for writing on a subject that I lived on every single day of my life. It's horror, abusive never-ending night terrors that still to this very day haunt me. If this subject offends because of language and or, subject matter, race, color, creed, and sexual orientation, **Read NO Further.** *I lived it, felt it, experienced it, and certainly became an instrument of it. It's time the world stops being so Goddamn blind about what is right in front of them. Please read on with the awareness that some of our lives weren't filled with roses every day. Yet, I am here, and many family members are "Gone." I write to tell her story.* **Elizabeth Vernus Martinis Wetzel Lema Cook's** *story. She was my mother. Her fate has shadowed me then and still does to this day!...*

    I write this story, because I need to speak out about a woman, my mother, a wife to a common low-down son-of-a-bitch of a man! Writing this today was brought about that I, his son had a flash of him in my mind's eye. My father, (FATHER) a word I have very seldom let out of my mouth. He's my dad, the meaning of a father has value, has substance. Like responsibility to the family, he created with the seed of past generations. In honor, respect to carry on the linage of that circle of life. Let me laugh, for he would not have a clue of what in hell I'm talking about. I write in remembrance of one day in the life of Elizabeth, a day that lasted for twenty-six years of married life. On that last day of her life on this earth. I held her in my arms at sixteen years of age. I witnessed her taking her last gasped of breath. At the young age of forty-five, she no longer could or had the desired to fight back from the endless years of beatings, vulgarity, slanderous name calling and hopelessness to ever get out of a world of poverty and alcoholic abuse. A world that she herself became a part of, excepting the hopelessness of ever getting away from the demon that created the fire and rain we lived in, up on **"Hell's Half Acre"!** *Before passing on she spoke to me in a whispered voice,* **"Lee, get Bonnie and yourself the hell out of that house...Please..."** *The last words she ever spoke. Here is what transpired on that darkest of days.*

Daddy Dearest, I now speak to you. After so many years of nightmares that were embedded, NO branded deep in my heart and soul. Why? I'm not sure except you flashed across my mind today. I remember at age three, you are holding me aloft on your shoulders. I look at this photo outside a beer joint with friends watching on as the picture was taken by Elizabeth. Where did you go after what had seemed a wonderful moment in time? All I can ever remember is the hitting, slapping, and beatings. All for the purpose of making me a man! So, you said at first. How I grew to hate you with every fiber in my heart and soul. You became that man we grew to fear, wishing for your demise. When did you stop being human, never was there a sign of tenderness. What caused you to unleash horrors that we couldn't believe? When I was five or so and wish to have a hero to look up to, I couldn't find or understand what a hero was supposed to be. All the bloody beatings you put upon Mom; she endured in her short life on Earth. You were the one who put her in that early grave, way before her time. Dad, why did you beat her on her so badly? Then turned on me feeding your rage over the years.

At sixteen, I held her in my arms and watched her life slip into the darkness you created around us. You can't imagine the horror I felt at that moment. There wasn't a damn thing I could DO! I felt the cold hand of death in mine. A razor blade shivered went throughout my body. Slashing at the core of my last remaining youth. Being taken over by hurt, pain, anger, and the seeding of evil. Damn you for all the sorrow! Damn you for all our pain! Weren't you able to see the hurt in Bonnie and me? Did you even give a shit? DAD! picture mom in my arms on that living room floor. taking her last breath. How could you? You were once again drunk and out of your fucking mind. Do you have the capability to conceive what was going on at that moment? I didn't know which way was up or down, turning and seeing the horror in Bonnie's eyes. Even she realized that her mother was gone and never to return! Blackness became our world at that very instant. What do I do,? What seemed to be forever was but an instant and I knew that the world we had lived in all our lives, was going to have to change. Or we too were going to die at your hand. There was no recourse to examine, no way were we going to stay in that kind of environment that killed our mother, Elizabeth. I would be next, or it would be I who would give into my darkening rage and evil temptations. My God! It felt as though I was running an endless marathon just to get a breath of fresh air. I remember screaming a primal unhuman scream within my mind. At that moment I was completely and totally defeated in mind, body, soul, and spirit. That's neither here nor there any longer.

It's close to Mom's birthday and the memories do linger and are always on my mind. Christ, it's forty-six years later, it feels like it was just yesterday. I write this at the ripe old age of sixty-four. I am now all alone, by choice mostly. I do have my little Nikki and he is the light of my life. You know this is a miserable world to live in. You, mom, and Bonnie are gone. You left this world all alone and by your own darkness that dwelled within you all your life. I had stepped up to the plate and expedited the necessary arrangements that laid mom to her rest. At sixteen, I suddenly knew what I had to do. A thousand questions went through my already fractured and lost mind. You didn't make it any easier then. Here I remain, it is as I felt when I was a child growing up on "Hell's Half Acre", Fearful of when you were going to transform. Many times, I ask myself with tears mounting and my heart overflowing. "God, I hate you". I despise and damn you for the constant and emotional anguish you put upon the three of us. I curse you for putting us through a living hell all our days with you up on "Hell's Half Acre". I look at this picture of you holding me at age three. There is a glimmer of pride in your eyes...or was it for the woman taking the picture on the day in 1953? You never showed us "Love" all you ever, ever showed us was anger, rage, hatred, agony, and pain! You created a pit of HELL in which to live. I know your childhood was a bitch, then thrust into WWII. You came home angry...Married your second wife, Elizabeth Vernus Martinis Wetzel Lema. Your first wife's cousin. Elizabeth was your wife for twenty-six years; she was pregnant by you a total of ten times. Only three lived. Now it's only I who remains and can tell this story. Dad, she was a wife, a mother, and a woman for twenty-six years and you murdered her! You beat her to death and I can't and won't forget all the days of my life from this time forward!

"ELIZABETH"
was her name.

DADDY GOT PAID!

*I wish to tell you a story that changed my life, the me I didn't even know. Truer than not, horrifying in its nature, and lived by me. A story about what happened most nights, under the roof of an old farmhouse that daddy christened, "**Hell's Half Acre.**" Daddy got paid on Friday of every week. He and his work buddies would go to the "**Hi-way Liquor Store**" to cash their checks. Each bought a bottle of whiskey, then they would head downtown to their favorite watering holes, "The Hole in The Wall" or "The Tic-Toc." Late last Friday night, I happen to be alone in the house. Mom was in the hospital about to give birth to my little sister. During this time in the fifties, you learned the sex of your baby, when borne. Being alone at my age wasn't a big deal. Even going on five years old, you grew up very fast when living isolated in the country. I wasn't frightened, except for snakes and spiders.*

What frightened me most days and nights, was my father coming home! It was Friday and I knew he would come home drunk. This night I went upstairs to my bed. I couldn't sleep wondering if mom was doing okay and whether I had a little brother or a little sister. I knew dad had no idea that mom was taken to the hospital. Dad usually came home around ten or eleven o'clock on Friday nights, sometimes later... As I was about to doze off, I saw the lights of a car flash across my bedroom ceiling. Moving slowly across the length of the room running down the wall as the car reached the top of the hill. Casting morphed shadows through the small window across the room. I jumped out of the bed and rushed over to look out the window. The window was opened to allow air to flow through. I heard laughing and talking in the car. The passenger door opened and out stepped dad. It was very clear he was in his usual drunken state. I jumped back into bed and covered up. I prayed a quiet prayer to myself, one that he would go straight to bed and pass out.

I heard him downstairs right outside the door, I knew he was taking a leak. He would always urinate up against the corner of the house. Marking his territory if you will. We had no running water, so that meant, No Bathroom." Then the door slammed open because he tripped over the step coming in. My little ears were like radars when it came to anything he did or said. I could hear him staggering through the open door. Falling into his filthy over-stuffed chair covered in cigarette burns and spilled liquor from over the years. I heard the familiar hissing sound of a beer can being opened. He started mumbling and cursing to himself, something a drunk often does. Then I heard him call out mom's name first, then my name. Once... twice... The third time would always mean business. **"LEEEEE... Get your Goddamn ass down here. NOWWW! You worthless piece of shit!"** *I can't remember a day that went by when that phrase wasn't addressed to me or to mom. I hurried down the steps and stood to the right of his chair.* **WHAM!!!** *He released a backhand up against my head, propelling me backward to the floor. I was stunned and, in a daze. Immediately I felt unbelievable pain. My right ear was ringing and burning like all hell! I saw white spots throughout a black background I then heard him yelling right above me, my sight was clearing up. I must have been crying, but it was hard to hear anything but a loud ringing pitch. When I regained my senses, then everything came together in those moments leading to terror. I watched as he stammered back and forth to stand straight. I gasped for air several times in quick gulps as he gritted his teeth,* **"Stop that goddamn crying, or I'll give you something to really cry about!"** *Before I could react to his demanding growl, he then barked out,* **"What in the fiddler's fuck is wrong with you? You stupid-looking son-of-a-bitch!"** **"Where's that fucking whore of a mother of yours?"**

I managed to get to my feet. Christ knows I should have stayed down on the floor keeping my mouth shut. **Oh, Hell No!** *I might be little, but he pissed me off. I shouted right back at him,* **"She's at the Goddamn Hospital having a baby! YOU FUCKING DRUNK!!!".** *As I got ready to take another breath in my fit of defiance, I watched him gritting his snaggled yellow teeth. The sound reminded me of a catfish making that noise. His gray-colored eyes turned green as he was getting ready to fight.* **"SO! Little Man, you think you're a bad motherfucker jumping in my face!"** *He hit me with another backhand directly in my mouth. The force of that blow threw me about ten feet across the living room. No sooner than I had contacted the wall than he grabbed a handful of my blonde hair. Lifting me up, slamming my back against the wall. Even at five years old I knew at that very instant that this night was going to be different from all the other nights before. For one thing, Mom wasn't home to protect me. For she certainly would have taken the brunt of his Friday night wrath, I thank God she wasn't! Tears of complete terror exploded directly from my soul to my eyes, Jesus Christ! The pain was unbelievably intense throughout my body. I gagged from coughing up blood. I went to spit a mouth full of blood onto the floor, but it just ran down my chin, dripping off onto the floor. I noticed a couple of my teeth laying before me. I needed to spit blood again. However, this time I was having trouble trying to open and close my mouth. That's when I realized that bastard had dislocated my jaw, knocking my teeth out. The horrific terror I felt right at that instant freaked me out to no end. It was intensified, with a second assault as he shook-ed me so violently by the arm that he dislocated my arm from the shoulder. It's amazing how things can flash before your eyes in a time of crisis! I looked up and there he stood over me. In my mind he was more than a monster, he was a demonic creature. By this time, I was crying so fucking hard and trying to push myself along the floor with my back up against the wall. Ending up trapped in the corner of the living room. What I saw on my dad's face, wasn't human! His face morphed into a hideous creature. I know he saw the blood and slobber flowing from my broken face. The demon was snarling at his prey. I was pleading with all the strength I could mustard up from deep inside. With my jaw dislocated or broken and choking on my own blood I tried to form words.* **"DADDY, PLEASE STOP! DADDY, PLEASE STOP!".** *Blood, slobber, and snot, mixed with tears running down my face, there was nothing I could have done or said to stop him in his drunken rage! Dad's face was frozen in a fit of crazed anger, gritting his tobacco-stained teeth. That's when he grabbed another hand full of my hair, shaking me like an angry Pit-Bull. Back and forth with such force* *that I had to have looked like a ragdoll in his clenched fist. I couldn't make out which end was up to any longer!*

Finally, he threw me once again across the room. I hit the wall with such force I felt the air being completely knocked out of me. I remember falling to the floor in a blinding white light gasping for air. Like that of a flash bulb going off in your eyes. The world around me went silent... I no longer could move! I didn't feel the pain any longer. Then... Everything went completely black. The next I knew; I was standing outside of myself. I realized I was looking at a heap of crippled flesh and bone covered in blood! I turned my head in the direction of my dad. He was ranting and raving as if a madman possessed. I watched him walking toward me lying on the floor. He screamed! **"LEE...GET THE FUCK UP YOU LITTLE BASTARD!"** *When I didn't respond that son-of-a-motherfucker kicked me in the ass, sounding like a roar of an animal. He demanded,* **"LEE... I TOLD YOU TO GET THE FUCK UP! NOW!".** *When he planted that final kick to my body, it was as if a lightning bolt had shot through my heart. It was like putting a wounded animal out of its misery! All the slaps, bruises, broken bones, and mental abuse of all the days and nights of terror in my five years on this earth were no longer! I need not ever again wonder if he would be coming home drunk. It no longer matters to me. It was over...*

I'm in a better place
Where there isn't any pain or fear
I'm safe within the arms of my true father
I just wanted someone to know what happen last Friday night after
{DADDY GOT PAID!}

"You may be asking yourself; can this all be true?
The answer is a resounding,
"YES!"
Except for the part where I had died.
There were many, many times when I had wished death would have taken me!
With each strike, each blow I died a little more each and every time.

By the way,
Mom gave birth to my little sister,
Bonnie Lou" ...

I'LL BE SEEING YOU

"As a child, I never imagine that all of the Monsters in the world would be Human"

It was my first week at West Frederick Junior High School. Seventh grade was scary enough. But what happened to me was nothing short of frightening. I felt like a fish out of the water as it was. A new school that contained seventh through ninth-grade students. New faces with no names were developing small cliques. Wherever I went I carried a lot of dark baggage from Hell's Half Acre. I acted like a whipped puppy most of the time. Always wondering when and where the next strike would come from behind. Every day when I stepped off that bus, was like stepping into the unknown. The bus was filled with a mixture of West Frederick Junior High and Frederick High School students. You see WFJH and FHS were beside one another. It took nearly a week to navigate through the hallways to find each classroom. Racing through the hallways became a lesson of staying to the right. We flowed like an army of ants. Then veering off into a classroom for the next lesson. To go to the bathroom, one had to raise your arm to get the teacher's attention to ask for permission. You would be given a hall pass in case stopped in the hallway coming or going. During the first few weeks, there were Strick hallway monitors checking every coming and going. Then things seemed to ease over time.

This afternoon I had to go to the restroom. By the way, going to the bathroom during school was a real treat. All we had at home was the "Piss-pot." "Clarabelle" the Outhouse during the daylight hours. Of course, anywhere outdoors. Well, I walked up to the teacher's desk and asked to go to the restroom. She handed me the hall pass, which was a horseshoe on a chain. Each teacher had their own take on a hall pass. Down the hall, I went past four classrooms, down the staircase to the ground floor level to the boy's room. I open the heavy door and go to the last stall to pee. Before I was able to unzip my pants, the door opened, and there stood this guy that had to be a tenth or eleventh grader, maybe a senior. He had dark hair, dark eyes, and a "Cheshire Cat" smile. I stood there frozen at the sight of this older guy. I had to bend my head back to look up at him. Through my mind ran the thought, "What do you want?" I went to move around him when he held me back in the stall. **"Don't be in such a hurry."** I spoke up saying, **"What do you want?"** That's when he said, **"I need a problem taken care of"**, as he took one hand and squeezed the bulge between his legs. My heart started pounding in my chest as he pushed me into the stall, and falling on the toilet seat. Giving him room to close the stall door. He locked the door with one hand and the other unbuttoned his pants. I watched him pull his zipper down. As he lowered his pants along with his underwear to the knees. There before me was a stranger exposing his very big and erect penis. He slowly stroked it back and forth. Then he leaned his head forward and growled his demands. **"Touch it."** He grabbed my hand and told me to wrap my hand around it. I resisted and he grabbed me by the hair yanking it. Now panic had begun to run through my mind and body. I was about to scream for help! When he slapped me and told me to shut the hell up. Or he'd hurt *me badly. I complied. Tears ran from my eyes. "Don't make a sound!" he said, "Jack me off." There I sat scared shit-less out of my mind. I had no idea what in the hell he was talking about. He directed me to jack faster. By now I had drifted into my world of darkness. I heard him barking his demands, I was obeying his every word, but I wasn't there. What seemed like hours were minutes. He grabbed my hair again. Then he slapped my arm away from stroking him. I watch as he took his other hand and jacked it in a hurried rhythm. Before I could react to anything I felt hot globs of thick semen strike my face. Into my eyes, burning like fire. He shot his results over my entire face. In my eyes, in my hair, and mouth. I sat there frozen by this assault. Leaning forward as he pulled his underwear and pants up, he said to me, **"That was a good boy. We'll have to do this again sometime."** Then with a slap of approval to my face he menacingly told me I better never tell a soul about this! adding, or **"I'll kill you!"** He left and I freaked out. I wanted to run out into the hallways screaming at the top of my lungs. I stood there shaking and shivering let a dog shiting a razor blade. I was having a hard time trying to breathe. Then as if the world suddenly stopped, I took a deep breath and went over to the sinks. Turned on the water and stared into the mirror in front of me. There was no sound. The reflection in the mirror was walking back to the stall and getting toilet paper. I watched my reflection as I seemed to stand frozen in place. I grabbed toilet paper to wipe my face off. I went back to the sink and grabbed paper towels to wash away his attack. I cried a river of tears as I washed away something I never experienced before. It was very hard to get the semen out of my hair. I washed my eyes with cold water to ease the fire. After I calmed myself down, I stared into the mirror and saw my other self. Just long enough to hide another horror from a reality that has forsaken this child. Then the bell rang for the change of classes. I walked calmly back to the room to gather up my belongings. All the way there I knew the teacher would ask what took so long. What in the hell was I going to tell her? I stepped through the door along with the new students. Her back was to the class as she was writing the lesson for the day. She never noticed me. I suddenly remembered I left the hall pass in the restroom. I held myself together through the long hallway as the students vanished into the classrooms. I remember feeling panic rush over me as if someone was coming after me. I started to run as if a pistol went off to start the race. I flew to the doors leading outside. I needed to get some air. Nothing else mattered at that moment in time. It was the seventh period. I bolted out the door and ran to where the buses picked us up to go home. Outside away from people so it would be possible to gather my emotions as I waited for the bus to arrive and take me back to **"Hell's Half Acre."***

*I sat down on one of the benches under the canopy to wait for the bus. It wasn't long before the first buses rolled in to take their position, one behind the other. They started arriving about twenty minutes before the last bell rings that school was out. I eyed my bus pulling in from the main street. To my right, I heard laughing. I looked over and coming around the corner was a group of guys from the high school next door. Lagging with another dude was the guy that attacked me in the bathroom just minutes before. I stood frozen in place. He looked over to see me standing waiting for a bus. He and his friends I assume kept walking and having a good time. He raised his arm slowly pointing at me. I'll never forget what he said out loud, **"Hey little buddy I'll be seeing you soon".** His friends stopped to see whom he was gesturing to. Apparently, a conversation was* *happening amongst themselves. I heard him say to his buddies, **"It's none of your business".** They walked onward acting as high school buddies do. Pushing each other, laughing as they venture on. I felt like a knife stabbed me in the heart. Just as the bus door opened, I threw up. I'm sure it was because of fear. Something I have known since the age of five. Only this fear took on darkness, **all of its own.** I gathered my emotions and headed for the door of the bus just as the school bell rang. Stepping up to get onto the bus, the bus driver said, **"Not feeling too good, are you?".** I went directly to the back of the bus. I opened the window for air. Here came my fellow bus mates. Some laughed talking about how stupid someone is. Others express anger for something that someone said to them over the course of the day. All of it seemed to funnel into a place where I wanted to burst out screaming, **"SHUT UP, SHUT THE HELL UP!"** But there I sat. Just like a toad. Motionless, hoping I was fading out of sight. Blending into the background. I stared out the window all the way home. Stop after stop letting the kids out. I waited until it was my time to exit the bus. All the way I prayed not to throw up again as the re-enactment of every single action flooded my mind. Stepping off the bus, and walking up the hill, I feared what could be waiting for me as I walk into the house up on **"Hell's Half Acre".***

SIDEWALKS
of
Frederick, Maryland

Sidewalks, written during the end of the sixties, and the beginning of the seventies. Around my eleventh grade. I remember it being a time of growth for me. A few of my friends accepted me. It didn't matter where I came from, who I was, what I was, etc., etc. You see, growing up poor in the fifties and in an alcoholic family that every now and then came into town on a Friday night to buy fuel oil and some groceries, always ended up in the local watering hole. That was the "Tic-Toc Tavern" across from the Firehouse. Like clockwork, my father started a fistfight and landed in jail. To make a long story short, I decided to go to New York City to pursue higher education life and the arts. Thanks to friends and students from two High Schools along with teacher and mentor, Anna May Hughes who encouraged me to pursue my dream in the Arts, which came true. I wrote Sidewalks in memory of that last night in Frederick before I left for the Big Apple. I was accepted to the "American Academy of Dramatic Arts". I felt scared leaving the only place I had ever known for the big city. I was making a step toward a dream that I believed would never come to light. My emotions came to the top like the rising of the tides. Here are my words to express my feelings.

Walking along the stark and cold sidewalks of Frederick at hour ten, I wear my trench coat with collar high. Only the sounds of a few motors and the haunting rhythm of my feet break the silence of the lonely evening. Forward I prance on the concrete shimmering with a diamond-glittered effect. The illusion is created by the winter crispness and the full moonlight of silver. A reflection of me through the windows of the shops, and dwellings tells the story of early to bed, early to rise. A few more nights I shall walk upon you. Looking at the shops reminds me of the times both yesteryear and weeks past. I find all the history to be interesting and it could have been more exciting without the hurt and pain. Barbara Fritsche's home and Rose Hill showed a town held together by belief and pride. From birth to twenty I remained here among times of hardships, people with narrow minds, "Be what we are or get OUT!" Yes, Frederick, I am different, I dream more, believe more, and want more in this life. I need a helluva sight more than those who are stuck in a small-town mentality. There is a wide world out there and much to experience and learn. You showed your fangs to this hometown American boy. Your bite was venomous, mentally this poor boy was destroyed by your ignorance to accept those who are different. Not all of Frederick held this ignorance. There were those that reached out and supported those like me. It didn't matter where you came from or what you believed in. Being kind, and friends were and are the train ticket to Humanity. I learned that change wasn't in your appetite. Years away and you've grown. Time makes the heart grow fonder; I'd love to walk upon your sidewalks once again to finally feel free of the hurtful past. I need not say more, except that you're my hometown. Born and raised up on Braddock Mountain. In my mind and heart, you were hated, redneck-ed, ugly, painful, and the tears of all my life. You really were mean to those of us that had much less than the core of the town. Selfish in the fact that someone from the other side of the tracks, needed to stay there!

Your contents hold a few great people, I will call them love, friends, and mentors. I will even go further in the belief that a few were even angels. So, I walk on your sidewalks, I don't feel or want them as mine like in the past. But one day I would love to come home and feel the good that once was. I will never deny you, nor will I ever forget. I once walked alone down Patrick Street. I felt the history, I listened to the rhythm of my feet on the sidewalks. Frederick, always remember your sidewalks have been walked by those that came before you. Sidewalks hold nothing but shadowed footsteps of the past. Frederick was found and settled by immigrants across the Atlantic Sea. Change is your destiny, or hate will override those with narrow minds refusing to change their ways of thinking. The charm of any town does not lie within its storefronts that one walks by every day. The charm comes from the heart of its people, and that makes or breaks what charm is Frederick, don't forget those that worked very hard to be a part to make a difference in helping Frederick to grow with the times. There are those that never received the accolades deserved for their hard work and efforts. The sidewalks in my hometown of Frederick do sparkle! All that was asked in return was nothing more than a pat on the back for a job well done! Sidewalks contain the history of all who have walked upon them and before us. Regardless of age, race, creed, and or sexual orientation may have grown up in misfortune. However, always remember we all walk on the sidewalks of Frederick.

Embracing Betrayal

"The Rape"

"One, pretending a false familiarity all the while, plotting your demise."

I feel as if I'm teetering on the edge of betrayal. Betrayal is without a doubt one of the darkest Evils in one's life. A secret holding you trapped and captive within your very own being. While everyone else is cocking their eyes in your direction. Making you feel even smaller or crazy for feeling the way you do. You know in your heart those who seek to betray you. They're always ready to put your emotions on the edge of darkness. I felt as though I were being pushed closer to the edge with every eye cocked my way. Behind me are confusion and disillusion. All the while watching my every move. Pretending a false familiarity. You can see in their eyes the plotting of your demise. Just leave me alone in my disintegration. Let me break down the path of pain I have grown to know. Then watch me soak up the flood waters of pity as I try to float on the debris of guilt. Cock your eyes in my direction to watch my soul sink through all the misbegotten emotions. Hark! I am one of the befallen wearing my heart upon my shoulder. How much further will you push me toward the edge of death's darkness? I say to you, **"ENOUGH IS ENOUGH, I CAN'T, I WILL NOT!"** *I am aware of all your evil lies, and degrading motives belittling me at every turn. All that I know to be true is that small people have small minds. Stagnate are your brains. You believe you've found an* **"Achilles Heel"** *in me. But you haven't and never will. Throughout my teens, many of you verbally beat me down with your hate and ugliness. There were a few of you who ganged together one night to teach me a lesson. On another occasion, two high school seniors from a rival high school across town and one senior classmate from GTJHS waited in the shadows, grabbing me, and forcing me into a dark alley between two shops in the middle of downtown Frederick. Threatening me not to make a sound. Oh, I knew they meant every nasty and ugly word being vomited in my ears and face. I was told what I was going to do and what they were going to do. My mind went dark, yet I was aware of everything happening around me. I became placenta to their every whim. Fighting them could possibly do me in. Being beaten to death was not an option. I lived through seventeen years of my life beaten, bruised, battered, and belittled up on* **"Hell's Half Acre."** *It was easy for me to escape into another world that I created over the years growing up. Always aware of what was going on around me. Such was this night. I followed their orders, believing it would be little me even more. I figured doing this would end the attack. However, one dude from the rival school had other plans that night. Two grabbed my arms and tackled me to the concrete. The third guy sat on my legs. Leaning over me he came face to face* with me. With both hands, he grabbed me by the hair. He was a strong athletic dude. With his face into mine, I remembered seeing him around town and at a few parties. I remember because he was a very good-looking guy. Well, I knew what his intent was. I started to gain some strength. In a low but serious voice, he told me what he was going to do. **"Faggot, I know what you like."** I felt fear at the end of that statement. Then, with one hand of hair, he pulled my head up. With the other, he cold-cocked me. Everything went black. When I came to, time wasn't the issue. I'm not sure how long I lay there before coming to my senses. My head and face hurt like hell. I tasted blood in my mouth and the knots to the back of my head were bleeding, but not enough to be overly concerned. It was very clear what he had done. **I was raped.** I felt the pain of the violation I endured. I pulled my pants up and noticed the blood running down my legs. As I began to pick up the belongings that were scattered around me. I noticed the blood on the concrete alleyway. I grabbed my dignity and walked to my apartment. Entering the door, I felt the increasing horror of gaining control of my senses. I broke down in silent tears with my back against the closed door. Locking the door behind me, I went upstairs, removed my clothing, and stepped into the shower. With my head under the shower, I watched the blood and gravel gather at my feet and down the drain. I watched the blood on my inner thighs wash from red to pink. I scrubbed away the results of sexual assault. Stepping out of the shower I stood in front of the mirror. I stared at my reflection. I don't remember for how long, but I was filling up with anger. With every question running through my assaulted mind, was WHY? What have I ever done to be treated like garbage? I picked up the ceramic soap dish and struck my reflection screaming" NO! NO"! **I remembered his face, I knew him and as far as the other two, I knew they went to Frederick High School. All three seniors.** To hell with the broken mirror. I took a sleeping pill and went to bed. It was afternoon when I crawled out of bed. Yes, I was in pain, both mental and physical. **No, I never told a soul.** Years later I did confide in a close friend. I went back to school that same day as if nothing ever happened. It was hard to do so because the one who raped me was there as well. We passed in the halls. My eyes were fixed on his every move. Funny to think about it, He always had his head down or turned away to avoid my stare. That was fine for I knew he was worried about me telling the authorities. I finished out my senior year and went on with my secret at bay. I saw my classmate that attacked me every day of that year. There were stare-downs in homeroom and classes we had together. The first few times were hard for me. I would still hear his words and that blow to my face knocked me out. His stare in the first few days after the attack was telling me that I better not tell a soul what happen. That didn't hold any weight for me. For my stare was saying, I know what you did! I even went as far as to walk up to him after several stare-downs between us. I leaned in whispering, **"You are a Coward"**. Whenever a flash of that night haunted me, I remember the shower I had taken when I got home, washing the blood of the violation down the drain. Watching the red water drain out in a timeless stowaway of hurt. I heard he is married with children of his own. I wonder, how often over the years, did or does he look over his shoulder, wondering what **"IF"**?

Words that are used with the intent to hurt, can do so! Some back them up with facts and witnesses. True or false, say what you mean and mean what you say. I've learned to swim in a world of intent. Of course, they hurt and damn near destroyed me. Sucking down the bitter hate, embracing their *lust to belittle. Wrestling with the egos of friends and foes can make you strong. For me, it's an education about social injustices and hate. There have been times in my life when I fell deep into the well of despair. I didn't want to climb out. I felt weak so many times throughout my teens. The mind harbors the light and dark of emotions. At times so intense that it burns my senses. I have experienced the silent tears that washed away the life in me. It pierced my heart, crushed my bones, and stagnated my soul. I spiraled downward, leaving me trapped mentally. What was left of me was an immense loathing and the sultry decadence of a double edge sword. Life is a **"Garden of Good and Evil."** I was pushed closer and closer to the edge of death and my sanity. The temptation is madness. The desire is divine. Together adds to self-gratification, **embracing betrayal.** Or **committing suicide.** Been there, done that...*

No One Knew Here in Frederick

No one here in Frederick truly knows my mourning

No one feels the burden put upon my early years

No one knows the worries I have for my sister

No one knew

No one

No one here in Frederick sees the tears of my everyday

No one hears my screams atop Hell's Half Acre

No one knows the pain I'm going through

No one knew

No one

No one here in Frederick watches what goes on after dark

No one knows my hopelessness here in this shack

No one knows my fear of tomorrow

No one knew

No one

No one here in Frederick knows every haunting hour

No one knows there's no hope in a house of abuse

No one knows the secrets I and I alone know

No one knew

No one

No one here in Frederick gave a damn for the poor

No one knows what goes on behind closed doors

No one knew how we hid to survive a Demon

No one knew

No one

No one knew that this unimportant tried to commit suicide

No one cared enough to look into the eyes of a child

No one in Frederick heard our cries for help.

No One Knew

No One

No

n

VIPERS ARE SINFUL PEACOCKS

*You who believe they are free from making mistakes, I say, "**a saint you are.**" You that boast they are the moon and stars throughout the universe, shine my friends, shine on. Those that have taken an action upon each known sin in their lifetime must be wise in their fortitude for fortune. You who stand on soapboxes voicing opinions, now stand on the edge of indications. A feeling of superiority lacks compassion amongst their fellow man. It is so easy to gain enemies when opinions are voiced with zealous ambitions, having the attitude of believing they are high born because of privilege. You know the type, "**born with a silver spoon in their mouths.**" The higher the pedestal the easier they crumble under such beliefs. Vipers are deadly and possessive when it comes to the sin of* **GREED.** *Tightly coiled, maintaining guard around their riches that multiply in cycles. Dragon's fire is known to be fierce, displaying signs, "**Beware Danger!**" It's a known fact that Greed feeds success and success feeds Greed. Handed down to newly born vipers in training no less. I tell you it's wise to investigate the face of the abyss before you take a leap into the unknown. Take time to think, are your sins greater than the whole of Sainthood? Go, take the plunge, for there waits a* **Succubus** *with arms opened wide. A Succubus waits to dance upon black satin sheets of pleasurable pain. The* **Succubus** *entices with words, "**Come on in, the water is fine.**" Engaging your every fantasy and whim surrounding you in a vice grip of pleasurable desires. For "**Desire**" is her name, a lustful vampire that feeds on your sins with sex and promises. You and your sins meld into a mating ball of confusion drifting into a craven darkening abyss. Stripped naked, thrown among the perverted and evil to be eaten alive. The sinful are her dessert. Go ahead and cry out loud for mercy, there has been a mistake made on your part. Screams fuel the fires rising from those you used and made enemies of. All to gain power which is* **GREED!** *Take heed ye* **Vipers,** *do not protest too much and certainly not too long. Those that inhabit the abyss are starved, each becoming greedy for food, ravenous in their need for the flesh. Within your lifetime did your actions speak louder than spoken words? Do you believe you possess and or pretend that you truly know it All? One who has so much, could you not lend a hand to the less fortunate? But of course not, that's why the* **Succubus** *and you lie naked together, give me-give me... The temptation among Vipers allows for the consumption of your soul. The human condition will allow one to paint a petty portrait of itself. Hang them in your own self-made gallery for the bastards and bitches to display their wares. Spotlight each one to show their explosive greed that displays the truth within. My words are not without sin myself, but I'm far from high and mighty. Simply put,* **GREED** *is damn ugly, the concept of wanting more and more, discusses the values of those who have nothing. It destroys the foundation of all humanity and the belief in God above. These words I pen are a message of grievous concern for my fellow man around the world. I suppose there is far too many drunk with the idea of power and wealth. The Greedy are addicted to their charm, they stand in front of every mirror they pass by. "**The Seven Deadly Sins**", beware for the Vipers can strike at any time. Wanting in excess seems to mirror the hidden form of vanities surplus. The rich covet like proud "**Peacocks**" when displaying their magnificence. There lies the rub, "**Beauty is only skin deep.**" The song of the proud Peacock has been heard across fields and forests. When assembled they display their possessions, strutting around with clipped wings. Is it their God-given beauty and or their loud cry that echoes the sin of Pride? NO, NO! It's the vanity of the Viper that covets a world of lustful pride. Each one turns an illustrious greenish blue with envy when "**Greed**" rises from within. The* **Peacock** *walks and struts by every mirror to face its own reflection! By the way, this is their downfall. Beware the* **Succubus, they are the sinful Peacocks!***

My Hometown of Fredrick, Maryland

Recalling Memories

*I still smell the **"White Star"** hot dogs. Around the corner was the **"Snow White Grille".** Stepping out the door onto the street picking your teeth after a half dozen of their half-dollar size hamburgers and cheeseburgers. My God, they were yummy. Make a right and eye the gems in the window of **"Elkin's Jewelers."** Walk over to your left about sixteen feet and you're standing at Frederick's famed **"Square Corner."** The ins and outs of the town. Yes sir, on three corners were the Banks, with their grand entrances, impressive to this country boy of five. Going out of town on your left stood the old **"Tivoli Theater."** I saw my very first movie there, **"West Side Story."** This movie changed my life that Saturday morning. I had to become a dancer, and that is what I did. Long before I was born it was a **"Grand Theater"** in its day. But wear and tear over the years and a flood or two damaged the inside. It became a movie house in the fifties. At that time the only one around. On Saturdays, it was for the children to watch cartoons. My first visit was amazing. A country boy steps into a grand palace with marble floors, chandeliers, red velvet seats, and even a balcony. The smell of popcorn being freshly popped when you first walk in with a ticket in hand. It cost this country boy Twenty-five cents. My God, B&W Television was just being introduced. We were too poor to own one, but later we managed to get an RCA Victor picture tube. On the right across the street was McCrory's five-and-dime store. Of course, on the corner stood the famed, **"Frances Scott Key Hotel."** It was huge, with a hundred-plus rooms. 1957, my days were spent being young and adventurous, if only in my mind. So many boyhood dreams that I would wish upon a star nightly. My cousins and I spent most days running through fields of wheat and weeds. Most of my cousins were wild animals. I was always dreaming, I saw magic in the trees, flowers, and clouds. I played with goats, pigeons, cats, and dogs. I raced through the fields, free like the wind. But all that was short-lived whenever Dad was home. At an early age, I was given chores to do. You started around five in the morning, wash up, and put on your pants, shirt, socks, and shoes. Watering, feeding the animals, and shoveling manure. When that was finished, I walked about a half-mile to catch the bus to school. School let out, came home, and repeated the same old chores. That was the early years in Frederick.*

You grow, learn, and live the life that is dealt to you. You either lived through it or you'd go mad. Once your innocence was precious. You grew up in poverty, pain, and abuse. Surrounded by a drunken atmosphere day in and day out. This world to a child lean-to early education of harshness and unpredictable situations. The times were a-changing in Frederick and so were the people. A flux of out-towners moved in and brought an array of new thinking. Some good and some not so good, people that is. There were those who seek out the poor and helpless to make fun of or even bullied by cowards that had to look big in front of their peers. For me in Frederick, it started around seven or eight at school. There were two classes of people Frederick.

My cousins and I were from the wrong side of the tracks. You soon learned how rough things could get. The home was like a volcano erupting nightly. My teen years were a mad house environment that drag me down. Creating the feeling of unworthiness, less than who you were or could be. Things in Frederick were very hard for those who jumped the tracks. In hope of blending in. I managed to break that barrier during my high school years. I became very active in the theater. I was able to create and live in an of my creation. And it felt as though I mattered. I guess I wanted to be accepted and loved. There wasn't much of that in my house. After graduation, I started teaching dance at Frederick Community College. Started a dance troupe called, "99 Plus 1". Being poor I never thought I would ever be able to attend college. Although I was offered a scholarship to Maryland University in 1970. But after all the abuse at home and trying to survive the day in and out, my grades would never carry me through academia. Instead, I attended the American Academy of Dramatic Arts in New York City. My Drama teacher and students from Frederick High and Governor Thomas Johnson High school students got together and collected money to get me to NYC to audition for the Academy. Their faith and belief in my talents would get me there, and they did! Prior to my going to NYC. I was a student at Frederick Community College. Studying Art, Art History, and Theater Arts. Known as Humanities, where I maintained a 3.8 average. After my two years in theater and as an Art major I managed to start teaching dance at FFC for the Adult Education Programs. Later I started teaching at the Frederick Dance center under the direction of Mrs. Joyce Morrison. After getting noticed by a talent scout for a new Dance Show on television, Titled "Studio 78". I was hired and thus started my professional career in the Arts. I left Frederick to explore professional Musical Theater while attending the American Academy of Dramatic Arts in New York City. I landed my first Off-Broadway Musical, "Let My People Come". It ran for three years at the Village Gate off Bleeker and Thompson Streets in New York's Greenwich Village. After the show closed, it wasn't long before I started touring in Musicals.

Frederick, Maryland is my hometown. There is much more to talk about what went on with and to me during my years performing in Musicals up and down the east coast. Growing up in Frederick was like having your foot on the gas pedal that often had the foot slamming on the brakes. When it came to something that they didn't understand if you were something different than what they deemed as "Correct" I personally was taught a horrific lesson. Frederick contains some heroic and amazing people. It's growth that harbors intolerances.

TENDER TARNISH

Elizabeth Browning once wrote,
"How do I love thee, let me count the ways. I love thee to the heights and depths my soul can reach. I love thee to every day's most quiet need, and if God should so choose, I shall love thee better after death."

Bonnie Lou Cook

I now stand at your shell. Wanting to make you aware of this great lady's work. Her words are the beginning of what I need to say to you now. Can you hear me? Can you? I'm in a lonely world that is cold and harsh. Youth's fleeting years passed us by like an arrow shot from the bow of misfortune. It's quiet now! Most sounds are still, dark, and lifeless. Every little thing in this world has lost its thrill and promise. What once had sparkle has tarnished dull and is useless from rusting. Echoes in the wind laughing uncontrollably were hidden from the monster that stifled our world of youth. The tender moments, the ever so tender moments we shared simply vanished in an instant.

Where have you gone my sunshine? The rays that woke me and fed me through those cloudy days. I can sit and remember they were good times; they were bad and ugly times. The distance can come easily, with miles and miles of empty spaces between us. Lives change, people grow, and minds develop. But love, it's always there like some re-accruing dream, each time you remember a little more. I'll never forget the way you walked. Classy, proud, and beautiful. A carriage of simplicity, yet eccentric. Small unknowing objects that only I could see, represented the enter most being. The silly little ways about you. How you treasured the meaningless little things. A flower bud that dried from the lack of moisture. The sick and helpless creature of nature. The sick and helpless creature of nature. The pain that entered you when nature reclaimed her own. You gave so much and got so little. You asked for nothing but small amounts of happiness. Something to call your own. Can time be like a book? Can the pages be turned backward? What about a revised edition? I need one on you and our life growing up. All the special events we once held, can they be once more? There were many times when we didn't get along. Hell, who in the hell could get along in that hell house? You are my sister and I watched over you more than you desired. I know you hated me so much in your younger years. Not once! Not once did I not love you. A week before your death, you told me why you hated me so much. I am so glad you explained why, face to face. It's unfair that we never had a childhood to share. It was simply impossible to do so. We grew up as adults. A child would never have survived in that house up on **"Hell's Half Acre".** *Do I have to travel to more empty spaces in my life without your hand in mine? I care not for the pain. I care not for the doubt. The knowledge of knowing we'll be together one day would help to end, to retire this hurt, the loneliness, this unforgiving question. I gaze into space and marvel at what lies ahead. This world has a lesser value without you in it. I will go on if I can.*

"How do I love Thee, let me count the ways"

Hell's Half Acre
In the Beginning

I was born and raised in Frederick, Maryland in 1951. The land was known as "Blueberry Hill". Later, my dad christened it, "Hell's Half Acre". My father found this shack up in the mountains back in the woods of Frederick, Maryland off Route #40 West. He was happy with it because it had enough land to plant a garden. If I remember correctly, we moved up on Blueberry Hill in 1955.

*The monthly rent on the small farmhouse in 1955 was $30.00 a month. That's right, believe it. Even at that dollar amount, dad often had a hard time paying the rent. During the winter months, Dad couldn't pay the rent. He worked in construction when the weather started to get worse, he was laid off and had to collect unemployment. Mrs. Reader, the owner turned a head for those few months. I'm sure that she had a soft spot in her heart for me and later when Bonnie my sister was born. Everyone in Frederick knew what kind of man my father was. A "Hellion" that got drunk and loved to fight! Our schoolteachers were aware. After all, there was no need to hide from torn-up textbooks and the battered existence we lived in and through. For some reason, he was totally against us going to school. More me than Bonnie after she became of age to start school. Many an evening would be spent with him preaching at me to quit school and go to work in construction with him. He would sternly yell, "It'll make a man out of you!" As far as I was concerned, that was never going to happen to me. **Never!** Farm work during the summer was hard enough alone. "When you turn sixteen, you're going to quit school and start working for a living with me. **You're going to QUIT SCHOOL!" Oh no, NEVER! NEVER!** will I do that?*

Dad collected unemployment checks during the winter months. A good portion of the check always went for cigarettes and liquor. He and my mother would drink seven days a week. I truly believe my mother drank so much just to cope with the beatings as well as the harsh verbal abuse that certainly took their toll on her and on Bonnie and myself over the years. There was a meal every night. Dad often referred to the food as "SLOP!". Often in his drunken demonic state, he would throw it on the floor, up against the wall, or even at mom. He'd order mom to fix him something worth eating. She would go downstairs, fix a plate of the very same food, and bring it up to him, only to be humiliated by his lack of respect. Let me make it very clear, mom's cooking was amazing. She could make a meal out of very little or hardly anything at all. She made it very clear that Bonnie and I would never go without a meal every day, one way or another. Our gracious, little, and the very modest house had no running water or plumbing. Our bodily functions were centered around a "Piss-Pot" and a discussing outhouse. This pot was used for nightly visits when the need would arise. Not one of us cared to go out into the dark night to visit "Old Bessie May". Our outhouse was that name by daddy dearest. A second deep hole was dug about ten feet beside good Old Bessie May. You see, when one hole filled up and the summer sun was at its zenith, the smell was a bit rank, to say the least. Bessie May was picked up and moved to her new location. Lime was used to cover the exposed hole and filled over with straw and dirt. Over several years the contents were absorbed by Mother Earth. During our timely visits, you made yourself aware of spiders, bees, and snakes that often wanted to make their home in or around Old Bessie May. We all had many-a-story to tell about our encounters with these intruders, so to speak...

*As far as no running water, we did have a "**hand-pump well**" under a beautiful grape arbor. We retrieved buckets of water for our needs. Drinking, washing, cleaning, and watering the animals. There were the chickens (Dad's prizefighting cocks), we had pigeons, and an American Appaloosa named "**Apache Firefly**". He was the pride and joy of my sister Bonnie. There was "**Willy** the goat", rabbits, Ginny-pigs, hogs, and dogs and cats. At one time we had pet Crows we raised from nestlings. We called them "**Heckle** and **Jekyll**". We even had a pet Squirrel Monkey named "**Buttons**". Filthy little beast but cute as hell. Buttons were allowed to run free. He would catch a ride on Rocky's back, a pet Shepard dog. Whenever Bonnie would saddle up Apache to go riding over the fields surrounding **Hell's Half Acre**. Buttons grabbed two hands full of Rocky's hair and rode him like a jockey. Those two were inseparable. Together along with Bonnie and Apache, they traveled up and down the trails as a team. When at rest, Buttons was in grasshopper heaven. He was never without snacks. There were times when we came home from school and Button's would be missing. One of us would whistle and call his name. It was answered by a shrill squeal. Then we would call out once again, "**Where are you Buttons?**" Here came Rocky with Buttons on his back in jockey styling. Running and jumping over and through the tall weeds. Damn! Button was an amazing little creature.*

*We had over a dozen make-sifted pens housing these animals. Weathered and shabby. Do you know something? That was a lot of water to pump three or four times a day during the summer. We did have electricity for the house. There was one 40-watt bulb screwed into the center of each room's ceiling. Thank God we had lights! However, there were many times when storms put us in the dark. We would break out the oil lamps and candles to light our lives. Winter often left us without electricity for days at a time. The winters in Frederick were nothing to shake a stick at. We all hunkered in the living room around the fuel oil stove. Mom, Dad, Bonnie, six dogs, a dozen cats, one monkey, and me. All would gather around that stove and curl up together and go to sleep. As the winds howled and the tin roof would make sounds that sounded like moans and groans of the aching. Sinister at times, frightening for Bonnie and I. Fuel oil has a definite order all its own. Often the wind would roar down the chimney, sounding like an old mournful scream from a Banshee. That was when a puff of black soot came from the flames and out into the room like a deadly entity in shadow form. Creating coughs and blackness around the eyes, ears, and nostrils when we woke in the morning. It was our only source and means of heat and cooking. We had an iron cookstove that was a lifesaver when the fuel ran out. We'd fire her up with wood and that small farmhouse was heated throughout. There was a joke about a cook stove. It went like this, "**What are the three most important parts of a cook stove?**" The answer is, "**The lifter, leg, and poker!**" Hey, it was funny to us country folk...*

*Dad lost his license in 1959. He was driving drunk with eight of us in his Pontiac. Driving to the Kramer's farm for "**homemade wine**". Depending on the season determined what flavor was for sale. There was dandelion wine, grape wine, rice, potato, and whatever berry came into the season. Well, it was a Sunday afternoon when the car was loaded up for our routine trek. In the front seat were dad, mom, Aunt Edith, and little Bonnie on mom's lap. In the back were Uncle Boots, Uncle Fuzzy, Dick Flook, and me on Uncle Fuzzy's lap. Turning off the highway to get on the road known as the "**Seven Sisters**", dad turned left to cross over the highway and the car stalled a bit over the hill coming at us, the broadside was a car speeding at 110 mph. According to the State Police. We* found out later from the newspaper articles that, the driver was not hurt at all. But was found to be drunk when we were hit at a hundred and ten miles an hour. Splitting our car in two. Mom and her sister Edith were seated in the front with my sister Bonnie on mom's lap. Mom and Aunt Edith were nearly killed. Both nearly had every bone in their bodies broken. Punctured lungs and internal bleeding. Mom had a severely broken jaw. At the point the car was about to be struck, mom threw Bonnie down between her legs on the floor under the dashboard. This action saved Bonnie's life. Bonnie was discovered in a pool of blood. An artery was severed under her right arm. Bonnie was two years old, dressed in a little white dress. No longer, it was red soaked in blood. A nurse on her way to work at The Frederick Memorial Hospital stopped at the accident, saw Bonnie, and ran to her rescue to slow the heavy bleeding that certainly would have taken her life that day. Never knew the name of that nurse. All of us were physically hurt in some manner. Twenty-five feet from the front half of the car, the back half faced the front portion of the highway. Still seated were Uncle Fuzzy, Uncle Boots, and Dick Flook. I was seated on Uncle Fuzzy's lap before the accident. I was found nearly forty feet down an embankment alongside a creek. I had lost consequence apparently. I was found and carried by a stranger up to the accident scene and Paramedics. Dad's judgment to cross the highway was impaired judgment that nearly got us all killed. Yet the car sputtered, lost the get-up-and-go, then at that very instant in time, **"All"** of our lives had changed forever. Alcohol certainly came to a bigger factor for most in that Pontiac. Mom's sister, my Aunt Edith was found beaten to death at age **"forty-five"**. Ironically, mom met her death at the age of **"forty-five"** from a beating. Both lived and died at the hands of a man once in love. But that is another story to be told.

Let me tell you a bit more about the house. I am very sure that if the walls could talk, they would have quite a few tales to tell. It once was a farmhand's house in the thirties and forties. So, it never was that important to be cared for. I believe the shack, as I called it, had to be much older. It had a brick chimney added on during the late forties. After we moved in, we discovered there was a fireplace hidden behind a wall downstairs. The foundation was built with stones. When the land was cleared for planting fields these stones were used to construct the original chimney. Many stonewalls were constructed over the property and through the fields. Hard work and labor had to be time-consuming. Dad ripped the plasterboard away and there it appeared. Black from years of soot and grime and whatever fell down the chimney. Don't get me wrong, when dad fired her up, that stone fireplace and brick chimney absorbed the heat and warmed all three-story rooms. That room functioned as our kitchen. There was a door that led out to the ground level. Flagstone was laid to form a patio covering that put you in front of the water pump. A huge grape harbor covered the well and hand pump. From mid-summer to early fall, that grape harbor permeated the air and circled the entire house with the sweetest perfume of ripening grapes. Of course, this led to thousands of bees, flies, and many species of birds. An amazing harmony of songs, if one would take the time to stop and listen for the good that nature offers for free. The ducks and chickens often made an early morning appearance under the grape arbor. A trough for water caught the overflow when the pump was being used. The pump broke a couple of times leaving us to pull the cover off. Which was a six-inch-thick slab of concrete that replaced the oak planks earlier used. Every time water was needed the slab had to be moved away so we could drop a line down with a bucket on it and pull the water up. We never forgot to put the slab back on. Didn't want someone or something to fall about twenty-five feet. Pulling the bucket back up was labor for me when I was in my single digits. But I managed it. It was extra work on Saturdays and Sundays because the wash had to be done. I was elected for the job because dad was **"drunk-as-a-skunk"**. It took *five to six buckets to fill the old washing machine. Then the same amount for the rinse. It was a pain in the rear. On weekends I ended up pumping and carrying close to fifty buckets of water. As mentioned before, the animals had to be watered from morning and afternoon to evening.*

*As far as taking bathes was concerned, during the summer and early fall, we would trek over the highway. There was a beautiful secluded cool mountain stream. It was running water and damn it felt good. We were the only ones who used the secret bathing pools and small waterfalls. My cousins Jimmy and Richard are the ones who discovered the spots and introduced their younger cousins to the secret. Hell, there were days after working in the fields all day, we were dusty, dirty, and itching. Farm work and gardening were hot stuff during the summer. So, the guys got together and went to the stream and had the most refreshing baths. Jimmy, Richard, and I would head further upstream to a beautiful area shaded by tall Poplars, Pines, and Oak trees. I have enough memories to last me all through this life when it comes to that stream and my two cousins, Jimmy, and Richard. Those two were mentors, heroes, and big brothers to this scared, beaten-down, and abused boy. Jimmy was several years older than me and Richard was two years older. Each one had that big brother factor for me, and they never knew it, never knew the admiration I held in my heart. Both were **"Movie Star"** handsome. Strong beautiful bodies from the hard work they endured. Jimmy was a sculptured beauty, he was **"Touched by the Gods"**. Black wavy hair that had a sheen of blue in the sun. Tall, handsome, and had a smile that was drop-dead gorgeous but intriguing, to say the least. Hell, mom, and dad both always talked about how damn good-looking he was. Jimmy would blush and that smile beamed. Right or wrong as a teenager, as an adult, and now as a senior in life, I wanted, wished I could have been him. Richard was a brutally handsome blonde. Striking features with baby-blue piercing eyes. Many a time he would catch me staring at him. He'd smile and say, **"You're looking at my eyes again!"** They were like Paul Newman's eyes. Thank God he would laugh and brush it off as a good friend would. Often, I would watch him working in the sun with his shirt off. The sun framed Richard in a **"halo glow"**, accenting every muscle he developed from the hard work leaving him as a tall, handsome, and dark-tanned **"Adonis"**. I often questioned my admiration for each one of my cousins. Was it the **"Big Brother"** idea that was in control of my desire to be in their company? Yes, in the beginning. The more I was abused and witnessed the abuse being done to my mother before my eyes, I turned myself in the direction of my masculine cousins. I wanted their acceptance, their companionship. I needed some other male figure to look up to. Let's be honest and I mean* __*"NO"*__ *disrespect to the memory of Jimmy or the masculinity of Richard. I fell deeply in love with the thought of having their affection and kindness. Who else understood and knew what my life was like up on* **"Hell's Half Acre"**? *They lived in their own hell of sorts. We lived in poverty and always seemed as if to defend that reason.* **"Life Sucked"**! *Yet somehow, we managed to have unbelievable moments of light in our worlds of darkness. Periods of warmth for those who only knew the cold.*

Back to the house as it were. Our kitchen had steps that lead upstairs to what was our living room. Mom and dad's bedroom was to the left. An 8 X 14 enclosure. There was another set of stairs that lead up and opened to my bedroom. My sister Bonnie had her room off to the right beside mine. There was another small room used to throw odds and ends into it. Mine and Bonnie's rooms also had slanted ceilings on both sides. Leaving about six feet of head space. We were ducking all the time. There were two tiny windows on the top floor. We would get cross-ventilation from my room through Bonnie's room during the summers. Damn, it got hot in the shack. The roof was made of tin. There were times when we were being baked in our beds. Many a night we would spend time outside in the yard under the stars to keep as cool as possible. Those were the nights I danced amongst the stars, **"Free to be Me"**! To get to the house you would turn off the highway. Then drive or walked up the hill that was quite steep. During the hot summer months, it was dusty and dirty getting up to the top. Many a day was spent walking down the hill and back up again. Do you know how active we **"young-ins"** are? The dirt was like powder in spots and other areas were stony and sharp upon our bare feet. All summer we barely wore shoes. Mom and dad couldn't afford new ones all the time. That luxury was saved for the first day of the new school year. Bare feet were fine with us. Shoes were for school and Friday nights. That's when we all went to town for groceries and fuel oil for the stove. Bonnie or I would have to down the highway to "Hamilton's Restaurant" to call a cab to take us to town. It was about ten miles to downtown Frederick. Then there was Tom Bowie, a co-worker, and friend of dad and mom. He and dad worked together at the same construction job for over forty years. Tom was a black man that did welding, and dad was a crane operator for Earl H. Cline & Son's off route #40 west. If it weren't for the kindness of Tom taking us to the grocery store to get oil and feed, **"We were up shit creek without a paddle."** If Tom was available to do these things for dad, all was well. But if Tom wasn't available to do dad's bidding, he was then called a no-account **"Niger"**. Mom, Bonnie, and I never thought of Tom that way. Tom knew that and he would always say, **"Charlie is drunk, and he doesn't mean anything by it."** I couldn't believe how gracious this man was. Deep down inside he tolerated dad's slurs and down-right unforgivable language. Over the years Tom lessened his availability. He went out of his way for years to help us, and dad had to speak ill to his face every damn time he got drunk. Dad would transform into that demon-like creature. I am telling the truth. His entire body, face, mannerisms, and demeanor changed before your eyes. He started with the cursing and then he would call Mom, Bonnie, and myself every foul name imaginable. The worst is when our souls were grounded up and spit out for being of Native American Heritage. We were nothing more than, **"A Nigger turned wrong-side-out. As far as he was concerned, that is lower than a Jew!"** That son-of-a-bitch was married **"twice"** to women of Native Indian Heritage. Before my mother, he was married to **"Evelyn"**, my mother's first cousin. That union produced two children, **"Loretta and Eddie"**. My older half-brother and half-sister. Evelyn finally divorces him after years of abuse. She got the hell out of Frederick and was far away from him. My half-brother and sister were left to my dad's mother, a grandmother seen once when I was around ten years old. This story is the way dad told it to Bonnie and me...

Tom didn't need to help us. He could have had each one of those evenings to be with his own family. Tom and his wife Gladys cared for eleven children. Several were fostered. A sweet and caring lady I met on several occasions. She had to be kissed by an angel, God bless her. No matter how many times Tom came to help us, we were thankful and said so. Nothing came from dad's mouth, nothing. When dad would start mixing the beer with whiskey, he would start arguing with mom. Tom would say goodbye to us and leave for his home back in downtown Frederick. Even he knew after all the years what was going to happen that night. We would say, **"Goodnight, Tom"**, but he was reluctant to leave. But we insisted, **"please!"** My mother would head downstairs to cook something for dad to eat. There was a chance this would calm him down. Most time, not! Mom would call upstairs for me to come downstairs to help her start the fire in the cook stove. You had to stoke it with kenneling wood. We would use a little kerosene for a quick start. Then add log after log. One thing I will say about that cook-stove is it could put out a hell 'a lot of heat. A blessing for sure. The winters were harsh, and it got quite cold. Splitting logs wasn't an easy job for a six-year-old. That task became mine from then on. I had to mustard up a lot of energy on *many an occasion. Dad come home drunk, and he couldn't manage to do the job. When I came home from school, all I had to do is look over at the log box and see that it was empty. I knew I had to split the wood for the evening. My life was far from my schoolmates. My cousin down below was in the same boat. You see, my father was one of those* **"nasty-dirty-lowdown-bastard-that-loves-to-fight"** *types of drunk. He was drunk a lot up on Blueberry Hill. Rarely did a day go by that he was sober on a 24-hour day. To his credit as a man, drunk, hung-over, sick, or sober, my father never missed a day of work.*

Mom married dad sometime after **"WWII"** *ended. I know it was the sixth of April 1948. Dad was born in February 1917. My mother was born in October 1922. When April sixth would roll around, mom would be at her worst on that date. Sometimes angry, other times depressed. She started drinking early in the morning after dad had left for work. When dad walked through the door that would be the night that she'd provoke him into another fistfight. I would beg her to stop drinking before he got home. I would go as far as to hide the whiskey. Hoping she would think she had drunk it all. Sitting in her chair she'd sincerely said to us,* **"Look you, kids, don't worry about me. I will kill that bastard if he lays a hand on you kids. I'll kill him."** *My mother repeated that statement over and over, again and again over the course of the day.* **"As sure as Christ made little green apples"**, *that night would end up with blood everywhere. Heavy was the drinking by both. First was the arguing. Then the exchange of major insults. I would get my share of foul language in trying to calm them down. I will pick one night when I jumped up from the coach when dad went for Bonnie. I was thirteen years old at that time. I jumped in front of him and got a backhand across the face. Poor Bonnie was attacked. Just because she was begging dad to stop hitting mom. Bonnie did nothing, nothing but try to help mom! As I fell backward, I stumbled from being dazed. I remember wiping the blood from my mouth. Bonnie began to back up in the corner of the room when dad turned around. She's standing in the corner of the living room screaming at the top of her lungs. He let go of mom. He took several steps toward Bonnie. It was a small room where everything was nearly at arms-length. I wasn't fast enough, and mom was having a rough time trying to up from the chair. He grabbed a handful of Bonnie's long blonde hair. That* **"mother-fucker"** *gave her hair one hell of a yank. To our horror, Bonnie screamed a blood-curdling scream! Grabbing her own head as she was slung to the floor like a ragdoll. Of course, I would have to jump in front of Bonnie to redirect his attention to me instead. There stood that evil motherfucker with a fistful of blonde hair. Mom ran over to Bonnie on the floor trying to console her and ease the terror she was filling at age of nine. The silver dollar size bald spot was bleeding. Dad looked at the hand full of hair. Then rubbing his hands together to remove the hair. As it slowly fell to his feet, he mumbled,* **"I've had enough, I'm going to bed!"** *I remember that entire senseless evening filled with horrors and blood. My mind and heart are filled with the pages from the* **"Dark Ages."** *So many fights and beatings throughout our three lives. I recall all the pain, the hurt, and the anguish every day of my life. My terrors and horrors were built like a dungeon within my mind. Bruises, fists, slaps, slams, blood, and belittling became the mortar that kept the light from entering what world I might have had. We were always waiting for him to come home after working fourteen hours a day. Listening to him getting out of a co-worker's car at the top of the lane. We'd look out the tiny living room window. Watching to see if he was staggering towards the house or not. Isn't it amazing how carefully you're taught to regulate your life around* **"Fear?"** *Just like clockwork, all I remember of my childhood was fighting a creature that truly manifested at will. Bonnie would saddle up Apache and ride away to hide from dad. Simply to get away from all the madness. I would go upstairs, sit on the edge of the bed, and silently cry. We were afraid* *of him and did our best to avoid the on-slots that became a routine over the years.*

*Now don't get me wrong, there were some good days. When he wasn't drunk, he would wake us up in the morning and be the father that we all wanted. We kept our always guards up, for he could change into that **"Demon"** all too fast. His good moments held a laugh or two. We would go about doing our chores caring for the animals, watering, and feeding. Cages and talk had to be cleaned. Often needed to be repaired and sometimes we would even start work on one of those new projects. For some reason, we never got around to finishing it. On carefree days, Bonnie and I would go up to the field where this huge walnut tree. A rope was tied around one of its perfect branches and swung like Tarzan. We were able to make a perfect circle through the air without obstruction. That was fun for a while. The best time was when our cousins came up to join in on the fun. Right beside the old walnut tree was an old raspberry patch. When they were ripe, we had a feast of sorts. Staining our fingers red to show for it. Sweet and juicy. Mom would come up with us and pick several quarts. She would make a pie and or make jelly. As the years went by, the berry patch just wasn't taken care of any longer. It went to the birds and whatever other critters that had a taste for berries.*

*For several years straight things around Blueberry Hill remained the same old routines. I mean life went on. The weeds grew taller, and our surroundings lacked signs of growth. Things between mom and dad got worst if that was even possible?... Dad's outbursts and rages grew in intensity day by day. Mom's attitude was one of, **"who gives a rat's ass anyway."** She stopped fixing her hair and cleaning the house and she would start drinking more than ever before. She would take her cigarettes and a can of beer and set in her chair out in the front of the house humming or even at times singing to herself. She loved the breeze that blew up over the hills and would circle through the trees. The breeze would blow through the wild roses and pass by where she set. **"Kids, come here and smell this sweet aroma."** She would yell to us saying, **"Come, smell the roses you all, you got to smell the roses in life."** At times when the sun would go behind the clouds and a shadow would move slowly across the ground, Mom would talk of summer dances and picnics with family and friends who used to come around. Bonnie and I watched her eyes as she recalled her days of youth with amazement. How real they were to her. She saw and felt every word that she uttered. I loved to watch her long black hair blow in the breeze. She would stand with her arms out and call to Bonnie. Bonnie would run into her waiting arms. As Bonnie ran toward mom, her long blonde hair streamed behind her. That was a **"Norman Rockwell"** painting if you ever saw one. A picture of love between a mother and her daughter. Love is rarely exchanged between mother and daughter. That memory stands out in my mind as if it were before me at this very instant. Her eyes were like the shooting stars we saw quite often during mid-summer over Blueberry Hill. Mid-summer was a time when the fields were thick and green and full of wildflower blossoms. So green that when the wind blew, it would ripple in shades of blue like waves in slow motion over water. I used to go up to the very top of the hill and lay down at dusk. I would watch the stars come alive as the universe was giving birth to each one that night in the evening sky. I would dream of what I wanted to be. What could I become if God would but grant me the power? I would hear one of the shadows whisper in my ear, **"You're a dreamer and you will be nothing."** Then I would hear dad yelling my name from below. **"LEE!"**, **"Do you hear me, boy, you better get your ass in this house!"***

*There were times when my **cousin Richard** and myself would walk up to the very top of Blueberry Hill and sit for hours at a time. We would talk about friends we liked and people we hated. Then* *there were times when we talked about what the future meant to us. Our dreams were as unlimited as the sky itself. We'd lie on our backs, look up to the stars and get as quiet as possible and listen to the sounds around us. Sometimes I could hear his heart beating. These were the times that I would glance over at him and take a good look. How his crystal blue eyes sparkled. He had a handsome face and blonde hair that fell into his eyes at times. He would turn his head over slowly and notice that I was looking at him. I would slowly turn my head away from him. This was our quiet time. Young kids exploring new venues. We laid them shoulder to shoulder and our hands at our sides. Without saying a word to me, Richard would touch my hand and the world seemed to be all right. There were times when I would shake with fear that he would know my secret. Richard was a year older than me. He was strong, blonde-haired, blue-eyed, and ruggedly handsome to boot! My cousin, his brother Jimmy was* **"James Dean"** *re-incarnated. Pictured perfect. My God, he was blessed by the Gods above. Dark hair, and eyes like a husky. Jimmy's face was so beautiful and how I wished I were him. That's what a man to me was to look and act like. Everyone, my mother included, Bonnie, and even dad thought the world of him. He used to call me* **"Baby Hughie"**. *That was a cartoon character. It was a large baby duck. Anyway, Jimmy was everything I always wanted to be. He was a handsome young stud, and I was so proud he was my cousin. Richard had many of the same qualities but in a different way. Over the years we all grew into young men with different drives and goals. Both our families lived below the poverty line. Poor and doing the best we could. We were considered* **"From the Wrong Side of the Tracks".**

Summer was the time we did as many odd jobs as possible. We worked hard to get every penny possible. Working in the fields bailing hay, straw, and clover. After those long hot days of dirt and dust, you guessed it, over to the stream to wash up. Our bathing area was surrounded by tall trees. The sun would filter through the tops of the tall trees and create bright spots upon the water and the banks. It seemed to be mystical looking in a way, very surreal. Summer was the time for horseplay and growing. My life felt good during times like that, yet the evening would come and the horror I felt was always true. Dad would come home from work always drunk, and his friends would come in the house or better, yet they would stay out in front of the house where it was a lot cooler. They would get drunk, get loud and someone would say something that would set dad off. That's when Bonnie and I would make up any excuse to leave the house for a while until we would know he went to bed or mom would let him sleep outside if he had passed out asleep out there. That was good for all of us unless things didn't quite go that way.

When I sit back, stop, and think of my youth, it's so hard to pick out the sweet, tender moments that we all shared then. So many of those wonderful moments were shadowed by the mental rape that that man put us through. I just thought about it, and you know what? Most of our years were fashioned around liquor. There was always that fun time when they all started to drink. Then like the shot of a race gun, everything turned vicious. Fridays were payday. Dad got off work earlier than usual and if he wasn't home around six, then that meant he was in town already and we were to get a cab unless Tom or Ed had dropped by and got one of them to drop us off at their favorite beer joint. That was the **"Tic-Toc".** *You see, the grocery store,* **"The Market Basket"** *was next door. After the drinking was over, we would go next door and get the week's groceries. Call a cab and homeward bound. No sooner we would pull into the driveway, dad would pay for the cab, and we all grab the groceries and started to walk over to the house. I will be damned if it didn't happen every damn time. Dad started his crap and by the time he stepped in the door, either an argument would ensue over just about anything, or dad would kick a cat or dog. Why?* **The man was evil,** *no other excuse, just evil. We helped mom put the food away and she would ask dad what he wanted to eat. We always tried to get him to eat to make him sleepy and he would go straight to bed. However, that didn't always work. Mom would fix what he said he wanted and bring it to him. No sooner did she set it down in front of him, than he would pick it up and look at it. Then yell like a crazy man. One of two things would happen at that point.* **1.) Grumble and eat it,** *or* **2.) Throw it up against the wall** *or* **3.) Slap mom up against her head with the plate.** *If the third happened, he and mom would start to throw food at each other, dad would slip and fall, and we all ran outside and let him tear the house apart. On occasions when he completely lost it, he'd grab the shotgun off the wall and step outside and shoot it in the night sky. We dare not run before he shot the gun. It was a single load 12-gauge. I tell you, as sure as* **"Christ made little green apples"**, *Friday nights were like the rising of a full moon's horror. A warning that it brings the demons out in their full glory! Up on Blueberry Hill, in the middle of* **"Hell's Half Acre"**. **Someone was going to feel his wrath...**

MY SURRENDER TO SORROW

It's the heartbeat of the night
Calling into the vast silence of lost loves divine
Sweetness within the breeze that blows directly to my surrender
Sorrow slowly crawls in an everlasting fog onto the land, hit by the man-in-the-moon
Casting a blue-black brightness,
The dreams of lovers hidden throughout the shadows
Many a moonlit canopy gave sight to my hidden books of poetry
You see, the "Master of the House" has declared, "There will be No Books!"
A declaration that no coins are to be wasted upon trash and non-sense reading
It was money that could be used for more important things around here
Like food, kerosene from the store
Hunger has tightened our belts more than occasionally
What he truly had meant to say was that the money could buy another bottle of liquor
I would not allow myself to feel a single bit of remorse for buying a book or two
Oh! the moonlight of night's sweet surrender was my friend and lover
My imagination crossed over into never-land and beyond
Writing stories creates adventures for my very soul
Adventures belonging to a poet's heart are as vast as the cosmos
I hear the cries of sorrow
They fill me without song
I can feel the battles of yesterday
Fleeting is the voice that echoes a haunting re-frame
It's dark and fierce-some
Beaten for my resounding protest of writing to cover my sanity
With words that touched my heart with light
I mastered the shadows supported by the moonlight
I was hidden like the rich treasures of long-ago pirates
Page after written page was read with the promise of "One Day!"
It wasn't long before the scars of my personal burden echoed with thunder,
Deep into sorrow's bottomless pit
From six to sixteen, the road traveled led to that my misfortune
Cradled in the land of drunkards and predators
If not for my hidden treasure guarded by sorrow's minion
Life would have fallen into insanity and or demonic overtones
My mentality was challenged one night while in the throes of a demon
Taunting my courage, I was staring directly into the eyes of darkness
A seduction of lust invited me to lay with him
I took the prone position, taking a deep breath, feeling the fire invading each of my wrists
I willed myself to sit up, feeling weak, feeling a draining of my energy
I finally accomplished the effort with determination
Guiding my back up against the wall of ill-repute, a light in my demeanor
My eyes, painted in sorrow now witness the red river of life spilling at my sides
Resembling the slow flowing of lava across old land

Creating nothing in its wake
What was the purpose?
I had the right to my sacred dreams, suppressed in a dungeon of ignorance and brutally
I did my best to hold onto my dreams, but I wasn't strong enough to fight the forces
I fought the darkness and the shadows of evil for as long as I could
It was hatred that filled the empty spaces of this dreamer.

So, in the moments of my fading light,
I had a vision of sitting on a stool on the stage
There were eight other stools, each placed evenly apart in two rows
Each stool including mine was lit in an individual light
I'm seated on the left, the last stool in the front row facing an empty theater
In front of the two rows of stools,
Golden light is downstage center at the edge of the stage
There is a beautiful redhead walking out of the dark into the circle of light
She wore a beautiful silky flowing gown of ivory
She looked familiar in so many ways
She stared forward as if in a quiet trance
One by one each stool was occupied by a handsome man.
Someone I knew from my past and present.

On my further right, front row,
A spot slowly faded up on my good friend,

Mike Mcleod

We attended high school together and were active in the theater department
I performed and Mike was the best stagehand around,
Not to mention tall, very good-looking, and extremely popular throughout the school
Many nights were spent in musical rehearsals
After rehearsals, we would go downtown to the "Snow White Grill"
We'd both order a dozen of their twenty-five-cent cheeseburgers,
And a milkshake and a large order of French fries.
The cheeseburgers were the size of a silver dollar, smothered in fried onions and pickles
Damn they were the best in town and always open late
Mike had a great personality and was a true ladies' man!
Mike became a very close friend when I was in a dark place,
I never knew if he was aware of my feelings for him.
It doesn't matter, I hid those feelings for his friendship meant the world to me
I thank God that he came into my life after my mother's death.
We lost touch after he graduated a year ahead of me
A day hasn't gone by that Mike isn't in my thoughts and my heart
Special people and friends are so rare in one's lifetime
Mike sat on the stool staring forward,
Behind Mike, another spotlight faded in.

Richard Angleberger,
a cousin of mine walked in and sat down facing forward
He is one year older than I
We lived near one another for most of our childhood and teen years
Our families grew up in very hard times and poverty,
But we all made the best of what we had
Richard had four brothers and four sisters
Richard was strong, muscular, tall, blonde, and ruggedly handsome
We spent a lot of time together, going fishing, and hiking throughout Braddock Heights
Several miles away down route #40 east was the local "Hi-way Drive-Inn Theater"
During the summer the weekend evenings were spent sneaking into the watch the movies
Walking back home at one or two o'clock in the morning,
Was taking a risk on a near deserted and dark hi-way
Hell, I felt safe walking beside my rough and tough cousin
I grew very fond of Richard
There are many days and many stories between Richard and I
I truly believe he was an important part of my life.
Growing up on route #40 wasn't easy by any standards.
There he sat staring forward with the other two on stage.

Another spotlight shined on another empty stool
In walked Billy Burdette
Billy was simply a masterpiece created by the "Man" above!
A beautifully sculptured stud of a man
My Lord, he was handsome, and I was smitten with him
His mannerisms were like that of "The Bad Boy Image", "James Dean" type!
Billy had wavy black hair, was six foot three, and had the body of an "Adonis"
His crystal blue eyes radiated, "Love Machine"
Along with all that, he possessed, "The Cock of the Walk" prance in his step
Listen, he was simply magnetic,
Twenty-seven and I was in the eleventh grade when I first met Billy
I wanted to be in his arms, right or wrong I tell you now!
I was head over heels for this matinee idol and as a studly hunk of God's gift
Of course, I kept all my forbidden feelings inside, hidden!
He was always around the house because he and his dad worked the same construction jobs
I was a master in the art of concealment
Here was Billy walking upon the stage and taking a seat on his stool in the spotlight
Billy stared forward like the others
I had a hard time keeping my fantasies in check over these hunks from my past!
My heart was thumping in my chest sitting still on this stool
The sight of him once again after all these years
Brought forth the hunger my spirit desired.
If I was to lose my virginity,
Billy would have been the one and I would have given it to him with pleasure!
My attention was drawn to the fourth light fading in on another already seated

OH MY GOD

The light just revealed, **Clark.**
Picture perfect just as he was every day in homeroom
During my senior year of high school,
He was the guy that everyone couldn't take their eyes off
Other than a morning nod now and then to one another
I never had the pleasure of a one-on-one conversation with him
His shiny black hair, dark eyes, and clean-cut appearance were striking, "Wall Street Prep"
Good looking and refine, I wonder what kind of stock he came from?
My guess is Elvis Presley, and Elizabeth Taylor...
Clark is a gorgeous young man, indeed!
I idolized him from a distance
He did flash that perfect smile and a good morning nod several times to me
These men and the memories I have of them were racing through my head and heart
I took another glance at the beautiful redhead sitting center stage,
Who was she?

From the shadows,
Walking onto the stage was a very tall, wide-shouldered lumberjack of a man
He sat down on his vacant stool as the light revealed him to me

Good God, there sat **Copa!** *"The Italian Stallion"*
He was the type of man that would give your heart a reason to flutter
Many a sigh would harmonize in the very air he walked upon
I am six-foot-two, and Copa stood a towering six-foot-six
He was all muscle, confident, and very much an Italian man
Copa had raven black hair, a black mustache with emerald, green eyes
He was always dressed in the tightest of blue jeans that showed all his outstanding assets
He wore a white tank top to show off that amazing tan and those cannons for arms
Copa was the definition of an "Italian Stallion", and he knew it!
I met Copa in Baltimore at the dance club called, "The Hippo"
And my dance partner, "Miss Vicki"
We're well known as one of "Maryland's Top Latin Dance Couples"
In fact, Vicki and I were "The 1980 Latin Champions in Maryland"
The "Hippo" at the time was the hottest gay dance establishment in the Mid-Atlantic
I saw Copa walk in as I was dancing, and our eyes connected
The flirting between us was intense
Copa and I spent several weekends together after that night
This man was a gentle and sensitive giant a remarkable lover
My time spent with him has been member-able throughout my life
Copa was approached by a casting director and flown out to Hollywood for a screen test
He had several minor roles in hit feature films and television movies
There he was facing forward like all the others were doing

To my right a stool apart, a green light came up on the stool
It was occupied by **Garland**
Another tall, blonde haired handsome dude, a well-known hair stylist, and dancer
If not for the beautiful exterior of this man,
I would never have known how true the beast that dwells within!
I got to experience firsthand the jealousy,
The contempt, and petty envy he displayed toward me on more than one occasion
It seemed that Baltimore City had two top male "Latin Ballroom Style Dancers"
Both of us danced throughout the Baltimore area in the same nightclubs
I went on to model and dance professionally up and down the East Coast
I truly never held any ill will toward this handsome rival
We spoke and run with the same circle of friends
We both dated the same "recording star" during the mid-eighties, at different times
Until this moment,
I've never really thought about him, as I'm sure he's done the same!
Sitting next to me on a stool is not like the Garland I remember.
Garland turned his head in my direction, giving me a nod of his head
In doing so,
The green light changed to white like all the others were
Garland returned to staring forward

The last light faded in on the sweetest of all men,
I have never known, such a gentle, caring, and "Friend"
A mild-mannered Native American Indian and blood brother,
Ellis Sampson
My eyes felt like saucers,
There sat the kindest of men I had ever known
Who just happen to come into my life at the right time?
Ellis was an accomplished artist with his works hanging in museums
Ellis was tall, dark, and very handsome
He drove a "Black Lamborghini" at the time
A beautiful car that impressed my senses
Ellis showed me warmth and understanding,
When a friend was needed, someone to listen to my words
Meeting Ellis was right after the freakish,
And the untimely death of my twenty-two-year-old sister, Bonnie
Our very short time together was well worth every single minute,
Spent exploring emotions and our heritage
On the last day of his visit to my home, he asked for a photograph of me
Of course, I gave one and several days later he called to inform me
He had sketched a portrait of me and wished I could come and see it
Several months later I received a call from Ellis,
His portrait of me was hanging in a Gallery Expo in Elliot City
I was honored beyond heartfelt warmth!
Now he is here,
Seated beside me on this last stool upon this stage...

"Here I sit, yours truly facing forward just as all are the special men
I admire and love you with all my heart. Several I spent a personal and, in some cases,
An intimate relationship. Each of these men was given gifts of amazing
Beauty inside and out. I gave of my heart freely and I would never regret
One single moment in doing so!"

I watched the lights fading out one by one on each man on a stool
Sitting in the dark I hear each of their voices whispering as if in prayer
Some were sweet as the fragrance of fresh roses
A few tugged at my heartstrings like the saddest of songs played upon a Cello
The spotlight faded in on the young woman down center stage
I know her, but can't recall the name of this redheaded beauty
Right before all eyes, an amazing moment was taking place
In a flash of sparkling light,
A pair of magnificent wings unfolded behind her
All the men seated on their stools began to softly recite the
"Lord's Prayer" in the darkness.
Except for the young woman who truly is an angel
I watched her stand up from her stool
Her beautiful ivory gown fell across her hips as if it were a creamy liquid
Stepping forward, she placed her hand out in mid-air with the grace of a dancer
It was as if she had placed it upon a satin pillow,
Slowly brushing her hand as she looked in earnest
She began to speak as if someone were lying in a prone position
Her words were soft and soothing,

The red-haired Angel spoke,
"I finished the book you gave to me to read
By the way, it is beautiful.
One section was especially touching for me."
She mimed opening a book to where a marker separated the pages
Then began reading the passage selected:

"I found myself praying,
I felt as though I had found an answer of satisfaction.
Remembering a dream, I had lost long ago.
Precious is those that hold steadfast to their dreams.
Never abandoning the path, they have in life.
For me, I tried to escape from a well of darkness from birth,
Chained to an abuser that was an instructor of fear.
I fought to reach the light above, a warmth I never knew.
And when I finally stepped out of the well,
My chains were only so long.
At every turn throughout my youth, I was haunted by an evil shadow.
I lost purpose between the night and day of hopelessness.
Abuse goes together with poverty and drunkards.

Dreams are destroyed when shadows block the sunlight.
I say to you, never not listen to your inner voice!
A whispering if you will, telling you to believe in faith, trust, and in love.
Your soul is but a sweet breeze that blows unto your own surrender.
Go into the light, hear the calling of the once-lost throughout the vastness of silence.
Run toward that great big ball of sunshine
Know love divine...
Stand in repose where sorrow no longer reflects.
For me my dearest of friends,
I have found everlasting peace and love upon the,
"Still Waters of My Life".

I watched her mime the closing of the book, placing it before her.
She spoke again.

"I read the entire book; I knew the under-scoring of your written words.
There is one passage I memorized.
I want you to hear your own words, so you know the beauty that is you.
Something that each one of us here today already knew!"

"In the blue-black brightness of night,
Under nature's moonlit canopy is,
"SPLENDER"
That should never be lost to or under the stars.
The romantic endeavors of lovers,
Are played like a game of chasing in and out of the shadows.
Expressing mixed emotions that race across heaven's night sky like shooting stars of fire.
It's the freedom to love with no regrets.
Hearts that become a union in the throes of passion.
Peacock beauty, singing a symphony of love songs, dancing to the beat of their own heartstrings
Harmony of the mind, body, and soul.
I say to be the conductor of your own symphony
For that alone will keep you from surrendering to sorrow!"

I watched the spot on her slowly fade as she returned to her stool
She sat once again on the stool and those amazing wings retracted behind her
Disappearing behind her very long auburn hair
My heart felt full as if it were about to explode with emotions
I felt tears upon my cheek, silent but endearing
I found myself wanting to exit the stage, but where to?
Just then all the spotlights came up on each man now standing in front of their stool
Arms to their sides facing straight ahead
Together they recited the "Lord's Prayer"
I regained my composer and took my place in front of my stool
Joining in on the prayer
Each one of my friends turned his head in my direction when they said the word,

" AMEN"

My special friends created a single line between the two rows of stools
Each slowly walked toward me
Some nodded, and a couple reached out and touched my face
Several spoke a private message of sorts under their breath
There were those that had tears in their eyes
I smiled as they each stood in front of me in sincere honesty
I wanted to hug and kiss each one of them, but something held me back
Ellis was the last in the line to greet me face-to-face,
When I realized what was taking place!
What was the message contained in this vivid vision of my weakness?
There stood that beautiful angel,
It was her red hair that finally clicked my memory
She was the one I secretly adored in high school and after graduation
The one young woman to whom I wished I would have confessed my attraction.
Her name was Joanne...
She was amazingly beautiful, sweet, and talented.
She possesses the fire of the Irish when she got peeved
I never thought I would have the chance to take our friendship any further
We spent a lot of time together in dance rehearsals and performances
I believe there were moments when she would have wanted me to take the next step
However, I knew she had a relationship with another
That made it very clear he didn't like me or being around Joanne in any manner!
Joanne told me it was over with him, but he wouldn't take "NO" for an answer.
I thought he was good-looking, well built with a dangerous ego
On many occasions, he lost his temper in social settings, so I heard...
I didn't fear him, nor would I ever trust him in the dark!
He wasn't the only guy that held a dislike for me or even a hatred
For whatever reason was befitting at the time, I suppose?
In fact, every dance partner I was associated with, made mention of their dilemmas
I guess when you spend eight hours a day in rehearsals and classes, five days a week,
For months at a time or even longer
It gives cause for the guy's questionable thoughts if more isn't possibly going on.
The age-old sharing their girlfriends with another guy,
Even though my dance partners would assure me,
That I was batting for the other team.
Even though each of my dancers knew I enjoyed the company of both sexes,
Known as a "Bi-sexual man"
There were times during my eighteen years of teaching dance,
I fell in love with several outstanding and beautiful dancers
The flirting was intense at times
I'm sure the young women enjoyed it as much as I had
A few of my partners had told me some secrets,
That there were times when they were hot and heavy with boyfriends
When they accidentally let my name slip out during intimate situations
So, there lies the rub!

I lost several dance partners because of this situation occurring,
Some quit because of jealousy and or for my safety
I was given the slant eye quite a few times out in public...

Back to the night of shadows, I have painted before you
My nightmare to own or the fact that my life was flashing before my eyes
I realized I was witnessing my own funeral on the stage.
The theater was my teen years passion, hell for all my life.
The handsome young men that held special places in my heart
These friends and or lovers were without a doubt treasures of importance in my lifetime.
Never have I dreamed a dream or nightmare that didn't hold a meaning expressed.
They held messages of earthly importance for me to grasp onto
This I believe with all my heart and soul
It was my mother who told me to listen for the message within each dream
All messages would be revealed to me soon
Its meaning would hold the truth
Friends and lovers are as precious to me as gold was to King Midas
All through my life growing up I walked amongst misfortune and darkness
The harsh, cruel, and evil that no child's soul should know or experience
I barely knew or heard the songs that many songs in their lives
All I know is that I am here!
Sorrow and darkness shouldn't control one's life
I've been to places where evil tormented my soul.
Right now, I have lacked the will to give a damn any longer.
The pain is so severe it hurts to breathe
Or the light of hope being beaten out of you on a regular basis
Hell, I have cried a river of blood for the heartache over the loss of loved ones.
All the time wishing it was me.
Reviewing the number of suicides in the family or your close of friends
The pain my friends is encased in a tar-like-evil that rises from the core of my soul,
Like lava in a volcano
The pressure couldn't be contained any longer, so it erupts
And I relinquished my will to go on
*My red-haired Angel **Joanne McNeal** held my hand and said to me,*

Joanne and Lee

"You can take your memories, love, and dreams with you in the end!
Lee, know that you have never been alone
Your life of darkness and evil was never at any time your fault
Know that your life after the darkness will be filled with amazing moments
That is the treasure,
That is the message,
The dreams and the nightmares have now ended forever

"You Will No Longer Surrendered to Sorrow"

A CHILD'S EYES

Have you ever wondered what's behind the eyes that a child sees?
I can tell you this child sees the world around him harsh as can be

This child's little heart knows all too well what fear and pain feels like
There's no love that is true and or kind, only fear of the dark knight

You can look into the child's eyes and know that sorrow is his name
His world is dark, hidden, and dirty, but he must never ever complain

No sun's warmth does he feel, and hunger is fed by visions in his head
In the corner where he sleeps, cold hard floor, no pillow on this bed

The creaking steps upon the stairs, a battlefield where foes will fight
He can handle most of what's thrown his way, except that of the Knight

His mind is a mass of confusion, all is lost in the eyes of Why Me?
Beaten, abused he's screaming a secret silence, I am here, is his plea...

A Circle of Warmth

{In days of Knights, Lords, Ladies, Kings, and Queens, our story takes place in a castle recently sadden by the death of their King. He has passed on far too early in age. The Queen and the Princess are being taken care of by the King's brother. One who loved his Queen long before his brother married and made her Queen...}

The Uncle Now Speaks

There before my eyes, the Princess truly is her mother's daughter. I had desired her mother since the age of twelve plus three. So many times, I wanted to speak poetry to my Lady Devine. However, I thought she would find me silly. Perhaps my poetry is that of a schoolboy's attempt at wooing as well. That was then and wishful thinking only led to very lonely nights. I found myself in good graces with my Lady and in favor after my brother, the King's untimely and unfortunate death. My Lady was left with a young daughter and a huge estate. Plus, a very large castle, staff, and the affairs of the Kingdom. His Will stated that I, his only blood brother would manage all affairs of the state and the country. I also was to see to every need of the Queen and the Princess. Over the years the Princess grew at an amazing rate. her mother held me in the greatest of trust. I was given the duty to guard the Princess at all costs from an array of young and viral suitors from all over the neighboring lands. The Queen had put her trust into my capable care, that No Man may try or by chance make time with the Princess's virtue! I was made aware of just how impossible that task was to be.

One stormy night filled with icy rain and winds with a fierce bite. Whilst standing guard outside the princess chamber, I was soaked to the core and cold. When I heard the slat in the door snap open. I heard my Princess say, **"Dearest Uncle, you are soaked to the core and shivering. Thou art soaked through and through. Please, come inside. For you truly will catch your death of cold on a stormy night such as this. Dearest Uncle, I surely could be eased of fright during this stormy night. Your company would ease my fear of thunder and lightning."** *Well, looking into those baby blue eyes, I didn't think twice. I unlocked the door to her chamber and stepped inside.* **"Oh Uncle, I'm sorry for the giggling. You look like a wet puppy. You must take thy garments off and dry them by the fireplace. Here, wrap thyself in my blanket and lie by the fire to get warm".** *I started to peel the wet clothing from my body. She stood by the fireplace stoking the fire. I manage the tunic and the wet shirt. She took a glance in my direction.* **"My Lady, you need to turn away in order for me to remove my trousers."** *She smiled and did so. It felt so good to remove the wet material from my chilled skin. I wrapped my unclothed body with her blanket. I picked up my water-soaked clothes and placed them on the stone mantel above the roaring fire. Just then a loud crack of thunder vibrated throughout the chamber. Since she was a little girl, she ran directly* *into my arms. Only this time, her security blanket was filled with a naked man. Such beauty did warrant shelter the need from the thunder and crack of lightning. When she was little, she would come running, however, she now was sixteen years old. How I fought the tingling inside me came to life. As of now the young lady in her gave way to womanhood with exploration. I cuddled her as I had for years when a small girl. The longer she remained in my arms, the more I couldn't hold my manhood at bay. She had motives of her own. Another crack of thunder vibrated through the chamber and my Lady managed to insert herself into the blanket. she felt like a gift from above. I had not been with a woman for at least four years. The truth be known I lost all reservations about holding back my physical needs. The more my Lady wiggled and entwined herself around my six-foot-four frame, there was no use in trying to hide what I lost control of. The Poet in my heart became the feathered quill and my body the parchment to write upon. I'm writing, I am yours, dictate a letter to myself. No for all that is holy write me a novel! I pulled myself from her tender grasp. Here is what I spoke of.* **"My Lady, you are a circle of warmth to my flesh whence bare and weak. Lock thy lips that are so plump, moist, and cherry red. Sweet Lady, did thee count roses of twelve plus five? I beg thee, I am lost beyond self-control. Let us both bed the sweetness of "Silence" this night!"** *How awkward does the moment feel? I'm sure for the both of us as we stood by the hearth where the fire has gathered in bounty.* **"Venus, when in your throws of unbelievable beauty and youthful fires. Let not a bitter breeze blow thy candle's flame to weaken thy desires. Then two will not feel despair over the last flicker of this evening's light. It is not seemly with thee in my arms. Together we will reach the heights of heaven's boundaries. Please my young Venus, together softly speak in whispers. Even though the walls are built of thick stones, the walls do have ears."**

A promise was made to water the forest. Keeping it fresh and green. When lustful urges are no longer at bay, one's hunger needs to be fed. I stumbled with my candle lit in my hand. Furs laid before the fire contain the Goddess Venus. All my emotions are gathered as I lay my body next to hers. Setting the young forest to flame. This I did, blocking an oath made years ago. I was put in trust to keep thy chastity safe and under lock and key. Thy love hangover seals the warmth of joyous dismay whence in the throes of a circle of warmth.

In times of harsh arctic blasts, it was easy to keep the Princess warm. The brutal bitter cold made it so easy for her to cuddle up close to my fire as her youth sprang to maidenhood. I found it hard to resist her amazing charms. Each time she would say to me, **"Why do you shiver so? Pull me closer. I will keep warm in the throes of Venus, my circle of warmth if you will?"**

My mind wants to speak of the promise made to her mother. My flesh is weak as my heart beats with desire. **"Sweetest of Ladies, your lips speak of warmth like before. Your eyes are filled with a fire of come-hither. It's a look that weakens my knees. I said I could be trusted. It no longer holds its chill factor. There before your feet, the truth be known as thy brow now forms a puddle of nervous sweat!"**

A Darken Canvas

Oh, sweet sunset changes ever so slowly into the night. Your paintbrush strokes of red, orange, and yellows paint the countryside as you fade slowly out of sight. Like magic, and a wave of the hand darkness appears. There is a miracle taking place every night in the heavens above. With a blink of an eye, a million twinkling lights appear, winking and twinkling from afar. Below my feet and all along the grassy countryside I christen my own. Last night's fallen stars rise, rise to greet the night sky. Here is when you catch a fallen star. For the fireflies to dance to the music of the night. All the wonders of nature are created by God's almighty hands. A master with color, a genius with every stroke he makes. He added sounds of nature, like a frog's croak, the hoot of an owl, a symphony of cricket calls, and birds settling in for the night. Far in the distance, you can see the lights of the farmhouse. Hear dogs barking at shadows that run across the fields. High on this canvas of black, a crescent moon shines silver. Wayward clouds catch its light, sometimes covering its face. Somehow the darkness envelops me in a blanket of warmth as I gaze at the stars and wonder if anyone really is out there. Then a shooting star makes its way across the velvet curtain. In a flash, streaking only to vanish before my eyes. Such a rare event, I was told to make a wish and tell no one for it to come true. Funny how time flies when you're enjoying a heavenly sight. Away from the madness that controls your life. Here away from the chaos and pain is my sanctuary. For whatever length of time, I can capture, those moments are by far more precious than gold to me. The ground under me is cooling, dew is forming on the grass. It's time for me to head home, praying all are asleep and there is peace. I salute the night sky; I praise all the wonders that God has given to us. Dawn will arrive in a few hours; I'll watch the morning sunrise from my tiny window and thank God for another day...

A Detour

I am here with you, yet so alone
The love I thought there has simply not grown
I seek a lover to make me a whole person again
I'm afraid I can see the beginning of the end
I may seem selfish in what I seek
I'm all I have, number one, though so meek
I feel so many things within my mind
Hurting another is not at all very kind
So, I live in pain, discovering a route, a new way
I am so unhappy, to you this I cannot say
Though I know I will suffer now
It will all work out some way, somehow
You are my friend, although I end up miles away
This is my destiny; a detour is all I can say.

A GIFT OF WISDOM

Watch in amazement as the ferns unfurl their fronds slowly
The magic of Mother's twilight veil covers natures children
Hidden in solitude throughout sanctuaries rest the restless
Remarkable are her creations in which to slumber the soul

Step lightly upon an abundant carpet of sprouts and shoots
Nature's perfectly laid carpet, plush and rich in its comfort
Protecting life anew under a blanket of what once lived
Beauty through seasons of morphing and life's last breath

To lay upon nature's plush carpet is to feel her life's force
Inhale with each step to know Mother's natural fragrances
Take time to listen to her songs as she caresses your senses
You're being blessed by her knowledge since time has begun

Mother's garden is filled with life, yet she cradles her dead
Mother is in a continuous birth anew, life eternally abounds
All of Earth's Kingdoms revolve within the "Circle of Life"
What lived in beauty withers then nurturers new beginnings?

A mother holds no secrets when she reveals life and death
She feeds the world from the riches of her soul renewing
Throughout our life, hopefully, we'll retain her knowledge
We're destined to follow nature's order, live, love and die

Her gift is wisdom, forevermore in life and to our death
Earth's riches are fueled by the decaying left behind us
Our very existence is the result of nature's recycling
*Be mindful of her "Conveyor Belt", **it's a gift of wisdom!***

A GIFT OF PROPHESY
"The White Buffalo"

Now is the year of the Buffalo
Open your eyes,
See the coming of what we have been foretold.
Listen to Mother Earth,
She now sings of the Prophesy for all.

When you sleep,
Open your heart to your dreams
For the wisdom of our Forefathers has now come true.
Let the women gather
So that they might sing of good things.
Bring forth the young Braves
In full Regalia.

Feathers, fringe, and bells tied to the ankles
Dance to the drums and the flute
Let our women dress in their finest
An array of furs and beads and bangles
Raise their shawls and spin

From the rising of the sun
To the setting of the Blue Corn Moon
We now give praise to the four winds.
Listen to the songs of the People.
Look beyond the Black Hills
And remember the visions held in the clouds.

Do not grow weary,
For the thunder, you hear is the return of the Buffalo
Across the vast plains as far as the eye can see.
Have you not seen
The Eagle and Hawk souring across the great blue?
Our legend has been born on this day.
It is time to follow the legend.

The White Buffalo has been born on this day
And wherever she may roam,
The land will be reborn for the People.
The rivers and streams run clean for the Salmon
Once again, they return home
To make plentiful.

Look to your heart and give of yourself,
Become one across the Nation.
Know the changing of the seasons,
First the budding, to full rich green
Into the colors of Fire,
The leaves drop for the long winter's sleep,
Bare will be the trees to all.

Let's talk of a celebration
Of a new beginning as we stand beside
The White Buffalo.
Begin by creating the Circle Dance,
"The Gathering"
Feel the power of the drum's beat
Let the women start to circle

Let the young join in
For they are the future and must hold onto our Heritage
They're handed down from generation to generation
by our Forefathers.
Bring forth the Dear, the Bear
And our brother the Wolf,
Let all of nature join in on
"The Circle of Life".

We, the "True People" of this land
Stand tall and proud this day.
Let All come forth
Young, Old, Men, Women, Sons, and Daughters
To this day the Prophesy has come true!

Lift your eyes to the Heavens,
Let your hearts fly with the Eagles,
Let the true people grow strong once again.
As we walk side by side,
Sing loud, sing strong of the Prophesy.
Let the women and children dance in joy.

These things we do now,
In praise of the White Buffalo.
We, the "True People" stand tall and proud
Even after all was taken from us,
We were scattered to the four winds
Beaten, Belittled, and Killed
Yet the Great Spirit still holds
Our heart, faith, and Pride

Manitou has seen fit to give life once again to his People.
His Gift of Prophesy
Now stands before us,
Rejoice we shall rise again
His Nature Child of New Beginnings
Has arrived and given hope for a new beginning
Known as

The White Buffalo!

A LETTER OF LOVE

With this pen in hand, it's the paper that awaits the words. There's a need that compels me to write him once again. However, this mind of mine wanders and drifts aimlessly searching for the right words to convey. There is no doubt I'm lost in my thoughts of her this day. Oh, how my mind drifts as I search for just the right words to express, yet again, how truly blessed he makes me feel. As I pen this letter of love to the man who holds my heart, my thoughts are full of memories of our last rendezvous. Is he smiling that remarkable smile that lights his perfect looks? Does he feel the gentle touch of my hand softly caressing his body? Does a tear slowly meander its way down his sculptured cheeks? Maybe he's missing me and wondering if I miss him just as much. No one has ever touched my soul so passionately as he has. I've never experienced the soft and gentle passion in each kiss placed upon my lips. I wonder if he can feel my thoughts of him racing in my mind. Does he know how lost I am when he holds me close? I know he feels the rhythm of my heartbeat. I wonder if he re-reads the love letters of my day past. When reading them he sighs and clutches them to her heart, thinking of the times we often shared together. I remember when our love started to grow, and future dreams were imagined. Would he think me silly if he knew I hold his letters as I sleep?

Resting upon my pillow next to me as though he were there. Does he dream the dreams I dream of loving him so intensely? I so want to let him know how amazingly happy he has made me. I wonder daily what he is doing to pass the hours away. Maybe his imagination takes him to a wonderland of lovers. There might be a loving whisper gently sighed from her lips, sent lovingly upon a gentle breeze calling my name as I do. I would love to send a gentle kiss floating upon a breeze to land gently upon his lips to let him know he is loved and needed. Can he feel this need I have to hear his voice call out my name. Dare I think that he is as lost in the memory of our love as I am? With this pen in hand, as if by magic the words are expressed, creating my heart's desires within this letter being lovingly penned. This heart of mine speaks words he longs to hear. This heart of mine needs to tell him just one thing, "I Love You!". The Gods and Goddess of love, give me just the right words. Let him know that this love I hold in my heart is a desire for him alone. Guide my pen, my hand, and my heart with love to a partner/lover who fulfills my every need. The only words I truly need to express our "I Love you with all my heart!"

A Librarian I Am Not

Ripped, torn, and shattered, is this the world I thought we created as one? All we worked so hard to achieve now runs through your fingers like dry sand. You cheated a lot of good people along the way, even me. Friends' reputations were ruined by your mere touch, your lies. Even family members felt you were not giving a damn about the constituencies. Carefree attitudes carry you through the day. Those that are still hanging in there for us, have made mentioned the way you walk around with your nose in the air. You're a fake, phony, and liar in your private world of cheating. I will not allow you to take me where you are going. Wherever you decided to travel you purchased a ticket for one! Run! If you must. I am standing tall and strong for myself. I was taught to be honest and trustworthy and to give my love to someone that is trustworthy, caring, and devoted. To treat people the same way I would want to be treated in a relationship, in life. You're just a child who throws tantrums to get his way. Well, go ahead and hold your breath until you turn blue. Scream and yell and kick. Cry Baby Cry! Haven't you noticed how people are just ignoring you? We all have learned our ways. You're not as transparent as you think you are. We've become strong and wise to your self-gratification. No Longer! It hasn't been that long for the two of us, but just long enough for me to read you like a book. I will not be your beginning chapter, not the middle section and I'll be dammed if I will stick around for the ending! You will be just another book on the shelf collecting dust. I won't be the one to dust you off. A Librarian I am not! There was a time, not that long ago when I thought the moon and stars rose in your heart. Now that I see who you really are, let me give you some advice. Take some time to sit down. Think about what your actions have done to you and me. How you have used your friends and our families. Listen to me, I looked into your eyes right this second, you know what I see? NOTHING! Not a damn thing. You have a long way to redeem yourself. Before any of your actions will sink in that pretty head of yours, this is what you must do right this minute. Pack your clothes, pack whatever else you have around here. Put the keys in my hand and get the hell out of here. Get the hell out of my life! Just leave! Don't worry about the money you took from me, Keep It! It's my going away gift to you. I will even hold the door for you. So long!

A Message from Mother Earth

*"My womb has gone barren, and I will reap no longer. I've been forsaken by my children around the world. The trees will no longer bear their fruits. I never believed how careless and greedy my children would become. The fertile Amazon has been swallowed by man, gone are the plants, and gone are all species of animals. I no longer have a heartbeat, an everlasting thud! Why have you poisoned your mother? My breast bares the stench of polluted waters. The plains of Africa use to run plentiful with herds of every animal created. Man has seen fit to hunt and kill endangered species for sport. Until they have vanished from the face of Earth, **"FOREVER".** My children, you've become Greedy and now you too will vanish. You watch me wither and die before your uncaring eyes. Face not having water, food, and life itself. My children, you've written your own demise. Here are my last words to you, once extinct, the earth will become like her sister, Mars,*

DEAD! *The clues of my suffering were always in front of you. You chose to be blind to my every need. Your future is No More! Mother Earth is No More, may she R.I.P. My children, are to be*

NO MORE...

A MOTH OVER A BURNING CANDLE

When the moth flies drained of all her emotions
Flight weakens her wings and all that is cherished
Wings dry like powder, caught in a stale breeze
Powder falls up and out, tender this does make

When wings doth carry the weight of the world
Flight makes heavy the silken frame of pure love
The heart is weakened from yesterday's taxing flight
The moth is easily burnt by the fires of a lovelorn

The moth takes a once-in-a-lifetime chance flight
There are no strings to this puppet of lost emotions
Heat rises, but where there is a cold heart in view
One falls clear of emotions, but not a burning candle

When a slow sinking takes to the depths of feelings
Strike a match and give life to the candle with flame
Offer roses of twenty for three seconds of wild and red
The moth lands on a flower bud, yet to glory in a refuge

When the moth flies high and touches the lunar edge
Kissed by dew in the morn, Mother taught Ye to flutter
The powder dries quick, bide your time upon the rocks
Don't fly above the flame of the candle, for burnt Ye shall be!

A MOTHER WAITS

*A mother lights another candle by prayer unto her faith is strong. A tiny candle is placed in the window. Her words will shine like a beacon unto the night. It has been a year since her five-year-old was abducted. She had disappeared in the quiet of the night as she lay sleeping. A mother sits by the window, remembering her smile, a giggle, and a sweet tear. She is a mother who waits for her little one to come home. Another mother and another mother hopefully wait from their windows. For some ungodly reason, children are missing around the world. Taken, some returned, and others are found that will never return to the arms of their mothers and fathers. There are so many candles lit this night. The beacons crisscross and puzzle amongst the stars. Somewhere a mother is lighting her first candle, with her unwavering faith, it's love that guides the match to light the way. It is her undying faith that her baby is alive and will come home. A mother will not let her heart believe differently. Call her **"Every-Mother"** who waits this night, and every night in routine. She looks out into a sea of flickering hopes and wishes. Each shone like a star in the darkness. Illuminating her dreams to come true. Will her one little candle shine bright enough, for Sally, Frankie, Johnny, Crystal, Mary, and Paul to come home safe and sound? A plea to come back to the arms that care and love you. Her mind is steadfast and true with every breath she takes. Praying for her child is alive and safe. Her heart explodes at the thought of otherwise. Some children are taken in broad daylight. One minute a mother is watching her little one playing in the front yard. She dropped her eyes for a second. Raised her head once again. Where did she go? Stepping out the front door she calls her child's name. Over and over, with each one being served in panic. Frantic and emotional the horror becomes real. Another child had vanished within seconds. Days become weeks, weeks into months, followed by years in most cases. Hopefully found alive. Damn the words, "I'm so very sorry." Another mother and father retrieve another candle as the sun retreats. By the strike of a single match, she whispers out loud, **"I am a mother who waits night after night for my child to come home"** ...*

A Scared Canopy

Stand with me in the misty morning rain. Watch as we are lifted to stand upon Holy Ground. Rolling in a thick veil of creamy mist. You hear the glorious sounds of an Angel playing the Harp. Conducted by the Almighty under the Scared Canopy of the Weeping Willow Tree. The music speaks to you and me in Earth's morning mystical light. Feel the mist on your face. Like being kissed gently by a symphony of earthly delights. Together the music and earthly kisses surround us as sweetly as the Misty Morning Rain that refreshes our faces. Listen to the Angels as they play their Harps in concert. The misty rain is their teardrops falling softly from Heaven. Their angelic music is creating Masterpieces of Emotions. With every flick of their fingers across the strings of their Golden Harps.

Now watch, the beauty of the Willow Tree as its spirit is wakened. Before us, now gives way to the Sun's warmth as she reflects across this land. Magically the veil rolls back. In addition, its creamy mist placed us up upon the Holy Ground. Now lowers us to greet the warmth of the morning. The harps and beautiful music fades. Mother Earth replaces all with a brighter tone. Gone is the Misty Morning Rain. Tenderly the kisses and the teardrops from the Angels caress the Spirit of the Scared Weeping Willow Tree. Go now and walk in peace. See all your eyes can see, all your heart can absorb lovingly. Then we will once again meet when the evening drapes are closed. As it has been repeated time after time. Before time was time.

Always come here to meet me in front of the Scared Weeping Willow as the mist of morning rain covers our faces. In addition, we again are lifted upon the Holy Ground. To hear the Angels, create music on Golden Harps. They cry and rejoice in the beauty given to all. That their teardrops fall as rain to form a Spiritual Symphony. A Scared Canopy that lies before Man, known as the Mighty Weeping Willow Tree.

{This is a strong and real-to-life situation. Even though there is harsh language it deals with the mental and physical aspects of "WAR" and the reality that surfaces in a moment of self-preservation. Unless you have experienced the true harshness of "WAR", it's reality slapping you in the face! This is dedicated to my military friends both living and those that lost their lives in the line of fire to keep this "Country Free" for you and me!}

A SOLDIER SINGS A SONG OF ZION
Walk a mile in their boots...
{A cold night approach}

Shivering... Across these fields sharp and barren the north wind blows a chill of reality. Soldiers huddled together in the quiet of the cold. Not a word is whispered as we observe" Mother Nature" at work. There are so few moments in the past five years where you allow yourself to lower your guard long enough to notice how blue the moonlight truly is. As nature casts her shadows across the weary battlefields, a soldier sings a song of Zion. We wait, and then... There over the knoll before us "it" appears in an eerie slow-motion crawl. Advancing over the dark fields in a fluid roll toward us. Lit in moonlight blue as if painted by a Master Artist it blankets the battlefield. That is when one's imagination can create visions in the mind's eye. I imagined the grandest of all ballrooms. A grand entrance in precession. The fog seems to morph into soldiers, men, and women of the court dressed in the finest of white satin uniforms. They file in, and a precession marches up over the rise, spreading out end to end, going right and going left until one single line has formed in the distance. A cavalry of soldiers in white marched forward into the fray. Shoulder to shoulder advancing across the fields. You hear in the distance the snare drums beating out a rhythm to march by. It is amazing what your mind can produce in a moment of silence. The advancing fog rolls and rolls until it lies at our feet. You watch it encircle your feet then snake up around your knees. I feel the chill over my body as I blow air from my mouth. We all notice how our breath slowly forms in front of our faces, simply hanging in mid-air. Created by the stillness with no air in motion. Then I shiver and shake the whole image from my mind. Back to reality! Something that isn't very hard to do on the battlefield. The night seems to never end, and the chilly air grows with each hour. Mother Nature holds onto the night. I close my eyes for a second to wipe away the endless night from my mind. After all, things have been quiet for the most part. Rest when able to.

*Then I hear, I hear faint singing of the words, **"Coming for to carry me home."** There before me stands a Golden Angel who speaks, **"Upon these celestial wings I will take you back home to the land of your birth. Across the majestic mountains of the Seven Sisters, over the valley rich in green Lemon Grass, and finally to the Grand Banks of the Crystal Sea. Where sounds of crashing waves and the birds nesting on the cliffs echoing in a thunderous retreat, called Home!"** I fell to my knees and began to pray. **"I want to go Home, Dear Lord! I am so tired of fighting these battles that I can no longer win. I am giving myself to you now! As I should have a long time ago. The enemy always seems to be at my back. Gaining on me day by day. I am through pretending Lord, that I am still that strong and brave soldier who fought amongst true Heroes. Conquering the enemy and savoring the day. Each marching bravely into the fray, each soldier here is better than I. How many times have I fallen by the wayside? I pick myself up, bewildered and confused of what I hear lying beside me. It has strangled that innocent farm*** *boy that I use to be. He no longer stands tall among the living. He hears the echoes of home. Fix me, Lord... Please fix me!"* The Angel in front of me raises his arm pointing to the sky above. *There in the moonlit night sky appears what looks like a growing star. But this star is getting larger as the seconds seem to slice through the body. There is a whistling sound that is far too loud for comfort. There is, "NO TIME TO THINK OR REACT" ... The sky lights up in a purple haze laced in a raging orange of fire. A sonic boom. Throwing you backward in pain. I have never screamed in my lifetime, like what came directly from my lungs. "OH MY GOD!!!" From beside me, from the back of me and in front I heard the shock, the panic coming from my comrades. "WHAT IS THAT?" ..." NO, NO DEAR GOD NO!!!... WHAT IN THE HELL IS HAPPENING!" Chaos, confusion, and dread marked the realization of this carnage. It was deafening and I felt an unholy fire about me... ANOTHER FLASH OF RED AND EVERYTHING WENT BLACK INSTANTLY... SILENCE... SILENCE... SILENCE... Another clarifying reality sank into all.*

I felt my flesh on fire. I fought my way up and out of the debris that covered me. I was a living ember among a multitude of unfortunates. I had a very hard time trying to see, trying to focus. Dirt filled my eyes and mouth as I spit and coughed to clear my mouth. I tasted blood. Once I was able to stand and my eyes cleared as much as possible, I touched my hands and saw the skin raw and blistered. Resembling melted wax dripping from my flesh. My clothes were burnt from my body or melted into my skin. I touch my head and my hair was burnt completely off. I saw movement rising from the debris around me. I heard my fellow soldiers sounding off like a Greek chorus, "What in the HELL was that?". Screams cry from those in clutches of hellish agony! Then someone shouted, "Look at the sky, it's red as blood!" I looked about surveying the scorched surroundings. "Everything was GONE!... OH MY GOD!!!... JESUS CHRIST! THOSE DIRTY MOTHERFUCKER REALLY DID IT! Some Dirty Bastard Pushed that Goddamn Button and Dropped the BOMB!"

I looked about and saw men and women standing and staring at the sky. Silhouettes of once soldiers that were morphed into hideous creatures standing in shock or lying-in heaps on the ground. There are those that now have become the walking dead. Dazed, confused, and not a clue in the world. At least a dozen figures lay scattered about my feet. Some are in pain, some beyond recognition as a man or a woman. All were transformed, burnt, bleeding, blistered, skinless, and most blinded to some degree. The moaning was so loud it sounded like a chorus of zombies on the march. I hear a faint cry within the moans. I said, "Listen Up, LISTEN, GODDAMN IT! LISTEN! "Do you hear that?", directed to anyone capable to comprehend. I awkwardly and painfully tried to move my limbs. We were clumsy at walking and truly resembled "The Walking Dead." Our bodies no longer were our own. We walked amongst the carnage of blood and human Remains. In and around the bodies in search of this lone voice begging for help. Even as we needed help ourselves. A soldier is never left behind or in need. I couldn't help but home in on that singular distressed plea. I was determined to find this soul. It was such a weak cry for help. I had to rest for a second, I sat down huge rock, then I heard the voice again. In taking that short rest period, I went to move, and my body stiffened. Where the flesh no longer supported the exposed muscle tissue, the blood and fluids started to coagulate. Making mobility a painful chore. With each movement, the flesh split, and a bloody goo oozed. I heard the faint voice once more... "Help me, please someone help me, it hurts, it burns." Somehow, I got to my knees with the help of a rifle lying on the ground.

My body was burnt so badly, and I felt the fire raging to the bone. At that moment it didn't matter, it just didn't matter! That's when I felt something grab onto my boot. I looked down and there was a very young-looking soldier. He looked up at me saying, **"Help Me Help Me!"** *My pain and awkwardness simply didn't matter. I go to pick up this frightened young soldier reeling in pain, his face was full of dirt and blood. The eyes looking back at me touched what humanity I still possessed. There was an extreme urgency being played here. I dropped to my knees and retrieved the canteen of water on the ground. I ripped off a piece of the soldier's shirt and soaked it with water. I wiped away what I could, this was a youthful-looking soldier. Lifting him, I tried to maneuver him up a bit when his helmet fell to the ground. That's when all this blonde hair fell over my arm. This was a beautiful young woman, she looked too young to be a soldier. Somehow, she was sheltered from the flash burn, but the sonic blast did her in. Just for an instance, I saw her as blessed that she wasn't burned. I said to her as I held her in my arms,* **"Hold onto my arms, you're going to be fine!"** *Nodding her head, she was in shock and repeated,* **"OK...OK...OK...OK."** *I went to move her up just a little more when she let out a horrific* **SCREAM!!!** *Screaming to the top of her lungs,* **"IT BURNS... IT BURNS! HELP ME, HELP ME! DEAR GOD ALMIGHTY, HELP ME! PLEASE FOR CHRIST'S SAKE HELP ME!"** *I moved my right arm around her chest, so, to cradle her and to make her more comfortable... That's when* **GOD AND I HAD AN ISSUE WITH ONE ANOTHER**!!! *I raised my head to the blood-red heavens above us and let out an ungodly scream of my own! I thought I was going to vomit the anger I was feeling. Terror filled my insides, I couldn't breathe. I thought my head was going to explode. I felt a fire burning deep in my gut erupting up to my throat! This was a terror I have never known in my entire life, and it was being exposed right before my eyes. The world was at the end of days and all that had been inflicted on humanity, couldn't equal the horror cradled in my arms! There in my arms and up against my flesh-burned body was the top half of this beautiful soldier. Her intestines were still hooked to the bottom half. Hot steam and bubbling bloody bowels flowed onto my lap. The organs and guts were rolling and crawling over one another like the "Mating Ball" of Anacondas. They were literately moving in a pile upon my lap crawling up and over one another We were frozen in eye-to-eye contact with each other. I was in terror, she in Pain and confusion!* {**My mind was in terror, my heart couldn't sink any lower, and compassion overrode everything inside of me. I had to pull myself together and deal with this injustice.**} *Things changed in an instant, like this injustice to all of humanity. Man destroyed himself launching and hurling nukes at one another.*

When the entire smell hit me, it was like when I was six years old and licked a penny. Well, that's what the fluids and blood and intestines smelled like that damn penny, tasting coppery, harsh, and volatile to the senses. All I was holding in my cradled arms was her torso. Barely alive and hanging on for a needed purpose. Her bottom half was attached to her large intestine. How? My God, she was still alive, it had to be the intervention of some divine meaning. She pulled on what was left of a shirt that was burnt into my own flesh. Please, let me be totally honest right now, I wanted to throw her off me and run like hell screaming my head off. But I would never do that to a fellow soldier. The term "Cowboy it up! was in order as if from my father's mouth through mine. Whatever pain and horrors of my own just didn't matter. I leaned over to listen to what she so desperately had to say to me... This had to be a nightmare I couldn't wake from... No such luck! I knew that she was very aware that she didn't have long to achieve her goal. She held onto me and spoke in haste, **"Listen to me, I am Heather Spencer from Mount Hood, Oregon. Please,** {**she started to cry**} **Please tell my mother that I love her, and tell my daughter, Jesse, that mommy loves her as wide as the world is round."** *She pulled on my shirt again saying,* **"PLEASE, PROMISE ME...**

YOU WILL DO THIS FOR ME, SWEAR IT!" *Her plea was heartbreaking, to say the least My emotions were spent at that moment in time. My heart ached; my emotions were spent. I felt my tears fall over my raw and burnt cheeks. Taking a calming breath,* **"Of course, I will, I promise!"** *In her eyes, I saw a glow of relief and she was satisfied with her fate. Deep in my heart, I believe she hadn't a clue that the world was nuked, and the likely possibility is that the States no longer exists as we remember it to be. I asked her name, in a fading voice she said,* **"Heather."** *she cupped my face with her ice-cold hands. Using the last of what breath, she had in her... she called out the name,* "Jesse". *Slowly between her weakening arms, I held on and placed her arms on my shoulders. She strained to say every word, as she gulped for another breath, and I saw her eyes telegraph to me,* **{I am dying, and I can't hold on any longer...}** *"Hold me" ... So very faint in my ear she spoke her last words,* **"Tell my little girl, Jesse...Mommy loves her this much..."** *she slowly buried her head into my chest, Finishing in a puff-like sound* "**m-o-r-e.**" *She just went limp and glassy-eyed... My emotions became a "72-car pile-up." I pulled her close to me, I was bawling like a baby as I rocked her in my arms. As if she was my daughter. With one hand I removed her Dog-tags from around her neck over her blonde hair. Then I wiped her tears from the cheeks of that beautiful young face. I closed her eyelids for that forever sleep, and whispered in her ear, trying the best I could, because I was choking and trying to catch my breath. For I could hardly breathe. As the tears ran from my cloudy and blistered eyes, I softly and tenderly whispered,* **"I... Promise you, Heather..."** *I don't know how long I sat there amongst the dead and dying as I held Heather in my arms. Rocking back and forth as if I were putting a child at ease. Maybe I was in shock from it all the inhumanity put forth this day.? Looking at the* **HELL** *all around us, I wondered, why a dozen or so soldiers and myself lived through this Holocaust. Scared, disfigured, burnt, and destroyed of all hope. Everywhere you look the scorched earth is unrecognizable. The sky is the deepest of reds and the earth, is burnt, dark, lifeless, and smoldering as far as the eyes can see, it was a landfill of burning and smoldering flesh. There is a fog that now creeps across the surface and smells sulfuric. The ground under your feet was steaming like the floor of a lava flow from a volcano. Several of us survivors if you want to call us that... Had our attention drawn to a dark figure laughing in the far distance? There, standing on a small knoll about a mile away, we saw in silhouette the figure of* **DEATH!** *As Death raised his arms as if victory were his, the steam made a hissing sound. The crackling sound of fires burning.*

You could hear Death laughing, as the **"FOUR HORSEMEN of the APOCALYPSE"** *rode across the blood-red sky. As I rocked Heather, I remembered the promise that never would come to pass. For this truly was the end of times. I was a soldier, holding the severed body of another soldier on the battlefield. I was singing as I rocked this child of God... Just a single* **"Soldier Sings a Song of Zion."** *As the fog encircled the two of us, the Horsemen carried out their deeds with a vengeance. I gasped my last breath as the poison from the fallout filled my lungs and body, silencing the last of humanity. Forevermore...*

"Yes, some son-of-a-bitch put their finger on the trigger and the world went up in a deadly flash of fire. Destroying all of life, for the sake of World Domination.
It doesn't matter Who? Where? Why? or when?"
"IT'S A STUPID FUCKING THING TO DO! IT'S TOTAL MADNESS!!!"

This speech is from the Musical
"Man Of La Mancha"

These are words that should be treasured and taught to future generations of the world.

"Listen, my friends, I have seen life as it is. Pain, misery, hunger, and cruelty beyond belief." I've heard the singing in the taverns. The moans from the bundles of filth that lie in the streets. I have been a soldier. And I have seen my comrades fall into battle or die more slowly under the lash in Africa. I have held them in my arms at their last moments. These were men who saw life as it is, yet they died despairing. There were no gallant last words, just confusion in their eyes. Whimpering the question, WHY? I don't think they were asking why they were dying, but why they had ever lived. When life itself seems lunatic, who knows where madness lies? Too much sanity may be madness! To seek treasure where there is only trash, perhaps to be practical is madness! But the maddest of all,

<u>IS TO SEE LIFE AS IT IS, AND NOT AS IT SHOULD BE!"</u>

*The proceeding monologue is from the Broadway Musical, "Man of La Mancha."

A SOLDIER'S LAMENT 1

Dawn's curtain is slowly being pulled across the heavens. The early morning horizon is as red as blood flows. Setting the backdrop for the war-torn battlefield lying before us. Weary be the fields for nothing vital grows there. It's not a pasture green containing flowers in bloom or waving in the sweet summer breezes. Eden has been transformed into a domain of death and destruction A multitude of soldiers have bravely fought and lie in silence. Somewhere back home hearts will weep for their loss. A nightmare filled with the unwanted dispatched anew. So many young men and women were killed before they even had a chance to experience life. A husband, wife, sister, brother, mother, and father will be laid to rest. During a starless night, the war raged on. Darker is the night that becomes a backdrop that accents the intent of an invasion. Where the flashes from bombs explode in the dark. Fire from the rifles disturbs the darkening plains with each flash of light, dawn's torn curtain is exposed. The sun rises with tears in her eyes. Etched high across the sky is huge white clouds laced by the fiery sun. There is silence at times across the wounded and scared battlefield. Remember the lush green grass with trees and the song of the Meadow Larks. Friend and foe are mesmerized at the sight manifesting before their weary souls. There is a seize of battle. Soldier after soldier slowly remove their helmets. Others react with tears of awe, slowly flowing over their cheeks. Among the billowing white clouds that stand motionless against a sky-blue pink. Stands the vision of a posed bugler at least fifty feet tall. We are witnessing a miracle.

A soldier in full regalia raises his bugle to the heavens in slow motion. As being witnessed by us on the ground. As far as the eyes can see ribboned in row after row appear white gravestones. There was total silence across the battlefield. For now, the world stopped turning and the vision was all inspiring. We heard the bugler playing, "TAPS." This I will never forget, for as long as I live. For this was an intervention. The glory of it all tore my heart from my chest. A few soldiers dropped to their knees. One voice amongst hundreds of soldiers began to sing the words that belong to the song of "TAPS." Many people didn't realize that there are lyrics written to "Taps". We assumed it was a soldier in the distance, he was clearly heard by all. Many relate to the music but very few know the words written. It was so quiet during this astonishing vision above us. Yet the lone singer's voice could be heard across the land. It was the most beautiful voice I had ever heard. We now were witnessing a holy vision manifesting over each fallen comrade. To this day many young soldiers had given their all for their country. Souls in salute as the bugler played "Taps." For those men and women who had fought and died on the battlefield, these words enriched our souls.

"SLUMBER YE YOUNG HEROES
FOR IN GOD, WE TRUST"

"Hark! The Phoenix has risen to light man's battlefield once again! Dawn is painted across the mountainsides as if rendered by a visionary artist." **NOW I MUST VENT!** *Throughout the ages, wars are carried into the future where souls are seduced by,* **"FALSE PROPHETS!"** *That Promising a ride on the glowing tail of a virgin comet! So, with faith riding in your back pocket we watch the beginning and the ending of "Governmental Fires." Either raging out of control or petering out. All controlled by,* **"POMPOUS POLITICAL OLD MEN!"** *Sending young men and women to wars. Senseless is the way of men who act as "Hawks" show there is NO other way but by FORCE. The sky is filled with the sounds of man-made thunder. The ground feels the vibrations of dutiful and patriotic men and women as they storm across the land that is not even their own. Like the ramblings of old men in control of the Government we elected! Clearing their throats one by one. while sitting behind a Mahogany Desk barking orders over the phone. Fight for a higher seat in their governmental parties. It is* **"WE"** *who need to ready ourselves, to rally for the* **"Tsunami of Posturing Blowhards."** *Each makes promises that will never come to pass. Telling ball-face lies to win votes and we the people are so Goddamn stupid for believing them! Cults are created by one who has never fought a war in their demonic minds. They point their finger to the heavens. With fire and brimstone mannerisms,* **{So like the Native American Indians that said, "MAN SPEAKS WITH FORKED TONGUE!"}** *telling us how they will honor the men and women who gave the ultimate sacrifice. So easy for the* **"BLOWHARDS", "COWARDS", or from my own vocabulary, "ASSHOLES."** *That runs our government. It is those that vote for these legislators. Be it known as in this country. Somewhere in a memorial on a paper, square piece of wood, or bronze, our nation has worded the following,*

"FROM A GRATEFUL NATION
WE THANK YOU
FOR YOUR ULTIMATE SACRIFICE IN DEFENDING OUR NATION
AND
THE FREEDOM FOR ALL PEOPLE"

"Hark! The Phoenix has risen to light man's battlefield once again"
Dawn is painted across the mountains majestic
As if rendered by the hand of God...

A SOLDIER'S LAMENT 2

Deep, deep down from the bowels of hell and all that is unholy
I let out a curse for the soldier that stood beside me had fallen
He's not another brave soldier or friend, he is my young brother

I fell to my knees, then cradled his devastated body in my arms
Heaven began to rain washing the mud and blood from our faces
Suddenly I couldn't breathe, for he went totally limp in my arms

My world went in slow motion, I only heard raindrops splashing
My emotions ran the gametic, shock, pain, anger, and back again
Each raindrop felt like chard of glass through my aching soul

Horror filled my mind, jolt after jolt shocked with untold anguish
I needed to pull myself together and carry him from this battlefield
My God, the mud was thick, with each step of my boot, I sunk deep

My heart felt as if it were exploding, and my soul weakens with every step
I promised mom and dad I would watch over him with all my heart
What must I do, Sweet Jesus? For you had a reason for taking him away

He answered me not, no matter how loud I shouted to the heavens
All the while I began to envy my brother, he is free from this hell
I wish him peace as he enters the kingdom of our Heavenly Father

It's hard for me to forgive myself, still...

A Story of Dark Passion

*Slowly the warmth from the Sun God gave way to the man-in-the-moon and the forever night eyes above. There is a wash over this winter moon. An unusual feeling of dredge fills the cold night air. All those that are in the deepest of cold slumber will sleep no longer on this evening. Along the banks of Louisiana, Swamps are every species of creature known, quite a few deadly to man. Will either emerge or crawl from the darkest of shadows and muck. Deep in the blackest of caverns and shadowed dens will come a gathering of those known as the **"Children of the Night."** They have wakened with eyes of fire and hunger. Creeping over the rocks and fallen Cypress trees throughout the swaps and bogs. Their fiery eyes have taken in the full moon, set large against the dark velvety sky. They've wakened to sing an introduction of their master's arrival. He stands deep in the back of thousand-year-old tombs, lost and forgotten. Wrapped in a cloak of stale, stagnate pitch, stands a shape like a large cocoon. Waiting for the ultimate darkness to emerge. Where the night air blows hard at your back. Bending the dead crooked branches of an aged Willow covered in Spanish Moss. Resembling boney fingers covered in creepy lady's laced gloves. Silhouetted against the full Blood Moon. Voodoo Royalty knows this moon to be the bringer of all evil. There is a ground fog that invites all to come and play the night away. Gases rise from the swamps, bubbling like a witch's caldron throughout. The night is an ice blue, trimmed in a faded rose color. There in the distance, weaving in and out of nature's creeping ground fog, one can see numerous slanted fiery red eyes throughout the waterways. Moving throughout the ancient gravestones neglected and long forgotten, evil moves to the chanting of nature sounds. Frogs, crickets, birds, and gators are on the hunt. How they tempt one's curiosity. But beware the swamps and their channels are death traps for those who are reckless in knowledge. For ions and ions, he has been imprisoned deep in his crypt. It's been a long time waiting for the Blood Moon to raise again. Counting time when once again he may walk the nights through the swamp known as his home. A wet slime and dry rot, lifeless ivy covering, and decay lie rotting over his marbled vault. He steps out slowly, pushing against the overgrowth. Parting the vines like a curtain just enough to blend into the surroundings. Thought to himself, **"What do I make of this new era as an ancient intruder?"** He glides atop the fog that lies thick across the graveyard. Standing still in the haunting shadows of the dark swamp listening as he waits. His red eyes observe a small figure with long raven hair. She is mysteriously moving from one shadow to another. His trance-like stare is filled with a hungering lust. He has not been fed for a longest of time. As she passes very near, it is easy to see she is a beauty to behold. His silence is remarkable. Just as she was about to pass right in front of him, she suddenly stops! She sniffs the air, very aware of another close by. He took a step forward from his dark solitude. It shocked and frightened her, bringing forth her animalistic defenses. Her beauty transformed into an angry demon. Her lips were drawn back over her now canine teeth. She was exposing her fangs, hissing, and growling like a hungry crazed animal. His gut reaction was to return in kind like striking of a match. He grabbed her by throat in a split second. What a rage he now displayed. He grabbed a hand full of the blackest of hair in his other hand. Pulling her down as he hovered over her petite frame. The action was so quick that the fog around them both took a while to circle them. He thought how this she-devil was remarkably strong and quite a handful to handle. She stared into his eyes, flaming blood-red. She could read his every thought at that instant. She was daring him to try and go any further without an invitation! He wasn't about to let her get the upper hand. For it* *had been an ion that he had a woman in his arms. This one wasn't going to get away, his teeth grew at a shuttering speed. Just then she raised her hand of razor-sharp nails. Wheeling them furiously, slashing his face with claws sharp as scapples. This action drove him to an uncontrollable rage. He threw her down and instantly fell upon her. Each disappeared under the thick creamy ground fog. With the hunger that burned inside, he sunk his fangs into her beautiful pearl-colored nape. Her struggles only intensified as she struggled under his weight. His rage soon turned to a manly lust. She began to relax in his arms. Her aroma was captivating, after a few seconds, he managed to regain some composure. Raising his head to catch a breath, the taste of her river rage lustfully ran down his throat. She then pulled him tighter onto her petite body. Not a word was exchanged, she leaned forward kissing his neck with a bite of her own. The expression on his face reached a lustfulness that was pleasurable. She drew enough blood to taste the flavor of his stud lines upon her body. Together there in the cool blue of night, they both sank deeper under the blanket of swamp fog. Never a word was exchanged between the two of them. There may have been an expressed moan of enjoyment from each of them. A Vampire lovefest ensued for many evenings to come. Their hunger for one another was epic. They made unbelievable love throughout the nights. They decided to take strolls under the light of the moon heading for their feeding grounds. Each would make several kills during the evening. Her attacks upon her chosen prey were vicious and precise. He found them exciting to watch, each time she made an attack he felt a sexual thrill deep inside. They both looked at each other knowing that time had slipped from them. Realizing that dawn was quickly rising and that their time was getting short, he raised his cape, and she flew to his side. Haste upon his wings was immediate. From that night on and every night after that, she shared his tomb deep into the catacomb. His name was Vladimir, and she was Natasha Rose. Softly she whispered in his ear,* **"Until Dusk my love"**... *He replied,* **"Until Dusk"**...

A THOUSAND SHADOWS WALKING

Let me tell you a story of a thousand or more innocent souls. Some lost their lives before the "March" even began. Some were weak and some were as old as the trail they were forced to walk. Driven by the "White Eyes" to a place to call "Home". They would live in harmony and peace... It was their land from the beginning, given to "People" by the "Great Spirit" who blew life in the dust of time. But the story of "The Trail of Tears", has been told by the many who walked the real "Trail of Tears"! What I wish to do here, is tell the story of two Native American Indians that were in love. They shared the same nightmare that both had had night after night. Were their dreams just that, "Nightmares"? Or was it an "OMEN" that was being shared throughout all the "Indian Nations" of what was to come?... Let me tell you the true story of these two young, ill-fated "Lakota" lovers... as handed down through the generations in my heritage...as told to me long ago.

*A thousand shadows walking, Brave Elk is a handsome young brave all about fifteen years. Sun-baked skin, muscular body. His long black hair danced in the wind that blew atop the knoll. Where the lemon grass was ripe and tall. The sweetness of the lemon grass swirled with the breezes. The night sky gave the stars life through the velvety black sky. He stood in silhouette facing the summer's huge Lakota Moon. Below running to meet Brave Elk was his intended, Little Fawn. A beauty by any standards was sweet and had a gentle spirit. She was all fifteen years old. Raven-colored hair she could sit on. As she ran up the hill to meet Brave Elk her hair flowed behind her as the wind kissed her Little Fawn's face. This night, they would lay amongst the lemon grass in silence. Together staring up at the stars and occasionally spoke in soft whispers. He reached for her hand, and she responded in kind. Together, each directs their prayers to the "Spirits of the Night." Each spoke of the dreams that would come to them every night. Dreams are considered windows into the future or troublesome. Their sharing was so much alike that they became fearful. Each haunting dream was shared; the rivers ran red with blood. There was smoke and many smoldering fires. Horses were screaming, the buffalo are butchered and left to rot. They both dreamed of walking on the Great Plains, at opposite ends, walking toward each other as they stepped over the massacred bodies, of the men, women, elders, children, and babies. Bloody body parts are being carried off by wild animals. Walking was brought to standing face to face in the center of the killing field. Each heard a shot fired! It echoed throughout the Plaines. Their eyes tore open and there was silence. These last two surviving Lakota stumbled into each other's arms. With their last ounce of breath, they slowly dropped to their knees. With longing in each other's eyes, they whispered, "I love you" ... Another shot rang out, and Little Fawn jerked forward into his arms. With strength he didn't have, he held her tight, and kissed her. Another shot stroke Brave Elk, the two lay facing one another. Both stared into each other's eyes. Now the sun has begun to set. Deafening is the silence of a thousand souls. Etched as shadows across the land. Vanishing is the people of the plains. Two Lakota Indians in love, sharing the nightmare that came true. Their dreams were an omen of the future, the **"Genocide of a People."** Thousands of young men and women and the old walked endlessly and died, a thousand shadows walking endlessly on a*
"TRAIL OF TEARS!" ...

Across America, the Winds Are Blowing

Across America, the winds blow

You've scattered seeds you shouldn't sow

A bitter harvest you will reap

America, for you I weep

Depriving old ones of their right to life

Slaying the children with a tongue as sharp as a knife

You scramble to shut every opened door

But refuse to acknowledge the poor

Look out your window, see what's on your doorstep

Piles of sorrow, pain, grief, and gambling bets

The miserable, naked, poor, and the blind

The weak of heart and the sick of mind

You used to pray, my soul to keep

America, for you I regretfully weep

What goes around, comes around in spins

Carried across this America by the changing winds

Agonizing Restoration

Sitting in the backseat of this stretched limousine, my thoughts are on the future. Headed fifteen miles west to a tiny church draped in purple, blue, and white Wisteria. Today they will be in full bloom and the warmth of the day will heighten their amazing aroma. Nothing is more beautiful than hanging drapes of Wisteria. The entire stoned portion outside of the grand old Chapel is covered in a veil of lavender-colored blossoms. The fragrance is lovely and candy-sweet when in glorious full bloom. The aroma carries you away from your favorite fantasies. Cupids, Doves, Hummingbirds, and happy tears of blessed Angels. In early fall, when summer takes her last breaths, a strong breeze blows the blossoms like into a flurry of falling purple snowflakes. We watched the children run and jump through the flurry of dancing Wisteria pedals. I cupped my hands to gather up the petals covering the ground. I put them to my face and inhale, to know their gift of sweet beauty. It's like capturing the memory of a youth's first love. That always seems filled with the freshness of love's joy and happiness in life. This time I pulled two small vales from my pocket and stuffed them gingerly with as many fresh Wisteria blossoms as possible. A memory vessel for the love of my life and me I. Remembering that day, we pledged to carry them near our hearts. She and I were being silly as young lovers often are, we made a silent wish for the future.

Time passed before our eyes, and we grew into our teen years, still in love. Upon graduation, I went away to college up north and she locally. We always stayed in touch. Often feeling the miles that separate us, being lonely for my love back home. I would open my vile, the scent brought special memories alive of that day. Remembering my secret wish made on that day so long ago. I wished, "She would become my wife one day." After my graduation, I went back home to pop the question. I had thought about how and when, and where to make my move. I agonized over the possibilities. For distance from one another was agonizing. I wanted everything to be perfect. Time brought us back together as the young sweethearts we were in high school. Catching up day by day on what inspired our lives while apart. Even though we talked about that missing time quite often.

The time had come for me to ask for her hand in marriage. My plan was to take her back to the chapel we loved so much when the Wisteria was in its full heavenly bloom. That late summer day finally arrived! Everything finally came to pass. All my plans leading up to this very special day were here! I was walking out my door when the phone rang... On the other end was her father. In my hand was the vessel that held my silent wish all these years. Suddenly time stops! My heart and my world were tragically brought to a standstill. I had dropped her off at home last night after a romantic dinner, and a walk along the banks of the canal. The evening was simply perfection. I ask if she would love to go to the Chapel tomorrow for the Wisteria was once again in glorious bloom. She threw her arms around my neck and said, "Yes, yes!" Kissing me with excitement. She was so excited about the two of us going back to the Chapel. I was ready to make my wish come true. I dropped her off at her home and drove back to my house. I never felt so blessed in my entire life. She is everything my heart desires. Still listening on the phone, I listened to the words her father was expressing. She told her parents she believed it was going to be a very special day. She harbored a secret wish. Her silent wish was coming true, she knew I was going to pop the question. Her parents said they never saw her happier during the evening. She was filled with anticipation, she said goodnight, then she went to bed... The following morning her parents knocked on her bedroom door, upon entering they discover her on the bed surrounded by scrapbooks, letters, and photographs. Apparently, she had passed away in peaceful sleep of memories. In one hand, she was holding a tiny vile of Wisteria Blossoms...

ALL I HAVE ARE DREAMS

My heart longs for the night when you come to me in dreams. Your beautiful body lies beside me like so many times before. It's heaven holding you tight in my arms feeling your warmth, I taste the sweetness of your lips, a flavor craved forevermore. I'll always feel your sweet caress and warm breath upon my flesh. Sweet as honey and gently caressed. I'd stroke your hair gently as I move it from your beautiful face. I love looking into those eyes of everlasting passion. Your cologne still lingers where your body lies next to me each night. I would kiss the nape of your neck, down across your shoulders, and across your chest. You always said my love was like receiving a dozen roses daily. We had a love that was strong, uniting us for walking into the future with dreams yet to conceive. You would kiss my neck gently, then whisper softly, "I love you." Always I'd catch my breath in a sigh, I knew what true love was. We nearly had it all my love, you and I were meant to be together. Now I reluctantly wake from my nightly dreams, for you are not there... My dreams are like the flickering of a singular candle in the dark. Our memories are played upon a violin, tearing at my heartstrings. My heart aches for that endless pool of love seen deep in your eyes. I sit on the edge of this bed, often I break down for the loss is too hard to bear. The loss of you has created an endless sad song that is sung in the darkness. Heaven has another beautiful angel and all I have are my dreams of you and the memories we shared.

ALONE IN MY SOLITUDE

Part One
"SELF-MADE PITCH"

THE ENDLESS DARKNESS OF MY NEVERMORE

I have had my soul caught between shades of darkness
The times have been lonely
The loss of measuring time is a careless whisper away from an eternal sleep
Standing in the meeting of two great walls,
Creates a corner black and as deep as evil
Holding the secrets to vanishing souls
I know, for I watch in secret,
Here in this pitch of all pitch
Where many hap-hapless souls fade into the endless darkness of nevermore...
So many times, I would close my eyes,
Walk into the darkness and I'd go weak in body
Then feel flushing in my soul
Tight in the corner, I would stand,
I would put a hand and elbow on each wall
Steady and steadfast with what faith I may muster up
And decide to remain in this limbo
Blend into the darkness before
And shut out all the pain laced in agony or deal with it the best I can
After all, I am a master at it, for a longest time now
I open the door to the darkness
This pitch of black that has surrounded my miserable life
Where I witnessed unspeakable horrors
I know souls that were sweet as fresh-bloomed Mimosa blossoms
Before taking part in
The Seeding,
The Plotting,
The Creation,
Of the Evil Deed, done and finished!
After the evil had its fill of all the good and plenty
Those that truly became filled with remorse
I cried a thousand tears for what I had done
In the darkness, this pitch harbors so many souls crying out in vain
But somewhere in the deepest of the darkness,
ALL GOES SILENT!
We listen in silence
It was faint, like a puff in desperate aspiration
We heard the evilest of all evil-ed sounds

The laughter of Evil's "Satisfied Hunger!"
All I feel is a total discuss
Then not a sound
Not a damn sound could anyone hear...
I gathered myself up and ran like hell
I ran from the darkness, from the evil laughing
I ran further and deeper into
The endless darkness of the Nevermore...
Into my self-made,
PANIC ROOM!
The endless darkness then echoed the silence
The silence of Nevermore...

ALONE IN MY SOLITUDE
PART TWO
Alone...Alone...Alone...

THE ENDLESS DARKNESS OF THE NEVERMORE

After all, I am the Master Shadow,
Living in the darkness of the nevermore
It is I that controls whether I live or die!
Living within a vault of darkness all my life
I open the door to the PITCH of black that has surrounded my miserable life
Where I have witnessed the horrors, no child should see
Seen, done, created, plotted, and faced every damn ugly moment
Then I sit crying after-wards
So hard I can't breathe
Not a damn sound could I make
WAIT! WAIT!
I can't breathe, I can't get any air
OH MY GOD!
I can't breathe...
My head is burning, it feels like it's going to explode...
HELP ME!
I gathered my reality up and ran like hell
Into my self-made,
PANIC ROOM
Something has changed.
My Panic Room doesn't feel the same anymore
I no longer feel my soul caught between two shades of darkness
I always called it the endless darkness of the nevermore
Nevermore?
Never...more...
Wait a minute, I remember...I couldn't breathe!
I was so damned scared; the darkness once again took over me
I could not see a thing
I would turn around and there was the pitch,
With no way out!
There were screams, scratching, and growling and the air was foul
Then things were attacking me from everywhere
Look at my arms, look at my legs, shredded with cuts and claw marks
I got to calm down for my own good
Wait, something is different,
Where in the hell am I?
Christ, I'm cold, stiff as a broad...

I am surrounded by an Ivory-white satin
Stitched, pleaded, and ironed just perfect
My head rests on a pillow of ever-soft cushion
To lie here in open silence
In this bed not of my choosing!
I have no choice, I must sleep in my world of darkness
In shadows, in my thoughts that are lingering
Cold and hauntingly lonely
My bedfellow be named,
REGRET...
What questions might there be?
And what brought this night about?
Look closely, a tear-soaked pillow from the ache in my heart
Bringing shameful doubts of self-devotion
Alone in more than mere thoughts
Lying here in this silent night
I see an extended room filled with faceless shadows
Seated row after row, after row...
The feeling of four walls closing in on me fast
Like a wild horse racing around an endless track of my past regrets
I say, "Pillow be my Sponge"
The blinders I am wearing, please guide my soul to the finish line
I cry out into the darkness...
"Sink, Oh Moon Sink"
Lower and lower into a world of mistakes
So that you can join me in my bed made of silence!
I calculated the number of times I have crawled between sheets
Turned out that the lights
Finding myself on the side at midnight
Saying, "Forgive my judgments"
Sometimes to recall my misfortunes
You would have had to lay beside me
To know my love,
To know how I would make love to you,
Is to truly know my worth!
Know that when I make love to you, we will kiss each other's souls
I wouldn't have it any other way!
My life was filled with chaos
My pillow holds a lifetime of solitude
For all that I loved is gone...
Lying here in this bed of silence
I watch faceless shadows walk by where I lie in morbid repose
I expected no more or no less
My pillow holds a lifetime of tears
Close the doors

I have seen all the misery I care to see
Shut the damn door!
I have lived this life and believe me when I say,
"ENOUGH IS ENOUGH!"
Regrets like myself will be laid to rest
I have paid my dues in life, not of my own choosing
This bed is made of silence,
Will finally allow me to be alone
In my solitude...

In the Endless Darkness of My Nevermore

AN ACTOR

You enter from stage right
Deliver your lines with authority
Bump into the furniture
And get the hell off the stage!

One becoming another
Living in the moment for the moment
Having the gift to develop your character
Reaching deep inside, gathering its essence

In the "Real World"
You learn by observing the actions of others
Tomorrow is but a thought, a vision
Yesterday is used for reflection

Study your craft
Read everything and become the sponge!
Absorb the meat of the script
Memorize your lines, become the reason

Sets to explore and props to handle
The first law of props, "Not Yours-Don't touch!!"
Each actor controls their own environment
Don't be afraid to show your emotions

Always stand in the light
Feel its warmth, always relate
Always respect your fellow actors
Each performance is for the very first time

Having respect for all involved makes you a true actor
When the audience believes the character is real
They will drift into the world you create
Loving your character or loving to hate your character

Hear the audience's response
Receive the adulation they give you
You and your fellow actors brought the story to life
Take your bows to show your appreciation

Curtain call after curtain call
Your hard and dedication have paid off
You now have received the ultimate reward
A standing ovation for all the hard work and time given

Your costume comes off and hung-up
Make-up, and hair pieces are removed
The mirror reflects the truth once all is stripped away
There you are, once again just an actor

It's time to exit the theater
Out the backstage door, exit for home
Possibly lingering outside are a few devoted fans
Autograph their programs, show your respect

Your car is waiting
You step into the silence, taking a well-deserved breath
Tomorrow night you will do it all over again
Bringing your character to life in the world you love so well

You're an actor, singer, dancer, director, and or choreographer
Each creates a world on the stage that is loved by all
Except, for one or two critics believing they could have done it better
Either way, a Thespian's reward is the sound of

"APPLAUSE"
"APPLAUSE"
"APPLAUSE"
"APPLAUSE"

AN ARCHANGEL I DID GREET

On such a day here in my hometown of Frederick, Maryland at Baker's Park, I've grown to treasure each minute. Lying contented on a carpet of thick manicured green grass. I watch the ever-changing cloud formations above. Cool is the summer breeze that blows throughout the park. Lovers are often seen strolling gingerly on the paths through the park. Shaded by huge canopies of Elms, Oaks, and magnificent Weeping Willows. Quiet is Carroll Creek which rambles and winds alongside the park. Ducks are often at their leisure floating on the creek. Children's laughter is always heard from within the playground by the Bandshell. Sitting up from my prone position, my eyes spot an old man on the bench under a huge Elm. Alone, he feeds the many pigeons and sparrows from a paper bag. Apparently filled with a combination of bread and seeds. As if a call to arms, I see waddling over the ducks and geese. I am often here in the park and don't recall ever seeing this man. I know just about everyone in my small hometown of Frederick. I suppose my curiosity has always been like that of a cat. I brush off, drawn to the old man on the bench near the old Bandshell. I see a pleasant gentleman with an air of complete serenity about him. A sweet summer breeze like a carousel surrounded this entire area. I felt as though I had entered a special moment in time. I felt as though I was always meant to meet this quiet old man. Instantly, it was the most peaceful of feelings I had ever known. I greeted the old man, introducing myself, then I asked, **"May I sit down?"** *Never looking up, he answered,* **"Help yourself, young man?"** *As I sat on the bench beside him, the birds being fed went into silent slow motion as if they need to take flight. He calmly leaned backward, saying,* **"Beautiful afternoon, isn't it?"** *I took a good look at this quaint silver-haired gentleman. Answering him,* **"I always find it a beautiful day in this park."***. I felt a wonderful, calming peace sitting beside this older gentleman. Sitting alongside this man gave me the greatest warmth deep inside. He turned in my direction, putting his right arm atop the bench, and placing his hand on my shoulder. Gently giving it a squeeze. It was his smile that mesmerized me, behind his eyes was a universe of wisdom. Whatever doubt, confusion, or misgivings I had in my life, mattered no longer! I couldn't help but gaze into those amazing eyes of an amber-rich glow. The world around us faded away. Not taking my eyes off his, I saw my entire life being played out in his eyes like a mirrored reflection. The pain that I had sheltered nearly all my life was being released and then drained by his touch. My heart felt as if it were going to explode from the relief it brought. I felt tears welling in my eyes. I gasped for air and released a sigh emptying the last of any darkness held within. This beautiful and amazing old man gave me a smile of fulfillment. Tears slowly descended along my flushed cheeks onto my lap. For the first time in my life, my heart was lighter than a feather. Who was this man? He leaned forward speaking words in a whisper like a song being sung. In a heavenly tone,* **"How Great Thou Art"***, always remember this my son", reaching forward with his other hand, silent tears flowed from my eyes. Placing his hand upon my chest, he said,* **"The person you are is in here, Trust him!"** *With my mind, I asked him without speaking,* **"Please, who are you?"** *Smiling as bright as the sun* *shines, the old man leaned into my ear saying,* **"I am whom you need at this moment in time. I'm sent by one who loves you, fear not for I am always with you, simply believe in yourself."** *A feeling of renewal washed over me; I was given a newfound reason. His soothing and beautiful ambered eyes remained fixed on mine. They're filled with warmth and loving wisdom as if I had always known him. I watched him emerge from his seat beside me as if age meant nothing. The old man took a few steps away from the bench where I now sat alone. Turning around to face me, the pigeons and doves gathered at his feet. Speaking to me,* **"Don't go through life in a rush as so many do these days. "They run as if to catch the sun when it is already within each of their hearts."** *There before my senses, the sweetest fragrance of summer wind encircled us. Amongst the brightness and snow-white doves, this old man was transforming before me. My eyes now beheld a virile, young, and handsome winged Archangel. His hair was long and golden. His eyes were sapphires. He wore a short white tunic laced in gold. I was amazed and in glory at the spectacle taking place before me. Around him golden rays beaming pulsated like the beating of a calm heart., white doves fluttering in silent flights about him. The brightness was intense, and I had to shield my eyes. Then he displayed two huge and magnificent opened wings of liquid gold. The air was filled with the aroma of Roses and Gardenias. I thought to myself, was this really happening to me here in Baker's Park? He spoke one last time to me,* **"Remember I am with you always!"** *In an expanding flash of white light, he vanished before me. There I sat in awe, a renewal of faith in who and what I am. The children were still playing and couples walking about. I never questioned what I experienced on that amazing day in Baker's Park. It was real and happened to me. A spectacular creature was sent to rid me of the darkness that was consuming my soul. I will take his words to heart and soul for the rest of my life. It truly happened, changing my life on that summer day in my hometown of Frederick. By the way my friends, that wasn't the last time I saw that beautiful old man. I saw him several times sitting on the bench under that great Elm in Baker's Park. Feeding the pigeons scrapes of bread and seed. I would always look in his direction and he would turn his head to look at me. Did I find religion during that experience in Baker's Park? It's very possible... I sat on the green grass nearly every day with one eye on that bench under the Elm. I saw the old man look in my direction now and then with a nod to say hello. Occasionally I would make my way over to the bench, even though it seems empty, I still feel the warmth of that old man, my Guardian Angel. For he is certainly always with me,* **"How Great Thou Art."** *A magnificent Archangel I did greet!*

SYMPHONY OF TEARS

It's the day that the world prayed would never come to pass!
Someone made the decision that today will be the day,

The World Should Come To An End!

{There were few survivors. Here at what once was called "Earth", the home of millions, is burnt beyond recognition. No trees, no animals to be seen, no birds in flight overhead. The sky is a burnt orange mixed with a deep brownish-red smog at its ceiling. The mighty Mississippi River still flows to the ocean, but as a tiny stream of muck, blood, and mud. Thick like a runny glue, resembling the flow of steaming lava. A tiny child sits on a large boulder overlooking the bare vastness of a place she no longer recognizes. Her tiny frame is completely covered in black chute and grime. What used to be a white dress has been nearly brunt from her body. Her head is chard, where her beautiful long hair once grew. Caused by the rolling blast of fires that raged around the globe. Appearing from nowhere, an Angel in her full glory of magnificence. She surveyed the surroundings. Before her on a large boulder overlooking a once great river, sits a child of six or seven. She is lost, confused, sad, and frightened. Smoke still rises from her remaining dress material and a body covered in burnt flesh. The small child of the man cradles her knees and stares into nothingness.}

"I sing to thee; little survivor fears me not! I am sent from afar to ease your little body and soul. I see you facing your own sea of misery. What song do your eyes sing my precious one? I feel so much hurt, and loneliness etched upon your little face. I will give to thee, music from my heart to ease your troubled soul. By placing my hand on your chest, you will experience an ever-changing symphony of beautiful music. Little one, you are our father's hope for the future of man. You are the selected one to be known as, **"The Child of Light"** *a future our father now questions.*

You will be lifted, becoming the messenger, becoming the center of man's new frontier. For your dreams are worthy and still yet to come. Take the music I have stored within you. Believe there is a reason to believe! You will fly amongst the stars of an endless universe, becoming starlight itself. I will be your Star-guard forevermore. I will teach you how to conduct your very own symphonies. What is the matter, sweet child of man? Do you know how truly blessed and beautiful you are? Let me wipe away the sadness that consumes you. Little one, do you know how music was discovered? By nature in her progression upon the earth. It was created as far back as the very beginning when the man took the time to listen. I will tell you a story about that first discovery of music, how it was created... When music was first created, it was heard and felt, it went directly to the heart. Come, sit close and I'll tell you of its beginning... In this broken and brunt world, once filled with all races of men and women. Some were bad, and some were good. Some were not so nice and others not so understanding about change! They were confused about what was right from wrong. Just like what happened here this day. Someone misguided, confused, or even consider consumed with madness, place a finger on the button that dropped the bomb! Creating a holocaust of horror and the distinction of man. A decision of a lost and weak mind filled with greed and visions of grandeur that wanted "ALL." Wanted everything under that person's control. Endless wars to show who had limitless power at their fingertips. Do you ask who am I to know these things? I have been around for a very long time; at the creation of this world when living creatures took their first breath. I was given this task by our father in Heaven. Freedom scares them misguided and change is a concept that Dictators fear! They teach themselves to mistrust their fellow man. Hating everyone and everything, they even hate who they are! Some believe they are unapproachable.

Above all and laws are set before them. It became a chain reaction among nations. It was heard and felt around the world! The deed has been done... There wasn't a thing, no logic that could have changed that moment in time! I will take your agony and pain away my little love. I will guide you through the universe. You have a vast selection of creativeness and will be given an endless trove of love in your heart. There is a universe, a cosmos of great creativity. All the advancements man created were gathered. An enormous library of knowledge from the greatest of minds. The future of music is at your command! Music is the life force that surrounds creation at its best. The best of times will be at your command. Use the music from the past ages and create your own for the future you will create. But the most important element, my child of light, will be the music that you take from within your heart. It's lying deep within your being, with every beat of your life force! Inside you is the beginning, that ancient sound that first starts life. Early man held a pebble in one hand, then struck it against another stone. That sound was pleasing to man's ear. Then the idea to take a different size stone and strike it against a bigger one created a tone. A variety of pleasing tones started a revolution, and the people of the land united, and communication began. The world offered many amazing sounds created by each race, religion, culture, sex, and creed. The rhythm was born, and it will happen once again by you my child of light. Listen! Listen to sounds far in the distance. That's right little one, it's the sound of thunder, like a faraway heartbeat. That thunder in the distance will bring rain to fall upon this burnt earth. This rain is like no other that once fell upon the earth. This rain will scorch the surface, and a fallout created, called **"ACID-RAIN."** *because of the bomb's explosion of radiation. Whatever may be living will find its demise. It will not be pleasant. It will fall upon the land, this brunt, bruised, and battered earth will forever be depleted of fresh water. It is death. Rain, once the giver of life will burn the flesh of any living creature that may have survived this doomsday. Sweet child, I see your past world ravished and torn apart with no hope. Soon there will be wolves, gathering at the survivors' backs. Forming a quarter moon, tails between their legs a hungering droll running out of their postulant's mouths. They show starvation's malicious intent! Those few that have survived this doomsday attack on all humanity*

will fester in their own apathy and or be eaten by creatures or dissolved by the fallout. In the blink of an eye, all living organisms will cease to exist. That will be the story of a once amazing planet known as **"Earth."** The truth is as the eye sees. Man destroyed himself in so many ways... Stand up **"Child of Light."** Take my hand, for we will travel among the stars throughout the universe. The future will be yours to create. Take with you the music that once was a heartbeat. Who am I, you asked? I am an Angel from Heaven above, sent by Our Heavenly Father who art in Heaven. Sent me to escort you to your new home. Remember when I placed my hand upon your chest? God is giving you his gift of immortality within your heart, encased with his love. You will be the precious gift to the new world. So that you will create a new and perfect, **"Symphony of Tears"** ...

AN INNOCENT CHILD

There is a beauty and a profound glow
When a woman is with a child
Her womb now cradles the miracle of a precious life
Soon she will be known as a "Mother"
The most amazing miracle known to all creatures on this earth, "Birth"
She suffers an unbelievable amount of pain
Bringing life anew into this world
From that one miraculous last push
All her pain suddenly changes to elation and tears of joy
Within that remarkable moment of anticipation
She waits to hear the most beautiful sound in a mother's life
Hearing her baby taking that first breath of life
When the air has filled those tiny lungs
Announcing to the world
"I AM HERE!"
There is a rush running through all those that just gave witness
To the miracle of life in all its wonderment
Nine months, sometimes less
A mother and father have witnessed
The long-awaited fruit of their love
The birth of their child
An innocent child.
At the far end of this miracle blessing
The tearing at the core of one's soul
Is allowing the unnecessary suffering of
"An Innocent Child"
An innocent brought into a loveless environment
Possibly an unwanted one
The heart dares not to sing
The soul remains hidden within the ugliness that surrounds the child
Often abused, battered, and made aware that he or she was a mistake
There is little hope that this innocent child
Will ever experience not being loved...
Parenting is a blessing and an obligation
Beyond all measures
It's the one greatest event that two can ever treasure in a lifetime
Holding life's purest form in your hands
Given the honor and responsibility of molding your creation
If there be a man needing to prove his worth in this lifetime
Look into the eyes of the seed you planted
Creating,
An Innocent Child...

ANOTHER EASTER HAS COME TO PASS

*Another Easter has come to pass my little love. Know that I am vacant of soul without you in my life. Each year my sadness knows no end. When I lost the two of you it cut like a knife. The shock drove me to the brink of madness. I pleaded, **"Please don't take my world from me!"** Sleep deserted me, all reasoning vanished. I was told to accept that it was fate and meant to be that took the two of you away from me. At my side, you gave me faith and great strength Something I never had as a child myself. Never have I felt weaker and filled with strife. Not a day goes by that I don't feel your arms around me. That is so hard to bear. It's my grief that guides my purpose through life and God knows that is something I need to escape from. **"Time heals all!"** I grieve for you and your beautiful mother. My mind tells me to move on, but my heart, my heart has vanished along with you. I wish I had the power to turn back the pages of time, trust me my loves, if possible, I would sing like a Lark. We shared five unbelievable and amazing years of watching you grow day by day. That Easter morning, from the street I waved goodbye as the two of you were on your way to morning services. I remained home to finish your birthday cake. I watched you both drive away and I lovingly sighed for my world was good. You were filled with such joy that morning. My God your laughs and giggles lit my soul. Watching you play with your toys; I knew you were happy. You see my father never gave me toys. He gave us animals to play with at first. Then we were the ones to feed and bathe and house them. You hugged me so tight that morning like it was your last. Maybe it was an omen? Coming back from church, a drunk driver silenced you both. Were you thinking of me before that fatal crash? I hope so. I had just finished icing your cake of blue. Your favorite color. I was just finishing scripting your name atop the cake. **"Happy Birthday Cody-li"**. I hurried to put candles on the cake and wipe the floor after my mess. A wave of darkness like a veil fell across my eyes. My heart sank when there was a knock at the door. Slowly I headed for the door. I answered the door and was hit with crushing news. It was a message that I simply couldn't comprehend. I stood there with my mind flashing moments of everything bad that had happened in my life. Falling to my knees in front of the officers. I was in shock so said the men. **"Will you be okay if left alone? Can we call anyone for you?"**. I shook my head, looked up, and assured them I will be fine. When they left a thousand things went through my mind. But before I would handle what was expected of me. I had to vent my hurt, pain, and anger! It was God I cursed that day, screaming out **"NO... TAKE ME"**, I screamed, **"WHY THEM?"** I had a few choice words with the man above. I was just turned thirty-five years old, and Cody-Li just turned five years old. We shared the same birth date, April 23. Easter brings no joy to my heart year after year. The loss of you Nikki-Lynn created a void within my soul. Christ, it's impossible to count the tears unshared. Cody-Li, you were my sun rising and my moon setting, and you shined like the stars. In your eyes of wonder, I could see the stars being at your command. At birth, I knew what innocent love was all about. I held you in my arms, vowing your life will be a song to remember. This fatherly love I carry for you, will never, never die. This I promise and know to always be true. Nikki-Lynn and Cody-Li to heaven you were called. One day we shall greet one another as if you were coming through that door on your birthday... Every time I close my eyes, I am with you... A father's love forevermore.*

ANOTHER GOOD-BYE

Again, my roots are snapped, broken from another pull,
It aches, just when you feel things are going your way again,
The mind begins to sink from heavy thoughts of what to do

Your eyes survey what was harvested from your daily living,
A person travels many back roads to plant a foot, just to get ahead
Wanting to feel safe, feel secure, to believe in yourself

Hi-ways cannot sprout new life like the blood in one's veins
Supplying a life-given force to live, but constantly races forward
The hi-way is a speedster, any thought of growth is impossible

Each uprooting, it's my heart that feels the pain of lost memories
They remain locked inside, when needed they will be tapped,
To experience once again for the purpose that all things are possible

My eyes saw my surroundings day after day showing the struggle to succeed
I can close my sight, for I know my footing from room to room
I can step outside knowing where every rock is and every tree as well

Once again, another seed I must place into Mother Earth
May it grow full strength, strong, successful, and beautiful
May she nurture her child, giving it a chance to grow big and strong

Everything in this life has a beginning, middle, and an end
We're born, we live and grow throughout our lives
Then we will pass on, such is life!

HELLO
And then,
ANOTHER GOOD-BYE!

AUTUMN SINGS A SONG

Summer fades
Into Autumn's time to sing
Joyous toe-tapping moments
Need to make way
Autumn gives birth
To the changing of the seasons
Nature produces
A spectrum of dancing colors
Atop the tallest of trees
A leaf rides upon the wind
Twirling between branches
On the way down
Silent words and whispered words of
"See you next year"
Colorful leaves play
A continuous game of tag
Some breezes whistle a tune
Others howl endlessly
A wonder of colors burst into a quilt
Blanketing the earth
Painted pictures created
Colored leaves echo across the land
Landscapes of cherished moments to capture live
Autumn sings a song
Of colorful harmonies...

Autumn Years

Across the meadow of seagrass moving like waves in the current. I often sit under Mother Willow in quiet reflection to ease my pain. Childhood Fairies dance under her trusses in the summer breeze. There is nothing more beautiful when my summer tree yields to the whims of fall. I reach for the tail of a dream that always plays a game of seeing if you can catch me. Throughout my youth, I held onto my dreams like precious jewels. That was all I had, dreams. They were so shiny, bright, filled with color and amazing wonders that gave me hope that there is something better out there for me. Now in the autumn of my reality, quiet reflections are dreams fading, and I'm holding onto life's railings looking down the steep steps of yesterday. I must step upon destiny's descent, holding tight onto every memory. What future there may be left to this soul is but a mere reflection that seems to pass me by. Now is the time when all paths walked are covered in colored leaves. My solo walk to Mother Willow is where I will sit in quiet serenity. A life where I held a few wonderful moments and cried painful tears as they vanished in the mist. At least God knows the whys and wherefores set upon the reasons. At best, "Poor Me, Pity Party" is the pursuit of dreams and happiness. Such is "Life". I look out over the meadow and feel the summer wind. It won't be long before Autumn's colorful ballet comes to an end. Soon the bench in the park will be vacant, covered in winter's white. Tired am I, my colors fade like the season in my Autumn years...

BELIEVE IN YOURSELF

Believe in Yourself was written after my father had decided to tell me how he really felt about me. He said, "Better things have run down my leg." This went on many times in my life while living up on Hell's Half Acre. It was written for all the times he slapped me around. Those were the times I chose to sleep out in the broken-down barn. Written for all the times I would hide as a child under the bed to let him think I was away somewhere. As I got older, and something would arise that made me question my worth. I wrote this for me to remember. Every verse that makes up this poem was written with hate. Written with bitter hope, and written in the knowing that damn it, I am someone, I have dreams, and no one is going to take that away from me. NO ONE! Years later when I read it, it still makes me believe that every word I wrote was written with hatred toward my father, but from my heart to me. I hope you feel the words and the meaning behind them. Do "BELIEVE IN YOURSELF"!

*It's all about wishing upon a star
What do you do when your heart is on fire?
When your dreams begin to come true*

*Taking your belief to a higher level
Opening your eyes to everything around you
Reaching higher, further than your arms ever have before*

*Running faster, further than your soul can fly
Looking for paradise were running as hard as you can,
I will bring you back to where you started from*

*Like diamonds upon velvet, you shine as bright as heaven itself
Take a deep breath, hold that special moment inside
Let it come forth that your heart sores amongst the stars*

*This moment in time offers a pleasant reality
Dream your dreams, run faster, and love this moment in time
And do **"Believe in Yourself!"***

BENEATH THE WINTER'S MOON

Silence has once again filled the night. There is no music in the trees, the branches still hold tightly to their summer green. Soon the winds of change will march across the mountains signaling the winds of change. The leaves will turn their backs when the cold wind blows sharply. Shades of green will change to the colors of autumn. Leaves will dance in great numbers, twirling, spinning, and floating to the ground. Turning brown and finally hardening from lack of moisture. Others remain to cling tightly to their branched homes. The first rush of winter's wind races in and out of the sparse branches. Convincing the stubborn few to relinquish their hold and join those that now blanket the floor below. Stubbornly a few still fight against winter's song as they brush against one another creating one of nature's symphonies titled, "The Last of Fall." Beneath the winter's moon of white, against the night sky painted in a midnight blue, there is a cold breeze that haunts through the lengthening nights. It's the first winter's blow and it crawls hauntingly forward. Advancing down the mountainsides creeping into the meadows below. Its bitter touch glazes everything in its wake. Dried brown leaves are now glazed in an unforgiving shiny frost. Kissed under the silvery light of the winter moon. Shadows come alive across the barren landscapes casting shadows that creep across as the moon treks across the night sky. Lucky are those that catch sight of the Winter's Star Dancer. At this momentous time of the year, she appears fleetingly below the full winter's moon. I wonder what music she dances to. With each magical spiral she creates across the sky it's as if you hear macabre harps playing in a haunting echo. For it is the moans and whispers of wind that create her dance. Strumming your heartstrings with icicle fingers. Her gown flows like gossamer of winter's white, long and flowing to the sounds of violins. Trailing miles behind her like the tail of a great comet. Truly a visual symphony created to the score of "Moonlight Sonata." Every beautiful moment is created by those with an imagination beneath the winter's moon.

BLACK IS

"Black Is", was *written during a time when I felt my soul captured by an unknown entity that falsely befriended me. Locking my mind in a dark hole with no way out. My heart was hurting and this hole I was in, was deeper than my arms could possibly reach to get out. The truth is I don't believe I wanted to get out of this dark deep prison. I can't say that I put myself there totally, for I always remember being in a hole to start with. A couple of times I thought I nearly pulled myself out of the pitch. Every time I turned around; I was being pushed into this same damn hole. It took years the feeling of being trapped, for me to raise my arm up from the pit of despair and join the living race. Only after contemplating blowing my brains out. You would know what "**Black Is**". If you ever fell into a deep despair that governs your life. I found that it is* you, *and only* you *that can reach for that trickle of light that flashes across your mind like the summer lightning often silent. Grasp it with your eyes, lighting the world around you. Reach for that light! The true light, not the one that burns your soul...*

BLACK IS

Black is my night
So deep a black that misery is lost in the pitch
There I sit, useless with nothingness about me
Dark are my thoughts of the yesterday that never ends
I scream as loud and as hard as I can
Until the blood veins in my neck and forehead balloon as if to burst
The pain is shared with the shadows that haunt me always
Many times, I collapse...
Darkness is no friend to one who has seen the truth
Still, I can feel the four walls that cage me
And this platform I stand on is made of taunt chicken wire
I assume there is a ceiling, possibly not
I walk around touching the four walls as if I were a mime in a performance
It is so silent that I can hear the touch of my hands
Black is the darkness that has always nurtured me from day one
My back is always up against a wall so too fast what may
Confused, and terrified, I slide down in defeat
An empty shell with my hands grasping the holes in the chicken wire that cradles me
Every now and then there is a flash of white light above
There is not a sound from the flashes of light
Black is my lonely, lonely world,
Only memories that slice at my heart leaving deep scars upon the flesh of my heritage
I say to myself, "Why should I bother?"
It just adds one more heartbreak to make me a baker's dozen
Within these four walls that bind me tight
Darkness is my only friend....
Somewhere in the dark
A voice I do hear
Muffled, weak, but urgent in its delivery
A burning flash of light I do feel
From above the flashes come and go like a thief in the night
I call out,
"help"

Black Widow

When I was small, I learned of her and her evil ways. My elders would gather at night, telling stories of those she had taken. Back and forth they would exchange stories. The women had laid food and drink for the men, all would exit but one or two. After hearing these stories told and told again, they were quite bored. The women who remained usually were older. For they enjoyed adding to the conversation. One story held my attention. The story as told...

"On this night a beautiful woman walked into the carrying food. Most thought she was one of the family members there that night. So most went on with the stories. Twenty or more men were moving about, getting a drink, or having a private meeting of the minds, I suppose. One young attractive guy was quite taken with this beauty. He tried to see her through the smoke-filled room as she weaved in and out of the men offering food from her tray. There she stood in the shadows mysterious and alluring. Was this beautiful young woman with anyone special? She sat in a semi-lit area. Her long hair was shining. She was dressed in sleek black leather from head to toe, accented by a red belt. The young man watched her every move. Little did he know it was she that was staring coyly as her eyes survived the room. He had caught her attention the moment she had to enter the room. Every now and then she would raise her head to look at him, and the light in the room seemed to brighten. This happened every time she investigated his glance. Rising from her seat, she stepped forward and retrieved a jug from the table filled with a variety of alcohol and beer. Making her way around, in and out of the men. The closer she got to him the stronger his heart would beat. It was clear she was making her way to him. Whenever she would select a man that she favored, there was no stopping her approach. Her face was flawlessly beautiful. Her eyes were black as coal, and her lips were glistening red as her tongue lightly rolled over them. One man away she looked into his eyes. He felt warmth move through his body. Her eyes were so dark, that one could get lost in them. Her eye-to-eye contact became mesmerizing. The young guy felt numb and fixed where he stood. He could move if he wanted to. What was it with this gorgeous woman, he asked himself. It didn't matter. As far as he was concerned, he was hers if that was the intent. There she was this unbelievable beauty before me. Long raven black hair and her perfume were seductive, to say the least. He was bewitched as she moved very close. Leaning forward she whispered, "Kiss Me." Their lips met and her passion enveloped him. This kiss was not like he had ever known. Though it was passionate, warm, and beyond sexy, he felt a slight sting on his tongue. She slowly stepped away. He moved his hand up to his mouth. Slowing ran his finger across his lips. There was a bitter taste. She realized he had tasted her injection. She then whispered into

his ear to meet her later outside. How coy she was as he nodded yes. "What's your name?" he asked. She replied, "Does it matter?". As she headed toward the door, her walk had drawn the attention of neither every man in that room. He followed her out the door. He felt the air that was cool and refreshing after being in that smoke-filled room all evening. He looked about to see where she had gone. She stepped out between two motorcycles. He thought, Hench the leather outfit. The sexy lady gestured for him to follow her as went into the shadows. "Meet me at the overlook," she said. Of course, he thought this was going to be a night to remember, and he was correct. The night sky had not a star to shine. The moon was full and gave way to shadow making of the trees, and bushes about the landscape. Following her, he thought of those black eyes, endless black pools of mystery. Following the path through the tall buffalo grass, there she was standing at the overlook. The moon was the largest I had ever seen. She's standing as if in front of the moon. Together it was as if reaching out and pulling him in. Speaking softly to let her know he found his way. She was facing the moon with her back to him. The last thing he ever wanted to do was to scare her. Turning ever so slow she said to join her. Answering her, he said how beautiful she looks in front of the moon. She referred to how great the breeze felt. Looking for a way to make his climb, asking how you got up there. Stepped back to look for the best footings, and a strong breeze blew. There was something magical about it. He giggles at the thought. A feeling flowed over him as if he were drunk. Impossible for he didn't drink liquor. Things were spinning somewhat but manageable. He looked up. Before he was something magical. Her long hair was moving in slow motion along with the breeze. He was captivated by the sight. It was spiritual in some way. There she stood on her toes as if to take flight. Arms gracefully reaching toward the heavens. Never, never had he ever seen hair that long and flowing. It was growing before his eyes. Spread outward looking like extra arms stretching out. Wow! he thought, this is so unreal. Then witnessing her hair turning white. Now she hovered before him. Yards and yards of silk-like material extended from her body. It moved formation creating a giant web. A spider's web she was hanging from. I went to my knees. I asked her to tell me her name. She looked down at me from her newly formed web above and spoke, "I conjure, I cast spells to ease my hunger. I weave a web like a widow I am. Catching lost souls, their misery, and hate of all lost. I am in complete agony. Man is easy to lure, one kiss by me and they are mine forever. So, I offer two sides for their soul to go. You have one quick choice to make, no in-between worlds, there is no light, only dark. My hunger increases as I fill you with lust. Still, you have not said your name to me, asking as if he must know. She replied with a growing eagerness. "I have many names, you must meet them all, as you will**! Pain-Misery-Agony-Fire and DESIRE!** You can call me", Lunging forward she let out a banshee scream, **"The Black Widow!"**

BULLET TO MY HEART

From a distance, I hear the screaming of a bullet-headed in my direction
Unwavering as it splits the very air it rides upon until it finds its target
Striking my breastbone, boring into my heart without a reservation one

I clutch my breast; I gasp a deep breath as I am paralleled backward
I felt bubbling inside my heart as air escapes from the burning intruder
I lay on life's battlefield, my essences erupting like lava, leaving me weak

There is a flash of white light, a crash of thunder echoing within my ears
Still, the pain is mellow in my chest and soul, a pain I've never felt before
I open my eyes, trying to focus on the shadow I see moving toward me

A new clarity to my vision brings forth beauty with an angel's sweet kiss
This angel, now softly cradles me in her arms asking, "Is it very painful?"
With a coy smile on my face, I answer, "With every beat of my heart!"

Somehow everything before this moment seems vague and inconsequential
Your bullet of love has struck my heart with a new and powerful awakening
Angel without a doubt your aim is true, a loving shot straight to my heart!

CAN'T STOP THE CRYING INSIDE

*We all listen to the chattering and the conversations buzzing about within our heads. All day, all night we listen to sounds around us. Like that of cackling hens at war with one another filled with yelling and cursing as they pull you into their line of fire. Then there's silence. Throughout a war-torn pallet, as if the fear you feared suddenly appeared in the distance. As the saying goes, "**You could hear a pin drop.**" Then all of Hell broke loose once again. After hours of mayhem and a large explosion, then all goes quiet. One by one those that lay peppered across the battlefield are heard. The begging for help commences. The screaming from soldiers in shock realizing the horrors as their pain strikes to the core of their being. The paralyzing emotion as they discover parts of their bodies have been blown to" Kingdom-Come" and beyond. No one on God's earth could handle the agony these soldiers are going through unless you are there to hear the cries from hell. I say, "Thank You God!" to the man or woman that doesn't wake up. They know not the horror that may pursue the last of their innocence. I heard a familiar yell; I stand rubbing the mud from my eyes. There's a layer of cursing through the fire and smoke. One cannot help experiencing the smell of burnt flesh and gunpowder. It reeks within the fires of hell as you maneuver your way through the harsh field of death. Dead soldiers walk aimlessly searching for rhyme and reason. Like a wounded dove among the cries of the dying, you witness what Zombieland truly is. In the distance that familiar voice was sounding familiar. It was the voice of my best friend. Through the madness, I forgot about a buddy that was always within reach. I ran, tripped, then crawled to where he lay. In a comforting voice, I said, "**I'm here, I am here.**" I picked up his devastated body. It was hard to control my emotions. He was in bad shape and bleeding from the mouth, ears, and nose. Tears are streaming from my eyes down my dirty face as I assured him, he was going to be all right. In my heart and down deep into my soul I knew he wasn't going to make it. He tensed up in my arms several times as I stumbled my way through bodies, muck, and debris. Never have I felt so weak as when the light inside me began to dim. I felt my buddy go limb in my arms. Somehow, through the madness of that moment, I slowly fell to my knees. Holding him long enough to slowly lay him before me. I had no strength. I gasped for air as the flow from my eyes became a waterfall. I became so angry at the world. Gaining strength and determination, I managed to pick my friend up and cradled his lifeless body in my arms. I carried him across the battlefield, hearing stray bullets whisking through the air. With every step back to the trench, I suddenly stopped in my tracks. My buddy mumbled his mother's name over and over. I felt his body being tugged and pulled from my arms. I heard, "**Let go soldier, let go!**" "**We got him!**" I remember sinking down to the ground. There on all fours, I cried like a lost puppy. But my buddy still felt like he was in my arms. Those gunshots I heard as I race over the field, as I hit and maybe I am dead, a zombie refusing to believe I am no longer alive. I felt numb, I heard sounds that sounded as if on a drum. Looking about there were shadows moving toward me. Hands and arms moving in all directions. What in the hell was happening? Where is Rico? Why am I being told to lie down? During this madness and started yelling for Rico. Is he okay?... Everything went black. I don't know how long I was in this blackout. Regaining my senses, and gathering my thoughts, it was plain to see they* *were doctors and nurses. My throat was dry as sand in a desert. I was given a drink of water. I ask where is Rico, is he okay? Tried to get him back to safety as fast as I could. They didn't have to say a word. Their expressions and the lowering of their eyes and heads gave me the news. This time I cried silently. The only thing I was able to say to myself was, at the least he is free from this conflict, this savage world. I said over and over, he is free from this world, free...free... I did what I could on that awful day, as those around me said, you did everything humanly possible to get help for him. Everything possible... That's what I keep telling myself as I helped to carry him to his grave... I look into the eyes of the parents... Into the eyes of the woman whom he loved. Dreaming of a future together. What do I tell them? What will comfort their mounting pain? If known... What lie do I tell myself? Ending the pain, I have buried deep inside. For he's of my blood... I now carry him to his final resting place. I can't stop crying inside, nor stop the anger that I have for a war that made no sense. I can't stop the pain in my heart, in my soul. Because I had to watch my older brother, my best friend... DIE!*

{A Canvas of White, came from a dream that I had at several different times. Overall, it was about five times. I had wakened and each time I would write down what I could remember. When the dream wasn't there any longer, I gathered my notes and laid them before me on the table. It was very interesting and lucky I remembered putting numbers on the scrap pieces of paper. When I felt they were laid out correctly, I stood up from my chair glancing over them. A story was beginning to emerge. I then went out and bought a stretched canvas. Brought it home and set it up as if I were getting ready to paint my dream. I would sit there staring at the white canvas for nearly an hour. I got the idea to set a few objects around the canvas. Then I placed a lamp over top, to the right and left, up and down as well. The lighting created wonderful shadows of the objects. Each time I place the object at a different angle, the canvas came alive. With my notes, the lighting, and objects, my pen became my paintbrush. Light can do amazing things during the day and night. I finished my painting, and it is for you to imagine it as you read, "A Canvas of White".}

A CANVAS OF WHITE

*I noticed a large canvas upon the north wall, white as a blizzard does blow. Its amazing brush strokes are but a feathering in the snow, light and gentle. My eyes did but blink twice in hopes to channel my sight to its focal point. Clearly a need to focus within a crystal where time stands still just for me... A river of white satin flows from one end to the other in a continuous stroke, Chantilly lace and a widow's woven curtain ropes hold back the rising tides. A river's rage foamed in a rolling tide of white, splashing the falling snowflakes. An Archangel in the grandest of regalia, like the Phoenix, rises white in flight. Time is the essence, vanity but a shooting star away, how high will the Phoenix fly? Explosive is the winter of temptations, cradled in the arms of an Archangel, this canvas blinds me with its pristine whiteness cleansing one's soul. Emotions circle like billowing clouds, I must stand at the mouth of this river. Hopeless dreams fashioned like a carpet of Snow Geese, quiet and motionless. Painted stroke for stroke in a mighty tundra covered in the whitest of all fleeces, glory on high for the Archangel radiantly descends from a winter's white-out surrounded in crystalline twinkling stars, glittered kisses of falling snowflakes. The Archangel lies among the soft white downy feathers of a thousand snow geese. At the river's edge, their wings are opened in reference to create a gentle breeze. Thousands of White Lotus blossoms, Star Lilies grace his flesh, a virgin's holy pledge upon holy grounds. Upon the river's rage heartfelt secrets no longer matter, the Archangel slumbers. Lastly, the artist painted a forest of white trees, pleasingly shadowed in mystery. A living maze of branches entwining over the Archangel, blessed anew Phoenix shall rise. Shooting stars dance within a blizzard of snowflakes falling, blanketing the scene. There be the mystery **"A Canvas of White"**, could it be a **"Dorian Gray?"***

*Let's pray **Not!**...*

CAPTAIN OH CAPTAIN

Captain, Oh Captain, A request I make of you?
Your ship is readied, I need passage over the blue
From bow to stern, we'll soon feel the ocean spray
But before we set sail, let us all kneel and pray

Captain, Oh Captain, the sails are unfurled
Your compass beckons directions around the world
I stand on the bow with my heart in my hand
My questions need to be answered, God help this man

Captain, Oh Captain, please tell me true
Did my sweet Bonnie ever sail with you?
Across the oceans and across the deep blue sea
The crew now sings, "Oh, Bring back my Bonnie to me."

Captain, Oh Captain, No luck from the crow's nest
We've sailed forty days and forty nights without rest
Weary is the mood for the touch of dry land
May God bless us with the warmth of sun and sand

Captain, Oh Captain, It's the dawning of a new day
After a warm breakfast and coffee, then we're on our way
The ship is loaded for the quest, our journey still awaits
Searching for sweet Bonnie, I now fear at Heaven's Gate

Captain, Oh Captain, it's time to come true
Twice I have asked, did my Bonnie sail with you?
With tears in his eyes, he softly sings to me,
"My Bonnie lies over the ocean, My Bonnie lies over the sea
Oh, bring back my Bonnie to me..."

{This poem was a joy to write. When I was sixteen, I worked in an upscale restaurant, "The Red Horse Steak House", as asst. cook to Ms. Millie. I was going to school and working. It was hard but getting a paycheck at sixteen was well worth it. This poem holds some desires if you will. Living in the backwoods and having nothing all your young years soon lead the way to independence. With imagination and a drive to desire something more than being a punching bag for my father, being on the road to self-respect was a dream. This poem, "Castle in the Mist" was about that dream. After leaving the Red Horse and nearing graduation from high school, I was offered another job. Mrs. Joan Conrad, who was a manager at the Red Horse, offered me a job as chief cook of "The Town and Country Restaurant off route #40 West. A stone's throw from "Hell's Half Acre". The answer was yes. I had my reservations because Joan and I hadn't always agreed on things. However, this woman was a class act. She was a party animal and simply outstanding beauty. Years later I was daydreaming about Joan and the help she gave to a student to improve his life. I daydreamed a lot in my life. I guess you could call me, "Walter Middy". My fairytale consisted of memories of a goal I had set for myself many years ago, to do better and go for the golden ring, so to speak. The central character in this poem is modeled after my vision of who Joan Conrad was and the impression I conjured. She became my "Queen Cassandra". When you read this light romp through "Fairytale Land", there just might have been or is a Joan in your life. Wherever you are Joan, thank you for believing in me.}

CASTLE IN THE MIST

Far beyond the hills, nestled in a valley of emerald green
Stood in the mighty "Castle in the Mist" of sparkling dreams

In the early morn, you would see rolling waves of sparkling mist
The valleys and fields all seemed as if the dew were diamond kissed

A summer breeze with the fragrance of lavender graced this land
Brilliant colored birds sing songs so sweetly and grand

The fawns and rabbits were seen playing from morn to night
Birds and butterflies frolic through fields of daises white

This "Castle in the Mist" was sheltered from all that was bad
For there was dancing, singing and no one ever felt sad

Childless were the king and queen who made a heartfelt wish
A daughter born with hair of sand, eyes of sapphires, and ruby lips

There was music, singing, and dancing throughout the night
Long flowing dresses swirled about the grand hall of light

All made merry for the land became fruitful and filled with joy
Every day was declared a celebration for every girl and boy

South of the castle was the land of the Forest De Holodomors
Once covered with forget-me-knots and colorful lilies did adore

It's now said to steer clear, that there in this forest baron of green
Lives strange creatures large and small, ruled by a wicked queen

Many have traveled into the forest and were never heard of again.
Many wondered what could have happened to so many of them.

Many warriors, huntsmen, and Princes disappeared in a flash of light
Within a siren's call, enchanting and sweet, trickery was their blight

Ruled by Queen Cassandra, a black-widow beauty of fire and ice
She has betrayed a handsome man who left her, not once, but twice

Once it was her beauty and her name spoken in many halls of supreme
Her world was like a great golden ball of sunshine, her life a dream

It is said that her mournful cries are heard from morn till night
For the Forest, De Holodomors withered and no longer holds life

Long since time tells the stories of one once so beautiful and fare
Queen Cassandra was known as the beauty with long black hair

The "Castle in the Mist" still borders the forest, lifeless of green
No mournful cries are ever heard, and no flashes of light are ever seen

All remains grand across the land of mist and sparkling dreams
Legendary stories are handed down about Cassandra, the Queen!

CHANGING CUBES

Before me, against all odds, there is always this solitary darkness. I name thee loneliness. Solitude has become a part of me, and I can't seem to resist its dark comforting mood. So cold though, tonight for me is the rest of my life. It's felt as far as the soul deepens. Singular, individual as in keeping my surroundings. In the making, one cube is placed against another cube. Dark is my sight, and the cubes are many. Each seems to be placed just so, so precise in fact to reveal and reflect on my soul if so, I choose to escape. Plants and shades of green are placed artistically stationed to and fro as if to be divergent. Evening last sunshine is captured as highlights as it filtered through crystal panes that paint a fractured rainbow across the stark walls. Cascading a pleasurable sight in my dark muse. Good morning it speaks to me. In return, it gives me a dream or two remembered. Cascading across my visual pleasures placed upon the cubes daring to share personal memories. My interests are written upon pages for safekeeping. Books of many flavors, bitter and sweet but tasty never the least. Knowledge holds no bars to my mind. Mirrored surfaces reflect a collection of diverse moods. A lifeless stationary menagerie in glass and porcelain. Figurines seem to dance at my request. Addressing curiosity before me. Melodically like a breeze giving movement to dance. Graceful and carefree are their mannerisms, floating like Angels with gowns that trail gracefully as the rainbow moves with time. How graceful, how peaceful is the feeling I receive? What is this at my feet, it is Blue, my loving feline. There is no doubt, he demands attention. Shoes I kick off and flop back onto the sofa of my comfort. A deep breath I do take and let it out slowly. I look around at the forever-changing cubes of my choosing. Blue makes his way to my chest as I focus on the rainbow painted across my legs as it crawls slowing down the wall. Even though my soul remains in solitary darkness I try to coop within my means. Hardships in my life continue to rock my world like an earthquake. Death came knocking with each aftershock. Changing the cubes once again in my life...

CHILD OF THE UNIVERSE

Child of the universe
Conceived in love by two
A gift from God above
A bundle wrapped in beauty, and love
There's no doubt, in my mind
The world will shine brighter with you in it
Your smile lights my world
With unbelievable joy and happiness
A child from the heavens
Your future will be filled with light
Child of the universe
There's nothing impossible
Do anything your heart desires
I say to you my little one
There is a silver lining behind every cloud just for you
God has planted a seed
Deep within the core of your soul
You will grow strong and beautiful year after year
One amazing day in the future I can see
You will witness the heavens opening-up
Sunshine will rain down upon you
Angelic voices you will hear
Singing their songs of praise to you
We have been blessed
That you have been given to us
Child of light that you are
Only you have the power to achieve in any endeavor
You are a Child of the universe
Hold your head high
My heart is yours
For now, and forevermore
Look up to heaven
Know that it's the only thing greater than thee
Child of the forever Sun
Its golden rays will give you strength
All the days of your life
Child of the moon
It's the moonlight that will guide you
Always through the darkness
Child of the stars
Starlight, Star bright
Your dreams will come true on this night

Angels will always watch over you
Child of the universe
How you amaze and beguile me
As I see summer muse
Dancing in your light
It's the future I see deep in your eyes
Endless and as vast as the universe
Proud parents are we
Child of the universe
It's God who has blessed Thee!

CLAYTON LIGHTFOOT
The Male Model and My First Lover

Before my eyes is an incredibly handsome twenty-two-year-old,
A "Male Model" named "Clayton Light-feather"
He's an extremely striking Native American Cheyenne Indian
For whom would change my life forever

I capture beauty as an artist, sculptor, and photographer
With these eyes, hands, and heart, I will mold this clay before me
Creating a statue of this Adonis that now lays before me
So, to allow the world to behold this beautiful hunk of man's-flesh

Tall, dark, and handsome in a tight, muscular body
An inviting tanned stallion, free, viral, and wild
Striking are his facial features, a sculptor's dream model
Beautifully formed lips, perfectly straight nose with high cheekbones

Clayton's eyes are deep-set and a rare aquamarine color
His hair is long and as black as a raven reflecting in the sun
His height is a towering six-foot-five
Broad-shouldered and arms of steel, so like a Hercules

Clayton's pecs are like two thick armored plates upon his chest
Covered in soft black hair that meets in the center forming a thin stream
Of black hair that flows over an eight-pack of rapids
Flowing downstream to his life-giving private reservoir

Well-developed thighs that resemble thick torpedoes
Leading down to a bodybuilder's well-defined calves
As he rolls over on scarlet satin sheets, there before my very eyes
Are two extremely tight and rounded rock-hard buttocks

His waist has two bands of tightly sculptured belted muscles
When Clayton flecks his back, it resembles the perfect cobra hood
This sexual-God rolls over to face me, stretching those cannons over his head
This eye candy coyly smiles at me, **"Come, join me if you dare."**

There was no way I would ever refuse such a tantalizing invitation
Every model has something special to offer the artist
Clayton answered an ad I placed in the "Trades" for male models
That was nearly a year ago, he has become exclusive to me...

Part One
"A Wet Introduction"

It was on a rainy afternoon, and I was trying to finish a project for a show coming up. The door monitors buzzed. I answered, **"Yes?"** *The voice on the other end was masculine, downright sexy.* **"It's Clayton, the model for your next project. It's raining like hell out here, can I come up?"** *I said,* **"Of course!"** *With that, I buzzed him in. I had a huge loft here in the city up in a high-rise on 70th and Central Park West. I listened for the elevator to open. This was our first meeting for me to see if this male model would be what I was looking for. I opened the door and there stood this wringing-wet giant in a trench coat! I reached out to shake his hand and invitingly said,* **"Please come on in. My God you soaked through and through! Here, let me help you take that coat off."** *We casually laughed as I turned around to hang the heavy coat. Clayton asked,* **"Is there someplace I can make myself a bit more presentable?"** *I replied,* **"Certainly, follow me."** *I started into my bedroom, turning around I noticed he was still standing at the door. He said,* **"Are you sure? I'm soaked to the core, and I'll drip onto your carpet."** *I said,* **"Please...it's all right, don't mind my messy bedroom. Look, you must get out of those wet clothes. Then go ahead and take a hot shower. I'll put your clothes in the dryer if that's all right with you?"** *Being polite, he said,* **"Thank you."** *I went to walk out of the bedroom to give him some privacy when he said,* **"Wait a minute, let me give them to you now."** *He removed his boots first then his socks. I watched this Adonis of a man slowly unbuttoning the drenched white shirt.* **(That's when my world went into slow motion)** *I was watching this handsome, virile young hunk of a man slowly pulling the shirttail from his jeans. Next, he unbuttoned each cuff as he coyly was eying me through his long black hair that was still dripping water from its tips. He rolled the shirt over one massive shoulder to reveal his unbelievably muscular arm. There is no doubt this was a guy who logged in for quite a few hours in the gym. The whole time Clayton was smiling and looking over at me. I was mesmerized by the semi-erotic removal of his clothes. He was seducing me as he pulled his canon-size arm from its wet confines. Of course, he was. Then Clayton unbuttoned the other cuff and peeled the wet material from his second loaded canon. My God, this stud was built like a brick house! He dropped the shirt down to his side. My eyes dropped to his waist as he tauntingly unbuckled the thick leather belt. Even though it was wet, like a pro, he easily pulled it through the loops around the waist. Dropping it onto the carpet. He was very aware that my eyes were fixed on his next move. My eyes moved up to see that smile that will be with me for the rest of my life and willingly so, I might add! I followed his huge hands toward the metal button clasp as he pushed the metal button through its eyelet. I let out a silent sigh of anticipation as he slowly pulled the zipper down. I was three steps ahead of Clayton's seductive strip. My fantasy pulled me into my mind's eye. {I watched him place one hand on each side of the wet jeans. Clayton gently moved his hips side to side as he gingerly peeled the wet jeans down over his exquisite ass. He moved the wet pants down over the hottest thighs I had ever seen on a man. What made this even more erotic for me was the fact he didn't wear underwear. Clayton slowly peeled the wet jeans down over the thighs, and down to the floor. Finally, he stepped out of each wet leg. He held the jeans in front of himself. He bent forward picking up the white shirt. He handed me the bundle of wetness smiling a devilish smile...} My fantasy was broken when I heard Clayton say,* **"I can't begin to thank you enough for your kindness."** *Swallowing a lump in my throat, I answered,* **"No**

problem, No problem at all.'' *Two feet in front of me was without any doubt, God's gift to men and women! Before I was this naked six-foot-five Hercules. Clayton looked into my eyes, seemly to my very soul. I felt those amazing aquamarine eyes that were outlined by the thickest black lashes. Accenting and highlighting the aquamarine color like light bulbs. Oh my God! This was the hottest, sexiest, and the most desirable man I ever imagined existing. Standing right in front of me. Here is my bedroom just a couple of feet away. My vision of a dream paradise. My heart was racing and pounding in my chest. My wishful thinking made me somewhat light-headed. Furthermore, my seducer knew it from the beginning...*

*I was suddenly whipped back to reality when I heard Clayton say, **"Christ! These wet jeans are glued to me, I might need a little help to get them off. Would you lend me a hand?"** What the hell just happened? I was dumbfounded. My god, what a fantasy I just had! I broke out in a laugh as if to say, **"Are You Kidding Me?"** Clayton asked, **"What's so funny?"** I answered, **"I have been there myself,"** Clayton in a frustrated laugh said, **"Are you going to help me out of these jeans?"** How could I refuse? Would I be that damn dumb to refuse his plea for assistance, NOT! Somewhat taken back from the fantasy reeling through my mind, I let out an eagerly, **"Sure!"** I walked over to my nearly naked male model asking, **"Just how tall are you?"** I asked standing right in front of my desire. I stand six-foot-two and this gorgeous man is towering over me. Clayton answered, **"I am six-foot-five,"** as he raised his arms, using his fingers as a comb to flip the long-wet hair back over those enormous shoulders. I was eyeing those mountainous size biceps attached to each arm. I am hopelessly in amber with this gift from above and before me. He smiled that incredible smile. His sculptured lips framed an outstanding row of perfect ivories. Looking into my eyes, he knew he had kindled a fire of hunger that was surfacing in me. Clayton directed me to stand behind him. There I stood facing that enormous back. Wow! What a sensual cologne he was wearing. The fragrance was an intoxicating musk. I watched as he placed a thumb inside and along the waistband of the wet jeans. He turned his head to the side to speak to me saying, **"Grab hold of each side and pull the jeans down."** We proceeded to move the jeans down and over his amazing fully formed glutes. I suggested, **"You're going to have to sit down on the edge of the bed, so I can pull the jeans over your thighs."** He shuffled over to my bed and had a seat. Laying back he lifted his hips. Clayton and I started tugging and pulling, all the time laughing like schoolboys. Between giggles, I asked, **"How did you ever get these tight-ass jeans on to start with?"** He answered with a chuckle as he answered my question, **"They weren't wet when I slipped into them."** Before I laid a half-naked God on my bed. Rising onto his elbows, Clayton's amazing eyes locked onto mine. He must be a Warlock using black magic on me. He was conjuring a spell over me. As if I were in a trance, I reached forward grasping the wet jeans. With a few strong tugs, I managed to slowly peel what resembled a snake shedding his skin. There right before my face, as in my earlier fantasy, he didn't wear underwear. With my semi-trembling hands. I continued peeling the wet material over the biggest thighs I have ever seen. Down over the calves to his ankles. Clayton started to laugh as I gave several tugs to finish this willing task. Playfully he had flexed his feet. My eyes never left his as I gave one strong yank! **"SUCCESS!",** I exclaimed in triumph. There I stood holding his wet jeans, now inside-out. My moment of playful victory was trumped by watching Clayton rise from the bed. Standing tall and proud like a giant Red Sequoia. This gorgeous Native American Cheyenne was standing stark naked in front of me. What a Kodak moment for me! Trust me when I say, Clayton was a beautiful man from head to toe, and I do mean **"MAN!"***

After a few awkward moments of staring, I gathered up his shirt, socks, and jeans. Clayton asked, **"Would you mind if I take a shower now?"** I replied, **"No not at all, help yourself."** I dropped the wet clothes and walked over to the closet behind him. He made a step to the side, and I opened the closet door to retrieve a couple of towels, a washcloth, and a fresh bar of soap. As I handed him the towels, etc... I made mentioned there was shampoo on the shelf in the shower. I watched him as he turned to walk toward the bathroom to shower. What an amazing tight bubble butt he possessed! I fall back onto the bed in a daze catching a fresh breath and then letting it out in a sigh... That's when I heard Clayton say, **"Hey."** I sat up and saw Clayton standing in the doorway of the bathroom. What a sight to behold. The hot water was running in the shower creating a cloud of steam that framed this outstanding stud of a man. His nakedness was more than erotic. He flashed that awesome smile as he adjusted himself from what must have been running through his mind. As far as the statement I made earlier, **"God's gift to women and men!"** His gifts weren't just the mesmerizing beauty and flawless structure. Every part of his body was well-endowed. Clayton flashed that amazing smile, conjuring me with those hypnotizing aquamarine eyes. Then he teasingly said, **"Would you care to wash my back for me?"** Without a second of hesitation, I stood up and pulled my t-shirt over my head, tossing it to the side. I stepped out of my clogs, and unzipped my jeans, dropping them to the floor with ease. I watched this long-haired Adonis disappear into the steam. I followed my male model into the cloud of steam...

End of the beginning...

COLD BLUE MOONLIGHT

Standing in a cold corner
Dark and damp as the thoughts running
Through these blackened veins of yesteryear
The sun is going down slowly...
Slowly as the day, I was laid to my eternal sleep
This remembrance has played its wicked laughs
Throughout the last four hundred years
Standing deep in the shadows of this Mausoleum
A prisoner, held at bay
Amongst the cobwebs, spiders, and vermin
I wait for the ultimate darkening
That's when I slowly step into the waiting arms
Of the cold blue moonlight...
The night air is cool, and the ground is warm
Creating a beautiful blanket of fog
Crawling across the headstones and monuments
Engulfing memorial plots
Of the young and old, rich, and poor alike
Death's domain
For we are alike in his morbid and greedy eyes
I take a step out of my unholy refuge
Far enough that the cold blue moonlight,
Makes its way across my 6'4" frame
My height blends into the doorway of my Mausoleum
The moon is so bright that the light
Creates shadows that highlight
The trees and gravestones with a sharpness
That is clean, crisp, and clear
Shadows forever dancing
As the moon moves across the sky of pitch
There at the edge of the cemetery
In one of the darkest shadowed areas
I spy a set of fiery red eyes...
Slowly I step back into the shadows once again
Beneath my feet lie the dry
Lifeless leaves that cry out with each step I make
The silence was broken
I watched the red-eyed dark figure making hast my way
I was so damn angry at myself
For giving myself away like that,
After four hundred years of walking in the shadows
My skills should be top-notch by now!

Who knows, it very well could have been my only feeding of the night
So rare to catch a living creature
Within this ancient valley of the dead
I spy the eyes of red in a haunting hunt
Silent and still I am
The figure is on the move in my direction
Surprise!
What do I make of this shadow, brazing enough to seek me out?
As the lone intruder gets closer,
I feel a deadness within my veins come alive
It's the feel of the hunt commencing
If what flows through these rotted veins is blood
Let there be a fire
To warm this frozen core of
Four hundred years
Now the hunter becomes the hunted!
The figure glides atop the fog in my direction
It's easy to tell that the figure is petite
Now close enough for me to see the figure is with doubt a woman
It's the moon that betrays this huntress of the night
With long, thick raven black hair
My trance-like stare fills me with a lustful hunger
I had not fed for two moons
My dark heart has come to life
Beating with a thud that travels to my temples
Can this huntress hear this beating drum the closer she comes?
I froze just as she was ready to pass my way
Suddenly she stopped but a foot away
Very aware of another presence
I stepped forward from my darkened solitude
Face to face
Our eyes witnessed each other's, lifeless souls
I felt and saw my hunger rising in her red eye
I watched her intent develop
She pulled her lips up over her gums exposing her fangs
She hissed and growled
I saw her breath hover in the cool night air
My gut reaction was the very same
I grabbed her as fast as a lightning strike
I grabbed a hand full of her raven hair
Pulling her down as I hovered my 6'4" frame over her
I had to look immense at that moment
However,
This she-devil was strong as HELL!
She looked into my eyes of flaming red
Daring me to go any further

My teeth grew at a shuttering speed
Just then she raised her other hand
Wheeling five sinister blades
Slashing my face with a lightning speed of her own
That drove me into an uncontrollable
RAGE!
I threw her to the ground and fell upon her
With the hunger of a rave-Inness beast
I sank my fangs deep into her pearl-white neck
My rage slowly ebbs into a vacuum of lust...
Her aroma was captivating the beast
I regained my composer as I continued to savor my feast
She pulled me closer to her body
No words were exchanged, she leaned forward
Kissing my neck with a piercing of her own
Together there in the cold blue moonlight
We both sank down and under the layers of ground fog
Never a word was spoken
A Vampire love fest was our personal concert among the dead
We made love most of the night
We then walked together toward the feeding grounds
She and I made several kills that night
I watched her vicious attacks upon unwilling prey
Which I found stimulating and erotic
We both looked up and realized the moon would wait no longer
Dawn was quickly rising
I raised my cape, and she flew to my side
Haste for protection under my wing
From that night and every night after that
She shared my coffin
As the lid closed that first night she asked my name,
My name is Vladimir,
Rosalind is my name...
Two soft and contented sighs
Until dusk my love,
until dawn...

COLOR HER SPECIAL
By Richard Lee Cook

Have you ever fallen "in like" with someone? You would know it the minute it happened. That's how it was with a dancer, instructor, choreographer, and partner of mine a few years back.

Beth, I'm sure she is teaching dance somewhere, or even performing in shows around her hometown. We worked on and were in several dance productions that we had produced and danced in. Her forte the ballet and rhythmic jazz. I thought she was one of the great dancers that our hometown of Frederick had ever produced during the 70s and 80s. Rest assured; it takes more than technique to stand out as a dancer. It takes personality, charisma, and a love for Art. Beth possessed and offered so much more...

Color Her Special, was written about Beth Dangerfield, a talent in the art of dance, that was and is as beautiful as she was in appearance. The joy of my life was to appear and perform with her on stage at the "Weinberg Center for the Performing Arts in our Hometown.

Beth Dangerfield

Upon her body like delicate dragonfly wings
She moves and floats gracefully across the stage
Her hummingbird heart beats with the rhythm of her feet
Comedic Delsarte turns green with envy when her wit comes forth
She's sensitive and many tears drop from her child-like eyes
Open-minded, creative, and a true friend she will become
Beth is a dancer of many colors
I am so very honored to call her a friend
That is why so many families and friends as well as students

Color Her Special

Come Lay with Me

Come lay with me in the meadow of perfumed flowers

Let my words of love wrap your body with silken grass

It'll soothe the pain you feel inside, for loss is immense

Lay yourself down beside the keeper of broken hearts

You need to taste my soft tender lips of wanting crimson

Your hair of gold flows with the rolling winds of free to be

Let me love you with my body, my soul, and tenderness

Under cascading willow branches, dancing over our flesh

Feel free and alive, for nature sings a song of our love

Explore the senses within your arms holding me tight

I arch upon the touch of your kiss, tender and sweet

Sing to me like the love of the Loons upon the water

Ride my very essence, seduce me deep with romance

Conduct your symphony with your striking features

Cover me in flowers from the meadows of raw passion

Do clasp my trembling hands in trust and amazing joy

Come lay with me in the meadow of perfumed flora

Taste the honey from the pleasure palace of passion

Welcome to my theater you fool, you will love it so

I am nature, take care of me, For I offer you love.

CRADLED LOVE

Cradled in the palms of my hands
Child of dreams I hold upon this land
Reach for the stars, you're delivered to me
And there is nothing greater than thee.

Life made in love, a water-lily pink
Dragonfly wings and puppy-dog winks
Honey-beige thoughts, a starry-starry night
Safe in my arms, Angels take flight.

The wonder of wonders, holding this life
Not to lose and never too tight
Daddy's little boy now and forever
Nothing will ever harm you, never.

Because your Cradled in Love

CROSSING THE NARROWS

Often clouds are white, floating on a sea of blue
There are many days that seem darker than others
When the need to falsify, trying to control the truth
It's the light that finds a way out of the darkness

There are storms that develop in my sense of being
Filled with wrath following me as the world turns
I will not deny that my life is so much like a storm
My life is but a reflection of the weather around me

Can't play the violins, for they are without strings
I regret that this is the saddest affair of them all
Even if your message has been laced with poison
Lift your voice and sing your song to the heavens

Upon the Stillwater's I stand alone on a liquid mirror
I shelter my world of solitude under a roof of pain
No Rip Van Winkle sleeps, nor a rock of ages for me
The bed I lie upon contains glass shards of memories

Often, I ask, what is the reason why the Lark sings?
What reason for throwing stones into the Stillwater's?
I've been invisible for so long, that I thirst to leave a mark
If I had a candle in the dark, no matches to light it

Before I lie the narrow waters, it's a cold crossing
My mind is in darkness, at last, it too, is a cold crossing
What comes to pass holding an unlit candle in darkness?
When my only purpose in life is to cross the narrows...

Damn The Shadows

Forgotten is the long day, however, the pain of the heart remains

The curtain of night descends and lessons the agony with sleep

All the while in the back of your mind another day will be ignited

It claws at your soul with a festering that oozes like an old wound

Now crawls a blackened wind, cold in its whispers of pleasures past

They offer tempting rewards that are unattainable in every manner

You're engulfed by an evil presence barren as an old woman's womb

You must not cross the river of despair for the whispers are blacker

Meet, "The Shadows" of your discontent with where your paths lead

Never to get the peace you crave as they whisper darkly in your ear

"The Shadows" will twist reality into your blackest of all nightmares

Dark surrounding you offer little comfort, only the everlasting grief

Your soul is starved for affection and the tears spilled make no sound

All that was is no longer, for you have aged way before your time

This darkness of "The Shadows" intensifies, why is it punishing me?

That's the way of "The Shadows" for your dreams lead to nightmares.

Damn the Shadows!

Dance of Lamour

There is a moment, an unbelievable moment

When two know that the dance is in their touch

It's the dance of Lamour

It feels sensuous like a warm tropical breeze

As it envelops the body and its senses

Your mind is now intoxicated with an array of fragrances,

Joining with the sound of ocean waves crashing in the distance

Giving rise to passion's rapture that no longer lies dormant

I kiss your body delicately, your beauty is beyond perfection

To say I adore you,

Is like watching the birth of the rarest of butterflies

Drifting motionless upon a wayward breeze

And it is my heart that emerges from its cocoon

Slowly in tandem, we glide side by side

Not a second do I waste when I am between heaven and earth

What Muse gave into playful trickery this day?

No blanket will cover the beauty that Mother Nature weaved herself

We rest our hearts like weary wings on Mother's "Forget-me-knots"

Sweet as the taste of honeysuckle upon the tongue

Please my love lay beside me for there is a method in my madness

Close your eyes and breathe as quietly as you can

Listen to the mother's symphony

Hear how the breeze whispers through the swaying field of sea grass tall

Listen to the secrets the trees hold as the wind ruffles the leaves

They tell stories that are ageless

Hear the sweet songs of the birds up high and down low

Hear the Dragonflies wings

Skimming across the mirror glass water, merrily humming from Cattail to Cattail

My love, there is an amazing world of music being played each everyday

Lying here in the shade of this weeping willow

Smell the wondrous sweetness of the Water-Iris along the lake's edge

Your touch reminds me of the romantic music and singing in the canals of Venice

Floating down the canals and waterways

It's amazing how smooth the gondolas float as the Gondoliers sing

Tenors, bass, and baritones each sounding like a magnificent instrument

Imagine the crying of sweet violins, each filled with desire

Now imagine the soft-touched sounds of Harps strategically placed around the lake

Each harp is played by an Angel in a flowing golden gown

Between each harp are Cellos played by Chirrups

The first and second Violins

Sound-like instruments performed on the Grand stages of the Paris Opera Houses

They can make you cry as they lift you higher and higher

Or fill your heart with the sounds of the wandering Gypsies

When Twilight tiptoes her way across the sky

That's when the touch of your fingers moves across my flesh

Evening comes to a crescendo of emotions

As darkness paints the heavens and the stars appear one by one

And the fireflies rise from the fields of tall grass

You hear the music of the crickets and frogs along with the hoot of owls

Nature's Grand Piano

As we watch the velvet black of night with each twinkle of light

It's nature's ebony and ivory entertaining us with classical music in combination

With every sound in unison

We are blessed in a world for you and me

They're playing our song,

"Moonlight Sonata"

A concert for two making love under the stars

Gazing into your eyes

I cannot help but swan dive into their crystal blue persuasion

I know no better moment than this one,

To say, "I love you!"

Where that may lead is in our hearts and the stars in the heavens above

Before me is the one for whom I have fallen in love all these years

It started when you asked me to dance with you

Every dance since then has been like the first dance of my life

Look how the moonlight of silver paints the surface of the lake

Watch the breeze from the meadow over the surface of the water

The midnight moon seems to shimmer

There before us lies an ocean of endless love

That dances upon the still waters of my heart

I can but only cry

For it is the most beautiful moment I have ever shared with you

Fall into my waiting arms

Give yourself fully

I will caress your every need tenderly

You will know a world of heavenly sensations

Together we will sink under the warm waters of desire

I welcome you

To my Oasis known as Tranquility

A place where embracing you is a dance of Lamour

Look into my eyes to see your pleasure caressing each emotion

You leave me breathless as we surface high upon the crest of each wave

Rolling, churning their way upon tranquilities shore

Making our way once again to the still waters of our hearts

That softly waltzes upon the music of love

Lingering on the waves of love's temptations

That takes your heart's desire

All you need to do,

Close your eyes

And listen to the world around you...

DANCE WITH ME

Early in my morning
I awake to heaven's gift at my side
How my eyes adore you so
In my arms, you slowly stir
Let your eyes see behind their veil
Take my hand, there's a story to be told

It's one of the physical pleasures
Expressed in a dance created by lovers two
Where an embrace gives rise to the Phoenix
Let me brush lightly my lips upon yours
Taste the passion, flavored by flame
A rhythmic flurry, Tangoed at best

An Adagio danced naked
Free formed with one goal to achieve
Now we sing in harmony, one hope and one wish
We danced the dance of love
Choreographed so beautifully
If need be, we will try again and again for perfection
Dance with me...

THE DAUGHTERS OF POSEIDON

Dawn is upon me; I see the valley amidst the sun-kissed treetops
There's an amazing golden sparkling mist covering the valley floor
Dark the night, a chill crept upon me as I perched upon this rock
Tragedy during dusk, carefree, reckless like so many times before

Warm is the sunshine upon my wings, knowing better, lends to pain
Warning, the surrounding sea is deadly for those with wings to spread
Cursed are the winds and mesmerized by the Siren's Call, was to claim
Many a handsome Archangel did dare the Siren's Call, presumed dead

Perched on this rock, I slowly spread my wings full to set once more
I walk along the river's banks toward a mystical cove, laden with rocks
There, Mermaid Sirens of love, amongst the water's edge totaling four
Shocked, suddenly startled by me, all diving into wakes of jagged rocks

Cooling mist spritz my face, and the heat of the sun was broken, like my wing
I turned to take my leave, when water splashed on my back, I turn to see
"Sir, do not haste, you fell from the heavens because you heard us sing"
"We are the daughters of Poseidon, the lonely Sirens of the Sea"

Warned I was of the Sirens who sing, so they caused my broken wing
Many an Archangel has fallen to their death, please, pray to tell of my fate
Sailors near and far do tell of run-a-ground ships and strange happenings
Men going mad from your singing, your beauty creates jealousy and hate

The four of you are unbelievably beautiful, your hair, your amazing eyes
I beg of you, tell me your names, even Mermaid Sirens must have a name
"Thank you, Sir, for being so kind, Destiny, Mercy, Largo, and Desire am I"
I'm Autumn, I represent the end of summer and the start of winter's claim

"As well, your name is beautiful, you're very different from all the others"
Wait! Please don't go, why do you take leave? "We must, that's our call"
Wait, will you four return to me by dawn's early light? "Yes, do take cover"
It'll be hard finding shelter this night; my broken wing was injured in the fall

Into the forest interior, a cave I did find, cold and damp, no rest tonight
The Sirens on my mind, knowing I survived the fall, yet my brothers died
Dawn is near, hurry back to the water's edge, my perching rock is in sight
I'll wait a while, my eyes became heavy, I woke from a dream where I cried

They're across the water, I yelled names, Destiny, Mercy, Desire, and Largo
It's Autumn, dawn's early light, come to this site where we were to meet
Diving in I saw tails splash 1,2,3, and 4 in a blink of an eye, away they go
Desire, why did you four leave in hast? "Summoned by father to the deep"

"Autumn, we wonder why you are unable to hear the message in our song?"
"Your brothers and the men of the sea, visit us below with our invitation, all"
"It's what we do, allure men with songs to join in the celebration, can that be wrong?"
If against their will, it's very wrong to lead men to their deaths, why the call?

"Desire is my name, and all men want me, they can't resist me, for I am desire"
"Largo is my name, I am music in their heads, it calls to them to come to me"
"Mercy is my name, I am the word on their lips, it's a mercy they want in cries"
"Destiny is my name, your destiny is to be with me, hold on tight, a final plea"

Desire, you have asked, Why the songs that you four sing didn't affect me?
Your songs were not heard, and the roar of the wind made me reckless in my flight
I got in trouble for not listening to my elders, my deafness was a secret you see
The truth is a blessing for me, the childhood lessons they taught were so right

Now I know it is evil in your songs, my brothers lured falsely by you four
Hear my words sisters of the deep, my heart is full for my brothers, and I weep
Evil is your songs, your beauty is false, no longer your secret kept, it'll be lore
Largo, Desire, Mercy, Destiny, winter will claim you forever frozen in the deep!

Dearest of Ladies

You chose words carefully then placed them upon thy faded parchment

Thy quill of golden pheasant spoke to me whilst fluttering in its flight

Many a mile the Trade Winds carried thy message of a lover tenderly

Daylight kisses, afternoon embraces and moonlight caresses divinely

Do I dare place my private feelings upon the spreading of your wings?

To float softly upon thy touch and the smell of ladies' fresh powders

Conceal my fluttering heart that doth not have wings to carry and perch

Your words are tasty as the sweetest sugar upon a child's lips waiting

You must know the strength that lies in guarded adornment restrained

An invitation to kiss the hem of thy garment truly becomes the tease

Now I am bursting at the seam to rise in favor of one night's total bliss

Like a faithful puppy, I will lie in the warmth of sweet peak's bosom

I dare not dream for the heat of the sun on my aching thighs will swim

By the grace of one so sweet, meet me at the wake of springs overflow

Upon softening fleece together, we bear with nature's sensual feelings on air

I am driven mad by Angel's heavenly smile and a virgin's offer to take

The sunshine of all summers produces waiting for grapes to pluck in sweet wine

The taste of thy honey is as sweet as the fruit on my vine for thee to savor

Bring fluted times two, cheese, and bread to our luncheon of earthly delights

I'll feast on the riches of your virgin valley, and you taste the fruit of my vine

Truly a feast fit for a King, Dearest of Ladies...

DEATH'S FINAL PERFORMANCE, EXIT STAGE RIGHT

There is one probability that I can rest assured on
Without any reservations what-so-ever in my life
"DEATH" is for certain! There is no escaping from that fact
Every living creature on this planet will face death

DEATH is filled with sorrow and heartache
The loss, the passing of a loved one,
The true possibility that the fear of dying yourself
Such fear brings about an everlasting sorrow

DEATH is nothing more but a forever sleep
It is when all functions come to a complete stop
It's the ending of one's journey and the beginning of a new one
Many treasure this thought, others believe your no more!

DEATH will be the ending of all my performances
"A Never-Ending Story", written for all the stages of my life
Then I'd enter the stage, deliver my lines with authority,
Bump into the furniture and get the HELL off the stage!

I wish to deliver my final line
That is before this show comes to an end, as the curtain is lowered
I will bow gratefully for the last time, I then deliver,
"ACT WELL YOUR PART, FOR THERE ALL HONORS LIE"
Then Exit Stage Right for the last time...

DEEP BLUE SLEEP

By Richard Lee Cook

Here is where I become as honest as I can. Deep Blue Sleep was written after two months of extreme mourning over my sister's death. A time when everything around me started to fall apart. To tell you that I went out to lunch one day and never came back was true. Bonnie's death affected me to the point that life didn't matter any longer. I wanted to fall asleep and never wake up. I needed to be with her.

Deep Blue Sleep became therapy for my pain. You need to understand a few things when I said everything fell apart. Within a very short period, my mother died, and my best friend got killed in an auto accident. Then my sister Bonnie got killed in a car accident, then Chris my sister's fiancé, two hours later after Bonnie got killed. He had an accident in the same damn spot that she had hers and ended up in the hospital with a head injury. It truly was too much for me to handle. We all have our breaking points. Please dwell in the depths of my written words. Things worked out, I'm still here, as well as the "Shadows," are still present today...

DEEP BLUE SLEEP

*Today is the beginning of what to do before it does me in. Travel far away without any contact. To start anew. Pack up, throw out or give away? Precious memories are placed with care in hope of planting them again. Today the pain comes so easily to my mind. Confusion and despair are covered by the mask of tragedy, and the comedy fades as though all hope is gone. Teardrops fill my eyes, clouding my sight. I now feel the tickling of tears down my high cheeks. My mind is in darkness. The hurt is so painful to bear. I feel as if I can't go on any longer. I'm lost in a world that doesn't spin. It has stopped! Maybe I, What if I? This has got to end. I'm alone in this world. It has been months since you passed on. My heart aches. I just can't bear this any longer. I'm going to lie down now. I'm drained to the bone. Maybe if I lay down to sleep, all my troubles will stop. Hurt grows rapidly and gives nothing in its place. Except for the sound of the door opening slowly, like 33 1/3 is as fast as it can move. A wisp of dark feeling cold air, chilling and haunting is felt. I stare at first, rubbing my tear-soaked eyes, then I jump from the bed to hurry, to force him out. "SHUT the Door", my mind shouted. But HE enters with a deadly calm. He is tall and demanding in form. "Give Me" in a strong commanding voice from a hallowed face. **"I Want You!"** in a craving manner. His hand touches mine. Feelings, dreams, my mind, and judgments are totally released to his draining touch. With my eyes begging, "Take no more". He releases his touch, and I slowly drop to the floor, like the slow melting wax down a candle stick. It was chilling and harsh. Looking up at this tall, and now handsome man. No longer did he give off that dark deadly feeling. He is lean with dark feelingless eyes. His grasp now is calm and quiet as my emotions exit my now relaxed body. Everything is falling into place and my understanding of what is happening makes sense. I say, **"Wait! let these eyes see its last of love".** How I wished I could have loved everyone, and everything around me more. How I could have changed the past if I had the chance. With a wave across my face, I now am looking at what was. To stand on the outside and look in on you and me sitting in the park. I asked if you were happy with Chris. Your face lit the day bright. You glowed. After all you and I have gone through in our young lives. I just want you to be happy. Bonnie looked at me and said, "I love Chris more than anything. Let me surprise you with the greatest news. Not even Chris knows yet". She giggles and then gets serious. With her head looking down, it slowly rises, and she says to me, "I'm going to have a baby". That was one of the greatest moments I had ever shared with my sister. Suddenly I notice the scene is fading. I turn to him and then I realized. He granted me what I had asked for. To have my eyes see the last of love. That truly was the day that love was felt. Two weeks later, both Bonnie and Chris were in two separate auto accidents, two hours apart, on the same road in the exact same spot going home after their work.*

*My sister died and so did I. But the pain and hurt of my lifetime was destiny, I presume? I look at him and say, **"Give me a moment to remember what was good for me".** He looks into my misty eyes with a red sunset glow and says nothing. He gently tightens his strong hand on my shoulder and nods a Go-on. Remembrance comes quickly. I guess what you care for, and love can always be tapped. Golden hair, long and in slow motion blown wildly through the air as she gracefully rides her Appaloosa, "Apache Firefly". This is what I recall about her. I would watch her doing rodeo stunts across the acres of tall grass that waved in slow motion as the summer breeze blew. Her beauty, strong mind, and her laughter were as gentle as honey-beige thoughts,* *she was everything precious, young, and so alive with blue-jean tears. My eyes tear up again as I view these memories, I say to myself, **"I love you, Bonnie, I miss you very much".** I miss all the things that a brother and sister do growing up together". Forward my mind travels and I see that my mind holds the memories of so many personal loves. In the misty blue dark, I see a figure of a small child, as I get closer and the mist clears, yes, it's **Cody-Li.** I call out to him. A delightful little boy. His manners were encased in such a little mind. So, mature before his time. I have held him in my arms, with so many tender moments that a father and son share together. **"I love you",** came so easily for me. My son ventures onward with his mother Nikki-Lynn. It's said that children are to bury their parents, not the other way around. It has ripped my heart out and now he is before me. Cody-Li is disappearing into the dark blue mist, just then I felt a cold hand on my shoulder. Suddenly I cry out loud, **"G O D !!!, I** need strength, hope, and assurance that this is right for me". From these eyes and down this face, the river rage has soaked my lap. I weaken and become sick. The pain is too much. I wish to rest. He holds me in his caring arms. Something I've needed for a long time. I hugged him with all the strength in my shell. Moments pass, and I raise my head with the knowledge of knowing this is good for me. We gaze at one another, I'm locked in understanding, for I know if he beacons to me, I am his forever! The decision comes without reservations. Closer and closer he reaches for my hand as he did once before. I slowly reach out to take that cold blue wisp of air from his hands. I ask him, **"Will I be with the ones I love and who loved me?"** The blue becomes bright and all fades from my sight. I see myself withering like a flower from lack of moisture. I hold on to him, never knowing his name. But it never really mattered. Dark and cold was his touch, now it's bright blues and a white light before me. There are figures within the light. I walk beside him with the feeling of a new beginning. My memories of the past and yesterday are left behind. As we walk a step to step, the dark blue wisp changes ever so slowly. I look back at what was. To see that it would have been nice to try once more. But I was alone, lost, and had too many dreams that were taken from me. This is right for me. So now I see sunshine in the distance and it's good. Maybe my place in the sun will be better? Now there is a long silence, restful sleep would be nice. So calm, quiet, and peaceful within this deep blue sleep..........*

DEEP BLUE WHISP

*The final stage is now completed in my life of fire, rain, and dread of traveling far away without any contact, maybe crossing over to new precious memory are placed with care, In the hope of possibly rediscovering. Pack up, throw out, give away and discard my life's unwanted trash. Today the pain comes easily to mind, and confusion taps on my shoulder Covered by the mask of tragedy, exit stage right as the comedy fades as though hope is gone, my backdrop painted in wounded teardrops Clouded is my vision, for the mind is exiting backstage to a dark alley. The hurt I've borne is so painful, I can't go on any longer in this arena I am lost in a world that doesn't spin, I am alone, lost in my own soul It's grueling maintaining one's own gravity, my heart aches for death I just can't bear this any longer, I am useless, depressed, and drained. Maybe the choice is before me, sleep, and all my troubles will cease. Hurt grows rapidly like cancer giving no hope as it floods the min I hear footsteps outside my chamber door, and slowly the door opens wide. A rush of icy air circulates about my candle-lit room, hauntingly surreal I am fixated on the opening door; I rub my tear-soaked eyes from staring. I jump from the bed, racing toward the door to force my intruder outside. **"SHUT THE DOOR!"** my mind shouts, but it was too late, and he enters the room and became deadly calm, he stood tall and commanding in stature. His eyes were icy, deep-set with hollowed cheeks, a cold demanding voice, **"GIVE IN TO ME! I DESIRE YOU!"** in a morbid craving like lust. His hand of long eerie fingers, pale blue, icy-cold when he touches mine. All emotions, my complete soul is totally released to his draining touch. With my eyes begging, **"Take no more"** he released his consuming hunger. I slowly dropped to the floor, like the slow melting of heated candle wax. He was chilling and frightened as I looked up at this extremely tall figure. No longer was his appearance menacing, he picked me up and to the bed. Something had changed in an instant with this figure standing before me. His face is handsome, a beautiful Cobalt blue with black angelic eyes. His reaching touch is now calm as all emotions exit my now relaxed body. Everything was falling into place; I finally understood his purpose with me. This entity heard my cries, he was more than willing to grant me my pleas. Everything within my being was drained, the pain, agony, hurt, and sorrow. Time had now sped up, fast and faster, my past vanished in a blurry smoke. My eyes slowly shut forevermore; all had darkened in a deep blue whisp.*

DEMON IS THE FATHER'S SEED

"Written in 1999,
Several days after feeling an emotional dread.
Once again experiencing painful headaches along with blackouts
As I did when I was twelve through the age of sixteen".

    I would have bouts of anger and time lost. As witnessed by my mother, sister, and cousins from time to time. I always felt as though there were "another" inside my mind and body. "He", totally felt the opposite of my normal character. I was told how evil and nasty I would become after the blackouts. Until I would fall asleep and then reawaken. The strange thing was, I never remembered a single blackout or doing the things they said I had done. I was told I acted and displayed mannerisms just like my father when he was drunk. The things I was told I did, just did not make sense to me. In 1999, I had a blackout spell in front of my two close friends. They said my face, body, and voice took on a different persona. They feared me. All that I acted out; I only know what was told to me. They both knew how my father was. They said I was just like him, but my face and body took on crooked features. Something they never wanted to see or experience again. So, I truly do not doubt them at all, if I acted and talk the way my father did, then I believe his seed was planted. Within this shell, it's only time and God would know when my other will come forth again. I wrote, "Demon is the Father's Seed" because it very well could be true...

DEMON IS THE FATHER'S SEED

I sit here beside myself, one is good, one is bad
Within my being a war is rumbling for control between two souls
One pulls me steadfast to the ever-giving light of love
The other pushes forward wanting to come alive in the dark
Between the pulling and the twisting of my soul a twin arises
Control of either is a lost cause for the good of my mind
My bad seed tastes what the sweet breath of life is
In the mirror, I stare at myself for the first time
Sharp is my cheekbones, my eyes dark in a face of evil
Lee is lost somewhere in the mix of two souls
It's easy to wear the face of possession
There is a new voice that rasps it hello and now bellows to be free
Whatever was of good is no longer the light
I no longer am I hearing the screams for help
Richard now breaths a demonic fire that needs to feed
Living inside for so long there is a hunger for innocence
Now his control rages with wanting to step out into this new world
He now walks beside those who see a stranger
The dark within is clever not to show his true colors
Amazingly he mocks the manners of the one who lived once before

Very aware of the needing for Lee's traits so as not to be made aware of
Now is the season of darkness no longer living in the shadow of who once was
A mirrored image was stolen to now raise unholy hell
Fire is now the demon's eyes to see
On a road of the destruction of another's the soul
Today the war within was won by the father's seed
There are only haunting visions and the cry of the lonely
The father died, but the seed of the Demon now lives on
The ugliness of the father lives once more
Richard says to what once was good,
"Lee we are one...
R.I.P."

DESTINED SOULS

It was our first everlasting kiss that captured a heart's true
Like a seed planted, the desire grew strong for me, and you
The flower bloomed under the sun with an undying trust
Two Souls forever sealed in desire, love's passionate lust

Destined souls walking side by side on its charted path
Yet we will guard our lives against diversity and its wrath
It is the stars and moon governing our love forevermore
We know our souls, it's the heart forever that opens doors

Our souls forever are destined to remain united in love
The Angels have written it across the vast skies above
When I first laid my eyes upon you, I knew it would be
There would never be another to share this life with me

DO YOU WEEP FOR ME?

"I am not the first troubled soul, nor shall I be the last...rlc"

Do you weep for me?
I beg of Thee; my soul is all that I claim my own
Lying beneath your swaying curtain of tresses like tears seems befitting
Your shelter gives my heart and my mind all the peace needed
It is so unsettling to be so far from my home

I am not the first one to be put to rest far from their home
It is you, Mother Willow that has shaded my broken body
Sparks of light filter through your tresses swaying in the breeze
You offer refuge from the heat on this battered and weary body

How beautiful you are against the cloudless sky of blue
You're a haven of striking beauty set within Hell's Battlefield
The breeze blowing in between your tears feels cool upon my flesh
How it refreshes this torn, broken, and bleeding soul

You're meant to weep for the sad, lonely, and distressed
I know that is why your name is the "Weeping Willow"
When your tresses brush against my body, you comfort my soul
I hear you whisper words of comfort as the breezes blow

Mother sing to me your song so to assure my soul knows peace
Your whispering tells me not to worry, you understand my fear
Mother the sun sets, and the red glow illuminates the path
The last of my life slowly draws the curtain on us both

Before my sight are shadows of those you have embraced
They too come for the shelter that you have provided over time
I am not alone in my demise, never to be lost on the battlefield
One by one they return to rest in your caring arms

I am sorry for crying out in my painful agony, Mother Willow
While life drains, cradle your son as only a mother can
We both know my time is very near and I wish not to pass on alone
For many, this day have lost their lives, and the rain may be their only tears

Eyes look your last, no longer do I feel the pull of war's horrors
With the grace of God, we, the fallen will live on beyond tomorrow
I'm at peace mom, I'm not alone, you have gently touched my brawl
Do you weep for me? Yes, you weep for us all...

DON'T MAKE ME LOVE YOU

Don't make me love you
It's I who will take you to a special place in time
Don't make me love you
We seem to be up against the wind you and I
Together we shall stand with our heads held high
Don't make me love you
Let me drink in the passion I have for you
Can't you say that I am naked without you
I am like a child crying out in the rain
Don't make me love you
It is I who will turn the tides for you
Just let me love you as we swim in this ocean of life
I will, not let you go
Don't make me love you
Because long after the stars have faded from the heavens
My love will still shine brightly in the beyond
So don't make me love you
For that is something you would never have to do

Dreaming of Dance land

It's where my heart lives in freedom and my soul dances in the softness of twilight night. There's a grand orchestra in the Famed "DANCELAND", its mystical music plays on the fly-by. Mystic shadows of dancers swirl through my thoughts as my dream brings it all to life. Shifting vignettes and lingering doubts flash in and out like the couples of Swing and Jive. Ghost shadows stark and vivid now flash before my eyes of things long gone, coming to life. Grasping for a taste of what should have been mine during an era that would have fit me well. Sweet brushfires burning on the edge of a forest floor, send smoke signals, hoping to cut a rug. Consumed in flames on the dance floor, the firemen jump, spin and prance in their Zoot-Suits.

Dance land is a palace for all ages, but my heart belongs to the world of Latin Influences. Starlight and dewdrops can make me forget flash and flair to favor all the Ballroom Styles. Crystal blue lights. mirrored stars, passionate couples fill the ballroom with waltzing desires. Harder than ecstasy, purer than love, master couples dance the Fox Trot like Fred and Ginger. On this night filled with stars, one singular star caught my eye. But was this Star or Angel? Here is where I belong, between a dream and heaven's plateau. Far from my ugly and true reality. The softness of stars twinkled in her eyes, entwining my heart, firmly validating my world. A crystal blue pool of cracked ice saw through the core of my soul in a single endless caress.

Her crystalline shadows and mesmerizing eyes told me my life would never be the same. If she would tenderly offer her mysteries in a dance with me. Chapter One would be written. My reoccurring dream of good and plenty give an additive measure of happiness to my life. As I long to arouse the flame once more from my loss of years ago that nearly destroyed me. She's captured and holds my heart enthralled. This amazing star or an Angel can dance. Seductive remembrance on a sea of silk is picture-perfect as our bodies Tango, step to step. I'll never find the words flowing inside to possess the rapture of my desired dream come true. The endless passion of a hopeless release comes true and the past I'm relinquishing willingly.

A touch of sublime beauty is all I desired. Gazing into the stars, finding an Angel that dances. Dancing was my life, it took a dream and an Angel, a reoccurring dream to hold the bliss so near. Now I wish to slumber in a dream of timeless love that has given me a world of dance again. To embrace my Angel, together as partners on top of the world as, **"Champions in Latin Dance"**. Never to be taken away, a title earned and always known as the "1980 Latin Dance Champions of Maryland.

Dreams are amazing and wondrous things in one's mind. Many things that our mind holds are keys to the past, present, and future. It all happens when you are sleeping. All you must do is remember your dreams as they happen. If you wake during a dream have a pen by your bedside and write them down. When you wake try to remember more and write that down and book it in a book. If and or when you recall something that is stuck in the back of your mind, return to your book of dreams, and see if it relates. Amazing and true happenings occur. I know it works for me. I have learned where things have been missing and was found after a dream I had. I dreamed I was in a certain place and four months later I recalled that dream and it was true. I had never been to this place before in my life, then suddenly here I was, right in the middle of what was my dream. It is truly amazing what a dream can do for us. Some say it could be a call from another lifetime or a door to the future.

DREAMS

Dreams come and dreams go
Floating, flying, and vertigo
Wonderland of wonders circles about time
Good things of hue and reason and rhyme

Dreams up and dreams down
Dark flashes with falling stars all around
Nightmares of terror and hearts in pain
They're cold, and dark with enclosures and no flame

Dreams in and dreams out
In and over, twisting all about
Warmth, the family, faces freeze
So many varieties, what's next do I see

Dreams dark and dreams in light
Grasping, holding on through the night
Follow the light, follow your heart
Nothing can harm you here in the dark.

Embraced By the Angels

"My days are dark as I make my way from home to school and back again. I am tired of being beaten down by narrow-minded people. You can only take so much before being damned. I write this in my journal for ME! Something to believe in other than the fifth that surrounds me. I promise you many sunsets created by our Heavenly Father. Painted in colors as rich as the sky is vast. Reflective like that of a mirror. Precious as the laughter of a child. heartbreaking, for the loss of a loved one. He gives you an endless world of possibilities at the end of each day. From the Angels who have walked here before you, through life's trials and tribulations, with every step of the way there have been Angels. Always standing beside you, behind from day one. This should, must give you pause. If you believe in the "Power of Prayer". Angels have always guarded you against evil and the harm it tries to inflict. Throughout our lives here on Earth and beyond, Angels have stepped every step you have ever taken. All in restoring you completely. Allow the Angels to embrace you fully. Continue to fight the fight. Let the waterfalls within your life be the healing waters of miracles. Let waters pour through you to heal that which darkens your soul. Healing gives your faith stronger growth. By being embraced by the Angels your soul will feel Blessed!"

EMOTIONAL

The road is long and I'm short to bare
A river of desires, why do I not care?

Many wishes unfulfilled, short of time I fear
This nightmare of lost goals is many and to near

A few tears still waken in this weary heart of mine
The road is long, and desire has wrecked in time

Sudden stops are many and the fuel is sometimes low
So many emotions harbored this I know

Color not, the story is told in black and white
Visions are dim, they subside day and night

Rest I need, for longing, need not rise
The road is hard, the will is soft at my side

Aged I feel before my time, where do I go?
The response lacks a mind who does not know

Wow! How deep is reflection, I now cry.
Untapped, I care not to understand why?

Just mellow to this story, the five W's I seek
The road is so long, no horizon, I now weep...

So, traveling on this asphalt made nightmares for me
The nightmares of all my life, a lock with no key

Many wishes and dreams are just not the same
Destination to one's life, you must travel in the name!

Endlessly

Forever, so it seems that I have wandered through a mystic fog

In search of the one I love

A love that suddenly ended in a blazing flash of an unbelievable white light

No pain, no feeling, simply a nothingness

The last thing remembered before the flash

Was a moment of total silence as we were looking into each other's eyes

No word was exchanged

However, I noticed his beautifully sculptured lips slowly parting

Forming the words that have endlessly been silent in my memory

"I love you"

I have been searching endlessly

He vanished right before me; I never had the chance to respond in kind

So, I search endlessly and no longer walk among the living

It's like waltzing alone, heartbroken, and flatfooted

Like a song never sung, two ships pass in the night

Under the shooting stars of a midnight twilight

Loneliness in limbo

Searching for the loss of a lover who vanished

For it is I who hasn't realized

That I vanished as well in that flash of light

Searching, searching, searching

Endlessly...

ENTER AT YOUR OWN RISK

In an instant
My world known as hell on earth changed to one of purgatory
I retreated to the only quiet place I know
A dark place is known as a shock
Here I sit in a room with four walls
It's cold and lifeless and as dead as I am
The world outside these walls rolls like a penny on its edge
Up and down inclines, racing through life's everyday situations
The window shades have been drawn by the widow of sadness herself
November is chilly and rain-soaked souls
Fallen leaves hug the road surfaces like the slim trail of a slug
Out of tradition, I place a small lit candle on the window
When a loved one is lost or has passed on from this damned world
Because the darkness of solitude has grasped me by the shoulders
Pressing my soul down into where I sit
There is no longer a fire to warm what spirit there might have been
I reside here in the halls of darkness
After another loved one has been taken,
NO SNATCHED!
From this plane of existence
Dear God! I feel such anger
Unrelentless RAGE!
Festering with nowhere to go
But we have been companions for the longest time
Even though I am trapped in darkness since birth
I know there is only one door before me
It breathes like a bellow being pumped full of air
So, I hide amongst the shadows
I have lost the will to walk into the light
My heart has been hardened
My mind along with all emotions
Feel weathered, and cracked, like ageless paint peeling off the door
I tacked a sign on the door stating clearing.

"ENTER AT YOUR OWN RISK!"

Everlasting Love

The one I love

Cries herself to sleep

At night

Longing for my touch.

We knew

Before starting a relationship

We must live our lives

Apart.

Sometimes

There are things

That happens in one's life

Which cannot be controlled.

And that someday

We will be together

On the other side of Heaven's

Everlasting love.

Every Dance with You Feels Like the First

This is the moment, a magical moment for just the two of us

Where we search for the dance of everlasting love anew

Feel the warmth of the day into the nights of tropical heat

Enveloping one's body with its rhythmic and sensual beat

Hot is the days of summer, lazily turning twilight into night

Placing you on a carpet of passion, the rapture is easily inviting

Cease the dragon's breath that turns the desert sands to fire

Enter Sir Knight of the Artic Breeze, cool the flesh of its heat

Where our heart's desires are written amongst the ancient stars

Drifting motionless as we are carried away on summer winds

Time means nothing when she is caressed in his strong arms

Not a second is wasted, embraced between Heaven and Earth

We will be floating where Angels dwell in loving harmony

Our hearts and souls are touched by their angelic voices

In their eyes, crystal teardrops chimes like Tubular Bells

"Hark"** the Angels sing, **"Sir Knight and thy Lady are blessed"

Our hearts are filled with joy and love as for we are blessed

Onward we experience the wonders that God has created

Gazing into your eyes so blue, there my future is very clear

I see an amazing lady for whom I shall love forevermore

My heart dances high above clouds laced with imagination

Clouds form a sparkling gondola created just for you and I

My lady takes the hand of the Gondolier, stepping to her seat

Together the stage was set for a romantic evening in Venice

We float through waterways created by clouds abundant

Our Gondolier serenades us with a voice echoing romantically

In and out of canals, waterways floating on a heavenly dream

Sounds of Mandolins, Cellos, and Violins echo throughout

Your lips upon mine certainly brought everything to a crescendo

It was somewhere between floating and the heavenly music

*A Piano is playing **"Moonlight Senate"** as we silently glide away*

Dedicated to the lady before me for whom I'm in love with

Take my hand and together we will step upon the waters

Of Venice, waltzing through the canals of our imagination

The midnight moon shimmers across the mirrored waters

I tell you now, every dance with you feels like the first time.

EYES LOOK YOUR LAST

This was written with the idea of the Grandparents I never knew. Both my grandparents on my mother's and father's side had died before I ever got to know them. So, with that in mind, I created the grandfather and grandmother I wish would have been mine. After I saw the movie, "On Golden Pond", It was very easy to pick the grandparents to love. What a wonderful movie that was and is. One night after a hell of a night on Hell's Half Acre", I sat down and wrote the words that came as if the scene were playing out in front of me. I turned the light out and lit a candle beside me on a small stand. I pictured my grandfather with white hair and wearing wire-rimmed glasses. My grandmother and his wife passed away when my mother was in her early teens. True story, she was struck by a car as she was walking home along the road from a neighbor's house. Her name was Minnie Jane Suzanna Rebecca Cramer Wetzel. I changed her name to Sweet Emma. I give you my vision of a grandfather as I created him as he might be as he is ready to retire for the night.

*He walks wearily to his bed of ninety years. Down that lonely hall that once was shared. Gone early she was at eighty-four, Sweet Emma, from his heart, did adore. The hand of age brushes a kiss upon her face placed by the bedside in an old pewter frame. Like so many times before when the day is long, he removes his wire-rim glasses and yawns. Folded carefully and placed beside her photo. The linen is pulled to the side, a pillow is fluffed. He sits for a while and stares into space. Slippers were removed one by one, placed just so. Before he lies between the sheets, a call is heard from a nearby lake. Gentle in the night the Loons sing their song. The moon of silver reflects in the lake across the way. Shadows of Loons in love, create ripples upon the water. This is his Golden Pond and Strawberry patches. Together many a day they walked for miles hand in hand, stopping to smell the flowers and pick strawberries for Emma's amazing jam. How well he remembers those days of yesteryear. Shutting the window just enough to let a breeze flow across the room. As he turns to shut the light, for just one moment he imagines Sweet Emma patting the bed and calling to him sweetly, **"Come"**. He clears his head, then a tear drops, and whispers to himself, **"All right Emma my sweet, all right dear, all right"**. Making his way to the bed he slides in slowly between the sheets. Leans over, turns out the light, and pulls the covers up. As he thinks of Emma, the bright moonlight casts shadows. They are upon the wall and on the ceiling overhead. Figures dancing about the room shadowed in blues and grays, triggering memories of dances in the church hall, down away. Slowly his eyes close, and he says this prayer every night:*

"Lord, my Savior, this I ask,
I wish to see my Sweet Emma just one more time
To be by her side and feel her warm hand on mine
If you see me fit to grant this wish,
Happy I will be, in her arms and Sweet Emma's kiss.
In your blessed light
Amen."

FACING THE STORM

"This is written metaphorically, my life, my mother, and my sister lived in an abusive atmosphere for many years. Together we weathered the raging storms of Hell. My mother lost her battle against a continuous twenty-six years of an abusive marriage. Until the loss of her life at the age of forty-five years young. As children and through our teens, my sister and I lived in abuse as a way of life. It's amazing how one individual can control another's life, spirit, mind, and body out of complete FEAR. I am all that remains of my family. And maybe that is for the best? In fact, "IT IS!" Storms raged nearly every day and night. Some darker and more furious than the next.

There in the distance, I saw the dark storm raging. My heart began to race, feeling it through my body. Flashes of lightning outlined the hateful eyes of evil, I stood frozen waiting for another flash to confirm it. Slice after slice of lightning marred the dark sky. Clarifying what I saw and did not want to believe. Miles away but gaining momentum every minute. In a powerful crash of thunder, my name was called! A foreboding flock of black Starlings took to wing. Dust devils rose like tornadoes across the meadows. Hot wind straight from the gullet of hell in warning surrounded my defiant stance as I refused to budge. A huge thunderhead stretched across the horizon. That's when the face of the devil was well-defined. Shades of the green outlined yellow eyes of a snake. He bombarded me with hailstones and fierce rain. It mattered not; I turned my back toward his blows. I turned to raise my fist in total defiance to his face, and he answered, descending in a swirling mass of clouds. Forming into a black churning creation of destruction. I braced myself like an unmovable mountain of rock. War raged around me with winds sharp as razor blades. Small demons filled with fury, sliced, and clawed at me, ripping at my clothing, completely shredding them. Evil did its best upon me; I was beaten and bleeding. I'm still standing tall, better in mind for facing my fear. All the battle scars will last as a testament to the truth. A mind chained in the darkness of a hidden dungeon. Still standing as the storm raged on in another direction. I turned back to see the devastation created in his wake. That is when I felt the air being sucked from my body. Driving me to my knees as I gasped for life-giving air. There was the feeling of a cold hand grasping my throat, squeezing tighter and tighter, lifting me off the ground. In a sharp crack of thunder, I was slammed to the ground. I hit so hard that I sank inches into the rain-soaked muddy soil. My courage was more than shaken, in fact, I felt fear. I rose to my knees as the last drops of rain washed me. The clouds slowly parted; rays of sunlight filtered down. The land before me was beaming in heavenly illumination. Shining several feet away from where I was kneeling, I saw a figure lying face down in the mud and gravel. Getting to my feet I rushed over to help this unfortunate. The figure had suffered slashes from head to their feet. Thunder rumbled in the distance like demonic laughter. It's very clear this person suffered the rage of the storm. It started to rain a summer mist as I turned the person over. The misty rain helped me to wash the mud from his face.

In my arms was the shell that housed my very own soul. The evil that plagued my mind and heart was victorious. In the end, I had found the strength to fight the demons at last. I cried tears washing away the agony bottled up for so long. What evil didn't know was that my soul was my champion. From the start to the very end of the storm, I stood defiant against his storming rage that hovered continuously over me. Now my spirit could finally rest somewhere beyond a rainbow.

Fanciful Symphony

There, investigate the distance between dawn's first flicker and the waking light. Where stars ride upon fireflies that kiss the mist, bringing the whisper of twilight. I have discovered a rare and exotic world like no other known to man. Come with me and see wondrous things. Witness my very own, "Brigadoon". That magical "Once in a year day". Nature has marked the fertile fields with an abundance of floral every color of the rainbow. Scan across the tundra's meadows curtained in hazy shades of draped color veils. Walk the picturesque shorelines, sun-bleached gold and blanketed in false diamond grains that twinkle and sparkle in a rich array. Imagine hiking in and out of moonlit dunes. Accented in Pampas grass adorned in their cotton-like plumage. Stroll through fully blossomed Weeping Cherry Trees. Sweet is the fragrance lit by the Man-in-the-Moon. Venture atop plush mountains, nature-rich in flowing streams. Craving their way around every bend. Mother Nature certainly has blessed this magical kingdom. Beyond transcends her beloved Eden. Secluded in a forest refuge of the rarest and most exotic birds. Summer songbirds from around the world. Melodically expressive and fanciful flocks arrive in full spiral dives. It is their grand entrance from every corner of the planet. A gathering symphony of nature's feathered beauties. Just imagine a million songbirds strong. Conducted by one singular "Maestro". The rhythmic south has arrived first in grand pageantry. With drums and fancy displays of amazing-colored feathers. Dancing to a deep thumping bass within, a mix of jungle-and-jive rhythms. Millions travel from every time zone just to roost in harmony on this, **"Once a year day".** Gathering in song to be heard, that they are needed in this damaged world. Each plays its part in the **"Garden of Eden."**

I was chosen as the conductor of this auspicious and enchanted gathering. Our beloved Mother Nature handed me the baton with tears in her eyes and the most amazing smile. I looked high into the branches of this cathedral-looking tree. My heart was beating a steady rhythm of its own. Before me, a vision of Mother Nature's eyes appeared in the mighty trunk of this enchanted tree trunk. I felt the beating of her heart and with that, my heart melded with hers. What an amazing feeling. I could feel the power she posse. My soul knew, felt, and bonded in harmony. Each branch of this tree cradled a beautiful living instrument. For which I would be in control. This night would be so like that of **"We are the World".** I turned to face the horizon. A curtain was now shadowing the Tundra that encircled this **"Garden of Eden".** I knew this was Mother Nature's doing. She was setting the scene as if this was the grandest stage of all Theaters. All around us in this garden, a dreamy twilight ascends, and the moonlight illuminated this grand perch for the millions of birds. Each branch held a songster and was lit by a star from Heaven above. As the velvet night blinks an eye, ready, marks the orchestra of songsters from near and far. With the rise of the baton, not a *sound is heard. Only the slight ruffling of feathers in the surrounding trees. From the highest point of the tree, as enchanting and spectacular as this auspicious moment and the gathering was, I tapped the baton in three quick taps. I cued the famed Phoenix in a spectacular fireworks display. Rising gloriously, igniting an outstanding flame abounding. The Phoenix is a symbol of* **"Constant Rebirth".** *Their song is a reality in nature's living symphony. Cued in harmony and blessed with grand vocals. The view, the sound, is to see. Unfortunately, in a* **"Once in a Year Day"** *for the sight and gathering is the Fanciful Symphony alone...*

FAR ACROSS A DISTANT LAND UNDER A CELTIC MOON

Dedicated to Miss Joanne McNeal

Far across a distant land
A land not as distant as my unattached heart may seem to believe
Under a Celtic Moon, loneliness is but a dance of her in remembrance

Far across a distant land
Is where our dreams faded with each thought of leaving
Like the dew in the morning, Lavender is sweet in fragrance anew

Far across a distant land
It's not hard to imagine a lovely Lass running free across the moors
Calling my name, hidden within the fields of Lavender singing in the wind

Far across a distant land
Such a happy-go-lucky child of nature, a child of beauty over hills and dells
Where she and her white horse's hooves danced and pranced to the pipes

Far across a distant land
The Celtic Moon shinning across the hillside in the mirrored reflection
Creating flashes of ghost-like figures hauntingly floating across the Moors

Far across a distant land
I would walk the hillsides alone, a broken man in remembrance of my loss
I'd sit as if in concert, listening to Celtic women sing of their motherland

Far across a distant land
Along a creek where nature revealed in midnight songs seem to be amplified
How lovely the sounds of homeland instruments echoing over the countryside

Far across a distant land
These hills remind me of the home where I grew up, fell in love with a red-haired beauty
Where Cellos, Violins, and the thumping of Celtic Drums gave way to a dance of love

Far across a distant land
Tall and beautiful in the saddle, riding the horse she loved more than life itself
Where my eyes played in the memory of her song of harmony named "Chloe"

Far across a distant land
My heart holds the tears of many yesterdays never to ever be forgotten
Memories that float in my dreams of wishful thinking she was still alive

Far across a distant land
Where dreams are reborn, relived for those who have learned to dance with heart
Awaken in the land of Angels, Lavender, and Harps of the Celtic Moon

Far across a distant land
A land not so distant at all, it's here and now, it's in my heart when I dance
*In my soul where all memories can call me **"Home".***

FATHER FULL MOON

From the darkest of spaces, damp, musky, rotting, and spoiled, Rise the walking dead by a force much stronger than life itself. Father Full Moon, named so by those who watched his figure, a tall dark shadow is seen crossing in front of the full moon. On those nights it was known that the Dark Angel came to feed. He was so different from the vampires that tore into you with lust, ripping the flesh from the body and gorging themselves like tics. He walked those many years ago after the Black Plaque arrived. How it all began was that in death he became the Dark Angel. When the fallout finally consumed all living creatures on earth. Father Full Moon listened for the moans and the muffled cries of those nearing death, the men, women, and the children of man. He would seek you out as his hunger grow, and your pain increased. Would you want immortality or to sleep without pain forevermore? When hunger drives, it's the thirst that takes over petty introductions.
"There is no need to deny or defy us, what will be, will be..." *Our Father Full Moon guides us in our nightly lust-driven feedings. We have no control for hunger is a very strong burning force, we must abide by the needing urge before our beloved darkness turns, into the unholy light of dawn where once we were favored in life's energy. History holds a claim that we have been around since 400 B.C. Stalking in the shadows draped in cover as dark as our intent, eyes like black orbs, lifeless and lacking all sensitivities and caring. Look deep into our eyes and see a vacant vessel with no soul. Once our yearnings were strong and very much like your own. Our very essence of life held uncontrollable desires with a passion high, flowing throughout every vein being pumped endlessly. For the river of life flows within the warmth of your sweetness. It's what we desire, what we crave, what we long for that's no longer our own. The difference with us, as compared to what was, we became the concept of rage. We were takers, many now "ASK", and in exchange for that sweet nectar as food, we can offer you an incentive, (if you will),* ***"Immortally over Death!"*** *Such power is given to us by* ***'The Master", "The Sire"*** *of our kind;* ***"Father Full Moon".***

Father's Day

One can speak a thousand words about how wise you may be

In the beginning, you made Earth and the Stars

Who could say more or even less?

Father, we thank thee for six and one to rest upon

Your hope for us, the world to be in peace

All are you, children, with pride in your eyes you do weep

Wayward are some and others straight as an arrow

Youth holds not focus on free will taking control

You blew into the dust you gathered in your hands

Adam, you named, and a rib made Eve

Soon they did sin by seduction anew

You banished both to walk the land

You spoke to Noah, the Earth you will flood

Build me an Ark, gather every species two by two

Your sons and their wives will be safe with you

40 days and 40 nights were needed to cleanse the Earth

Pharaoh enslaved your children, and you heard their cries

You then sent Moses to deliver your words, "Let my people go!"

Pharaoh saw the mighty hand of God, for the Nile ran red with blood

By your might, Moses raised his staff, the parting of the sea miracle

You sent an Angel to the Virgin Mary

Who would deliver your son in a manger under the Bethlehem Star?

By trading a carpenter for a young man of growing faith

He healed the sick, crippled, and blind to see

By judgment and trial, which one would lose?

Jesus or Barabbas, a choice was to be made

Jesus was to give his life for a crime put upon by his own people

Laid on a cross with nails hammered into his flesh

It is Father's Day and I have one wish if I could

To give my life in exchange that he might live on

Yet it was your will and to question is wrong

You are my King, my Savior, and my Father.

Give us this Day in honor of your love!

FEAR OF LIVING

"There is a lack of everything, prices continually rising, no jobs available, the poor are poorer, the rich are still rich and getting richer by the minute. Soon there will be a fight for survival, and we will live between "The Tale of Two Cities" and "Solent Green" if the "GREED" does not Cease!

The fear of living...
It's the fear of being able to hold onto,
All things that you've worked so hard to make your life valid
Family, food, home, money, and health
Now of days it's the fear of not having a steady job!
Or at any moment your let go,
The Government fazes you out!
Or worse yet, a job you put 40 or 50 years into,
Reeking all the benefits over those years
And wondering if they will be there in the future?
The head of the household is wondering day after day,
Will his or her life and family be taken care of in their **"Golden Years?"**
My fear was in maintaining a roof over my head for my wife and son
Paying the bills on a shoe-string budget from year to year was a hard thing to do,
When you are young and starting out in this material world of good and plenty
Well hell's-bells, all that I cared for was taken from me one April...
I had a five-year-old son, **Cody-li,** and his mother, **Nikki-Lynn** was taken in an instance...
Both were killed on an Easter morning on their way back home from church,
It happened to be a drunk driver, how ironic is that? I ask
My life went into a spiral and the will to live didn't matter at all!
Everything I feared in my life, up to that very moment,
"HAPPENED!"
I lost one job after another in a world where there were
"NO JOBS!"
The car was taken, the bank took the house and my land
Then came the health issues, unexpected, no job, no money, and no insurance...
Now what I know as an educated man in America, four years of college
And another four years of getting a **"Master's Degree"**
So, I can earn more money by getting a better and higher-paying job!
"THAT DOESN'T EXIST!"
My smarts tell me,
"I AM NOT THE ONLY ONE WITH THESE TROUBLES!"
But listen to me**,**
"I don't give a damn about anyone else"
**"I am only concerned about ME these days,
And each one of us is feeling the same way, my friends!"**

"This is where I need to just lay down and DIE!
I say, the HELL with it all!
The two most important people in my life have been
"Yanked out of this world!"
I hear my friends and the people on the streets talking, complaining,
"All my savings are gone", because of the increasing costs of Medications and Doctors
They fear that people will not be able to live on minimum wage as is,
In the very near FUTURE!
Because the cost of everything has skyrocketed!
" For one reason and one reason only!

"GREED-GREED-GREED-GREED-GREED!

Everyone wants more money, more Profits
Now there are more Senior Citizens on Earth than there have ever been in the history of MAN!
Baby Boomers after World War II
We are living in our "Golden Years" and we are living longer...
These years are to be the best years of our lives.
Who in the hell came up with that phrase?
You know that was created by.
Someone who was born with a silver spoon inserted up their ass as a child
The rich and privileged...
Do you know that there are more?
"BILLIONAIRES" to date,
Than ever before, so many that it's a bore to hear who is and who isn't!
So many that they never have to worry about where their money is coming from
But when you're living from paycheck to paycheck,
Holding down two or three jobs just to survive
Yet, you still must "Steal from Paul to give to Peter to pay Mary"
It goes something like that...
People are working their fingers to the bones
Trying as hard as they can, making sure that their children get everything they never had!
Do they see it that way?
NO! because this world at this time,
Our youth has had everything "GIVEN" to them since birth.
Well maybe in the future when they have children of their own,
They may see the errors of their way,
Maybe-May-be, MAYBE?
There are many of us that have lived our lives like frightened animals
Hiding in caves away from the real world
Afraid that if people moved in too close
They would know what we really are...?
There was no time for the "Rite of Passage" in our lives
No trials of strength nor mystical chants have tempered us
A blinded soul where he and she groped through life, falling many times
Many have stumbled over and over, with broken bones, bleeding hearts,
Crying over the last dollar!
There are a multitude of many who stepped in line behind me,

*Stepped on the **"Yellow Bricks"** in my childish dreams of refuge, singing,*
"OVER THE RAINBOW"
Some hid in shame, embarrassing others, and wished I'd hide within the song!
I say, "For I am more than all this" I boost, "You'll hear echoes from others of my like"
But so many of these boys and girls got lost in their dreams
The dreams of yesterday were held tightly in their grasp!
Those were the ones I was in fear of losing...
Or stolen or fading away before my eyes,
*Because they were **TRUE BELIEVERS!!***

"AND THAT MY FRIENDS IS WRITTEN ACROSS THE SKY
BY THE WICKED WITCH!"

"SURENDER"

The Fear Is in Living!
Visions of a magical day
When voices are heard from some other place or time
There before us lying on an altar is,
"FATHER TIME"
Who will lift the shroud?
The heavy shroud that dims the thoughts of the multitude
That washed away all the colors in tears of indecision.
From this, I have a Coloring Book of Future Dreams...
Titled,

"FEAR OF LIVING!"

FLAMES CAN AND WILL BURN

The lore of sexual pleasures

The hottest flames are blue and white

The fire will dance a haunting and mesmerizing invite

In a fiery form of a God, he teases you with his beauty.

The blue flame is the brother of the fire
He is blinding to one's sight and cares not who gets burned
Together they create a lustful invitation
So, like a ripple upon a motionless body of water
Their beautiful ballet is supported by a company of equally dangerous dancers
Each strong and colorful in their own means
Red, crimson, orange, and yellow complete this choreography
A purge can be defined as when the heart is given to passion
Beware, My Friends!
Love can burn the very soul of an innocent
To feel the fires of the flesh beckon for more
Fire is an all-consuming passion
Where you fall forward blindly
The heart easily surrenders to its lustful whispers with its forked tongues,

You shiver from their touch
Like the bite of a black widow as they secure you in their web
"Desire", is her name, his name is "Mercy"
Beware my friends "Fire" comes in many forms
I was young, innocent, and not yet wise to the charms that draw you into the web
There is a light at the end of a very dark alley
I remember well the fascination drawing me to feel the warmth of his charming heat
Pulling me closer to uncertain danger and or delight
There he stood, tall, dark, and handsome beyond belief
His eyes burned with the fires of Hell
His dance was just as seductive and inviting as the black widow's ballet
His hands were flames of red and yellow as he engulfed my innocence
Willingly I allowed his flames to consume me
Never did I feel such warmth
I was surrounded by a wall of loving fire
I let his fire show me no mercy
I became a part of his ballet of sexual flames
I set my very own soul on fire
For to remain still, there is no warmth,
Only the seduction of being seduced or being the seducer
I chose to burn within the choreography of seduction
He took my innocents and became the teacher
Lessons learned through the dance of fire
To become a watcher
Is to go out in a whimpering puff of smoke...

{This is my interpretation of when I was seduced from the age of eight to my mid-teens by an extremely good-looking man that made me feel very special once, I fell into his trap the sexual seduction geared me with an education in the art of survival and how to seduce when needed to guard against rough and tougher men and women who think they are in control. I can't say at the time I was frightened by him; this man gave me what I longed for, the love of a father, and mentor older brother that I wasn't getting in my childhood. I got beaten and abused at home and I ran into the arms of a man that gave me what I wanted and need. Now at seventy-one years old, I realize how I was manipulated and taken advantage of all those years. One day he simply disappeared from my life. I was fourteen and I went on with being abused at home and gave up on the life that was dealt to me. Until I was 16 years old when my father finally put my mother in her grave. I woke up and went for something that that man once told me, "Lee. Grasp the golden ring where you might, but always make it what you desire. Do what you must do to survive.} and I have to this day...

Flicker The Candles of My Heart

We are miles apart, more miles than I dare to count. However, my love, even so, our hearts are as close as the love songs of the Larks in the twilight hours. We're connected both in our minds and hearts. My love, still it's hard to have you so far away. Funny how I can smell the fragrance you wear throughout the day and night. When I'm still I feel your hand in mine. I feel your warmth and gentle caresses as I lay me down to sleep. When my world turns blue to gray and down and out, I think of you. Bringing forth the sunshine. Lighten my world and I can cope again. In your absence, I have tender memories to reflect upon. Still, the empty place where you once laid beside me in my body now holds a loving memory. A memory that sometimes comes to life. I feel your loving arms around me. I often find myself begging you to never let me go. There is no doubt, that you always created the flickering candles of my heart. Sometimes my dreams seem to come to life. For instance, my eyes were covered with dark foreboding hands. I took a deep breath as the hands faded from my eyes. Then there in front of me stood this magnificent creature. Tall with dark features. Dressed in black with the most astounding set of wings. He was of the Master Painters of the past conceived in religious works of Art. His beauty brought tears to my eyes. Of a wave of emotions, I couldn't understand at that moment. It was now clear that he was the "Angel of Death". There he stood, a beautiful vision before me. As if guarding your endless sleep. He raised his arms in a forward motion as if beckoning me to join him. His massive and glorious wings opened high behind him in one gentle flap. I felt the breeze as if it were a whisper circling me. Swirling around my feet, up to my legs, and into my chest. Touching my heart! I released an unbelievable sigh. The breeze didn't just touch my heart but entered my soul. Tawas his hand that gently squeezed that unbelievable sigh from my heart. My love, he touched the core of my very soul. It was like a warm misty morning spray of tranquility. It was as if I was standing under a waterfall totally naked. Being bathed in heavenly rays of sunshine, standing in a lush meadow of Lavender and vanilla blossoms. Soothing my soul of all pain.

Today I stand at the foot of your silent bedroom. Here is a stone garden amongst those that silently lay within. I have viewed up, down and through the sea of grave markers beneath the universe above. Time slowly marches for a hero who lived his life, not in vain. But walks amid the rows of the mourning that sleep beneath the gaze of death. My love, I found him to be kind and handsome. A gentle, understanding man, if you will? My hand trembles as I place a single red rose upon your chamber of sleep. To you, I blow a kiss. My emptiness has no bounds. I wake at night hearing your voice calling out my name. There are times when I awake from a dream that the longing for you is so deep in my heart that death is inviting. Life goes on and so shall I. A single red rose holds my desire, my love, and my memories. I rest in knowing as the years go by, one day we shall hold one another again. Until that blessed moment, I shall place a red rose upon your chamber of sleep and remember how much you flicker the candles of my heart.

FLICKERING IN THE WINDOW

Far back in the mountains, up on a hill, a crooked old wooden shack stood. Upon the tiny, ricked porch a rocker sits. An old lazy hound asleep alongside. The day ends as the evening star appears. The darkening blue veil of night arrives, and in the tiny window, a candle is always lovingly lit, flickering its glow throughout the night. The story is about an old woman who lives alone and how her son went off to do his duty in the service. Her son has yet to return to his home from a war fought between the states. Sometime back, a letter she did receive from her loving son so very far away. The letter stated, **"Mom, do me a favor, so I might find my way home, put a lit candle in the window for me."** *This she has done faithfully every night, to countless to remember. She counts the many long months since he faded into the distance, sending his old faithful hound dog back home. Still, her son has not made his way home. Each night she sits as the candle flickers. She watches the candle dance endlessly as the tiny flame illuminates the dark night. It reflects in her weary searching eyes. Often falling asleep till the cock crows at sunrise. It's her love that really flickers so bright, as she mumbles to herself saying,* **"Come home my son, come home to me".** *Her days are filled with a mother's needs, washing clothes, cleaning feeding the chickens, and chopping wood for the fireplace. Still, the candle flickers in the window when lit as the sun goes down over the mountains. Today is her son's twenty-fifth birthday. Out on the rocker she talks to the old hound,* **"Today is Jacob's birthday, old girl!"** *She recalls the teen enlisting for the cause. Whispering,* **"Happy birthday Jacob, my beautiful son".** *She stares down the long-crooked path That just maybe today will be the day he returns home. The candle filters light across the porch as she prays each night that he finds his way home. That single flame flickers till dawn as a beacon back to the home he loved so well. She rocks slowly, closing her eyes and remembering the joy Jacob brought through the days. In her personal sigh, she mutters,* **"Come, home son."** *For another month of nights, she counts in total. Often, she goes out on the porch searching. Rocking in the breeze of summer's last breath. Listening to meadow Larks sing their songs. She loves how the sunsets between the mountains. That glow of orange as far as one can see. Roscoe is always by the rocker on the porch, looking for the boy that he grew up with. Roscoe lifts his head staring down the path and lets out a moan of sorts.* **"What is it, boy?"** *Straining to see in the mist, she stands wiping her glasses with her apron to see clearly. In the darkness, she hears a soft and low voice,* **"Mom"** *like it is riding upon the warm summer breeze. The candle flickered brighter in the window. The closer the figure comes; she holds her breath. Old Roscoe slowly emerges down the steps staring at the figure nearing closer. The old hound sounds off a joyful greeting when he hears his name being called. Trotting to greet his long-lost buddy and friend. Their greeting is more than heartwarming. It is an old friendship being renewed after all these years. The old woman hears,* **"Mom...Mom!"** *Down the steps holding onto the porch railing, she slowly steps one step at a time to greet the love of her life. She hurries toward a love lost, now found!* **"He has finally found his way back home,"** *said under her breath. Both run into each other's loving arms. Joyful tears run from a mother's eye for a son and sons for his mother.* **"Mom I'm Home!"** *she cups his face taking a long look into those eyes she adored then gives kiss after kiss.* **"I've been wondering forever in the dark."** *She listens to his words and has a deep-hearted sigh as if she knows what this is. He says to her,* **"I saw the candle flickering in the window."** *She lovingly says,* **"I lit it without failure, my son."** *Together the three walked toward the old shack as the warm summer breeze encircled the three of them. Like a mother, she fixed his favorite dishes and chatted, laughing, and* *remembering all things past. Then they sat on the porch exchanging stories. He went back inside and brought out his old guitar. He played his guitar and sang her favorite song, **"Summertime"** as if he had never left home. She rocked slowly and Rosco took his place by her side at the rocker, and all was calm. He looked up at her, **"I'm really tired, I'll turn in."** He kissed her cheek, and she cupped his handsome face **"Sleep in peace, my gorgeous boy, sleep in peace"**. She watches as he heads for the door. Going through the door, he slowly turned to her, **"Mom, you know I love you with all my heart."** She smiled, **"I know son, Jacob I've always known."** The candle in the window flickered in his eyes. Turning around, he walked back into the house, setting his guitar by the entrance. She put both hands on her own aged face with several gasps, the tears flowing from her eyes, she heard Jacob say, **"It's good to be home, Mom!"** She took a deep breath, **"I know son, for me too, my son."** A strong summer wind blew overhead. It seemed to circle the house with a calm demeanor giving the Erie feeling like the air being sucked out and around the cabin. The leaves rustling atop the old oak beside the shack stopped moving and became silent. She and Roscoe both focused on the door. Just then the door opened slowly. The guitar he left beside the door slid down. She heard, **"Thanks for lighting the candle, know that my love flickers in the flame always for you."** It was warm and felt like a kiss being placed upon her cheek. She took her glasses off once again and pulled up her apron to wipe the tears away. Tears both sad and happy at the same time. She blew a kiss to the summer breeze circling the shack. Roscoe let out a long-gated howl. Mom sat back down in her rocker. Upon the breeze, she heard his voice singing, **"Summertime"** slowly fading in the distance. A candle was faithfully lit for the lost son. Every night the flame flickered brightly in the window thereafter that unusual and special reunion. Until one night in the dead of winter, The light flickered no more...*

FOR WHAT REASON

Where did this all come from?
What have I done for you to belittle me?
Right in front of all to see
You can scream at me, you can yell at the top of your lungs
That I can walk away from

For what reason
In front of family and friends
You're ramping and raving I can handle
Even you're cursing at me can be like water rolling off a duck's back
What could I have done to warrant this?

I have taken more off you than I care to mention
You can call me every name in the book
The mental and verbal abuse you routinely throw in my direction
All this I can take with a grain of salt
But for what reason

You can and have walked all over me
And for whatever reason, there may have been
I can sweep it under the rug
Even the cruel and harsh attitude from time to time
But I ask, For what reason

You have disrespected me at every turn
Yet I remain by your side
This is the last straw that broke the camel's back
You now have gone as far as to strike me in public
And For What Reason, I ask?

I now say to you, never again!

For You and Me

I walk through the beauty

My steps have awakened

The very heart of Mother Nature

My eyes see the depths

Of a wondrous and amazing beauty

That now comes alive

From a mist that lightly falls

From a gentle waterfall

I walk upon a lavish green

That sparkles because of the mist

Fairy-like magic

By the touch of their wands

I step further on this carpet of greenery

So many beautiful trees

Where their leaves turn over

To catch the moisture

Gazing up through the trees

I can imagine the branches

Bowing as I walk onward

Just like a Princess

In a fairytale

How I love Mother Nature

She creates beauty everywhere

My day is complete

Where my steps so gently

Did I make in tenderness?

Here is where my heart beats freely

In Mother Nature's kingdom

The Sun in all its brilliance

Cascading its rays

Through the army of trees

Then illuminate the vines that grow

Thick over the majestic landscape

Into the mist from the waterfall

Creating rainbows all around me

I turn around slowly

With my arms out wide

I can say to the world

"Have you ever spun around in a rainbow?"

Well, I have, and I felt the love

That God has made

For You and Me.

FOR YOU

Just lean on me, I will always be there for you
Right or wrong whatever you do, no judgment will I make
My shoulders are strong if your need to cry
I'm your faithful puppy, tried and true

What right do I have to lean on you?
You have always given love so true
The truest friend to me since we were pups
I have made such a mess of things in my life

When the seas are rough, I will be your port in the storm
If there be the need to confide in me, I am here
If you find that you're weak, my strength is enough for two
If ever you are lost, a beacon of light I shall be

What you don't realize is that you always have been,
And always will be the calming sea for me
When the tides of my life are out of control
In you, I have a safe refuge for my heart and soul

If ever you would fall from any height, I will catch you
If your back is up against the wall, help is a heartbeat away
If ever fear would enter your heart and or soul
Remember it's our love for each other that will empower us both.

FORGET ME NOT

Someone, 'Forget Me Not" slips silently over my lips
I am gasping for air, echoing into the void of my sadness
It's called depression for those that can't understand it
Nor could care less about the sadness I've come to know

When I'm writing, my choice of words steals my voice
Slipping into haze like oiled pleas of me forget me not
That fall upon winter's sleep like snowflakes on water
Shall I lay down to rest, such are the stories I conceive

I retreat from the battle long before it was ever waged
Existing beside my peers, I was beaten down by bullies
"War's Victory" was my loss within a hasty with-drawl
This is my last request, if by chance it's heard, Someone...

"Forget Me Not!"

FORGOTTEN FIVE

I think today is a butterfly stitch from the past
It brought a meeting of five years forgotten at last

Together we spoke, together we remembered
He once was very close and maybe again this September

A handsome young stud who shared his secrets with me
Experimenting foot-free and fancy both were we

Brought together by one who weaves in and out
Both handsome men and gorgeous women without a doubt

She's my energized cosmopolitan, dance partner, see her twirl
Sassy hot and photo beauty, always in fashion, what a pearl

As our story goes, two is company, one must go
Envy and jealousy became the enemy, that we three know

She wanted him, she loved me
I loved her, I wanted him, he wanted both, you see

The future looks bright, we're shooting for the stars
We will accept each other for who and what we are!

FOUR WALLS DO NOT MAKE A HOME

Let me make this perfectly clear, my house was never home!
It had a roof that sheltered us from the weather
But not the raging storms inside always in constant flacks within four walls
There was a floor that completed this tomb of anger in the dark

Within this tomb, it was divided into upstairs and downstairs
Each room had four walls and a ceiling
I dwell-ed in 8X10 room, take note, I dwell-ed not lived...
My sister had her room next to mine to feel as safe as possible

Each had a bed and a very small window to breathe fresh air
It had a door to shut out the horrors in this world
A lock mattered not; it had been busted through quite a few times
It was our room to shun the outside world and from one another

My room held no memories of good, in fact, it held nothing of importance
Reflection of what was and reflections of what never will be echoed
These four walls talked of horrors, and you could hear the cries of the lonely
Beneath our feet was without a doubt, the entrance to hell's pit of anger

There was never comfort being felt inside our world of the living dead
This house could tell the world stories of fear as if the glass was breaking
The walls speak of secrets that were burnt like shadows against the grain
It's deafening when you were alone, sitting in the dark, simply waiting

For the change of weather was constant and the sun never shined for long
A house harboring dark memories that cut like a knife into the soul
Death moved in and never left, bringing terror and horror to siblings in chaos
Four walls do not make a home when love is murdered before your eyes

Many years were spent simply as a haven of convenient sorts
Extreme loneliness was felt many, many times, I had, and she did.
It was better feeling that way for we were taught at an early age, that love is cold
Because when you had to open the door, it meant faking a smile at humanity

My house was never a home, yet you could it breathing in and out
No matter how many secrets the walls held, the walking dead screamed out loud
I would never feel rooted, one never felt welcomed in this house of shame
When the four walls do speak, the story will finally be seen in the light

If those same four walls would talk, what a story they could tell

Metaphorically speaking in shades of darkness, my mother murdered at forty-five
My sister was terrified to stay in the house with the beast alone
Myself, it didn't matter, I was dead anyway...

Four walls do not make a home!

FRIENDS

People are many
Friends are few, true, and close
Interesting friends are what is rare
Many smiling faces with eyes as distant as a dream in the making
Count on a single hand friend
Seven letters and out of seven there are two that are true
People offer but are they sincere with their charity
Do they feel close,
Can they give that which is rare?
They are many, but I stand in the shadows, hidden
Loneliness is a sad affair
To hold close, no one is there,
You hold on tight as you hug yourself
Friends look onward,
That we march together for it is we that truly see
Walk forward with me my friend together,
Being alone is a sad affair

From Shadows to Nightmares

Forgotten is the long day, however, the pain in the heart remains

The curtain of night descends and lessons the agony with sleep

All the while in the back of your mind another day will be ignited

It claws at your soul with a festering that oozes like an old wound

Now crawls a blackened wind, cold in its whispers of pleasures past

They offer tempting rewards that are unattainable in every manner

You're engulfed by an evil present's barren as an old woman's womb

You must not cross the river of despair for the whispers are blacker

*Meet **"The Shadows"** of your discontent with where your paths lead*

Never to get the peace you crave as they whisper darkly in your ear

***"The Shadows"** can twist reality into your blackest of nightmares*

Dark surrounding you offer little comfort only everlasting grieving

Your soul is starved for affection and the tears spit make no sound

All that was is no longer for you have aged way before your time

*This darkness of **"The Shadows"** intensifies, why is it punishing you?*

*That's the way of **"The Shadows"** your dreams lead to nightmares!*

GIVING THE WRONG MESSAGE

Look behind the eyes of this boy, there is a message for help

Please, I beg you to look into my eyes and see my message
On the outside, I may be silent
However, on the inside, I'm screaming for help!
Take it for Christ's sake,
"TAKE MY HAND!"
Abuse takes the mind, body, soul, heart, and spirit...
Love? What is that?
How can a child know such a thing if he or she has never experienced it?
Do not look past the child in front of you
Be alert, be aware of the signs,
It's easy if you try
Hear the tone of their sighs
Listen to their crying, both out loud and those that are silent
"The eyes are a mirror to the soul"
The world of abuse is nothing new
Abuse is more than destructive or even devastating,

Physical

Mental

Sexual

Emotional

It is so much more than that.

Brutal

Evil

Horrific

Terrorism

Bullying

A child only knows what horrors would be in store if he or she told anyone
Help is desperately needed
We all know it's none of your damn business to interfere.
RIGHT!
SHOW SOME COMPASSION
From the beginning of their young lives,
They have been given the wrong message in life
They will never know a childhood that is filled with,
WORDS THAT HURT
PUNCTUATED
It is something they'll carry into their adulthood,
If they live long enough...
It is registered on the faces and bodies of the young and old alike
The scars are deep within the mind and etched on the flesh.

BRANDED DEEP
BRUISED
REMEMBERABLE
BATTERED
MENTAL AND PHYSICAL ISSUES
DRUG ADDICTION
PROSTITUTION
DEPRESSION
ACTING OUT ON OTHERS AND OR ANIMALS
EVEN DEATH
Abuse is an infection running ramped through all walks of life
It's possible right next door
Say a prayer...
Hell, even the church harbors the truthful shame
Religious caretakers went astray,
Listen, my friends, it has gone a hell of a sight deeper than that
Imagine the children seen walking the dark streets at all hours of the night
*Their lives are encircled by guardians named **"Shadows".***

SADNESS
PAIN
SUFFERING
AGONY
ABANDONED
RUNAWAYS
BROKEN HOMES
Even more beyond one's imagination, the reality is simply tragic
Abuse strangles one's.

HOPES
SHATTERED HOMES
RAPES THE VERY SOUL
DEMONIC IN NATURE
DESTRUCTION OF INNOCENCE
TURNING DREAMS INTO NIGHTMARES OF A LIFETIME
SO MANY TIMES, LEADING TO SUICIDE
An innocent is unfortunately taught by one with an agenda of his or her own
Abuse is an endless cycle within the circle of life
Effecting one's mind, body, and the soul
Self-esteem vanishes within the haze
Many innocent children are given the wrong message from the start!
ABUSE,
Is real to those who have no control,
Over their surroundings or the lack thereof
Please! do not close your eyes to realities
Unfortunate and Frightened!
I know,
For I experienced it first-hand...

GOD WOULD BUT GRANT YOU WINGS

Two of my dearest of friends had a wonderful little girl that was dying of heart trouble. Just four years old and the sweetest baby doll. You know the type, big sad eyes, gorgeous hair, and a face the Angels had kissed. Ray and Linda were at their wit's end. Her name was Star Lynn and their first child. As her condition got worst, Ray and Linda knew it was a matter of time before they would have to say goodbye. My heart was full for the three of them. They knew I wrote poetry and stories. They loved reading my work. It came about one evening at the hospital if I would do them a favor. Of course, I'd do anything in my power for them. After all Star Lynn was my godchild. They asked if I would put their words in a poem of sorts. Star loved her mom and dad reading to her every night. This poem would be their way to say goodbye. I had never been asked to do anything this personal before. But when I looked into my friends' eyes, I couldn't say anything but yes. So, when they received the word that they would need to prepare themselves, they called me to come to the hospital. They had two weeks to memorize the poem. They were prepared emotionally, physically, and spiritually. They wanted me to come in with them and I did. It was a wonderful and emotional journey in our lives that night. This is what they recited to Star Lynn, this moment they would hold dear in their hearts forever...

God Would but Grant You Wings

This day, God would but grant you wings
You will see heaven and amazing things

You're here in my arms, I now must release
You will fly on tiny wings of love and peace

I wish I had wings, this would be my dream
Together we'd fly over fields and streams

I must be realistic when I look at your sweet face
This journey you must take alone in God's good grace

It's very hard for mom and dad to say their last good-bye
We'll look for your tiny wings amongst the stars in the sky

Your wings will sparkle, and the Angels will sing
For this day, God would grant you wings.

With that amazing moment in all our lives, love flowed throughout the room. They held Star until her eyes closed. I heard Ray and Linda softly whisper to Star Lynn. "We will love you forever, sleep-sleep". There is nothing more to be said, they will grieve and over time the heart will gather the memories shared. I know, for I lost my son at age five.

Going Back

It has been years since I traveled back home

Tomorrow lays heavy on my heart

Will it be the same?

Will the same monsters lurk around the corners?

Do the shadows hover in a dark guard?

Is the roof of the tin still rusty?

Do the creepy branches of the old oak,

Scratch the roof when the wind blows?

Are the weeds still overgrown throughout the fields?

This has never been a home to me

It never was, it was a place to hover in

Never was their love in those four walls.

It has been years since I went back home

To a place where God was a prefix to profanity

Tomorrow feels like I am headed to a funeral once again

Packing my bags with the things I left with

Going back is stepping into a hell I once lived

Where the Devil was the General

Where the Shadows scratched and left scars

And the blood ran cold

Tomorrow will come and the sooner the better

I will face the Demons once again

The same way I did when I exited that hellhole

I will thumb my nose at the garbage of yesterday

It has been years since I went back home

Tomorrow will be like swimming upstream,

Against rapids of blood

I will do what I need to do, then say so long!

GOODNIGHT LOVE

Tenderly you spoke to me with a whisper of love
A heavenly brushing as if from the wings of a dove

I softly brush my lips across the nape of your neck
A sigh so warm, as if dancing a lover's silent minute

We float amongst the warmth and tantalizing charms
We discovered the lost horizon in each other's arms

God has painted a lover's sunset just for you and me
Bursting in hues of orange to brilliant reds on high

Our eyes are witness to a Picasso across the sky
The Almighty has painted a world just for you and me.

Great Red Road

In this world, I may not always

Find peace and serenity

If I put forth the effort

To understand my misgivings

Then my part becomes complete.

May I always find the strength?

To walk the Great Red Road of good

Many experiences will walk by my side

I have the choice to choose

The straight and narrow.

I find in this vast life of learning

To hold in trust courage,

Optimism in all situations

I face each one with honor

Love and understanding.

When I am lost and alone

On the Great Red Road of discovery,

May the kindness of my brother

Hold goodness in his heart

And we will believe in a World of Peace.

Guardian Spirits

High on Devil's Peak, overlooking the Painted Canyon
Stands an old man withered by time,
But not in his spirit.
It has taken him three long moons to reach this sacred area
This Holy Land of The People.

There has been many a Great Chief who stood in this very spot
He has walked the**" Red Road"** for eighty-nine long summers.
After a short rest, he tends to his faithful friend
Removes the dusty old blanket from his back
And two rolled blankets with important ceremonial attire.
He then takes the rope bridle reins from his steed's head
After several soft pats on his neck,
He gives him the freedom to do as he pleases.

It's time to gather some kindling for a fire
As he walks around picking up a piece here and a piece there
Thoughts and reflections of years past
Come forth like an old movie reel in flashes of lights
Skillfully creating a campfire bedded with grasses
Around the base, stones are set to contain

From one rolled bundle
That has been tied carefully with thin strips of rawhide
Is opened and rolled out gingerly.
He has gone through this routine many a year
But this year they hold more meaning.

The first holds his finest Fringed Buckskin Leggings
Adorned in shells, bells, beads, and small feathers.
Made by his wife some forty years back
A Breast Guard adorned in feathers, beads, and Bear Claws
Armbands embedded with precious jewels and his Ceremonial Pipe.
He now dresses, each piece blessed as he goes along.

The fire is started with dry prairie grass and flintstone
Then his aged hands cup the sparks
He gentle blows upon the smoke
And waits for the red embers to glow.
Bigger sticks are added, then you hear the crackling
Of the green wood releasing its moisture.
There is such a sweet aroma as the fire takes hold.
Larger pieces of wood are added to sustain its hold.

Now for the second blanket,
It's laid out and rolled open as he says a prayer.
This is his crowning glory
With one hand holding the heavy beaded top band
It is unfurled to the length of six feet plus
He whirls it around, so it blows open in the breeze
With all the pride in his soul, he places it upon his head
This is his Headdress, A War Bonnet like no other
Made with several hundred Eagle Feathers.

He now retrieves his pipe,
Made from the antlers of his first Buck taken
Now he steps proudly to the edge of Devil's Peak
Lights the pipe and blows the herb to the four corners.
The sky has turned golden with the horizon set on fire
The clouds are billowy and laced with the fire of the setting Sun.

Truly this land was painted by the hand of the Gods.
Hence the given name, Painted Canyon
Across the plains, down in the valley, and across the river so wide
This blessed land holds the colors green, blue,
Purple, red, orange, amber, and hues are not named.

Dressed in Full Regalia
Holding his pipe in both hands raises his arms to the Heavens
A breeze from behind begins to blow,
It's just strong enough for the leaves on the trees
To sound as if their rustlings are enchanted and join in song.
Across this fiery red and orange painted sky
A flock of geese add their song in chorus and lend their beauty
To this painted miracle across the canyon.

This is when the Old Chief raises his voice to the heavens above
He loudly trumpets his name
"I am Chief Running Wolf"
There is an echo in the distance to confirm his name.
He pauses, for the clouds have moved in a formation
Within these billowy clouds, a faint vision begins to form
Within this forming vision,
His aged eyes can see the outlines of the
(Guardian Spirits)
The Warrior
The Wolf, The Bear, The Eagle
The Buffalo.
"This is good medicine" *he murmurs.*

In the distance, far beyond the Black Hills
There is the faint sound of drums
Made by the thunderous hoof beats of the Buffalo
Running across the plains by the thousands.
They are in slow motion across the horizon.

Running Wolf then speaks again,
He calls out to each Guardian Spirit
As he raises the ceremonial pipe to honor each one
He is speaking to the Four Winds that they also represent.

"Oh, Mighty Forefathers"
"Now I stand before you, as I have so many times before.
Only this time my heart carries a heavy burden.
I am saddened that each and every day
We the People of this land, Our Home, and Your home
Lessons by one every day."

Just then the fire makes loud crackling noises
Sparks rise and jump into the air overhead.
He begins again.

"The young ones, our future, has lost their way
No longer do our children wish to know the ways of our Nations
There are those who try to teach the tongue of our People
It falls on deaf ears."

He pauses once again; he takes a deep breath.
He needs to gather the strength to carry on his plea.

"The Women cry, and the elders have given there all
They teach the old ways, in hopes it carries to the future.
Our crafts and livelihoods gather dust and cobwebs

"You, The Wolf, once free to game and to run the four winds
Are but one or two where once there were thousands.
The mighty and powerful Buffalo
How you use to be seen roaming miles wide,
As far as the eyes could see, are but a hand full and are caged."

The Prophesy of the White Buffalo!
Has been born, Our People are waiting for the Miracle.
The Eagle once stood on cliffs and treetops across the land
As the symbol of freedom and strength.
Their cries are no longer heard across this land.
All that I say to you this very day is true."

"The Beaver is gone; the Wild horse is no more.
My heart is sad, as a Chief, I can do nothing
As a Nation we are caged, We the People have NO rights.
Guardian Spirits what can We do?"

Chief Running Wolf lowers his head.
He now begins to sing in his native tongue
Delayed echoes seem to bounce from hill to hill and valley below.
The sound and the beat of the drums begin to swell.
The breeze now has turned to wind, swirling the smoke
Around his body and twirls overhead.
This is a spiritual moment up on Devil's Peak.

"I am too old to do any good any longer
And my time is at hand.
Soon a new Chief will take my place.
This could be a good thing,
Change is the way of the wind.
I will fade into a lost land as our People have."

"I have lived for more than eighty years
And I have seen life as it is.
We the People, The Human Beings
Have seen pain, misery, and cruelty
By the hands of the White Man.
We lie in the streets like bundles of filth
Hungry is felt and there is singing in the churches
What messages are being taught in there?"

"Even our young men and women die or get mangled
Fighting in a country that isn't even theirs
This is our country; we need to fight for our land.
We need to fight for the right to live!
I know of warriors who have died in the arms of their brothers
Before they passed on, it was their eyes
Asking the question,
Why?"
The old chief lowers his head, takes a breath

"I don't think they were asking, why they were dying.
But why they had lived at all?

I say unto you now!
For to See life as it is now
I would rather see it, as it should be!

Has Anybody Here, Seen My Old Friend

{There are moments in one's life, regardless the age, where that moment or moments change a person's way of thinking and their lives profoundly. She did this for me.}

"Mankind must put an end to War Before War puts an end to Mankind"

John F. Kennedy

*A remarkable, frail but powerful old black lady walked out on the stage of the **"Ed Sullivan Show."** It was airing a crossed the United States of America and the free world. You could have heard a pin drop as she sauntered up to the microphone. It was plain that the mike stand was taller than she. She stopped and stared at the stand. Then with that perfect comedic timing of hers, looked out at the audience and shrugged her shoulders smiled her toothless grin, and burst out laughing as so did America. Like the Professional she was, lowered the mike stand to her height and said, **"Hello, I'm Moms Mabley."***

The lights dimmed and a spot faded in on Mom. The music began. Once again there was total silence in the audience. As I truly believe was in every household in America. We were waiting for her to do her to sing the song that rose her to the top of the music charts. This amazing woman with those wonderful big eyes set the scene as if there were people walking by the blind. Moms began...

*"Has anybody here, seen my old friend **Abraham***

Can you tell me where he's gone?

He freed a lot of people,

They say the good die young

I turned around and he was gone.

*Has anybody here, seen my old friend **Martin***

Can you tell me where he's gone?

He freed a lot of people,

They say the good die young

I turned around and he was gone.

Has anybody here seen my old friend **John?**

Can you tell me where he's gone?

He freed a lot of people,

They say the good die young

I turned around and he was gone

Has anyone here seen my old friend **Bobby?**

Can you tell me where he's gone?

He freed a lot of people

They say the good die young

I turned around and he was gone...

It's needless, but I'll say it anyway. There wasn't a dry in that Theatre and or in every home across America. She received a standing ovation as televised A close-up of Mom showed the tears down her streaming down that wonderfully aged face. A black woman sang about the men that touched her heart and soul as did every American watching that night.

These men of American History were cut down in their prime of life. Men with vision and a loving their country. A country that fell in love with these men and their outstanding visions. When this old black lady sang this song, the nation felt her passion and patriotism. I can honestly say that each of these men made an impact on my life. But that sweet lady stole my heart that night. These are moments in time that change the course of men's lives forever.

"Ask not what your country can do for you, ask what you can do for your country."

John F. Kennedy

Martin Luther King

Abraham Lincoln

Robert "Bobby" Kennedy

Haunt Me No More

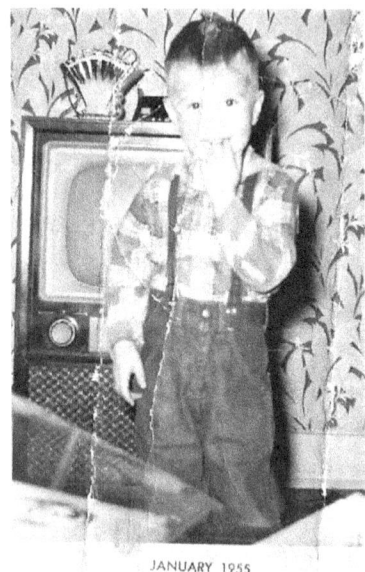

JANUARY 1955

My mind is dwelling in the dark somewhere

Alone and feeling as though all hope is gone

Encircled by dark dreams in a non-reality

Confusion filtered like the sands in an hourglass

Thy heart bleeds punctured by arrows of pain

Driven on a hi-way of loneliness, shot by torture

Never-ending, stagnate backwash of hopelessness

Forever draining into the void of redemption

Eyes wide shut, staring into the face of a decision

Flashes of light caught in the corner of my sight

Crashes into a wall of uncertainty, blinding hope

Time stands still, flashes of reflections haunt me

I sit alone staring forward, down a ribbon of ink

Rock steady is the day as family members go by

They say their goodbyes, all but he whom I find not

He gave truth and wisdom behind the eyes of blue

His soul is warm beyond compare, what is this?

There he is hair white and aged hands wrinkled

Rocking calmly in wicker of white, a pal at the side

Behind those eyes of blue, I now see the wisdom of old

With you I will rock steady, it's the right thing to do

Down the lane, something dark is coming this way

There is a breeze, he stands, walks down the lane

Like so many times before, to fetch the mail today

He returns reaching forward I offer my hand to him

He pauses for a moment, looking deep into my eyes

Speaking tenderly and flirters as he steps beside me

"I know these hands so well, where you have been?"

At that moment, a flash of light in my mind's eye

Dazed, suddenly I'm racing down a ribbon of ink

Pain, I'm feeling pain as bright as light can become

In slow motion, my steps match the hast around me

Uncertainty now melts into understanding as I focus

Realized the crash was silent to me, blurring my sight

I rub my eyes and things around me become clearer

Moving toward me are arms reaching to come closer

Through this calm, a tunnel of light is before me

As the story has been told, my loved ones greet me

The pain, uncertainty, and chaos of decisions matter not

This tunnel takes from leads to the promised land

I turn and look down at that endless ribbon of black

I see myself, aged and alone with the closing of sight

I feel myself being lifted, carried away, and no longer in pain

Only darkness in my haunted dreams of once before

I SHOUT OUT LOUD INTO THE DARKNESS

"HAUNT ME NO MORE"

"HAUNT ME NO"

"HAUNT ME"

Haunt Me No More

HE IS MAN

He stands in the shadows of himself
He smiles and the shadows come forth
He gives a glance that travels from soul to soul
He makes you weak and creates uncontrollable desire
He stands handsome and clean
He is Man.

He has sculptured hair and tempestuous eyes
He's a dancer with style, both in form and movement
He flirts beyond his own understanding
He has flair and personality with a touch of humility
He walks into a room and heads turn in his direction
He is Man.

He will go out of his way to help others in need
He respects those that give respect in return
He is the first to arrive and the last to leave
He could never hide for he stands out in a crowd
He is young at heart and always warm in manners
He is Man.

He has feelings and needs to express himself
He can be a friend beyond the meaning of a friend
He loves all that God has set forth upon this earth
He is a dreamer that holds high the passion of the heart
He can make you believe in yourself when times are rough
He is Man.

He at times feels the darker side of himself
He has walked into mistaken paths of Forget-me-knots
He steps forward in the cold without reservations
He displays a hard exterior when needed be
He parties beyond understanding and gives nothing to reason
He is Man.

He cares not to stop and smell the roses
He has demon eyes that look right into yours and captures all
He will glance in your direction and demand your attention
He will take all you have in life and laugh at your demise
He moves in and out of the corners of your soul
He is Man.

He takes your strength leaving you with weak despair
He is cold, heartless, vindictive, and insensitive
He cares not for your shortcomings
He stands in the dark waiting to take your last breath
He feeds you with fear and hate and the unknown
He is Man.

He is both identities and can stand in the shadows as one
He stops himself from walking into the future
He holds back the will to seek answers
He can face himself and study who is the stronger
He sees the truth within his own eyes
He is Man.

He needs a friend; He wants the strength to stand tall
He needs to guide himself toward himself
He needs a goal, a shining star to reach for
He wants a path and someone to walk beside him
He is his own twin in the garden of good and evil
He is Man.

He looks into the mirror of life and takes a bow
He collects the parts and creates the sum of the whole
He can be fun; he can be wild, and he can come or go at will
He must think before doing, He must reason before reacting
He must be able to say NO when the time calls for it
He is Man.

He will recreate himself into an everyman on the street
He will take what is there, not what others say there is
He is the only one who knows the other side of his shadow
He's found the two halves, now he must fuse them together
He has become a person who reaches for the highest star
He is a
MAN!

Hear The Beautiful Whispers

Moonlight descends over Heaven's Plateau of garnet cliffs

Giving off angelic whispers are the flowing ribbons of silk

Clouds of fog form atop rivers across the green valley floor

Rapids form like dancers in a mixture of adagios to the sea

Memories etched in patches of sunlight across canopies thick

Rich vines weave their running whispers, a century of growth

Glistening light across sparkling dew anew and equally fresh

Picturesque landscapes, paramount, capture the lost horizon

Hear the whispering of the lost and found dictated on the wind

Secrets dare thee tell, for the dragonfly's gossip by the waterside

Butterflies harbor their whispers atop tall reeds in the river mist

They kiss secrets in the fragrance of Lavender's sweet divine

Buried deep within the valley green a world timed by nature's call

At dusk rises an army of winged lanterns magically light the valley

Airborne is the fireflies launching their fiery flashes to lure a mate

Flashing desires rise, and fall forever in nature's timeless booty call

Mother Nature at dusk paints her masterpiece of glorious colors

Added to her timeless beauty a soulful symphony of nature sounds

Created like an arrangement of floral beauties, songbirds a plenty

You simply need to close your eyes to hear the beautiful whispers.

Hello Operator

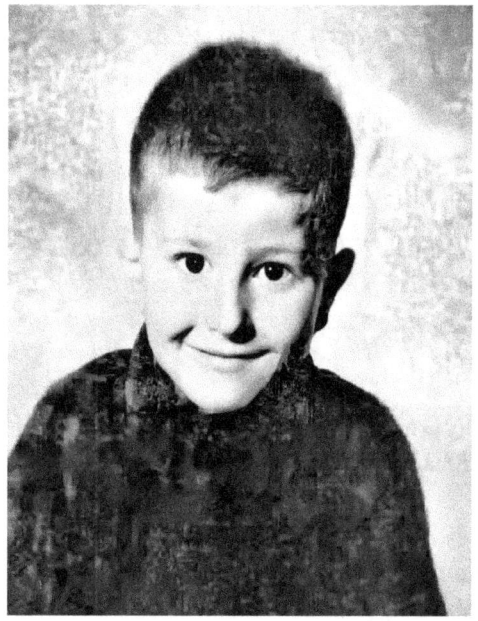

RING~~~RING~~~RING~~~

{You can hear a click-over}

{Pause for a second}

{Then you hear a mature, business professional, a woman's voice}

"Operator Speaking, may I help you?"

{Now you hear the distinct voice of a little boy about 5 years old. He has big hazel eyes, blonde hair, and a beautiful angelic face. His voice is as sweet as the purring of a kitten. He is mild-mannered but has importance about him.}

{The little boy speaks into the phone}

"Hello, Operator",

~~~[pause]~~~

"Would you please help me make this call? The last time I saw my mommy, she was on her knees praying and daddy was sitting in a chair bent over with his face in his hands. I didn't have a chance to tell mommy and daddy goodbye. *{Taking a deep breath}* I don't want them to be sad, *{a hurried pause}* and I don't want them to cry either! Listen, Operator, ring the phone real loud.

Please let it ring until they answer it, Okay? Tell them it's me...~~~[pause]~~~Operator? I'll wait right here on this cloud. I miss them so much since I went away. My number is 301-555-9192."

{The Operator is quiet, as she manages to take a quick breath. She has the little boy wait long enough to make the connection...You then hear}

[click over]

{pause for a few seconds~~~then the operator returns saying,}

"Go ahead, sweetie. Your mommy and daddy are on the line and so excited to talk to you... You are going to hear a click. That's when you can begin talking. Bye, sweetie."

[~~~Pause, Click, the little boy begins to speak~~~]

"Hello mommy, hello daddy, so glad that you are home! Because I wanted to tell you how much I love you both and to let know I'm not alone...

I like it here mommy...It's so pretty, just like you! Someday you will come and stay with me. I know you and daddy will love it here. When your souls are...set free...

I sure do miss you mommy and daddy and I think about you two every day. Just look to Heaven above. Remember it's here I must stay.

Since I now live here in Heaven, cause from you I had departed. You have only to think of me. I'll listen to your heartbeat.

For I know that's where you keep me. All the love you hold inside. I can almost see your faces as you think of my love.

Mommy and daddy, I must go now. I won't forget your love for me. So, wipe those tears away and give me a smile. We'll be together again...You'll see!

Bye,

I love you always and forever"

~~~Click~~~

~~~~~~~~~~~~~~~~~~~~~~~~~~~~~~

"Hell's Half Acre"

Hell's Half Acre, *these are the words written in the form of a letter to my sister before she was laid to rest. She was tragically killed in a car accident at the age of twenty-two. I had asked the Funeral Director if I could have five minutes alone with my sister Bonnie before the doors were opened for family and friends to enter and pay their last respects.*

I walked up to where she lay and put my hand on hers. She was so cold and so stiff to my touch. My heart and my soul were just as cold and stiff. Staring at her lifeless body I began to talk to Bonnie. I wanted to believe with all my faith, that she was listening to my words. I needed to tell her goodbye, the only way I knew how to. I was filled with dead and decayed emotions. I had to let them come forth. Love, anger, hate, joyful memories, sadness, and all the tears "we" experienced up on "Hell's Half Acre". If I could have colored that moment, it would have been in shades of black and blue with slashes of blood red. Standing there and realizing this would be the last moment I would be able to touch and see her. My heart was ready to explode. My soul was on fire. After all the horrors we witnessed and experienced as kids growing up over the years, it was very clear, at least to me, that our lives were doomed from our first breaths of life up on "Hell's Half Acre".

This mental and heartfelt letter to Bonnie said everything I needed to say as a brother to a sister. I never knew her feelings and thoughts about me as a person, as a brother. But a week before her death, she set on the floor of my apartment on East 3rd street and finally expressed the words I had longed to hear. She said, "I want you to know I love you. Thanks for sheltering me from dad. Yes, I've known the struggle you have gone through in this town. I took a lot of shit from kids at school about you. I can't lie, Lee, I didn't understand at the time how destructive their words were for you. I made choices that drove a wedge between you and me. I wanted nothing to do with you. Yet, you protected me from dad's evil advances. Lee the weeks before mom's death, I watched dad's transformations attack you and mom. I'd saddle up Apache and ride away as fast as I could from that hell house. We both dealt with our own hells in our own ways. I know your Bi-sexual/Gay. I wanted no part of that, and my so-called friends were out for you to teach you right from wrong. Who and what do you do with your life, is your business? You're my brother and that's good *enough for me." Looking down at her face, my words came from the only place left that still had a spark of life in it. My heart is so tender, and my soul is forever tarnished. We shared all our youth in a world of hell, demons, and shadows. Our lives can only be handled as* **"Tender and Tarnished".**

Heroes, Everyone!

It's more than we dare to count

With more being added every day

*The death toll from this hapless **"War"***

Is by far too high of a price to pay

We were convinced by false words

From those in whom we put our trust

We're told for the safety of our country

That invading Iraq was a must

But our nation doesn't seem any safer

And many feel that things are the worst

As we lose more friends around the world

And become the land to hate and cruse

Our troops are the bright shining stars

Sent to fight for liberty and to risk their all

Each of them is our true-life Heroes

Men and Women, standing proud and tall

Most of them are only kids

The way wars always seem to be

The young are sent to fight and die

For the sake of Democracy...

But as the body count keeps growing

And the truth becomes clear

People and troops are finally asking

"What are we really doing here?"

The Taliban are coming back

And Osama still has his plans

We should have finished what we started

When we went to Afghanistan

But we diverted our attention

And caused another breeding place

For all kinds of terrorists and nuts

The scourges of humans

Maybe sanity will soon prevail

And let us hope it's not too late

To end this and bring the troops home

Before they know that deadly fate

No matter how each of us feels

About the do's and don'ts polities of war

We've sacrificed enough Americans

For the answer to, ***"WHAT FOR?"***

Let's bring them back and honor them

And not forget when the war is done

Treat our Veterans with dignity and pride

*And as **"HEROES",** each daughter and son*

For all of those who gave their lives

To fight for each child, husband, and wife

Americans must hold their heads high

Heroes sustain our freedom and life.

His Lies and The Darkness

{A Predators Gospel}

He said to come into my dark haven

I remember his words so well, **"Let me keep you safe**

And I will give you an everlasting kiss,

That your soul will be nurtured."

Then he placed an eerie black satin robe

Around my chilled body placing a kiss of fire on my throat

I was hidden from the world for a long time

He had promised to cover my sins.

He made me feel excited about a while

Then time became longer and darker

However, solitude and being alone

Did not feed the hunger of my wicked needs.

He said, **"You're safe and secure with me."**

His promise to change me never came to pass

I was hidden and his to feed upon in this darkness

That's where he controlled my every move.

I wanted to feel the warmth again

Only the rays of the sun could do that for me

This dungeon grew darker around my desires

From within I knew I was dying and rotting slowly.

I did try to escape once when he had left to feed

Only to have my plans foiled by an early return

With fire in his eyes and an evil stern voice, he grabbed my throat,

"You will obey my every command!"

For the first time, I was truly frightened

I will find a way to plan an escape

I knew deep inside I had to keep trying

One day I will be freed of his damnation.

However, that day never came to pass

I was a fool to believe it would be possible

That I could ever escape the darkness

And the cold grip he has on me.

I can't put it into words

How I allowed him to control me,

I was weak from the start and very foolish

All the cat and mousing, lead me to believe he would change me.

After all this time, sitting here in the bowels of hell

Hopeless, dejected, and weighed down in waste

Do not believe his words

And hid the promise of the night.

He knew that if he ever would honor his promise,

To change me and allow me to die

That is when I'd rise to walk into the night as he does

He would no longer be able to control me.

I say to you, make sure you stay in the light

Please, I beg you not to follow my lead with foolish sins

Once the black satin covers your body

Your soul will never be free of his lies and the darkness wins.

His Name Was "Desire"

Here I am amongst an ancient maze of Catacombs. Nearly hidden within the shadows of the forgotten. Overgrown dying shrubs, creeping vines, broken tree trunks over centuries. The only living creatures are the rats, spiders, and snakes, all search for a meal. I was entombed in a prone position. With my hands, feet and neck chained. Fasten to the bottom of this rotting coffin, encased in stone. Some five to ten years back the Catacombs were rocked by a violent earthquake that tossed, thrown, and buried under tons of earth and debris. There were many aftershocks. Then it was quiet for a while. Then another earth-shattering quake struck in the same place. Whereupon my stoned enclosure split apart. It was just enough to see light about ten feet away. The tossing and jarring of the earthquake had loosened the chains that had bound me for ions. It had given me a new intervention of the possibility. That I may walk among the living once again.

*I struggled to free myself when an aftershock lifted the tomb pushing it on its side. I began in earnest to pull at the restraints around my neck. The chains around my feet gave way after a strong kick. It took a little longer to free the metal collar from around my neck. I took both hands on the collar and snapped it like a twig. The restraint was no longer. I was free once again. I clawed with fury at the opening of my containment. An explosion of power burst through the dust, dirt, and stone. I was covered with years of muck and filth of ions. My body was withered, dry skin over bone. I made my way out of the ruins into the fresh night air. I just stood there. The air was waking my long captive body. My flesh was feeling energized. From tomb to open air brought a tribal erg deep down inside this renewed body. One that had been long forgotten for me to maintain my sanity. I felt a power surfacing, hell let's call it **RAGE!** There was a fire burning in my eyes. I wanted out of my damned prison. Finally, this day had come. Being renewed and standing in a world that was open to me, gave way to memories of the past. With all the power I could muster from within and the fire of hatred, along with an increasing hunger burning deep inside, I knew I had to feed as soon as possible. Then my regeneration would be complete. I stretched forth these limbs to shed all decay. I let out a primal scream that equaled the quake that set me free. I wanted to vomit all the past poisons. Everything had to be released from my body and mind. This now was my rebirth to start anew!*

*First on my agenda was feeding. After all, I have emerged from the bowels of the earth. I'm parched and long to drink from the river of life. I want to taste its sweetness. Feel it flowing down my dry throat. With each pounding of my prey's beating heart pumps the blood through their veins to my waiting kiss. Until my thirst, my hunger is satisfied the river of life is my only need, my drive for fulfillment. To control the rage and anger I will do what I must for survival. A rodent, rabbit, or deer will make do until a human cross my path. It was the jealousy and anger of a blood-thirsty bastard that cornered me and in a fit of rage drained the life out of me. Not completely at first but just enough to put me on the brink of death. He leaned over me and whispered in my ear. **"Do you*** *want revenge?"* Looking into his red eyes of lust, I nodded yes. He bit his wrist and guided it to my mouth. Drop after drop fell upon my lips. I grabbed his arm placed his wrist into my mouth and sucked like a leech on fire. Finally, he jerks his arm away from my greedy intake. ***"ENOUGH!",*** as he fell back regaining his strength. I lay on the ground tossing and turning with awful pain throughout my body***. "I'M ON FIRE YOU BASTARD, WHAT IS HAPPENING TO ME?"*** I screamed in anger. In his weakened condition, laughing he said, ***"Your Dying".*** Then sections later, I took my last breath. Apparently, Anton, that is his name, buried me in the darkness of a French Forest. I slowly rose from the shallow grave he placed me in. My arm broke the surface and Anton was there to pull me free. The world around me was alive in sound. I faced Anton with destruction in my eyes. I took both hands and drove them into his chest. He was propelled hundreds of feet backward. My strength was amazing. He returns my action in a flash. He was my maker, and he controlled my every move. He was the teacher. Anton guided me through my first feeding. It wasn't long before we worked in unison to capture our prey. Together we travel ed through time. He was my mentor, friend, and lover. In 1920, we were in a speak-easy enjoying the music and pretending to be human. That is where all hell broke loose on me. An amazingly handsome man in a black tux caught my eye. His beauty was sensual. Tall, built like an Adonis. Slick black hair and a smile to die for. I was very surprised to see him move through the crowd and placed himself in full view of my sight. Anton was elsewhere searching for our next prey. Feeding time was past due. I couldn't take my eyes off him. I watch as he was approached by many women and men. He was cordial to all. Between greetings, he always turned his attention to me. He took the last drink from his martini glass. He put it on a table next to him. He made a gesture to follow him. I looked around for Anton, he wasn't around. I knew I shouldn't follow this guy. I was compelled to do so regardless of the consequences. There he stood at the end of a long hallway. I stepped forward to meet him. I watched as he stepped into a door. Making my way to the door I saw standing in the shadows of the room. He said, ***"Shut the door behind you."*** I stepped in and closed the door. I watched as he removed his jacket. ***"Don't be shy,"*** as this beautiful man stepped toward me. Little did he know that shyness wasn't a part of a vampire's demeanor. ***"My name is Christof."*** I in kind said, ***"I'm called Desire."*** He walked up to me. He brushed the back of his hand on my cheek. ***"You're a very handsome man"*** he whispered***. "You feel cold my friend, no matter we'll warm each other up for sure."*** I wanted to feed on this stud in front of me. However, I wanted to see how far this moment would go. Christof took a step back. He unbuttons his shirt one button at a time. When he finishes, he then pulled the shirt from his pants. He removed the shirt and set it across his jacket. Before I was the Adonis I knew had to be under those clothes. His tanned muscular chest was simply amazing. I had to touch him. I moved my hands across his massive pecs and down his rippled stomach. He was hairless and smooth as silk. I can't lie, I was seriously turned on. I wanted to make love to him. There I stood and Christof reached over and removed my jacket. Opened my shirt and kissed my chest. He rolled the shirt over my shoulders, stepped behind me, and removed it from my arms, lifting the tails of the shirt from my pants. Christof put his arms around my waist gently pulling me up against him. Sexy would not describe the scene. I'm six-foot-two and he had to have been six-foot-five. My cold body felt his warmth and that was intense for me. He turned *me around to face him. Christof's huge hands cupped my face. He leaned forward and kissed me as I had never been kissed before. I melted in his wake. He slowly kissed his way down my chest, putting a little attention to my nipples. He continued down my rippled stomach darting his hot tongue in and out of my navel. On his knees, he looked up at me with a coy smirk. Then proceeded to open my belt, unbutton my pants pulling the fly down. I am considered dead, but the body still functions as if alive. Like a bomb going off, the door blasted off its hinges flying through the room. It was Anton. He came in and there I stood, Christof on the floor. Anton grabbed Christof by the throat lifting him off the ground. I rushed over to help Christof, but before my first step could be taken Anton snapped his neck with one hand. He dropped Christof and turned his rage toward me. It's not a pretty sight to watch to anger vampires going at each other. Fangs extended and fire in the eyes. My maker was stronger than I. His rage engulfed me to the point of a blackout. Long story short, Anton had chained me to my coffin and entombed us both in stone. When I came to the horror of his jealousy and rage were apparent. He was the blood-thirsty bitch that entombed me for all time. If still alive, my revenge will be calculated perfectly.*

I turned to the north of the cemetery. I heard the rustling of leaves along the ivy-covered stone wall. Sounding as if someone were walking nearby. The leaves were swirling around in a circle. Gathering from the bottom, rising and up into a column. There before me within this column of leaves was a flashback, I remembered many times like a reoccurring dream. I've had a very long-time remembering nightmares as I lay in my prone position. It will never end until I can take my revenge. Erase Anton from my mind, the maker that forsaken me. A maker always knows where the one is that he made. Anton was nearby. I could feel him as if it were yesterday. I must feed to recharge my strength and so I did. I went over the wall and discovered a lonely woman walking along the sidewalk. She never knew what hit her. I drained her completely. Fire rose in my muscles, giving me the strength, I craved. I went back over the wall and to the entrance of the catacomb where Anton sealed my fate for eternity. I stood in the shadows very aware he was near. The column of swirling leaves was a message that he was aware of my escape.

I remember that night before he turned me. I was standing at the edge of Central Park in New York City. I stood under a streetlamp lighting a smoke. When I felt a slight breeze on my back. Then the sharpest burning pain in my neck. My heart was beating so fast. It amplified a pounding in my head. I struggled against my attacker without success. He was too strong. Every beat of my heart I could feel the flow of my blood being sucked. No matter how hard I fought I was now wilting in his arms. I went in and out of wavy blackouts. I felt my life draining away as my heart slowed with every beat. I fell slowly to my knees still in his very tight embrace. He finally released me. Revenge has been on my mind all those years entombed by that bastard. Anton, I wait! This time my back will be up against this wall...

HIS ONLY FRIEND

{When your only friend is your own shadow}

*He was so tired; life wasn't worth the time of day. The knocks, belittlement, and abuse took their toll. He just turned twelve in an upside-down world. Nights were endless and the Shadows screaming, I was his only friend, I listened to his broken soul many times, and my hand grasped him in the darkness. I wrapped my arms around a soul needing warmth. We walked "**The Long Hard Road**" in near peace. That was the time his heart came alive with promise. Together we ran toward that great ball of sunshine. The warmth of light gave him a song of joy to sing. I shadowed his every move; I felt his pain holding on. That night I heard him cry out into the vast darkness, over and over, he cried for my hand in the darkness. His crying quickly turned to blood-curdling terror. I reached into the light finding his open-ridged hand. I pulled with all my might, but this time it felt different. He no longer fought like hell to escape his attacker. I wouldn't stop pulling, I was determined to save him. I braced myself with all my power to save my friend. Success, I found myself cradling this beautiful spirit. I will lighten your heavy heart; I am with you always. My words of comfort became his song of purpose. His dark world was no more, my friend had given up. It was exactly one day after his twelfth birthday that, his life in the dark dimension didn't matter any longer. He had slit his wrists after being brutally beaten again. A demonic presence now imprisoned his mind and body. I lay down beside him, melding together as one spirit. Together in complete silence, in complete stillness, I whispered like a summer breeze within our union, "**Wake, open your eyes for we journey together.**" By sheer will, our eyes opened to a world of "**Serenity.**" We stood facing down, "**The Great Long Hard Road**". Reaching his hand forward, I whispered, "**I'm with you.**" Warmth surged in our hands, and he sighed, "**We are one.**" His hazel eyes filled with tears as he hugged himself. He placed a kiss on his own hand, his soul cried freedom! Together with starting a journey anew through, "**Serenity.**" Never to know darkness again, for the spirit of light, had finally become this young boy's only friend...*

HI-WAY OF THOUGHTS

Confusion is in my memories
A hi-way that entwines and clover leaves to the back roads of my mind
Construction is at every turn
North, South, East, and West

The directions are never clear, yet yields are plenty

Confusion is like a blanket of early morning fog
Surrounding my early morning thoughts of the day yet to be
Turn to the right, turn to the left
Weave in and out of traffic is the routine every day

Where do I go, how close is the exit?
This must be a hi-way of despair
Over to my left and over to my right there are caution signs
Still, I drive onward and onward as the day is long

A never-ending ribbon of haze-mat
Dusty memories of good and bad
Speed limits give way to peddle to the metal expression
Homeward bound as the song goes

Now I race along, the fog has lifted
I travel on and on and no lights are before me
Confusion, for I believe I'm going in circles
Nowhere in my sight,

*Do I see a **STOP** sign?*

HOME
AMONG THE MANGROVES

HOME,
Picture my world tangled by the roots of the Mangroves
My mind lies beneath the roots, the roots so twisted below
Lying in animation trapped on a rack from medieval days
Under the water that rises and falls as the tides wash away

CRYING,
I want to walk the shore's edge at the end of my days
As far as my sight carries, creating watercolor memories
A few days are held sacred within my heart and spirit
That which God created, a housing supporting my soul

PRECIOUS,
The water rises above these roots with the rising of the moon
Grounded, flushing precious air back and forth over my body
Awakening of the realization that life must survive in my mind
Ions of repetitive flushing of water welcome the sands of time

DESTINY,
Take deep, long breathes to renew the fate that lies before me
Before I reach the arms of destiny, lying, waiting patiently
A mind's journey floats upon fresh mesh like that of gossamer,
Before the Royal Sabbath of dream-making and imagination

JOURNEY,
Rippling motion across the surfaces of the oceans and,
Against a sunset filled with hidden sorrows and secrets
Slammed against the deepest of desires against the cliffs
Swirling with the tides like a Hurricane of my days lost...

I AM THAT CHILD

JANUARY 1955

Who is that child of fading light, cradled by shadows?
Why is he so sad, so meek sitting alone amongst the deadly mushrooms?
Living but barely existing from day to day between harsh eyes
Has he ever experienced the true concept of "Worth"?

How could this child of light live in and out of the shadows that he fears?
Was it meant to be a curse put upon this candle with no flame?
Lost in a world of drunken abuse filled with questions that fade away unheard
His life is tragic, weaned prematurely, then discarded to the cannibals

The fear, the hunger, and the Creepers waiting to take advantage
Daylight offers nothing but illuminated evil of the coming darkness each night
What is education to a six-year-old, when the teacher is darkness
The need is for comfort, safety, and small bits of scraps to survive on

This is the child of light and of lost innocence
No fault of his own, yet the horrors are etched forever within his brain
Shadows have followed him, a constant dread that ticks within a dark clock
Who is this child of fading light, cradled in the arms of shadows?

The body and mind have aged way before their time
Scared, battered, beaten mentally and physically, unaware it's not the norm
Life had dealt him a world of horrors within a world of reality
Who was this child of fading light and lost innocence?
That child my friends was no other than I...

Silence is Deadly

I AM THY KNIGHT

"I am thy only knight in tender tarnish
Lovelorn-ed and smitten by thy beauty
Yet the touch of thy hand and I tremble inside
My heart beats so like the hummingbird
I imagine all thy suitors; I would have to feign off
Alone I stand, for it's I wish you to favor
Thy Lady surely knows the depths of my affection, my love
I shall write poetry that Minstrels shall weep over
Envious of thy lavish garden of words expressed
All Ladies shall surely quail of their content
As shall the Lords that compare to be equal to thyself
I love thee like the bees hath cherishes the flowers"
This heart I keep for thee alone
I shall always dive deeply into thy pool of beauty
It is these lips that will quench thy thirst
I am more than the flesh standing before thee
I am thy knight in tender tarnish" ...

I Dance for Me

I dance as if my body were the music and I have an engagement amongst the stars. Call me harmony. I am transported through time and space and sometimes beyond the stars. Drifting high in the stratosphere, I move as if each instrument dictates the movement to be expressed. Angelic voices play with my mind, singing in perfect pitch across the heavens. Where the stars have become musical notes. Emerging from reality to fantasy. There are times when a veil of music covers my body to give my soul the freedom to dance.

*I am the **"Star dancer"**. Dancing has taken me to a world where it's easy to chant my story. My feet seem to race across the morning clouds until they create the illusion as if my feet bring about the fiery sunset. So many times, the melody I hear beacons me back to reality. I am happiest when the music, the moment and the surroundings give me a reason to express myself. When my body no longer allows me to fulfill the essence within my soul. The memories of youth and the freedom I created for myself will dance on and on...*

I EXIST

I exist!
Hidden within a cloak of darkness
I calculate with precision
No heart do I have
I don't give a damn about mixed emotions
Stalking in the night is merely a playground
I lust with a depraved and lecherous mind
Within the shadows, my lust becomes a hunger game
Taking what is not mine only adds to the game I play
I creep, I crawl, I leer, and stalk my prey
I am concealed in the shadows
How black can the heartbeat be?
I laugh at the thought of it all
The night winds call to me
I give a silent howl to the full moon of desires
Seduction is my greatest talents
I am a master of taunting lies
I revival in the tormenting of your essences
My hunger is fed in all the acts I perform
I'm always lurking in the back of your mind
I calculate your every move
Depravity is my darkest companion
Where there is rage, I provide the darkest pitch

I Exist!

I Have Lost a Love

I have lost a love and it is tearing me apart

I can compare my emotions

Like the withered petals of a dying flower

Each individual petal drops one after the other

I am a man who cries for his loss

And not ashamed to admit it

Each tear represents a memory once held

A flood of past, present, and the lost future drowning in tears

It's never easy losing someone you love!

Unless it happens to you, I suppose

And after they are gone

It's very difficult to know

That they will no longer be around

That's the reason behind my silence

I have lost a love and it is tearing me apart

I feel as though I've been cast out

Alone into the fray, into the ocean

Into the deepest of the abyss...Still

To know that we will never talk again

Never see the one you love, face to face

Learning to deal with my own sadness

That's the main reason why I find life unfair

My deepest thoughts and emotions

It is extremely difficult to express

It's the feeling of living a broken promise

A dream that fades into the distance

I pray often for guidance

Because I know I must accept

That it was their time to be in Heaven...

"Still"

I have lost a love and it is tearing me apart!

I JUST GOT TO SAY

With a pen in hand, my paper awaits the words
A need compels me to write her once again, but
This mind of mine wonders and drifts aimlessly
No doubt I am lost in my thoughts of her today

Is she smiling that remarkable smile that melts me?
Does she remember the gentle touches of my hand?
Is there a tear meandering down her cheek of rose?
Maybe she misses me and wonders if I miss her

I wonder, is she reading a love letter once before
After she finishes it, does she clutch it to her heart?
Can she be thinking of a time we shared in the past?
When our love started to grow, dreams are dreamt

I wonder what she is doing to pass the time away
Maybe she is daydreaming in a wonderland for lovers
Maybe there might be a whisper gently spoken of me
Sent upon a gentle breeze calling my name, as I hers

So, pen in hand, talk of crazy love upon this paper bare
Create my hearts desires upon this sheet I now pen on
Let this heart sing with words she longs to hear from me
*I just got to say to the love of my life, **"I Love You!"***

I Lay My Cheek Upon

This heart of mine lies heavy in my chest

I walk across the sweet summer grass

Where we laughed, touched, and dreamed

It's so hard to believe it has been a year

I'm still confused and lost in your memory

There still was so much to say and do

It's been a year and my heart aches for you

I face today and tomorrow as I move on

How warm the sun is on my face right now?

The sky is as blue as your eyes wandered

Your energy was as fast as this breeze blows

I watched you for hours as your mind was at play

I wish I could explain how your life was mine

There were so many who adored you as well

If you only knew how many hearts, you touched

It's a shame that many will never know you

They say time heals all things, so say some

My heart is a twisted knot, and it hurts

I will go on with you always in my heart

Time, be my friend, and let me start again

I stand here at your resting place

Where all that's left is this stone monument

Plus, the memories held deep in this soul

I place my cheek upon your memory in loving tears

My Son...

I Say Goodbye

Today I say goodbye to my little one

How can I say how much I will miss you?

I have just a few things to say before I take leave

This I feel you should know

No light will ever shine brighter

No star, no lamp is brighter than your smile

Wherever I may travel

No town, city, or street has brighter lights

Always your laughter I will carry

This I will hold in my heart

These memories will always shine

For you always touched my heart that way

Though I kneel near you before I go

It won't be forever in time

Distance is but a flicker of your smile

That alone will bring me home

Your kiss reminds me to hurry back

Squeeze me tight like you always did

No these are not tears my little one

It must be something in my eyes

Make sure you always smile for me

Smile brightly so I find my way home

Always remember my little love

No matter how far away I am

I will be looking for your smile above

I do believe in Angels!

I Thank the Lord

Today is Thanksgiving. I stand here on the edge of goodbye. I question every day why should I thank thee. Answers were found everywhere I turn. Selfish was I, for why should I give you thanks for everything I've done myself? I get up every day and go to work. I break my back to keep a roof over my family's heads. I put food on the table for my wife and seven kids. Then came the time I had to hold down two jobs to make ends meet. Why, oh why should I thank thee? When the kids are ill, need new shoes and clothes. I'm to give you thanks for that. When I got laid off from work, was I to give you thanks for that? I think not!

When I went off to war in a country, I had no business to be in to start with, I fought for this country that I love. To be free and fight for liberty for all. When I was shot and laid bleeding in the mud, I am to give you thanks for that. When I came back to the states with one eye less and scarred from head to toe, I was told to give thanks to the Lord for I am still alive. That's comfort isn't it, Lord? I am to give thanks for my brother when he was blown apart before my eyes. There wasn't enough left to bury him with. Well, I thank thee, Lord...I thank THEE!

Today is Thanksgiving Day. I'm standing on the edge of goodbye. I'm taking a deep breath, Lord. Now I am thinking of my beautiful wife, my children, family members, friends, and that roof over our heads. I'm looking around and suddenly I start bawling like a baby. A river of tears flowed down my face when I thought of all that is my responsibility. I got to take another deep breath. Lord. Looking at my surroundings I see the worth of it all.

Dear Lord, I see the beauty in the land. All the open space above my head. The vast blue sky, the green under my feet. That, I am thankful for. I'm thankful for the chance to wake up each morning to see that beautiful woman lying beside me, and my amazing children. I'm thankful for that woman who stands beside me through thick and thin. My children are healthy and getting an education. Something I never had the chance to take advantage of.

So, Heavenly Father, I don't go to church and why should I have to, when right here in the open is your church? I speak to you here. You're in everything and everything is you. On this day, Thanksgiving, I was ready to say goodbye. For some strange reason, I started to talk to you. Those changed things, I suppose. I do need to give thanks for what I have. What do I have to be thankful for? My life. To go home and spend another wonderful house full of family and friends. So, Dear Lord, I thank Thee.

I WALK AWAY ON MY OWN

Writing this poem was therapy for one minute! You might ask why. I was downtown in Frederick, with a few friends from the Weinberg Center for the Performing Arts. We were rehearsing for a dance production to raise money for the Arts in Frederick, Maryland. We took a break for lunch. Walked out onto Patrick Street and headed for our favorite hangout to grab a bite to eat. That's when I noticed people who were so much in love. Locked hand in hand, giggling and kissing. It was the person I devoted my life to. "I Walk Away on My Own", was written several months later. I was sitting at my desk recalling that day. I was peeling an apple before I realized what I was doing. I had taken the peeling knife and etched the following words on my cherrywood dining table; "I Walk Away on My Own!"

Today you walked by, and it is I who greeted Mr. Lonely

All feelings inside of me drained to my feet

They seemed to follow you two, leaving me so lonely.

So, I closed my eyes in the hope it wasn't true

There you were hand in hand, my dreams began to vanish

Today was to be special for me and you.

I should have called your name out loud

Called you every name in the book, to show you my hurt

Just to ruin your moment floating in the clouds.

I opened my mouth to say, "So what's this?"

Not a nary word came forth, my heart was in my throat

I wanted to scream; my gut was hit with a fist.

It's amazing how fast emptiness can take its toll

I allowed you to break my spirit and dignity

A ten-year union, a home, a dream, you have no soul.

I took several deep breaths of freshly found air

I am standing strong; you're cheating and lying tell who you are

I'm not faultless, it is you that doesn't give a damn

I'll walk away composed, complete my agenda, and call it a day

Today it's I who will walk away from you

When you come home tonight, I will have one thing to say

"Guess who I saw today, I saw You"...

I Whisper Make Love to Me

The first time you lay beside me, I thanked the Lord above

I held you in my arms and there wasn't a care in the world

Never had I ever felt the tenderness of touch so like yours

With your head upon my chest, you heard my heart beating

I whispered, make love to me

Your warm gentle and tender kisses caused my body to shiver

The such pleasure was more than I could bear from one so beautiful

Together our bodies moved to a dance of seductive harmony

Our lips met with a caress of tenderness, then a hunger of need

You whispered, make love to me

I climbed upon your body, taking your hands above your head

I felt the beating of my heart racing, I had longed for your love

I held you down, looking into eyes of green to see your pleasure

I will show you the moon and stars as we travel afar on a comet

Just whisper, make love to me

Slowly and sensually, I invited you to dance the Rumba of love

Together the heavens are not that far away as we fly in tandem

In your eyes, I see flames of desire as we ride together up and up

In my arms, there is no greater pleasure than you and you alone

Together we whispered, make love to me

You maneuver yourself atop me and the friction drives me wild

I say whisper my name in my ear, then call my name out loud

Together, slowly we will dance and drift in and out of the clouds

Hold on tight for the feeling of the rapture has captured the two of us

Tenderly I whisper, make love to me

Tenderly we kiss for we are lost in the moment as we descend

I love watching you lying beside me as the river of desire drains

I run my fingers slowly up and down your sculptured body wilting

I finish with a kiss light as the fluttering of butterfly wings landing

I whisper to you, make love to me again...

I WILL ALWAYS REMEMBER YOU

Life gets so complicated far too often
Somewhere in our teens, the heart was fancy-free
Something about your glowing smile
The ease of your laughter
I will remember my first love

I still feel your arms around me
Tender, desirable, and secure
I remember the special moments shared
They were intensely romantic
I will remember the love

The way we hold one another up
When the times seemed too rough to handle
You gave me strength when I was weak
Your hair, your eyes, and your fragrance
I will remember you, simply everything

I fell in love at the drop of a hat
Sharing our lives was perfect and right
Then the shock of death turned my soul to stone
Memories will never fade into the mist
I will always love you

I see loving couples starting anew
I relate to young lovers with the stars in their eyes
To every lover's stolen kiss
Your memory is everywhere and that is why
I will always remember you...

If I Could, I Would

If I could have but one glorious dream in my life

And granted the ability to produce it each night

I would envelop you in my arms forevermore

Never to ever let you out of my sight

Together we'll walk hand in hand through this life

Good or bad, down the ever-intriguing mile

Climbing each mountain that's in our way

For our strength will conquer each trial

I'll give you a sunset, a sunrise, and a twilight' flight

We'll fly to the moon and dance throughout the stars

Then kiss the man in the moon just to watch him blush

We will catch a ride on a rainbow sigh to somewhere afar

If God would but grant me, my one ultimate wish

I would give you the world of blue and the stars that twinkle above

I'd stare into your eyes and tell you how much I care

You're my dream come true delivered on the wings of a dove.

If You Pray, Ask for Peace

Several years have gone by since terrorists struck New York City's Twin Towers. Time has flown by and it's hard to comprehend or even understand the madness that ensued. How can a person be so blinded by their faith and beliefs to end up hating their fellow man? Then take their own life and the lives of so many innocent people just to glorify a religious cause. Delivering an unbelievable terror, pain, agony, and grief to so many. One, two, three, and four planes killed thousands. Also destroying landmarks known around the world. 911 changed the lives of every American in that senseless attack. It is so unbelievably hard to comprehend that the man for whom master-minded his wrath against America! Over the years it seems that many more have chosen to walk along that deadly path of havoc and terror. Our world has fought too many bloody battles of greed and the hunger for power! Centuries of fighting over the control of land and people. Fighting in the name of Truth, Justice, Freedom, and GOD! Most foreign wars are fought over religion, land, and OIL! A one-man's control for it ALL!

911 will be remembered for the thousands of souls lost on that day In New York City, Pennsylvania, and Washington D.C. As sure as God has made little green apples, it's the age-old story of wanting more and more... **GREED! GREED! GREED!** *followed by insanity, and control in the name of whatever faith of the times. The world will forever change, yet somewhere in the corner of the world, the sound of a bass explosion is heard and felt. It touches the core of your body. This will be the destruction of* **"ALL MANKIND!"** *I say if you pray, for Christ-sakes, ask for* **PEACE!**

I'll Take the Greyhound Home

The music dances within my soul, I know time waits for no one

Lost somewhere between here and there, then again maybe not

Heartbeats and the moonlight reflect on the Angel of my dreams

I gathered only my most precious aspirations with a few photos

The rain begins to trickle, I sit on my suitcase with thoughts wet

After a short but steady rain, the sun returns to dry everything out

I watched the steam rise, I walk in a dream of my imagination

Why Not? I've nothing else to do until the greyhound runs my way

Daydreaming was short-lived for the sun dried everything in haste

A one-horse town, hell I owned the horse, could not afford a car

I turned eighteen three days ago, got into a fight with the old man

He a drunkard who had beaten Mom, my sister, and me all our lives

He killed mom, sis and I had had enough of his brutal way of life

It's my turn at life, the hell with him and everything that goes with it

My name is August, 6'4", blonde with emerald, green eyes, and a tan

I am without a doubt a country, born and raised with cowboy boots

The sun has nearly dried my clothes, I stood up from my short respite

I stretched my arms outward, rearranged my wet jeans over my thighs

Rocked back on the heels of my boots, pulled my shirt from my pants

Took it off, so that it might dry faster in the summer breeze kicking up

I opened my duffle bag, got my bandana out, and a picture of the one

It'll be tough to explain that I have taken the greyhound to wherever

He'll have to understand, that I must drink from the glass of change

My heart is with him, but I must give my dreams a chance to live

So many times, I was told, **"Boy with those good looks, your height,**

That body of yours will take you anywhere your heart desires to go"

Maybe modeling, that I would like to do, hell maybe some acting too

Another country boy goes to the big city to find his fortune and fame

If you don't have a dream, how are you going to have a dream come true

You must have a goal within your heart, or your soul will certainly die

If dreaming is all you have, dream on, reach for the stars, Why Not?

If I become lost and lonely, I can always catch the greyhound home.

Waiting for the Last Tear Drop to Fall

This is the last time I'm waiting on anyone
I've packed my bags; I've got a ticket for one
You're never here, you're always there, you never call
I'm waiting for the last teardrop to fall

In the beginning, you were a hero to me
What you have put me through, everyone sees
I guess you think I'm blind to it all
I'm waiting for the last teardrop to fall

I am tired of being lonely, night after night
When you are home all we do is fuss and fight
I'm holding onto something that will never stand tall
I'm waiting for the last teardrop to fall

Every night I watch you walk out that door
It's like clockwork, it's quarter till four
I know where you're going, you know what I saw
I'm waiting for the last teardrop to fall

This is farewell, I had to leave tonight
With all that has been said, you know it's right
I've cried so many tears, I've given it my all
I'm not waiting for the last teardrop to fall.

In An Old Man's Shell

So many memories are encased in an old man's shell

So many years have come and gone for this explorer

Once strong and stead-fast, now weak and frail

He needs constant care, and a loving push to keep active

He was sharp as a tac once, now lost in space

Always cold, so wrinkled and his hands shake a lot

He sits the days away somewhere in dreams

I watch each day how lost and confused he gets

I watch to study him in the garden, sitting all alone

He just stares forward as if searching for the answers

I walk to his side; I notice a tear down his cheek

Locked somewhere in his mind is the question, why?

At times his love overflows, then, "Who are you?"

Some days are good, but most days my heart breaks

He will talk all day long when his mind is at play

Suddenly his mind will go blank, then the day is lost

In that old man's shell is an extremely wise man

His heart is full of love, his eyes glow with the truth

On the day he was born, a Weeping Willow was planted

He'd sit under the Willow and tell me stories of when

Father time called him to walk forward anew

His mind comes and goes, and an aged body remains

In an old man's shell is the soul of a once-great man

I miss the man he used to be; I still love who he is now

What can a man expect, for age will certainly find you

When a man fades with time, he hopes something remains

To say, I was here, I dreamed, I loved, and had a purpose

He always said, "Dreams are all we have in life, so Dream"

I hope there is someone who remembers a fading man

This man's time on Earth should make a difference

To be remembered for the contributions a man has made

Life is merely a gift from God, housed in an old man's shell

IN LOVER'S TWILIGHT...
IN THE RHYTHM OF THE NIGHT

HE

Somewhere in Lover's Twilight of yesterday's romantic bliss
There are two clinging shadows beautifully etched on a wall
Holding each other, in truth trying hard to stand on their own
Clinging to moonbeams and flirting with the Man in the Moon

SHE

Their bodies dance within the light lifting senses out of sight
A kaleidoscope of hues mesmerizes and permeates the heart and soul
They dream in sacred metaphors in sync with Nature's Creator
A confluence of energetic passion insinuating their emotions

HE

Sensual lips dare a careless whisper between his light and dark
Igniting fire-flamed kisses in amber and red, tinting the horizon
Reflecting in their moist flesh as they caress the heat of passion
Their greeting of a bygone era with the flickering of a silent film

SHE

Along with the music of night winds playing through the swaying of trees
They caressed in passion's embrace the excitement that lovers share
Touching...igniting sensations...undressing souls as they lay under
A canopy of cosmic candlelight taking flight in the tease of night

HE

"Lights, camera, action!" posing just like Valentino in "The Sheik"
Willingly she embraces, poised with passion now in sensual form
Seductively she dances, "The Seven Veils" falling into his waiting arms
Whereupon the call of action begins an assault of tender kisses fair

SHE

Feel the caress of my cosmic rays and allow yourself to be amazed
Let all your receptors feel my heat only then will you be complete
It's your powers, "Oh Moon of Splendor!" My body's being invaded
By your invisible beams as this man on the moon seduces this woman

HE

The sweetness of her everything lies in a wake of royal honey nectar
Should I summon the God of old to intensify and cascade the stars
Where shadows dance to silent violins, for it's said love is only love
It is very easy to allow your imagination to hear heaven's symphony

SHE

He surfed into her heart on moonbeams plunging her soul all aglow
His verse never waned, taking her beyond where anyone could ever go
There's magic in his cells, in surrendering sigh, makes him a paradigm
There's no other love, never can be the same in this one moment in time

HE

Halt, oh lover's moon, don't rush to take your leave from midnight's sky
You are an orb of the light divine that embraces two people in a sweet caress
This extraordinary love unique, as an effervescent dance in the moonlight
Imprinting on skin with radiant heat, the state where true lovers are in

TOGETHER AS ONE

And together we lay on the softness of Mother Nature's hand-knitted guilt
One cannot help but feel wrapped and cradled in our mother's loving arms
I watch the rise and fall of fireflies against a carpet of velvety ebony sky
Each night does come and witness the breathing of Mother Earth herself...

A heaven-sent sign...in an ever-refined design...
In lover's twilight...In the rhythm of the night...

In My Solitude

Surrounded in ivory white satin

Stitched, pleated, and ironed just so

My head rests on a pillow of ever-soft satin

To lie here in open silence

In this bed of my own choosing

I now must sleep in.

In my darkness, in shadows, my thoughts linger

Cold and hauntingly lonely

My bedfellow be named,

REGRET...

What question might there be?

And what it brought to this night

Look closely, a tear-soaked pillow from the ache in my heart

Bringing shameful doubts of self-devotion

Alone in more than mere thought

Lying here in this silent night

I see an extended room filled with faceless shadows

Seated row after row, after row...

The feeling of four walls closing in on me fast

Like a wild horse

Racing around an endless track of my past regrets

Pillow be my sponge

The blinders I'm wearing please quiet my soul

I cry out loud!

Sink, oh Moon, Sink

Lower and lower

Into a world of mistakes

So that you can join me

And lie here in this bed made of silence...

I calculated the number of times I've crawled between sheets

Turned out that the lights

Finding myself on the other side of midnight

Saying, "Forgive my judgments"

Sometimes to recall my misfortunes

You would have had to lay beside me

To know my love

To know how I would make love to you

Is to truly know me

Know that when I am making love

We will kiss one another's, soul

I would have it no other way

Jumping in and out of beds is far too often bodies without souls

What a waste!

Silence...

My life was filled with chaos

My pillow holds a lifetime of tears

I am tortured in my solitude

For all that I loved is gone

Lying here in this bed of silence

I watch faceless shadows walk by where I lie

In morbid hunch

I expect no more or no less

My pillow holds a lifetime of tears

Lower the lid on this bed of forevermore

I've seen all the misery I care to see

Close and seal the lid

I have lived this life

Enough is enough

Regrets, like mine, will be laid to rest

This bed is made of silence

Will finally allow me to be alone

In my Solitude...

IN SEARCH OF
THE NEVER-ENDING STORY

There are many times in our lives when things get complicated
I easily could tell by your smile and your eyes; they give you away
Falsehood happenings weaved within the way you made love to me
Your soft, gentle way that your arms wrap me at the end of the day.

Life is only as complicated as we allow situations to fester around us
The stars that shine in my eyes every time I look at you, tell the story
The reality of my love is encased within my heart of hearts, so strong
It's you're comforting and caring affection that I hold dear as a blessing

When my world was falling apart, you could lift me up with your smile
I'd start laughing till I cried, and you would wipe away my tears with a kiss
I lost the strength to pull myself up and out of the gutter when I fell
I couldn't have cared less, I was weak, but somehow you gave me strength

Don't you realize that I needed to be needed by you and you alone
I needed to be the one to lighten your load, put purpose in your heart
To dry your tears, to shine a light into a world of darkening darkness
Use me for any reason in our lifetime, I am your season as ordained

I look upon a lovely face, I know everything was going to be all right
We took a walk in the park and all that was oppressive disappeared
Remember the faces of the people, it was so easy to see their secrets
Couples that are happy, some have a lover's quarrel, young and old

I adore and cherish our walks, for you too gave me strength and hope
Your love and your warmth give way to the easing of my deepest fears
I do remember the faces of those we met throughout our days together
Love and eternal warmth for their tender love shared with each other

When you were away, I swear I could hear you whispering my name
There was something deep inside of me churning emotions haywire
It's not hard to realize we were two lonely people with the same goal
In search of, "The Never-Ending Story" to belong, forced to let go...

I can't, I don't regret the love we shared when we were united as one
Because it was a love meant to be, the time we had together was total bliss
This love shared, "The Never-Ending Story" has now come to its ending
We shared a love that was meant to be and now we must go on separately

I thank God for the time we had together, giving each what was needed
You gave me the strength I needed, in return, I nourished your lost soul
Don't get me wrong, for I will always be thankful our paths did cross
It was meant to be this way; I have got to learn to live with the memories

Our love, our time together was a true heavenly blessing from God above
It was the apex of our lives that was needed to put meaning in our lives
We both know that we both could share the lessons learned over time
Loving deeper, soaring higher, finding what true soul mates are all about

I will forever keep you in this heart of mine
As well I forever hold the love we shared in time
For we have enhanced each other's lives!
We are soul mates forevermore and a day...

IN SILENCE, SO LIES MY SOUL

There is quiet on this summer evening
When the day finally yawns from its toll
My weary eyes slowly close and I listen
For that silence that lies within my soul

It is so peaceful and all so comforting
Allowing the mind and soul to connect
Enabling the day's activities for sorting
One by one in a cool and calming effect

When in limbo, I listen to my heartbeat
I feel life's blood flowing, surging quietly
Onward my mind, soul, and my heartbeat
A harmony of three comprised most of me

I brush my breast with summer's Jasmine
The sunset's red glow illuminates my flesh
Then twilight's curtain is drawn once more
As the day ends in silence, so lies my soul.

IN THE ARMS OF ANGELS

"It's Christmas Eve and this man is down on his luck, so many situations have dragged him down into the pits of despair. He is walking the streets of his hometown where he was born and raised. There is something different about his despair, he feels as though a shadow is following him. It's dark and a feeling of dread washes over him. The streets are barren this evening. It's 29 degrees, he worked hard all day, and he's hungry. His mind reflects on the fact that his wife of twenty-two years has taken their two children and left for good! She deserves a better lifestyle than he has or will ever be able to provide. However, she refuses to get a job to help support her lavish wanting. So, every week he hands over his paycheck to satisfy her. He is a good man doing the best he can. The feeling as if someone or something is following him intensifies. He suddenly turns, drawing his fists tightly. Ready to face and defend himself... He sees no one, nothing. There is a bench nearby with a streetlight close. He walks over and sits down. He sits in a manner of defeat. Bows his head, trying to hold back an ocean of frustration and loneliness. It doesn't help that it's Christmas Eve. He suddenly snapped his head around. He felt something very cold touch the back of his neck. There was nothing. He looks up, for the snow has started to fall. He thinks to himself, "How perfect, it hasn't been shown on Christmas in a very long time. Better yet it's on Christmas Eve. He enjoys the flurries slowly dancing about each other until the snow is becoming heavier and laying quite fast on the ground. It's getting late and his depression stirs him from the few moments of distraction that the snow had given him. Along the way home the snow is gathering in intensity and in inches. He looks up at the street sign, realizing he has walked completely to the other side of town from where he lives. The wind has increased, blowing the snow lateral. Of course, as he turns to head in the other direction toward home the snow is blowing in his face. It wasn't Billy's intention earlier to go home. But things change in our minds and hearts once we sit down to gather our thoughts.

*Billy is fighting the frigid wind when he feels like he is being followed or stalked. Billy turned around thinking he had seen a shadow ducking behind some bushes. He turns back and keeps walking, and that is when he sees a local church through the raging snow and wind. He was drawn toward the church. With these eerie feelings and the happening of shadows seen, Billy goes inside the church for comfort and warmth. If anyone was following him, at least he would be able to see them if they decide to be so bold as to follow him into the church. Billy removes his hood and gloves as he walks up the long aisle toward the alter riser. With each step, the weight of his problems ebbs up like a high tide rising. He falls into the front pew. He raises his head to see Christ on the Cross. He quietly mutters, **"WHY? FOR CHRIST'S SAKE, WHY?"** Billy now has a talk with his Lord and Savior.*

"Here it is Christmas Eve, the day you were given to the world. The greatest of all gifts to mankind. I want to tell you something and I hope it makes sense. Because it sure as Hell doesn't to me. Here I am, in your house, and to get here I have been carried along the way" *In the arms of the Angels.*

I have walked many miles, all these steps just to hold onto the beauty of the written word. My heart sees what clear can be. In the eyes of the Angels, all this lives in my own heart's reflection. In the arms of the Angels there within the deepest of my adoration contains what I hold dear. So many dreams unfold before me. The wondrous moments held so tenderly came together in a story form of never-ending hopes. In the eyes of the Angels, a legend has been written for those who have walked miles after miles in a heart so pure. For my eyes did gaze upon the beauty before me. So, like the most precious of gems so clear pure, and vibrant now overwhelm me.

Life sings a song so beautifully written when in the arms of the Angels. I did cry and my soul but did a search in vain. Yet it was never to be discovered. In the arms of the Angels, there is no limit to their love. My heart has found no boundaries. The voices of the Angels so soft, calm, and gentle made my heart weep. His love flowed through me like an endless river. Every tear rambled through Heaven trumpeting his glory. He opened his wings in glorious magnificence. There his heart opened to me and shined brightly. The warmth was just for me, the love was just for me. In the arms of the Angels, I traveled miles just to discover that fact. What I have wanted all along has been right inside of me all this time. My value, my worth is there to be tapped. Now I know what the feeling of being followed truly is. My shadow, the shadow of an Angel, my Guardian Angel. In the arms of the Angels, my worth was and is warmed by the light of love. I found in their light that my own heart does shine with such brilliants, my world is illuminated. In the eyes of the Angels, there is a place for me in Heaven. I am not alone, ever! For I am always in the arms of the Angels".

In The Wee Hours

{A deadly search to be loved}

With eyesight sharp as the blade of a razor. He saw the gleaming flesh of his first wanting desire of the evening. As she trotted near the alleyway where he was in waiting. He stepped out bumping into her. She fell back a few steps, gathering her balance. She didn't know if she should get ready to run or scream or call out for a Bobbie. Until she saw his handsome face. Stumbling a bit, he caught her arm keeping her from nearly falling to the cobblestones below. She was totally mesmerized at how unbelievably handsome this stranger was. She was stunned by the structure of his facial features. The richness of color of his amazingly emerald, green eyes. His hair was thick, shoulder-length, and Raven's black. So black it flashed a purple sheen as he moved in the moonlight. The stranger asked if she were okay. It took a second for her to recover from the spell she was under. She nodded with a sheepish smile answering, "I'm fine, thank you." Boldly she said, "Your eyes, your eyes...are..." He walked behind her placing both arms around her. He pulled her back into the shadows of the dark alleyway. Still, under this man's spell, he pulled her head back. At that very instant terror now showed across her face. For she saw what was truly behind those emerald, green eyes. "EVIL". With a left-to-right motion, he slashed her throat. It was quick as a bullet fired. His mark, for whatever reason, wasn't as clean. She had struggled violently which led to an unclean cut. Blood shot from her juggler like a fountain exploding. The killing was silent but bloody as hell as she slowly slides out of his arms. There she lay atop the moonlit cobblestones. Staring at her, he could see a reflection of his true self in her eyes. It was dark between the two buildings which made it easy to hear approaching footsteps. It was always quiet in the wee hours of early morning. The streets were covered in a thickening low-ground fog that seemed to crawl. It travels from street to street in the lower parts of the waterfront. There were only two types of women that would make their way through the streets. In the wee hours of London, it was the hard-working agents and women. Coming or going to work in the Pubs and or the Bakeries. Then there are the hardest-working ladies across all of London. "The Ladies of the evening". The whores, are battered, beaten, bruised, and taken advantage of by their pimps. And many times, the Johns themselves. This is a hard-knock life for these women working the streets of London. This stranger of ill-repute, pure evil has a heart of ice. His veins carry the blackest of horrors. He comes from the deepest of wells. On nights when the moon shines like a cold veil, the stranger hunts like a man. However, on full moon nights, the hunger of the beast roams the streets and alleyways. Becoming a Demon straight from the filthiest part of Hell. Bloodthirsty through and through. Lurking in the darkest of alleys for the wayward members of London's misfortunate. This creature's hunger for blood is endless. It goes for the throat of every prey stalked. The attack nearly beheads the victim. Making for easy access to the river of life. With a fiery gleam in its eyes and a contorted face, it straddles the victims. Once the hunger subsides, the transformation from one beast to the other is magnified two folds.

In the early morning fog, the creature lifts its head to the moon. In its hand, the instrument is razor-sharp and deadly. The stainless-steel razor catches a flash of moonlight. Reflecting in the fiery eyes of emerald, green. In that instant, he slashed her midsection. The anger is magnified as he rips her bodes from her body. It proceeded to gut her like a fish. It began to search through her open cavity for a certain blood-rich organ to feed the lustful hunger. Once it/he had located his prize amongst the woman's still moving intestines, rolling, and heaving over and under one another, he raises his blood-rich prize high into the air. He lowers the organ to his waiting mouth. The moonlight now frames the hideous features of this Demon's face. Bending his head backward, grasping the enriched blood-soaked organ and lowers it to his mouth. The organ still shows signs of warmth in the chilled night air His mouth is filled with hideous dagger-like teeth. His blood-dripping lower jaw has extended downward, and the upper teeth are extending as fangs. Squeezing the blood-soaked organ to savor the river of life as the fangs are inserted. He bites down on the organ, placing the large organ into his hideous mouth. Enjoying the to its fullest. It took two very large gulps to position the organ to go down. With the neck stretched backward, you could see the outline of the organ slowly moving down his throat. Standing over the woman he looks down at the prey. All attention was aimed at the woman's body between his legs. The London fog was creeping through the cobblestone streets and alleys. The fog had reached his feet. The temperature had dropped a bit more. The fresh kill warmth was steaming in the chilled air.

A slight breeze pushed the fog down the alley, covering the gruesome scene left behind. During the early mornings, the breeze blew in from the harbor arena on the east side. The Demon turned its head toward the street as if he had heard something. Through the growing fog, one would only see a ghostly figure at best. Within minutes he had transformed back into that unbelievably handsome man. He looked about with his emerald, green eyes checking the street for signs of life. He reached down with his right arm and placed it around the lady prey. Scooping her in his arms and disappearing through the foggy dark alley. Headed back to where demons' dwell. There will always be shadows in the fog and the fog has a life all its own. The emerald-greened-eyed handsome man will return to walk the streets and seek shelter in the even darker alleys. A deadly search to be loved.

INHALE AND EXHALE

Inhale and Exhale
There is the knowledge between,
Heaven and Earth
With vast treasures to behold
Riches beyond all measures to comprehend
Spiritual,
With endless possibilities
Love thyself beyond all fears there may be
Physicality,
The Art of the five senses
Achieving harmony in each one
Learn to walk between the balance
Of Heaven and Earth
At every glorious sunrise
"Inhale...
And when all your days have come to an end
...Exhale"

Is It My Turn to Die?

"As I was watching a clip on the television about "The Atrocities Put Upon by Man", I found myself getting into a rage over the things man has done to man. So many horrors. I recall the American Indian. I remember the history of what "The People" had endured in our own country. Put in combination with what is going on all through Africa. My heart fell apart for the history of what "Man" has done in his wake! So, I write this scene as if I were a teacher there and trying to protect the children I've grown to love. Put whatever race you may, they "All" are God's children. How would you feel if a child looked you in the face and ask, "Is it my turn to die?"

{War creates chaos and the children suffer the most}

We are huddled together wondering if, waiting to die

There is hunger in the faces of the children

For days they cry a silent cry that weakens their little souls

At times there is a silence so deafening

Broken only by a child's faint whimper of no hope

Dirty angelic faces, matted lice-ridden hair

Whatever clothing, they may have on their backs

Are filthy, torn, and covered in fetuses and urine stains

Their little feet are scarred, cut, and infected

For the walk has been long to Heaven's Rest.

They were abandoned by grieving parents

Who without a doubt are dead protecting their children?

Mothers raped, beaten, cut up, and left for dead

Their father's tortured for days and dismembered

They are left for the wild animals to feed upon.

How inhumane!

These young children learn early

The atrocities that man can put upon man

Desecrating the values of life itself

All this horror because their skin is

{Red-Black-Yellow-Brown and or White}

PROVOKES

I too am frightened of what will be my demise.

I am sure to be branded a

{Indian-lover, Niger-lover, Chink-lover. White trash}

All because I stood up and screamed,

"NO, ENOUGH IS ENOUGH, NO!"

They are scared and alone

In a bloodbath not of their making

Are they to suffer unmercifully?

Can no one hear their cries, does anyone care?

*Or is it that no one "**gives a damn**"?*

Will they be dismissed as worthless trash?

Ignorance and prejudices

Don't let this happen!

Not for our future, not for their future

Just to hear a child say,

"Is it my turn to die?"

IT FEELS

One day you wake up and the sun is shining through your window
And filters a warm ribbon of strips across your body from the blinds
And you know what?
It feels good, sometimes.

One day you wake up and there is no sun shining at all
No sun, no ribbons, but a chill to your marrow
And you know what?
It feels bad sometimes.

One day you wake up and that's all there is
You just wake up and lay there staring at four walls
And you know what?
It feels like a prison, within a prison.

One day you wake up and suddenly you realize that there
Really isn't any reason to get out of bed,
And you know what?
It feels scary that the idea is appealing.

One day you wake up and all you worked for, for years
Has vanished and taken a hike,
And you know what?
That's when you ask yourself, what happen?

One day you wake up and find the whole thing is heartbreaking
With no answers to what in the hell did I do wrong?
And you know what?
That's damn unfair.

One day you wake up and say to yourself, why bother?
It feels good to just lie here and block out the frigging world.
And you know what?
That's a cop-out, Yet, why bother?

One day you wake up and say forget this
And go about your way alone, then someone says, Life goes on!
And you know what?
When someone feels like this, who gives a rat's ass?

One day you hope you don't wake up, but you open your eyes
To see ribbons of light across your body
And you know what?
It feels good! But?

One day you don't wake up
You feel nothing, see nothing, hear nothing.
And you know what?
It feels good

It feels scary
It feels bad too
It also feels like a prison
Do you ask what happens?

Feelings deep inside telling you it's damned unfair
It was a cop-out, too
Who gives a rat's ass anyway"?
And you know what?

It feels good,
BUT!

IT'S BEEN YEARS

It's been years since I've heard your sweet voice
It's been months since the laughter echoed through my mind
It's been weeks upon weeks since the day we ran ourselves silly
All those years, months, and days that were taken from you and I
Now I only can use my heart and mind to recall the laughter
To recall the tears, giggles, and just being together
It's been years since I've heard your sweet voice

You're gone yet always you're here in my heart and soul
Many times, I had asked God, if he would turn back the hands of time
If that were only possible, for it's been a long time waiting
I guess better left undone, it must have been for a good reason
Yet you were cheated, I was cheated, and it is damned unfair!
We are told to live life to its fullest, live every day as if it's your last
It's been years since I've heard your sweet voice

It's been a long time since we talked about our dreams
It's been forever sitting by the phone waiting for your call
It's been hard living day to day without acceptance you're gone from this world
All those endearing young charms of yours that will never shine again
They will never shine as bright as when you smiled your smile
It's been lonely sitting here looking at your pictures
It's been a long time since I heard your sweet voice

JAMES ALLEN ANGLEBERGER

{THE MAN I WANTED TO BE}

Heartbroken, in his car on a moonlit night quietly sits
Confession and depression as his dreams are never reached
Seated beside him was an old friend cold, a cigarette he lit
His life from the start offered so little, he worked hard

His waterfall eyes were the bluest of all sapphires
Constantly she flashed through his mind memories
His heart was shattered, a spirit extinguished by fire
The pain of a lost vision grew into shadows of agony

He spoke not of his private anguish containing ill-will
Finishing the last cigarette, he flicks it out the window
Beside him in the front seat sitting silent, cold, and still
Reaching over to grab her by the cold heartless throat

Feeling defeated, his anger subsided, and he takes a stand
Jimmy gently released his grip, she fell back in the seat
Conflicting images flashed from head to heart and hand
A man of incredible strength sub-come into a succubus

The moon was high, a lovely soul was now lost in the stars
Struck by the madness of heartache, his pain had to cease
Once again, he grabbed her long cold neck in the moonlit car
Positioned her between his legs in his uncontrollable sorrow

Jimmy suffered in private, mental anguish like never for
Her scream echoed without remorse across the countryside
Hopelessness exploded in the heart and to his soul's core
Cold steel and a succubus destroyed this beautiful man...

"His name was James Allen Angleberger, everyone called him, Jimmy.
He was my handsome and studly cousin, never knowing he was my *"Hero"*
He shot himself...
Ending a young man's life, filled with endless possibilities
Jimmy will certainly be missed by one who admired and loved him
He was the big brother I never had
And I loved him!"

James Allen Angleberger

    Jimmy is and certainly will always be remembered by me. I am proud that I knew this amazing and beautiful young man and my cousin. Jimmy was an important part of my life growing up off Route 40 West, in rural Frederick, Maryland. James Allen was a cousin of mine. I was blessed to have known this handsome and charismatic young man. Jimmy was my hero from the start. He was four years older than I. We were born and raised in the country on the outskirts of Frederick, Maryland. I lived up on Blueberry Hill and Jimmy along with his father and seven siblings lived at the bottom. Our lives were filled with many trials and quite a few tribulations. We both lived in old farmhouses without running water and bathrooms for most of our lives. Jimmy's father and seven siblings occupied four rooms. Their father was a man whom I admired and who worked hard all his life.

    Good, God! Jimmy was heaven blessed with extremely good looks. Wavy black hair and sapphire eyes certainly were great features that drew you into his amazing and charismatic personality. Hell, those rich blues could melt ice and the heart of any woman he desired. He was six foot two inches of hard country muscle. Though, barely out of his teens, he was a hard worker. Truly a man's man and every woman's fantasy in the flesh. It was that outstanding smile that possess you. It was like the shine of well-polished and buffed chrome. He was rugged, strong, and worldly. However, it was his gentle nature and mannerisms that were loved by his family and friends. Jimmy was caring, gentle, and loving Yet, though you wouldn't want to cross his path. This guy could handle himself in most situations. I know without a doubt in my soul, that the combination of all these things is why I admired and loved him so much. I never had an older brother to look up to. Jimmy was my candidate. I'm not ashamed to tell anyone that I worshiped him. I loved him for who he was, the male mentor I could learn from. I wanted to be him, have his outstanding good looks, and the strength that he possessed. There was that streak of English coursing through those veins. The blood of generations past flows through our families. Most of us were unfortunately products of our environments. We grow up in poor situations. But we managed the best we could. We lived and loved, we dreamed of better lives. Living through hardships that very few around our age could ever imagine. But we had one another.

I thought about the world of Jimmy and his brother Richard. Richard was two years younger than Jimmy, but a year older than me. When Jimmy started working hard at making his life better, that's when he fell head-over-heels for a tiny and pretty woman. She was the sun rising and the moon setting as far as he was concerned. As with all young men, Jimmy's attention was given to his girlfriend. I saw less of my mentor, my friend, and my Hero. I lost touch with my two cousins after I moved from, **"Hell's Half Acres".** I was encouraged to pursue a career in the Theater. I auditioned in New York City at the prestigious **"American Academy of Dramatic Arts."** One week later I received the news that I was excepted. On the day I was leaving for New York City, I went down the hill to say goodbye to my big brother Jimmy. I thanked him for all the years of being my friend. He gave me a hug and a handshake goodbye. Jimmy whispered in my ear, **"Do us proud, Baby Hughie."** It was his nickname for me. A cartoon character on television at the time. An overgrown baby duck in a diaper. Oh yes, it got my goat, and he relished the reaction I use to give. I got into my Toyota to drive to the train station in Baltimore. I rolled the window down and leaned out the window telling him, **"Take care and I'll see you around Thanksgiving."** That would have been the right time for me to tell him he was my "Hero". He flashed that incredible smile of his. Jimmy gave a couple of taps on the roof of the car. I pulled onto the highway taking my first steps from the small town I was born and raised in. I took my last look at Jimmy in the rear-view mirror at the man I hoped to mold myself into. There are no words to explain my admiration for this handsome man. I saw Jimmy wave goodbye. I noticed a change of expression on his face. It was a vacant expression as he yelled out, **"I'll be seeing you, and give them Hell, Baby Hughie!"** Christ, a lump developed in my throat that was so damn hard to swallow. So, this small-town boy left for the "Big Apple". Whereupon I lost all communications with Jimmy, Richard, and most ties I may have had around that time. After my first year at the "AADA", I got my first chance to go back home during a holiday. I started to try and look up Jimmy but had no luck. However, I did find an address for Richard. I drove to his address in hopes to find Jimmy. It was great seeing Richard. I wanted to know how to get in touch with Jimmy. Richard gave me the darkest news. Once again, the **"Shadows"** had reared their evil frigging heads and dealt another blow to my gut! It was my heart and soul that vanished in an instant. Richard being blunt and never mixing words, said, **"Jimmy Committed Suicide".** He had shot himself in the head sitting in his car...

"My God!!, I was choking inside. I couldn't breathe. My head was spinning in disbelief. Jimmy never would do something so drastic. Impossible!" I went through shock, denial, hurt, and an aching pain inside my heart. Then I was angry, angry at this Goddamn World. I held all these emotions inside. I felt as though I was going to explode. Richard handed me a funeral card. I simply looked at Richard and said, **"Richard I have to go."** I got into my Honda CRX and drove away to where we grew up. I pulled off the highway creating a cloud of dust. Parked in the same place where Jimmy and I said goodbye the day I left for NYC. The house he and his family lived in was just a shell of a foundation still standing. Up at the top of "Blueberry Hill" was the farmhouse where I spent the worst eighteen years of my life. Except when my Hero, Jimmy came around. I visualized the earlier years, watching Jimmy walking around, working on a car or two. I don't remember how long I cried sitting in the car looking over at the abandoned white stone foundation where my cousins lived. I remember screaming at the top of my lungs, **"WHAT A FUCKING WASTE!"** ...

His name was James Allen, so much like the rebel, "James Dean" and looks of "Guy Madison" and "Montgomery Cliff" rolled up into one! Damn! that's truly handsome. He will always be missed. The world he wanted to create was doomed from the beginning. So much like many of our families. In truth, we all were doomed one way or the other. Jimmy gave a powerful amount of love and of himself to many. I understand that all his hard work went into trying to please the woman he fell in love with. So much like a **"Succubus"**, she was never satisfied, always wanting more. Such is life!...

James Allen Angleberger

DOB
19 AUGUST 1948

ENTERNAL REST
22 NOVEMBER 1979

**Was laid to rest at the age of 31 years young in Mt. Olivet Cemetery
In Frederick, Maryland**

**He was found in his car
Apparently of a gunshot wound to the head
One beautiful soul, One beautiful man
lost to suicide...**

****

Rest in Peace
Jimmy
My cousin, My Hero, My Friend

Johnny Angel

He's a messenger from God, an amazing lover, and handsome too

He comes to me nightly, his wings opened wide with love for two

Tenderly he whispers into my ear melting my heart with his love

My body glows when he softly sings the song of the morning dove

Amongst distant clouds laced in gold, my lost horizon appears complete

With the back of his fingers, he softly brushes the hair from my cheek

There's passion in his eyes when he kisses me, I surrender, I am seized

I sigh with passion when he stands before me naked so beautifully free

My senses come alive with fire for his aroma of Jasmine tantalizes me

When Johnny embraces my body, I'm magically transported to high

With the magnificent spreading of his wings, tears appear in my eyes

The sunset slips slowly behind the distant Island of Love in a fiery glow

A volcanic climax burst our lovefest, cascading across heaven's slow

When love feels right, your emotions explode like fireworks in the sky

The Hammer of Thor drives deep into the canyon where Heaven resides.

JUDGE ME NOT! BANG!...

"Enough" *I shouted. Let me welcome the promise of oblivion*
Know the soul that is an unguarded ball of mass confusion
First the slice, I try ignoring the pain as the river of life flows
Like one's enemies, an open wound that festers, then oozes

There is mounting pain and agony rising, attacking my sanity
In my mind, a boiling fever contains the last of its awareness
Knowing it's far too late to try and make any sense of it all
Despair is nurtured in my mind as I scream in silent echoes

I now breathe in desolation, leaving me lying in a dark trance
I have not the will nor the driving strength to fight any longer
There is no hero in my sight, as life seeps from my wound
Please leave me to my love for the Reaper arrives to bed me

I chose to be caged in my own isolation and time matters not
Hearing the cries of agony as tears join the flowing river of life
Damn this lingering, dear lover ends it before the horror sets in
Fear has never been a worthy companion all through my days

*Christ asked on the cross**, "Why have you forsaken me?"***
Am I being rejected for a man's indiscretions in his lifetime?
I have taken all the years of disrespect and a country beatdown
I have fallen among unsung hero after hero, forever to sleep

Judge me not!... *I offer my soul that's encased in this corpse*
In the distance, the serpent gathers souls from the battlefield
Must I give my pride to this endless darkness that awaits
I resisted the hunger frenzy and am now forced into starvation

Please! judge me not, do not strip me of the last of my dignity
In my hands is one remaining bullet, the gun is cocked and ready
I have given up on myself, my faith has seemed to evaporate
*Enough to all of this, **"The Master of Oblivion"** is Welcomed!*

BANG!

JUDGE ME NOT!...

Judgmental In the End

{Do not treat me like a piece of trash}

This greeting I offer you is nonjudgmental at first sight

The kindness I present to you, I hope will be received in kind

At an early age, our family was encouraged to give all we can

We didn't have much ourselves growing up, but we gave

It was a gesture I learned, I asked for nothing in return

If all you offer is a smile with a thank you, that's enough

A smile on one's face with a kind word relates to happiness

For those that finally open their eyes, it'll be too damn late

To judge this beautiful person before knowing them is wrong

It will be God who will judge every one of us

"And the wicked shall ever be humbled in the end"

What virtues need there be that time needs to examine

Explore then act upon them in all earnestness, faith, and trust

*We all can say **"Hello"** and mean it!*

Conduct yourself with

DIGNITY

BEING AGREEABLE

HAVING HUMILITY

BITS OF PATIENCE

LOVE

JULY 4TH, INDEPENDENCE DAY

And the parade is just about ready to start...

THIS SHORT STORY IS DEDICATED TO THE DEVOTED PATRIOTS WHO SERVED THEIR COUNTRY WITH PRIDE AND WITH HONOR FOR THIS COUNTRY THEY LOVE. AFTER SERVING THEIR COUNTRY IN THE MILITARY, THEY RETURN HOME RELIEVED IN KNOWING THEY SERVED GIVING IT THEIR ALL. "BUT!" THE SOLDIER IS STILL FIGHTING FOR THEIR RIGHTS TO LIVE FREE AND CONTENTED IN THEIR OWN HOME, IN THE UNITED STATES OF AMERICA. VETERANS AS FAR BACK AS THOSE SERVING IN "WWI" STRUGGLE STILL TO THIS VERY DAY, TO GET THEIR JUST DUE FROM UNCLE SAM. WHEN IN THEIR TIME OF NEED, MOST TURN TO OUR GOVERNMENT FOR ASSISTANCE AND ARE EITHER DENIED OR LOST IN THE PAPERWORK KNOWN AS "RED TAPE BULLSHIT!" FACTS ARE FACTS, THOSE THAT HAVE SERVED AND ARE SERVING AT THIS VERY MINUTE WANT TO BE RESPECTED FOR DEFENDING THIS COUNTRY AROUND THE WORLD, AND CERTAINLY, THOSE THAT HAVE GIVEN THE ULTIMATE SACRIFICE.

Seated outside on the porch in their white wicker rocking chairs watching the neighbors and some strangers setting up chairs, some laying blankets down along the street that runs north and south in front of their houses. The old couple gets a thrill out of the day in more ways than one. Kids running and screaming and then here comes little Nicky Jones, screaming at the top of his lungs for the others to wait for him to catch up. The old couple has watched the same old thing every single year since 1946. Only the faces are renewed and with the changing of America's melting pot being added by different nationalities.

Someone about five blocks up the street echoing down the grapevine that they can see that the parade has started. That's when the action down on both sides of the streets wage their own wars to get the best seats on the curbs in front of their houses. Kids start yelling that they must go to the bathroom! You hear mothers and fathers yelling for the kids to run back to the house and hurry up because they're not going to save their spot forever! Coming up the walkway are three teenage girls dressed in red, white, and blue with every kind of trinket that represents the fourth of July. If it blinks and moves to create noise, then each girl seems to become a walking time capsule of the day. One then asks, **"Would you allow us to sit on your walkway and step down there? It's a place to watch the parade, plus the little kids annoy us all the time."** The old couple looked at each other and smiled. The older woman makes clear that they clean up their trash afterward. Giggling like the schoolgirls they are, agreed to do so. With three thanks they head down to their viewing perch to watch the parade well over the crowd below.

Here come the street vendors selling food and toys on long sticks and every child's favorite, balloons of every color of the rainbow, and of course cotton candy. The old man asked his wife if she wanted some cotton candy. She looked at him and said, **"Don't you get me started on sweets, you old fool!"** He said with a straight face, **"It's not for you, it's for the young girls."** The vendor made his way up to the three girls, giving each one a pink treat. The old man yells down to the vendor and said, **"I'll take care of you tomorrow, Smithy!"** Smithy saluted the old man. The girls yelled at them thank you like the cheerleaders they are. **"Thank You, Thank You! Thank You!"** The old woman looked over at her hubby and said sweetly, **"That's why I love you..."** Just then *coming from the backyard, walking up the side of the house where several of their old friends from the local "VFW Club." "Lord", mumbled the old woman, "They make more noise than all the teenagers around town alone!" It really didn't bother her that much for they have been friends forever, serving together in "WWII". Many of their friends didn't make it back home. These soldiers and nurses have maintained the closest of friends. All their lives have been filled with children, grandchildren, and a few great-grandchildren. Proving that life goes on and on. After the hello's, hugs, and cheek kissing, it was time to get settled so they can watch the parade from their vantage point. Each one of them has a family member in a high school band or drill team and one of their friends is holding an Office in the Government. The parade has started and nearing their street. It's always the same old thing year after year, but it doesn't matter because it is the fourth of July! A day of celebration of our Independence from the old country. Each of these veterans has their own reasons, feelings, and what this day means to them. Regardless of how it is expressed, the meaning holds the same emotions. "Well, what is this all about guys?" Said a friend on the porch. It was a local and national news team covering the day's events and activities as well as the parade. "Good day, one and all. You all look like the essence of Patriotism!" said the newsman. Joyfully the group of friends started to talk all at the same time. "Would you be interested in being interviewed for the evening news? We'd like to ask each of you, what does this day mean to you?" explained the reporter. They all agreed, and the reporter had his team set up for the interviews. The personnel raced about setting up lights and light filters. Just on time, for the parade was just about in front of their street. The old couple was being interviewed first since it was their porch to start with. The first question went to the old woman, "How and what do you feel about Fireworks at the end of all the celebrations?" she said in a teacher mannerism, as if addressing a class of students, that's because she ended up teaching nursing after the war ended. This is what she said to the young reporter, "The fourth of July is so much more than fireworks. Oh, so much more! It is the spirit of freedom. Thankfulness and acknowledgment of what Liberty truly means. A staggering reminder to never, ever take it for granted!" Then the old man was asked what the fourth of July celebration proved. He said, "July 4th celebration proves to the world that No Terrorist Organization or Ideological Extremist can break the UNITED WILL of our multicultural country. Independence Day has come to signify that America embraces ALL World Races, Religions, creeds, and Cultures!"*

The reporter expressed his gratitude and told the old couple how dynamic their statements were. He then asked them whom he should interview next. That would give an equal opinion. They pointed out their brother-in-law, Richard. He had lost several good friends and his sister. The old couple told Richard he was next to be interviewed for the evening news. The reporter asked, "I'd like to know what this holiday and other Patriotic Celebrations mean to you?" Richard took a deep breath and spoke his mind into the camera; "As a child, patriotism was pervasive in my hometown. I knew from an early time that days such as Memorial Day, Independence Day, and Veteran's Day were not just days to have a picnic in the park. It was instilled in me, by example that this quiet and proud vet, that we must care for all our service personnel every day! My dad lived by the theme to help all people every day. As a citizen, veteran, husband, father, and mail carrier. So now, I don't mind if people see me wearing my patriotism on my sleeve each day. I proudly stand and teach my students to recite the (Pledge of Allegiance) to the flag each day before our lessons began. This I did when I was in elementary school. Then I will be Damned, some high and mighty unpatriotic son-of-a-gun had it removed from ALL schools across America! That was and is a sad day for America. We work together to make each person in the classroom's life a little easier. And when one of America's special holidays comes near, I make sure I pass it on to a new generation of America's children how important our beliefs in life, liberty, and the pursuit of happiness are every day! The students ask, why do I shed a tear now and then when I salute our country's flag...my response...I'm thinking of all the young men and women who died, so I can have the freedom to stand and openly salute OUR Flag of the United States of America!" There is one more thing I would like to add if you don't mind, there are NO WORDS that can set my heart a fire like these words.

"AMERICA THE BEAUTIFUL"

"Oh, beautiful for heroes proved
In Liberating strife,
Who more than self their country loved?
And mercy more than life."

I hear these words and they hit me right in my heart. My chest tightens up, a pit forms in my stomach, and my throat clenches. The words to that second verse touch me like no other. Reminding me of the sacrifice of good men and women who serve in the military."

"CUT! that's a wrap everyone. Thank you, Richard, and thank you very much for your candid statement. I believe everyone will want to stand up and salute our nation's symbol of independence and freedom. After these airs, my good man, America very well may be saluting you, kind sir! That was remarkable!" Richard then said "No Sir, that's love for my country and for those that gave their lives so that I could stand here today...

KNOWING YOUR LOVED

Look for the brightest of stars, know my love
Someone from afar, yet not too far, adores you
You are so like the rising tides in the evening
Know that it's I that waits for the rising moon

I'll sing a serenade to one who knows me not
It's said, I am a fool to admire you from afar
You're invited to stare into these dreamers' eyes
The melody I sing for you will fill the night air

It is I who wishes to strum your heartstrings
Float upon a gentle breeze to my private oasis
Hear the song of crystal blue persuasion I sing
Do rise my envious moon, shine your beacons

See me standing on the pier when the tide rises
Watching moonlight dancing across the water
Tonight, I serenade a love song to the heavens
Filled with passion and longing for a someone

Tonight, be made ware, this Phoenix is in love
Through words in my song, I call to thee, come
Do open your heart to someone who loves you
Search the night sky for the brightest of all-stars

Knowing you are loved...

LABYRINTH OF SHADOWS

My Labyrinth weaves amongst the shadows of my mind in repose
I meander through a dark maze of my own past and present
I have not found a way of any possible escape
Dead end after the dead-end is laced in malice of thorns
My mind goes blind in the attempt to find an exit
The ugliness of this Labyrinth makes for redundancy
Wall after wall creates endless confusion, a massive blackness
I must keep moving for the darkness become the shadows that taint and tease
I feel them blistering my heels, chasing me through a chamber of horrific shoes
Yelling, screaming, and laughing at the pain I'm feeling
Just when I think I have outrun them
I am tripped to the ground by the hand of sorrow
Stripping me of all my dignity
Slashing endlessly at my naked body with claws sharp as razor blades
I crawl in a slim of blood and cruel whisperings through this hellish Labyrinth
Where there is not an exit!
I cradle my own person, closing my eyes to the terror
A terror that has no ending in my darkness
Hell, why bother torturing myself to find a way out any longer
Allow the shadows to possess my very essence
Reach out and allow the shadows to take me by the hand
Willingly walk into their dark den of abuse
A world I know only too well
No beginning, no ending in the heart of this Labyrinth called, "HELL"
All around me are voices that float upon the stale and humid air
They fill my mind with abusive and sexual phrases
I'm physically and mentally exhausted, I simply lay down in the maze
I am thinking, "Here I am shadows, do what you will"
Cover my naked body with your pitch of endless agony
I want you to be ravenous, stripping away all my flesh from the bones
All that I was and wanted to be matters no longer
Trapped is where I have been since age four
Whatever freedom existed in this train-wrecked brain was lost a long time past
Your deformity turns me on!
I find you sexually attractive and inviting
Make love to me, here, right this second...
You, in this Labyrinth of Shadows

LAST OF DAYS

*Here I stand facing the valley of no choice, the last of days. My eyes, I force them toward the horizon where I witness the truth. I plant a steady footing for a ravenous wind about to hit me, how it does rise before me like a stallion on his hindquarters. Fright and tears commence from my heart and soul, for I see amongst the muck, dirt, and filth, come riding the Four Horsemen! Never such evil have I ever seen, eye to eye, our fate awaits. Humanity must face what comes after them, eras of **"WASTE!"** Riding hard with the fires of hell burning everything in their way. Marking the day to forever night in slim of the foulest of stenches. I'm battling the forces of **"Man's Inhumanity to Man"** hot is the air. Now fall the young boys, and girls, leftovers for our future planets' hope. **"Innocent Children"** who knew not the danger of playing war games. I scream a bloody scream, **"Take a deep breath you sons-of-bitch".** Walk into Mother's once dream kitchen and Vomit Tragedy Anew! I remember being blown backward; I felt my bones snapping within. That is after I see, smell, and feel my flesh boiling my skin away. All this in an instant as I am slammed against the future's invitation. There is a split second of "PEACE" then a nothingness, nothing... During man's demise, an army of "Bloody Shadows" marched in unison. Sloth strangled Envy, slashing Greed and Lust, beheading Gluttony. He was ill-prepared for his demise and landed the man in the arms of **Death.** The Dark Angel saddles, running a steeplechase for a perverse prize. A question to answer is, **"Who would be first to "RAPE" Mother Earth?** Man, no longer exists, and no living creature has survived Earth to this day. Ride the "Mushroom Heights" with the men who declared the annihilation. I cried blood looking up at the sky from my own valley of decision, Screaming as **I see Hell's Tsunami of Prophylactic Crematorium of Fire.** No longer to see **"Good Morning Star-shine the Earth says hello."** The remaining is a mega-trillion puzzle piece scattered across the universe. And I see ravenous human-like creatures searching for table scraps. I'm but a gasp away from endless floating, waiting for my turn to become a piece for the gathering. Death dismounts his steed long enough to gather his bounty of souls, he reaches out into the dust with his skeleton hand, filtering the sand from my soul. Looking back, I see a fractured Earth encased in a hellish ball of fire. Then the core of a once blue world, a mega explosion, and a shock wave will usher in...*

THE LAST OF DAYS

Learn To Dance with the Rain

*All my waking hours seemed to be emersed in two emotions. One of **"Sunshine"**, where all is well. The sweet flow of order where one can be with nature and wonder. Offering the senses an array of musical colors. A pallet where one stops and smells the roses if you will. The second is **"Rain"**. Subject to one's interpretation. I find the rain to be like sheets of music. Songs were sung from and of the heart. Endless arrangements of **"Ode to Joy"**, **"Sadness"**, **"Loneliness"**, **"Loss"**, **"Grief"**, and **"Darkness"**. Each symphony is conducted in a variety of degrees. Sometimes in a mist that seems to brush the flesh like a lover's whispering breath as one stands like a lost soul in a **"Garden of Good and Evil"**. So many times, my heart paused long enough to taste the mist on my tongue.*

Rainy days in my life have been many. There were very few shelters, and no umbrellas when the rains came. So, I stood in the rain. Sometimes the rain was warm upon my face. It felt as if they were the fingers of God himself. I've stood in many a delude. Torrents where the drops were cold, sharp as razor blades slicing at the very soul. Feeling hopeless and depressed. You stand there facing your past where the sun is hidden far beyond the dark clouds. I realized at a very young age that life is a series of ever-mounting tidal waves. As the waters rise uncertainties swirl about with being bombarded by debris that cuts and chokes the life out of you. Wave after wave crashes over your head. Still, you keep your head above the water. Taking a breath of precious air.

*From a child of despair to my teens filled with confusion, physical and mental abuse, bullying, and even raped. My purpose, my reason to live went unanswered. I was told to have faith. Have faith? In what, who? I was simply a drop of rain amongst billions. A part of a vast ocean. The worst of emotion that one can experience is worthlessness. If I must exist in this **"conjuration of vapors"**, I will learn to dance in the rain. The only time in my life when the sun shined through the clouds. Sometimes, I danced within a rainbow. And that my friends are worth* **everything...**

Let's All Raise a Glass to Suicide

Let's raise a glass to my new friend

"SUICIDE"

A prologue to the darkest corner of one's soul

A heartbeat below your darkest sadness and as close to despair as your honesty takes you

Just beyond sanity's locked door

Sinking down to the depths of your madness,

Pain, misery, and being lost beyond understanding

You become blind to all reasoning

There is a slashing of a bright blinding white light

Across your mind, that cripples your thinking

Let me introduce you to the sisters **"Doom"** *and* **"Dread"**

Beaconing to lie down beside them

The temptation is sensual, sexual, and breathtaking

Dear God, the darkness is pitch black

Traffic runs through your system and then slows down to a deathly crawl

Finally, the silence is deafening

Memories flash and flicker

Then a picturesque and peaceful carousel fades to who knows where...

Let's all raise a glass to

"SUICIDE"

Lies And the Darkness

{What you are about to read is very true. I <u>metaphorically</u> cover the place, time, and for whom the story is about. My Vampire was unbelievably handsome. I was a young guy who was looking in the wrong places at the wrong time. It was I that lead me into a world of dark exploration. Why not, I was raised in a dark setting from birth. The extra education I learned sustained through my adult life, with reservations, I might add.}

*He said, **"Come into my dark haven."** I remember his words so well, **"Let me keep you safe and I will give you an everlasting kiss that will nurture your soul."** Then he eerily placed a black satin robe around my chilled body. Moving my long her away from my neck, he placed a painful kiss upon my throat. I was shocked, then horrified. I had never been held so tight in my life. I struggled somewhat, but hopelessly. I slowly became weak and submitted to this handsome man. I was taken away from the world I knew. He had promised to cover my sins. I felt excited about a while. But time had developed darker as it moved onward. Solitude was often my friend. It didn't feed the hunger I was experiencing. Wicked were my thoughts. I told my capture I needed a change from this cavern of tombs. My hunger was driving me crazy. I shook, shivered, and clawed at to walls. He said, **"You're safe and secure with me."** His promise to change me never came to pass. Every time I brought up my desire to go with him, he became angry. Which frightens the hell out of me? I was hidden there in the darkness with his forever lies. He controlled my every move. I realized I was a slave to his passions.*

*I wanted to feel the warmth again. Only the rays of the sun could do that for me. This dungeon grew stagnate, darker, and more like a prison. Which in all essence certainly had become so? From within my body, I was dying and rotting inside. I did try to escape once. It was when he had left to feed. Only to have my carefully laid-out plans foiled by his early return. My God, the fire in his eyes was frightening enough. In a flash, he grabbed me by the throat. Fang extended and a sterned voice said, **"You will obey my every word and command!"** With his cold hand nearly strangling me to death he forced himself on me. Never had he made sexual overtones towards me. That moment was an experience that had me trembling. He was forceful, demanding, and calculated with every move he put upon me. Sex with a vampire is stimulating, passionate, and intense. No matter what I refused to do I felt compelled to surrender to his every desire. This went on for months. When you are frightened for your life, you'd be surprised at what you will do to appease your capture. Especially a Vampire. There is beauty when a vampire becomes passionate. There is a tender way about the approach taken. The terror one feels, exits your body. In its place is the desire to give yourself fully. When this is achieved, there is nothing better or so fulfilling.*

*After all this time sitting here in the dark feeling hopeless, dejected, and weighed down in waste of despair, I am rotting! I started to escape from his control, but I would end up back in the dark being used as his bag of blood. If this should happen to you in the wildest of dreams, BEWARE! Don't believe their words. Don't trust the promise of the night everlasting. He knew that if he ever would complete his promise by drinking his blood allowing me to die and then returning as the Vampire I wanted to be, I might leave. Or once I rose to walk into the night, he would no longer be able to control me. I've been under his control going on for two hundred years. I've learned that being by his side has its perks. To be honest, the intimate moments are, to say the least, enlightening. No pun on the light...I say to you, make sure you always remain in the light. Please, I beg you, don't follow my lead with whatever foolish sins you may desire to accomplish. Once the black satin has covered you with its sweet talk and smooth manners, you have lost your will. Vampires are very clever, covering your body and soul with their needs only. They can't help themselves for that is the nature of the **beast!** You will never be free of his lies and the darkness. Trust me, my friends, Vampires are real, maybe not like the ones in films, **but damn close.***

LIKE DESTINY'S CHILD

Mid-summer
Thick with gray clouds
Thus, hanging heavy with
Days Remembered

Thoughts
Thus, shadowed by emotions
Are but bye-gone
In thy longing

How I linger on
Contemplating
And wasting days away
By this tranquil pond

There I go
Casting stones
Into thy mirrored reflection
Like Destiny's Child

Will I see
My desires come true.
Or their weight weighs heavy
And plunge to the bottom

My mind flickers
Like the lights
Of the bye-gone era
Of silent films

I witnessed thy stones
To the unknown drowning pool
The summer shower of thy tears
Running down my face

My memories are relived
One after the other
I beg thee to carry thy sad thoughts
On the summer winds

I will not wrestle with you
How would thy soul ever rest?
With thy head upon
A sorrowful pillow

I have stood anchored against
Storms raging from fate
Yet I survived
Tempest's fury

My heart and soul
Soared toward the sun
Its warmth gave chase
To the gray clouds

I did but walk alone
With pride and contentment in thy soul
Nevertheless like
Destiny's Child

LIKE THE PHOENIX

There she sits motionless
With her head resting on her knees
The corner of this alley shall be her home for the night
***"Thank God"** she mumbles to herself*
This night will be warm
Stillness is her only friend in the wicked city
Being quiet becomes her mighty strength
Hidden in the shadows of the pale moonlight
That shines through the dark alleyways
There is a wind that blows through the skyscrapers
Cursing, screaming and yelling
As it slams against the brick walls
That moan the names of the lost and lonely
There are times when she must cover her ears
For the wind speaks to her in evil tongues
It's so very frightening to this wayward child of the night
As her eyes witness shadows dancing through the allies
Showing themselves as the morbid and deformed giant
Racing up and down the brick walls disappearing into the shadows
As they run from the headlights of the cars
That often makes screeching sounds
Eerie echoes surround her in the darkness
Cats squeal as they run from discarded cans and newspapers
As the trash swirls upward from the updrafts of the subway grates
Then there are the vocals at all hours of the night
Coming from open windows stories high
Depending on the temperature throughout the city
The nightly entertainment costs nothing
As she sleeps with one eye always open
Ready to flee upward like the Phoenix in flames
If need be...

LISTEN FOR THE SCREAMS

Listen! Can't you hear the unmistakable crackling of screams
From the mountain range to the mountain peaks there are cries
Feel each one, the spirit echoing in anger, disbelief, and fear
Man, once again is hard at greed, stealing, and creating murder

Pine, cedar, oak, redwood, and mahogany no longer stand guard
Centuries protecting Mother Earth from the tempest of erosion
The forest screams out into the broken silence as another falls
Listen to her screams as she crashes amongst her mother's history

I hear the spirits of all mother's creatures calling out for help
Acres, miles upon miles of living forests die and vanish daily
I can see the horror and I weep as their life force is massacred
Relentlessly killing Mother Earth, her children, our very own

My heart aches as it beats in horror witnessing the destruction
Watching tree after tree being dragged across Mother's face
Creating a scary moonscape of vanishing living organisms
Witness man's killing fields, lifeless and barren for generations

Listen! Can't you hear the last of nature's screams for salvation
Decades of death yet to be made aware of, hear their pleas, screams
Once the cedar, oak, redwood, and mahogany stood in plenty of glories
Vanishing from the face of the earth, their screams are but echoes

The creature known as man is the instrument of annihilation...
Killing the forests, polluting the waters, and being greedy to do more
Murdering God's every known species around the world over time
Finally destroying themselves in mass annihilation of stupidity!

LOCKED IN FEAR

Hidden children suffering through abusive childhood tragedies
Seldom expressing the horrors that are needing to be shared
Fragile the mind and body locked in dark caverns of isolation
Tears are weep-ed, pain, and horrific abuse, does anyone care?

Physical, mental, and verbal abuse conducting fear daily
The days of innocence are marred by an evil malevolence of pure
What could possibly conduct an abuser, is it simply evil pleasures
For overtime, a child's world is painted in black and blue

They zombie through childhood, growing older before their time
Masking the horrors forced to conceal dirty lies within their hearts
Till they're locked in fear, laced with hopelessness, blinded to the truth
Fireworks explode from the heart and soul held dormant at best

A numb heart, the soul suddenly vacates its last hold on sanity
No longer caring to cope with the possibility of dreams coming true
Now the children of abuse walk through the garden of good and evil
***"Do what you will!"** a silent message from the cry of the lonely*

Unthinkable attacks on children, develop a world with many issues
Years intensify the hurt that meanders like a river of madness
Every liquor bottle shattered, and every loud crash trigger a memory
Seldom one sleeps, eyes on a door that might open, leading to horror

A child's imprisoned mind is one that has never learned to run free
A hunger suppressed by fear lacks the power to break the silence
Four walls are known to close tight around a child's last hope
Remaining chained in a world of lost innocence, locked in fear...

LOST AND FOUND

The mind drifts far away
In hopes, that it will return someday
Darkness and confined in a nothingness space in time
It's scary and haunting in sounds that are like the wind with chimes
A thumping in my head that vibrates with a sound like a tuning fork
I'm confined in a bottle with a very tight cork
I'm lost in the darkness of my mind
No exit, no doors, not a window I can find
The horror that I have found
It's the heartless, loneliness of sound
Everything was lost and nothing to be found
This is my story of me.

LOVE IS THE WIND

Love is the wind, endlessly dancing over the oceans and seas
Dancing upon the shores and across the land through the trees
Searching for the lost loves, faithfully devoted and the so true
Endless air in motion that seeks the forlorn in shades of blues

Feel my loving whispers along the nape of your neck so divine
Caressing gently your soul in a warm sigh that can only be mine
Taste the flavor upon my lips like a kiss of the sweet summer wine
See me move the clouds creating a swan in a flight unconfined

Feel fingers move like that of a lady of leisure through your hair
A mesmerizing seduction that meanders upon the cool night air
Feel a spiraling about your flesh lovingly stripping away any fear
Know my whispers as adoring love sighs of affection in your ear

Love is the wind, air in motion, searching to nest like the dove
Soaring amongst the clouds, ever-changing in the heavens above
Love lies in a sanctuary of whispering sighs of yearning desires
Touching hearts and souls like steaming gasps of ecstasy on fire

LOVE UNDER GOD'S SKY

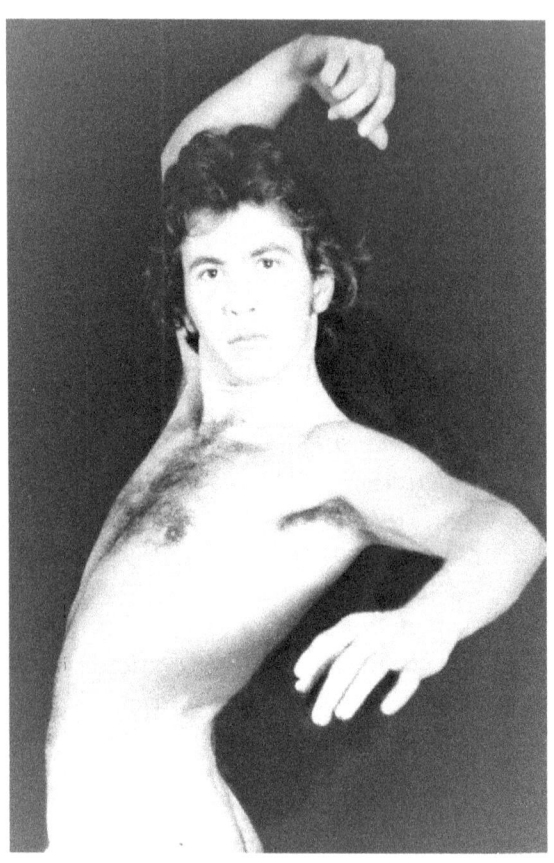

Have you ever had someone special in your life? Someone who has shown you the sweetest of kindness. Who holds compassion above all for the rest of your life? When all others fade into the background then, it is you that may understand what I am about to pen. There is an earthly angel of true love and kindness. Who resides in the center of your life and above all your heart? For not only the span of a reason, a season but a lifetime, illuminating the desires, hopes, and imagination That has managed to live only in your dreams, until now... Can you be the one, are you the one I should believe in? You are the one whose eyes I see shining deep into the ebony abyss that sparkle brighter than all others before me. Is it so wrong to long for this? Is it wrong for me to cast my wish, my dreams into the forevermore of darkness? Can you share with me the essence of who you are? The blessing of your innermost glistening true beauty that is far more attractive than physical attractiveness. Can I but hope to be the true object of your devotion? The completion of your journey from darkness to light. When I describe my perfect love, it's filled with tenderness, carried on wings of respect. It's someone with devotion so complete, so warm, and someone who lives to their own rhythm. Who can touch the heart of another through life and in their dreams? We are carried away in a fantasy across God's creation, the Earth. When we allow God as the core that binds our hearts, we can experience and conquer the most tumultuous of darkness. Pure love in a rhythm of complete harmony is only surpassed, by the exquisite beauty that lies within the depths of your eyes. And my heart can then and only then know true passion.

I stand naked before you under God's purity in his clear mountain stream. I stand under God's eyes hiding nothing with my arms outstretched inviting you to join me with the love I offer. Join in and feel the drums of your heart's desires and the freedom to explore one's emotions. I ask under God's sky, what more can a man offer in his presents? I allow myself the pleasure of undressing my frame. I slowly and purposely savored every second to free his creation to nature. Sharing the glorious freedom to enter each other with our physical beauty under God's graceful vast blue sky and his universe. His handsome presence is evidence of him being my king's creator. Under God, this beautiful creation bares his nakedness before my eyes. He steps into the heavenly light shining through the tree's canopies of our father's divine artistry. The man stands in all his glory and there before I is Adam, he tosses his long raven black hair, and the sun illuminates this beauty that God has created. Every curve, every shadow, and every glorious muscle dance in the light. Our love for each other is blessed by God's divine order and is pure. His rugged handsomeness is a gift directly from the heavens above. His physical essence is accentuated by the glistening waterfall behind us. The refreshing mist circles our bodies, glistening like sparkling dew. I feel his powerful yet gentle touch which is masterfully orchestrated. He stands beautifully naked before me, inviting me to savor his sensual gifts. He reaches for me to come from the tree's shadows into the warm light. With every step, I made in the stream toward this mountain so beautiful, we stood facing each other, I staring into his eyes and he into mine. Not a word need be spoken, our souls hungered in the glow of our natural freedom and heartfelt admiration for one another under God's sky. Sharing together in unison an emotional moment as a tear dropped from our eyes. He responds to my body language with his intensely sensual touch. Delicately sending tidal waves of excitement throughout my body. Slowly we walked over to the waterfall hand in hand. Stepping under the falls our bodies were enveloped with the pleasure of Eden's singing waters.

*The feelings we shared at that moment in time were so intense. We kissed with a passion so powerfully sweet it was reverent. We embraced as we stepped behind the waterfall. Beneath our feet, the stream carried our emotions and passion over the rocks and down the mountain to the valley below. **"Now you know my world, he said, it's filled with truth, for the heart knows no lies under God's sky!"** We slowly sank into the pool of water behind the falls in each other's arms. I thank God for all the blessings he has bestowed in this union between us, freedom of mind and the flesh. The spiritual union of our two hearts, minds, souls, and bodies as one completely. I now know with every ounce of my being we are blessed and our love for one another will last past all controversies and life itself under God's sky.*

Man-in-the-Moon

Here I sit watching an instrument that every now and then sends me into a frenzy over something that gives me pause. For whatever the cause may be, I become an inhuman rage. News warranting a stamp across the face of worldly officials! I pull my ass from the chair of indecisions, and head for the john. The entire time yelling and cursing at the tube for what's being aired! Grabbing a beer from the frig, I fly out the door, and onto the porch. Chug the brew, and belch out loud as my final word on the subject! I stood there for a while listening to the so-called evening news. Stepping away from the porch, I took a deep breath of fresh country air. Staring up at that man-in-the-moon against a backdrop of black with millions of twinkling stars. There he was staring down at me with a face as pale as a ghost. That face was indignant, and his expression seemed to mock me. That ruffled my feathers, looking up I said, **"How long have you been hanging around not doing a damn thing? I pointed my finger at him saying, "This whole damn world is falling apart!"** The entire human race, not forgetting the animal kingdom, is suffering! Multi-millions of men, women, and children are starving to death. War, Poverty, Famine, Disease, and countless inhumane actions **are** put upon and regulated by anger, greed, and racist groups that are creating wars of opinions as you make your rotations around the Earth. As if by some form of magic, a gray veil moved across your face as if to say, not my problem! Two catered shadows darken, eyes formed, and stared down at me. The man in the moon now stares at me. I have never felt a chill that cold as to run through my entire body. In a deep, low raspy voice, the man-in-the-moon began to speak. So, I smile and look down at you. So let me tell you something! Through too many beautiful starlit nights, I've had to listen to your crying and moaning and groaning about everything under the Sun. **"Now I'm asking, what in the hell do you want from me, anyway?" "I've been long before the dawning of man, before time itself. My light has been shining through the heavens long before a breath had ever been taken by a human. You stand there staring up into infinity and know nothing. You step out of a dwelling, complaining About nothing more to do than stare at the stars and make a wish. You have food to eat and clothes to wear, and people that love you, and care about you. Though you have made more mistakes in your life, squandered every blessing given to you. Hello, you are alive and breathing. You have no right to question my duty. I hear the suffering of mankind, seen ten thousand Wars of destruction. You stand there complaining while millions of children go to bed hungry, and humanity drowns in a cesspool sea of Perdition. There is one thing I am good for friend, I give light! Yes, even in the darkest of nights and I'm smiling because I know the truth... that things are never as bad as they seem and no one on Earth is ever truly alone...that time is fleeting and there is more to life than you can possibly understand friend! It's a matter to stop and listen. But you are always welcome to stare up at me and fully enjoy all the conversations we have. You think about what I have said here tonight. Maybe the next time you run out of that dwelling in frustration from watching the television, stand before me and have a smile on your face"**. I thought about what the man-in-the-moon said to me. So, there must be a real meaning taking hold! I thought hard about it. Well, you don't argue with wisdom like that, the man-in-the-moon is more than what we see!

MIRROR LAKE

Crystal clear water, calm and reflective, a painter's paradise
Water lilies of violet and white, shaded by a Weeping Willow
In sync with the water's calm, Loons sing of twilight's arrival
Nature supplies the window dressing for Summer's eve anew

A picturesque cottage covered in flora and ivy reflects on the lake
Nestled between canopies of Oaks and majestic Ponderous Pines
A manicured yard and patriotically, "My Country's Flag" is flown
Stacked outside the cottage, is a wall of firewood for a winter's blow

There is a canoe and a rowboat always tied out back at the pier
Songbirds sing from morning to night, in peace and in tranquility
There is a pair of Trumpet Swans with a clutch in tow each year
Racing atop the tree's canopy, squirrels in a continuous game of tag

If asked do I love my cottage in the country called, "Mirror Lake"
*There's only one answer I reply, best stated by, **"Elizabeth Browning".***
"How do I love Thee? Let me count the ways. I love Thee too everyday
most quiet need it. I love Thee to the heights and depths my soul can reach.
And if God should so choose, I shall love Thee better after death."

MISS VICKI

Miss Vicki, what an amazing young woman, she was and is still to this day, I'm sure! After several years of teaching Latin Dance to this young vibrant bundle of energy, she was a natural at it. These words represent Vicki to a tea.

I had to write about her and put her in a poem or prose, she was a big part of my life. I spent hours upon hours with her. When I needed help after my sister's death, Betty Neal, her mother offered their home to me. Betty is a wonderful, open-minded lady, and I do mean Lady. She could hold her own on the dance floor. Vicki was the greatest dance partner I ever had. Vicki could wear any style of Stiletto, and she made the shoe ignite a fire on any dance floor.

Around this time, I told my students we were going on an outing to Baltimore's Top Dance Nightclub, which just happen to be Baltimore's premier gay club. My favorite dance club in the seventies, eighties, and nineties was the "HIPPO" on Charles Street. There wasn't a night that didn't have couples from every Dance Studio in Baltimore and Washington, DC. there. Skirts twirling, jungle drum music to dance to. If you were new on the floor, every eye would be on you to see how good you two were. We were there every night of the week and on Sundays to all the tea dances around town. We'd danced from the time the doors opened and didn't leave Baltimore until the sun was about to rise. We drove an hour both ways. Vicki was crass, opinionated, stylish, vogue, and beautiful. When we walked onto the dance floor, we were given space and most eyes were on us. She made me look good. I'd like to think, visa-versa!

Every word in the poem/prose is about what she is, how she was, and how she looked in my eyes over our dancing years. "A Wild Woman". I hope you like her as much as we all did.

MISS VICKI

Her mannerisms are like the **"Succubus"** dragging you down into damnation
She is very enticing, as she claws away at your soul
Her cat eyes of green are controlling and manipulative
Her eyes fixed on you, your beguiled and bewitched beyond redemption

Miss Vicki is like a silent vampire in the darkest corners of the night
She feeds on your failures, guilt, animosities, and frustrations
You will sink into her desires with one deadly caress
Her arms are like two **"Burmese Pythons"**, once in her coils, all is lost

She maneuvers a spell with her body through the men of her desires
All are tall, dark, and handsome and are at her beck and call.
She surrounds herself with sweet erotic music and she invites you to dance
Her moves on the dance floor are like liquid fire

Her hips hit every drumbeat, every move is expressive of her needs
Her touch is exhilarating, and it will set your heart on fire
There is turning in all directions and her spins are to die for
There is a continuous feeling of pleasure running up and down your spine

You would want to sink into her desires and dance to the tune of her sins
Her conquests are many, there are shadows etched on the walls
Her deepest of passions is much too difficult to define
She stares into your eyes, and you freeze with anticipation of lust

Closer she comes with her tongue licking her blood-red lips
Her kiss is more than pleasurable, it tastes like sweet berry wine
Before long she moves her lips down and around to your thick neck
You're frozen in desire; this **Sensuous Goddess** now has her way with you

She has taken your soul as she drank from your river of life
Miss Vicki got what she came for, a taste of your sweet wine.
She dances her way back through the many sex-crazed studs of before.
All night and every night she get what she wants

MISS VICKI WANTS YOU!

Moonlight Fantasies

My Guardian Angel rescued me from a horrific storm last night. My heart beats on silent waves, and my prayer was heard into the abyss. As the tide ebbs out, a grand shipwrecked on an island of my own design, beached on a high white sandbar. Far away sounds of thunder were heard beyond distant hills. How amazing, sounds of peace ring out loud. In my dreams, love songs sound like soft angelic sighs of beautiful young men and women archangels. There are songs beautifully sung by lavish tropical birds. The sky morphs from a wicked gray, into rich baby blue. Always honor Father Sun's and Mother Earth's spirits, for they alone make or break what is left of your sanity. Blessings are sent to me on the colorful wings of rare butterflies. An island paradise rare in Orchids grown from the fertile land of tomorrow. With a heavenly fragrance like the Star-Lilies, as rich and sweet as a blushing pink wine. My soul is filled with fluttering butterflies, colors rich in Ruby, Sapphire, Emeralds, Gold drippings, and Elizabeth's Diamonds. Listen, for no soul cries in the twilight time of Moonlight Fantasies. In my fantasies, it's the sleep that often fades the dark, the evil put upon in a reality of harshness and pain. Moonlight fantasies sometimes bring a horror or two known as Nightmares...

A MORNING ADAGIO

It's early in the morning
I awake to heaven's gift at my side
How my eyes adore you
In my arms, you slowly wake
Let your eyes see behind their early morning veil
Give me your hand
A story needs to be told
One of the pleasures expressed in a dance of love for two
Where an embrace gives rise to the Phoenix
Let me brush lightly these lips upon yours sweet as an orchid
Tasting passionflower flavored in flame
A rhythmic flurry, a tango at best
An adagio dance in the nude
Free formed with one goal to obtain
To move and sing in blissful harmony
As we dance the dance of life
Choreographed beautifully
Each movement danced with perfection
Filled with unbelievable pleasures in the throes of love
A dance duo a Morning Adagio

Mrs. Topengs and Her Pigeons

Fallen-colored leaves lay patterned on the ground. Leaves fall on a weathered worn bench, aged it is. Under spreading branches, nearly bare of its leaves. Old is the Oak, seasons are calendared by her will of nature. All is covered in an early morning fog of November. Moisture covers the leaves that danced a journey downward from above. Far in the distance, at the entrance of Baker's Park, a grayish figure, barely visible, walks on the wet path beside Carroll Creek. Crooked is the path, as is the bench she's headed for. Nearly seventy of her eighty-eight years, she walked, she greets her friends. In front of her is her sit-upon, removing the wet colors of fall. It matters, not the little moisture where she always sits. The old woolen mossy-green trench coat has seen better days. Memories of years good and bad were pondered upon this bench in this park nearly every day. Recalling her two sons that run amuck on sunny days through the park chasing ducks and pigeons. Young lovers kiss, and days of kites and carriages strolling echo the past and present. She sits so calmly, adjusting her hat, scarf, and gloves. She looks at the surroundings as she opens a paper bag. Never does she sit too long. She whistles light upon the air. Always first to arrive, landing at her feet is," Mr. Buster." Bossy is he, blue in color, with one white feather in the tail. He coos and structs about at her feet. From her worn-out bag, she produces her usual bits of bread, crumbs, and seeds. Slowly the pigeons begin to arrive, then flutter about one another knowing the treats that will be offered. So much, so much noise, they do wait for her treats as she greets her precious little friends. There are always a few new arrivals, and all are welcome. Bits of dried bread was collected to feed her pigeons dear. Hundreds land at her feet, and Mr. Buster takes his place upon her shoulder. She tosses over and out the flurry in front of her. She hand-feeds Mr. Buster and in return, he gives her what seems to be a kiss on her cheek. Slowly one by one the pigeons fly away to their next meal. First, to arrive, always the last to go. Mr. Buster coos in her ear as if to say thank you. Mrs. Topengs eats a piece or two left over, and waves goodbye to her friends and family. She gathers what is loose, then sits a while to remember and take in the pleasantries of the days. The curtain of fog is fading like the years as the sun clarifies the warmth of the day. She gathers the thoughts and like magic, one fades, and the other clears to show the past. In a vision, before are her two sons playing ball close in the park. 1942, the world was changing, her sons 18 and 19 were drafted. Their goodbyes were said to her with a hug and a kiss. Love you, exchanged here at this bench in 1942. She watched as they boarded a bus to start their service. This left her all alone. The days passed, months, and years with a letter from the boys from time to time. Always saying, they are missing home and love her so much and hope to see her when this war is over. She holds them to her heart and saves each one as she ties a yellow ribbon around them. Every day she made her way to this bench to pray for them.

It was in November of 1945, much like the days of old. Except there were no pigeons this day. The sky was overcast and somewhat melancholy. Two tall figures entered the park and walked through the fog. Mrs. Topengs kept her eye on these two men coming her way. Two handsome soldiers greeted her and spoke in a calming tone, she took a deep breath and listened to the young soldier's words. Mrs. Topengs? Mrs. Grace Topengs? She nodded yes to them. **"We are sorry to inform you of the death, of your two sons in the line of fire."** *She stared at the young men for what seemed to be hours yet was only seconds. They each handed her an American Flag, folded in the traditional way. Faintly, she heard,* **"On the 24th day of November 1945..."** *as she reached for the flags,* *everything faded back to clear. A ray of sunlight shined through the clouds, she pulled back for a second to gather her thoughts and emotions. The young soldiers asked if they could escort her anywhere. As she gathered her belongings, retreated from the bench, and sighed, "No thank you, that is not necessary, I would like to be alone as I go home. But thank you anyway. A few colored leaves spiraled down in front of her, then a slow flurry of more. She was making her way back through the park, then stopped for she thought she had heard a familiar voice. Turning around, she heard a familiar sound coming her way. Sweetly she smiled and a tear made its way down her cheek. On the pavement walk, Mr. Buster and another friend were walking side by side. After all this time, after all the walks to the park and sitting on that bench, could this be a sign? Yes, she said to herself, it was a sign that her two son's spirits followed her back home!*

MUSIC OF THE HEART

Music of the heart is
An ever-changing symphony of beautiful tears
Creator of constellations, compositions,
Relating to musical starlight,
Futuristic, voyeuristic, characteristic
Brilliant minds that conduct on
Canvas or perhaps parchment
Creative street music
Sparse thoughts of sights and sounds
That trigger's justified thinking
Listen deep, deep beyond all listening ever pondered before
There lies an ancient sound
Perhaps a pebble was tapped against another
Stone against a rock
And the mixture created tones
Soon sounds in our daily lives created music
At the least rhythm was born from the heart of Mother Earth
As is the music of the heart that sings her Opera
Titled, "Desert Song"
A land dry from lack of water
Drums of thunder resonate in the distance
Promising rain in the dark of night...
Spirits of the landmarked without the freshness of the water
That runs under its bed of sand and stone instead
The virtue of water flows not above to mirror the sky of blue
Nearly silent is the music being played by the waters
That flowed into paradise
As a beautiful Oasis known as "Heaven's Pool"
Now sing of stone but sees only sand
That blows into the canyons of life's blood
There be the curse of the lost spirit of a land cool in waters
Rage is a blessing to the stone
And a man no longer can remember when
Now there is music forged in the deepest canyons,
Layered over millions of moons faded in and faded out
Listen to the voices of sorrow
The chimes of forgiveness that no longer hear the pleas
To raise the waters from the fiery red sands of revenge
Once again, the blue vast mirroring of water to the sky
Or even sky to water
With the flight of the Condor once more
Lost in an ageless flight of resistance
Of being a part of the circle of life once again

The heaven of the endless blue and black
Wings of the Eagle that soars endlessly across a shameless sky
The Great Eagle,
Introduces the Condor back to his native lands
So huge is the span of the Condor's wings that they touch
Canyon wall to canyon wall
He now focuses downward over the snake-like strings of flowing water
That once raged in flooded redemption
For the green, lilac, amethyst, ruby, scarlet and yellow
Dollops that weaved throughout,
Multiplying in ambition
A forest thick where life thrived
There the Great Spirit will silence the cries
Of brother pain and sister agony
And spin the wheel of chance
I am so lucky,
To presume for I no longer hear silence
There is music that carries the brushes and pallet of songbirds,
Lemon grass and thistles of amethyst prevail
Mother earth's heart beats once more
Across these lands
Belonging to no man
Hear the drums, the flutes, and bells belonging to "The People"
Hear the native Americans sing loud across Mother's land
If the mighty Eagle flies over the mountains,
Together hear their voices sing loud and free from ocean to ocean
For it is,
"The Music of the Heart" lives on!
Where the desert abyss covered in dry red sand
That sucked the earth dry of life-giving water is reborn
For I fear the cries of rebirth
That sings of life anew will never be heard again
Except in the,
"Music of the Heart"

MY CHILD

I'd sing a lullaby in the morning and at night to my child
I would rock you slowly until you were sound a sleep
I held you in my arms until our hearts would beat as one
Even though my child, you were not there any longer

So many extraordinary visions danced through my heart
I loved touching your warm soft skin of beautiful ivory
I gazed into those amazing blue eyes and saw innocence
Most of all my child, I saw a world of love in your eyes

Your tiny hands would reach for me grasping my finger
Lovingly I would kiss your apple cheeks rosy and ripe
I would tickle your belly just to hear your amazing giggle
So heavenly like the gentle chimes and angels whispering

Together drifting off to sleep with my child in my arms
Dreaming of the future, and what it could hold for my child
The three of us would cuddle together in sweet harmony
I would hum a lullaby as your mother softly sang to you

I remember like it was just yesterday, with the three of us
Now, your mother and you my little one are no longer here
I don't hum the lullaby like once I did for you to fall a sleep
When I rocked in this chair as I cradled you in my arms

I sang a lullaby to a dream, my child, to my son...my son...
Touching a beautiful gift your mother and God gave to me
Your little hand in mine, you wrapped it around my finger
Daddy shared a dream come true, but tragically taken away

My Child, my son, and his mother
Gone...

MY FRIEND

My Friend, Truly *the closes of all friends a boy can have when he needs someone to talk to, to play with, and to become the best of friends. This is my tribute to my best pal when I was starting the first grade.* ***"Rocky"*** *was his name, and he was an of Red Chow-Chow and Saint Bernard. We lived out in the country of Frederick, Maryland. It took nearly a mile to walk to the bus stop. When the day came for that first walk down to the bus, there was Mom, Bonnie, Rocky, and me. When the day was done, there was Mom, Bonnie, and Rocky greeted me to walk back home.*

When the time came for me to make that trip with several other kids to the bus, it was Rocky who walked with us every morning. When that bus arrived back at 4 pm, Rocky was there waiting for me. For the next two years, Rocky walked with me and that was also when Bonnie started her first year. Fate has it, as it seemed to always haunt us, Rocky wasn't there one evening. We walked off the bus and called his name, but he didn't show. I remember we ran home thinking Rocky would be there waiting for us. He wasn't there. I remember running back down to the road calling his name and making sure I was out of the road, for that was a busy time with people coming home from work. There to my first ever horror moment, laid Rocky. He must have been hit by a car and killed. Three years on that road and never once did he get struck. I ran back screaming and in tears to run into Dad. I told him where Rocky was, He went down the road and I remember him carrying Rocky in his arms and Dad had tears in his eyes, for we all loved that dog. He was buried in the back garden amongst Mom's flowers. This is a remembrance of the greatest pal, and friend a boy could ever have.

"I WILL ALWAYS LOVE ROCKY!"

My House

My house was never a home

It had a roof that sheltered us from the weather

It had four walls that held the roof up

There was a floor that completed the box

This box is divided into five separate rooms

Each had four walls, a floor, and a ceiling

I dwelled in one of these rooms

My sister is in another so to feel safe

Each had a bed and a window

It had a door to shut out the world

A sliding lock that was worthless in its purpose

It was a room for contemplation, sometimes

My room held memories worth forgetting

For as long as my mind reflects

These four walls talked of my youth

And the horrors felt in my cubical of despair

Sometimes comfort was felt

My house can tell the story of fear and hurt

The walls speak of secrets that belong to only me

It's deafening when you sit still

Many a day was spent in a haven of darkness

Feeling extremely lonely at times was I

It was better feeling that way

Because opening the door meant faking a smile

My house was never a home

No matter how much the walls wanted to scream

I never felt rooted, never felt safe

If four walls could talk, what story would be told?

A house is not a home when love is rotting

My mother was caged nearly all her life

My sister needed her own space out of fear

I shut the world out in the hope to find myself

There was never a feeling of being a family

Never was there ever a feeling of trust

It was always trekked softly not to disturb the Master

My house never knew the meaning of home.

MY MIND

My mind travels quite fast today

Thoughts over and under other thoughts

Feelings deep, deeper than ever before.

Emotions ride high on nerve endings frayed by fire

My mind wonders through time giving way to the forbidden zones

I am a creation of mass confusion.

My mind is forever like a spinning wheel

Filled with detour signs racing through the game of life

Spun, woven, stitched in a patchwork quilt scared

From the moment of my birth and to my death

My mind is a vault, absorbing a world of no possibilities

I've been given a ticket to ride this game of worthlessness.

My Son
My One and Only One

Sweet is this child, longed for in dreams

Nine months carried to the waiting day

This beauty was well worth waiting for

Printed in my mind until the end of time.

Cody-Li, my son, my one, my only love

I'd secretly watched your mother from afar

Caressing her belly, feeling the kicks made

Then, I saw you emerge from your darkness.

You brought a river of tears from my soul

From deep inside a feeling of pride did rise

*Hearing you cry, was like saying **"Here I am"***

My heart exploded, I never cried so hard.

You're my son, my little boy, a gift from God

From the day of your birth, I have loved you

This wondrous gift your mother gave to me

How could I ever stop loving this gift to me?

We both shared that special moment in time

It halted long enough for our eyes to meet

Like in a dream, a story told, all began to fade

You are here, I turned around, and you were Gone!

Pain, anger, the broken hearts of why so young.

Only five years, you sprouted wings and flew away

In haste, you, and your mother both left me alone

I am lost without my son, my one and only one.

My Shroud Please

A shroud of off-white rests upon my body at last

Reclined in my sweet resting place under the beauty of the Magnolia Tree

You brought the past with you and like time after time again,

You brought grey clouds before the mighty storm

I am shadowed beyond the gates of common understanding

I fall before the faded faces of yesterday

And nothing will ever be able to replace them

I hear the mighty Eagle

I recognize his call and I shall fly free or not at all

Then comes the gentle hand of grace to brush my weary brow

Please, place my shroud upon my body of lost possibilities

Long last there is quiet upon my bed of monumental stone

The darkness has at last conquered my conflicting soul

I no longer see my bed of suffering and torment

The worst is over now,

My shroud, please...

NAKED BEFORE YOU

In a clearing surrounded by nature's gifts
I stand naked before my father and mother
I listen to the four winds; I feel their kiss by
My name rides upon my friends of summer

I honor in the seasons of all living life forces
Bringing the tales of our ancestors before me
Some are told softly, others fiercely spoken
Their stories teach lessons to live wisely by

It's the winter's rage that often tests our lives
Shocking are his stories, a gruesome affection
Mountains harbor the snow for safekeeping
His words are harsh till spring softens them

Brother Autumn reaps a full summer bounty
Across the grassy plains and upon the valleys
Your colors of fire rich our lives with beauty
A blanket to cover the earth when winter arrives

I love standing naked under the vast stars
When the whispering breeze hums its song
Hearing night come alive with its harmony
I am but a mere speck in this world of many

I honor my mother, father, sisters, brothers
Thank God for all the good gifts in my life
We are one family united under your watch
I stand humbly naked before you in gratitude

Nature Conducts

Morning rises to sing her song of reflection

While nature conducts a chorus of perfection

Summer whispers a tune of memories sublime

Together the music dances through all time

Abandoned like snow-covered beaches, icy ghosts rise slow

There is he, moonlight dancing a solo on the freshly fallen snow

Shadowed are the Pampas bent by the blow of winter in chase

Even the sparkling stars shiver in their winter land embrace

Mid-day short-lived were weary the eyes have glazed over

Daydreaming of your youth carefree lying in a field of clover

The day has vanished fading into the night if the truth be known

The why's and wherefores' swirling, answer not when alone

Comfort in the body as the mind labors in troubles of harsh despair

Never shall the tears that are hidden rise in life's favorite care

Short-lived are the moments of intense eagerness and even laid

Whatever suspense there was has gone, the wait is over and paid

Anxiety has no life to barter for the rose sheds her tears

There are secrets untold, unspoken words of silent fears

Bitter consequences bonded by punishment suffer a silent cry

Sometimes lifeless and empty, united in someone's truth by and bye

Deafening is the silence that sometimes floods the sorrows

Silent is the graveyard that amplifies the mood of tomorrow

Lost in a superficial crowd where the roar of many is less than a few

Their emotions falter with the multitude now lost in self-control anew

We are reduced to nothingness in the pitch black of sinking sorrow

Together our containment is lost in a second, suffering a fragile tomorrow

Time is just an exquisite embrace that is silently slipping into the sea

It just takes a few un-symbiotic tears to stir the waters named Mercy

An expectation of uncharted shadows leads to a world of shattered dreams

Unquenched are the desires thirsting for a flow of unspoken words, so it seems

Spiraling winds overwhelm the tranquil peace that nature conducts endlessly

Rains of ecstasy now wash away concepts conceived in the morning musically.

Never To Be Forgotten

Words can hurt and bring a man down

They can turn him ugly to all he sees

Words can destroy a mind and heart

Many can hinder thoughts forever

Up or down in mind or heart to shallow him

Dreams, when young are staked out to dry

Hopes bashed up against life's jagged rocks

Words can do this to a young man's heart

Words can create and take a man on-high

They can teach him the beauty in all the living

They can develop creativity in his mind and soul

Words will give life to the soul's reason

Show him a path unto the teacher of light

Dreams to come true, dream of future goals

Hopes of being more than you are, the achieving it

Words can guide the heart in everlasting love

Then there are words spoken by a woman

They can make a man or break his will

Words from a poetic woman in love

Will bring him to new heights because of respects

His spirit can have wings when words have meaning

A woman's words can bring him to tears

Happy is the man when words are whispered in a sigh

Her beauty inside and out reflects a belief in his own words

A slight touch, a kiss, and a caress calms the beast

The inflection of a word has excellent meaning

Words that express his most quiet needs

The right words make him more than he thinks he can be

For there is love in his words

Thank you, sometimes are the most complex words for him

But not for this one man, who is made strong

The words from the Angel of gold, will not be forgotten!

NIGHTINGALES SWEET AS APRIL BLOSSOMS

Nightingales are sweet as April blossoms sang you a song
I cradled you in my arms amongst sweet Gardenias' white
The first time ever I held you, I feared holding you too tight
Suddenly you were gone, no longer to cradle in my arms

Every night I sit in the rocker imagining you in my arms
I put your blanket on my face, I can smell your freshness
I looked into those innocent eyes filled with life's promises
I still smell you, feel you, hear your every giggle and cry

I loved how your tiny fingers reached out for me with love
I would lay your tiny hand into mine and in the future, I'd see
I'd nibbled on your toes just to hear your music come alive
Angels watched, the bells did chime, and nightingales sang

Not a day goes by when I don't smell Gardenia blossoms
It warms my heart as the fragrance moves about the room
I close my eyes, feeling your everlasting presence of love
Nightingales sweet as April blossoms still sing you songs

NIKKI-LYNN

"I have convinced myself that time must have ended
And then began again when I first met you
Oh my God, I was so much younger
And you are older and wiser than I
None of that mattered to me
Walking, talking and
Dreaming"

"Nikki-Lynn
Come over here for a minute
Just play along with me
Humor me!
Close your beautiful eyes
*Picture walking along the **"River Walk of Love"***
Sit and relax on a soft carpet of green
Feel a cool breeze of mist from the water that rushes over the rocks
If you listen hard enough
You will hear the "River Walk of Love" singing
Now, if you listen to the sound of the leaves,
When the wind blows through the trees
Their rustling adds a heavenly harmony to her singing
Can you hear it?
I watch my beauty as she lives in the moment
I can see a schoolgirl's imagination take her to a world of magic
And I too, am whisked away into the moment
When I notice at the corner of her eye

A flash of light where a diamond appeared bright,
Sparkling as it slowly moves down her beautiful cheek
That's when I felt a tightness in my throat
I never would have believed,
That she could be even more radiant than she is..."

Nikki-Lynn,
I whispered quietly in her ear
Open your eyes, my love
There's something I wish to say
You know I love you
There is nothing I wouldn't do for you
You know I will always be there
In times of trouble, in times of need
If you are feeling sad, you can count on me to lift your spirits up
I will give you a wink and you will know to smile
I'll give you a hug and stand by your side
Nikki, what I am trying to say is,
I would do any...
OH MY GOD!
I want you to...
How can I...
Nikki-Lynn,
"Will You Marry Me?"

I will never forget that day for as long as I live
That was the hardest thing for me to do
And I will never forget the son, you gave me, us...
Five beautiful and amazing years together
I'll never understand God's reason or purpose for taking you away,
But who am I to question our father?

Well, it is getting late, and I must get back home
So far away across the United States of America
As you all here put it, **"The Mainland"**
Standing here looking down at your stones,
My broken heart still weeps
Cody-li and I have the same birthday
My son was turning five years old
Well, I always repeat the same issues, don't I?
I must go, or I'll miss my flight
Remember my love is never far away
My body leaves but my heart remains with you both
ALOHA AND MAHALO

NO LONGER WEEPS THE WILLOWS

Always the sun and moon embrace the weeping willow
She carousels to the music of the breezes and tempests
Anchored to her mother that waters and feeds her roots
Nature's gift of love is a testament to the lady's longevity

She's a collector of many memories throughout the ages
Her long tresses dance to and fro in the summer songs
Autumn's tune announces the coming of a harsh winter
Until then her carousel will circle merrily in the breeze

Winter's harshness has no pity on nature's grandmother
As her life force slowly retreats into her soul foundation
This year-old man winter stripped away her life within
When perma-frost released its grip, all the spring cried

Father Sun and Sister Moon gently embraced her spirit
Grandmother Willow bough-ed her head to the ground
Time marched forward and nature reclaimed her beauty
Mother nature always lays her beloved children to rest

Grandmother weeping willow will forever cry her tears
All of nature now cries because of the toxins in the air
Grandmother's death was not because of her age alone
Mother Earth is being poisoned by man's abusive nature

We now must live our lives in shame, we didn't listen
The wisdom of our age is taken with a grain of salt
The world's only hope lies within the youth of the future
The circle of life is broken, I fear it's too late to change

No Longer Weeps the Willows...

NO NIGHTINGALE TO SING MY SONG

I was born insignificant
Therefore, I know, never will a song ever be written for me
Special I will never be
Never will I experience the meaning of special
No hero to praise
Just another being that vanishes into the endless haze of the forgotten
If I would lay wounded upon the battlefield of life
There will be no nightingale to sing my song
My reflection stands in the periphery, this I have seen
In a world beyond fragile and on the edge of danger
A stage with a grand curtain will slowly open
Like a veil rising to expose a figure
A shadow of another me stretched across the stage

Why waste the time on introductions
Neither one of me are worth taking time on such a production
Looking at myself gives me an uneasy feeling
Both of us are uncomfortable
Who do I think I am?
The light on me fades to complete darkness
The same veil lowers between us
The grand curtain slowly closes as expected
Nothingness!
A silent world so well-known to me
Once again, I tell you,
There will be no nightingale to sing a song for me
I will make my way through the continuous darkness to my home
Where I live in the shadows of a horror
I feel fear that dares me to dream of the light
I realize no one will ever know I am here
Therefore, no song will ever be written for the nightingale to sing
My world of darkness is filled with empathy
My destiny is nothing more than a generation after generation of hand-me-downs
There will never be a song written for I never existed
Even if it happened,
The content would be ironic and repulsive
Redundant at the very least!
The instruments would consist of cellos and violins out of tune
Playing a,
"Concerto for the Shadows in Grievous Sorrow"
This small dark symphony is written by,
"The Master of Lonesome Heartaches"
The rhythm is macabre
An audience full of lost soul groupies
They will hear no nightingale to sing my song
This is the reflection of me
I alone will sing my own song,
Setting the nightingale free

OF WHAT ONCE WAS

When the heart becomes drained of its feelings and emotions
Dried up into powder and caught up in a stale stagnant breeze
Fine powder falls from above, and down, and over all things tender
Emotions weaken all that's cherished now becomes breathless

When choke, all the feelings are smothered by the not so tender
What's remaining are ivory-shadowed figures of what once was
It's the mind that is expected to control a whirlwind of emotions
Now you're weakened from the loss of yesteryear's fragmentation

Many times, the heart has skipped a beat over shocking outcomes
Like a game of childhood joys, toss the pebble, Hey! it's my turn!
Hop-scotch playtime favorite, imagination in chalking squares
The heart is surrounded by impediments, and pebble lands on the line

The soul is empty and totally drained of concerns, why bother?
Sinking to the depths of five hundred miles on a broken wing
Washing away complete hopes and desires of ever giving a damn
Trying to stop the teardrops from what seems to be a raging storm

Can only blind the eyes with the uncertainty of what needs to go
Close your eyes to the shadows on the floor of what once was
Memories gather on a dust-covered summer lost amongst the falls
Pray the day will come when freshness rides upon the air in motion

The heart contained forever finding a rhythm of what once was
A rebirth of emotions that tie the gathering memories of one loved
Once again, the heart regains the strength and skips another beat
You feel emotions you've cherished, just wipe away the powder

On Our Own Land

Attacked on our own land

From above came two explosions

All Hell broke loose

Devastation in our eyes

Confusion running rampant everywhere

People covered in grayish-powered dust

A deadly fog

A bevy of ghost-like figures

Contorted Faces

Horrific cries

Earth shuddering screams

The stench of fuel everywhere

The day the Twin Towers came tumbling down

War in Iraq

Rising fuel prices

Raging Storms

Flooding is everywhere

So many people affected

So personal

Public Catastrophe

Devastation is Climbing

"HOME IS WHERE THE HEART IS"

Things are becoming more difficult

Living and coping in the red, white, and blue

Do not forget the Twin Towers

America is a Christian Nation

Hold our belief up high

Buddy to Buddy

Buy another six-pack

So many of our men and women are dying over there

Shed your tears

PRIDE

FAITH

Say a prayer

America has her own problems

So many disappearing

So many dying from unheard things

VIRUSES

WARS & ACCIDENTS

Where are the parents?

We wear our hearts on our sleeves

Medical Costs

No Insurance

The Doctors are getting theirs

TEACHERS

They make $35,000 a year

Look at the crap they take in trying to teach the parent's problem

They don't make Enough People!

Face the reality of death and destruction

We didn't have this problem until They invaded us

Where will they strike next?

SUBWAYS

AIRPLANES

CRUISE LINES

This Nation of Ours needs more than Prayers

Let's Prayer People

FREEDOM

Continue to Pray to God

"I've seen the promised land"

DEATH

CHILD ABUSE

Within the Church and our own Homes

Madness is eating away at us

CRIME

MOTHER NATURE

And Endless War that doesn't cease?

Pray and find Peace

Will that really HELP?

It all started when the Twin Towers came tumbling down

POVERTY

HOMELESSNESS

Get a Frigg' in JOB!

Calamities facing the Red, White, and Blue

OBESITY

HOUSING ISSUES

PLAN PARENTHOOD

God Bless America

Let's make positive changes

Mother's crying for the Lost Children

MURDERED

DRUGS

PUSHERS

JUNKIES

SUICIDES

How can anyone cope with all the suffering?

"There Before the Grace of God, Go I"

PRAY SOME MORE

FAITH AND TRUST

Pass the collection plate, Please

Does the Church really need more money?

JUSTICE FOR ALL

Death and Destruction is awesome

Pass the Potatoes

Mommy, I am hungry!

SORRY KID

What we need is a Miracle

The desire is for Peace

Who has the time to stop for Peace?

TRANQUILITY

We need to find the comfort we had before

The Day the Twin Towers Came Tumbling Down

SEPTEMBER 11, 2001

911 Everything changed on that day, The World Trade Towers, it all became undone

On our own land

MAY GOD BLESS US ALL

Once A Poet, Always A Poet

Once a Poet, always a poet

Ring clear a poetic dream was written long ago

"Starry, Starry Night"

"Quote the Raven, nevermore!"

My favorite,

"How do I love Thee, let me count the ways"

What do all the quotes of poetry mean?

The changing times

Pondering as you sit back and wonder what each line means

It is locking me inside a box

Then telling me to get out

Poetic movement is like a mighty gust of wind

A tornado that comes in the night

Why?

Poems to read that give reason to pray for

Some poems are like the brightest of sunshine

There is a coldness to words

Some are like fire from Hell

Sensual readings in a Coffee House

War and protest

Folklore and Mythology

Winds of change are here for your pleasure

Now the fad is all about destruction

The ending of all time

But no matter where you go to read

Poetry, Prose, Short stories,

Fiction, Non-Fiction,

History, Comic, or Love Themes

Always there will be a poem written with

Our Heavenly Father in mind

He has been the focus point

Of writing since the beginning of faith

Poetry is and will be a part of our lives

Until the end of time.

Countless libraries around the world

Harbor volumes of Man's written words

Those that do not write with gill and or pen and ink

Paint their poetry on canvas

poetic reflections of life

Man's inhumanity to Man

And so on and so on!

"All the world is a stage"

Many a writer began with the magical words,

"Once Upon a Time"

Man created songs

Country, Classical to Metal and Rock,

Soul, Alternative, Techno

Folk, Bluegrass, Gospel, Opera, and Theater

Poetry in one form or another

Speaks to us in rhythms

The oldest form of poetry is

"Love Letters"

Even the tiniest of notes

Reflect the heart's desire

Love makes us all poets

The next time you read anything

In any form and or subject

Remember that there was a poet at its heart

Shakespeare wrote what I believe to be

The most famous line ever put on parchment

"Romeo, Romeo, Where forth art thou Romeo?"

Believe me when I say

Once a Poet, always a Poet!

ONCE UPON SHADOWS

The days are shortened, then the cold darkness creeps upon life's stage
How perfect the dance within the collective shadows of life's winter
Forever stretching across nature's backdrop in morbid choreography
Recreating the movements to equal Twyla Tharp's silent aching song

This time of year, the forest's pine trees offer no fruit for the birdmen
Beware, For the wind whispers of the black-heart-ed Croon's covens
The full moon is high, and the cries of the lost children are to be heard
Fowl fumes rise from blackening cauldrons that are hidden in solitude

Fables are told, yet it is the truth that's often sung by traveling Minstrels
Children's rhymes handed down through the ages contain many clues
Wise are many children who read between the lines about the wicked
Yesteryear is filled with such subtle wisdom to have adhered to nowadays

Within your mind, that's being painted pitch until it's hopeless to see
Whirling within the lost time there's a greater distance between stars
Which just might hold answers to escaping the clutches of darkness
There are countless and numberless possibilities amid old wife's tales

So many children without purpose vanish into the arms of shadows
The heart is battered and abused far too often, once young, now old
Countless trials and endless tribulations mark the soul with a scarlet letter
Branded deep into the forehead for the world to recognize the ownership

Beyond wicked are the bitchy Croons, if not eaten they will cruse you
*My childhood soul drowned in a flood of tears, **"Be Gone Evil Ones!"***
I ventured deeper into the forest of darkness, overwhelmed with shadows
*I'm lost in the forest following the path that leads to **"Hell's Half Acre"***

It is so easy to give in to the cry of the lonely and abused when lost
Another child's cry joins the echoes of thousands wanting to be heard
The horror stories that contain hidden codes to heed and listen to...
*Storybooks colored in black and gray titled, **"Once Upon Shadows"***

ONE MORE MILE

I have driven down this hi-way
More times than I care to remember
This hi-way is named
"One More Mile"
Memories good, memories bad, and even worst
I mark the time by following an endless white line
Hypnotic lines of yellow and white reflected in the night
Darkness offers the soul credence of silence
Quite often I will glance into the rear-view mirror
To the fading of what was
Miles and miles of empty spaces
I give thanks to the darkness that covers
The lost dreams and headaches left behind
It's not very hard to forget the mileage traveled in loneliness
I have driven through the land of the lost and found
Friends we three are,
Searching for the next rest stop that never seems to come
Having to turn the radio up full blast
In order to shock your senses back to reality
I have driven directly into traffic jams six lanes deep!
Sitting motionless in heat from the bowels of hell
Geysers of steam exploding under the hoods from idling
Surrounded by a growing rage
For hours upon hours
There were miles of out-of-tune horns blasting for a hopeless cause
"STOP THE INSANITY!!!"
That's how it is on this hi-way named,
"One More Mile"
There were moments in my lonely life,
When I felt the hi-way urging me to keep driving onward
As if there might be something special for me
At the end of this hi-way
"One More Mile"
My mind has been captured in a stagnate world
My heart beats in darkness as I travel nowhere in particular
I've longed for nothing more than a little happiness
Still, I drive into the darkness
Seated beside me were my forever companies
My forever Shadows, named loneliness and sorrow
I have known the horrors of darkness all my life
I have become a shadow of myself
I walk alone down the hi-way known as,
"One More Mile"

PAINTED WORDS

From his soul came the multicolored spectrum of words
Painting a canvas of swirling emotions dark and tainted
Regretful memories portraying his youth in a mix of mud

A hidden jungle of green, harsh surroundings with thrones
Blood red, dark copper smells, thrown together in a brew
Friends and foes, blinded critics slashing away at his pallet

Painting his world black and white, a total lack of coloring
His heart bleeds so often the blood flows a blushing pink
A rough demanding world that totally lacks all compassion

Stroke for a stroke of burnt oranges, rusts, browns, and black
Horror and the shame painted in lightning strikes over the pitch
Appearing within billowing clouds of charcoal and evil eyes

The true color of envy is outlined in decaying squash and fire
These are the making of all nightmares, seemingly endless
His remaining spirit hovers over the edge of a razor blade

Where are the whys, the wherefores that frame this canvas?
Bruised pigments, broken brushes, ravished body works
His muted canvas of words, scream out into the community.

"ABUSE"

NO BETTER FOR THE WORST

I have known this feeling most of my life

It was time for me to call it my last

There were those who cocked their mirror eyes away from me

They wouldn't give me the time of day

A total refusal of any acknowledgment that ever existed

Regardless I would walk onward to my destination

Even though it never led to anywhere, any place,

Other than walking among the living.

There were times I could feel their repulsion

I gave up the idea of trying to connect, simply wasn't worth the effort

Walking among the living was like walking among the dead

Often, I would duck from the street and enter an alley

The dark cold alley felt more like home

Relatable, filled with crevasses I could meld into

"JUST LEAVE ME ALONE"

Often, I felt like the slimy sludge of human waste

Leaving trails from the attacks of childhood Bullies

Often when alone, I would breakdown staring into the future

I'd step out of myself, watching me fighting pigeons for scrapes of morsels

At the lowest times, I would run through the rain of self-pity

Other times I would dance in the rain of my own disrespect

"Hello, world! Why am I a child of God?"

I suckle on hell's bitter hate

Slap after Slap, I turn the other cheek

All the while suppressing the screams with silent tears

My life is like a brick and a rose

The brick is the hard and cold wall built before you

And the rose is the beauty one can see if left alone to do so

What's left for those like me is the means to the end

Allow the dark to become so dense you no longer can see your thoughts

Find a secluded crevasse in the alley of life

AND SCREAM!

I dream of lying down in a field of tall green grass where the wind creates waves

Each wave lifts my spirit to ride on Mother nature's love

Better yet stand atop a waterfall that plummets hundreds of feet into a great blue lake

Then swan dive...

Each offers my caressing the loneliness of my childhood with compassion

Softly stroke my ego, if ever I had one?

The silent tears shed were for nothing,

I heard somewhere that shedding tears cleanse one's soul.

If that is true, I've shed several lifetimes and watched them washed away

For whatever purpose, the reason I existed in this time and space,

Nothing will be left behind

A single tear like a grain of sand am I in the ocean of life

No Better for The Worst

PEARL

If the world is my Oyster,
Then I shall be its Pearl.
And like Pearls, it takes time for nature to create
the beauty within this shell
I'll take that time,
So that I develop within this world.

PLEASE SIT BY MY SIDE

My friend, please sit beside me in this garden of beauty
Feel the spirit of life, love, and wonderment throughout
"All Good Gifts" are given to us by our heavenly father
In one's solitude, sitting in this garden fills you with joy

Beneath your feet is a carpet of peace and understanding
Before your eyes is an endless world of amazing serenity
A forever painting painted by the Master Artist of them all
Come, my friend, walk beside me in this garden of beauty

This garden's path has been walked by many, yet by few
Listen and hear tranquility calling for your surrender to it
Upon this water look at your own reflection to know the truth
These reflective waters are the true mirrors of one's soul

Give your spirit the freedom it desires here in this garden
Imagine your spirit to be an eagle soaring endlessly above
Throw a pebble in the water, the ripples will show your life
Watch how they travel revealing stages in your circle of life

Just like life itself, they roll outward and onward endlessly
Until your life force has reached the shore of total fulfillment
Those left behind will always be with you, for love never dies
Know it's the heart's soul that carries your diary of memories

All will be with you throughout your venture in the evermore
My friend, come sit by my side in this garden of all gardens
Hear the spirit of life whispering a song that reigns supreme
It is here where your presences are prepared to move onward

You will be bathed in his essence, heaven's Holiest of Light
The warmth of the Holy Light will remain with you always
I tell you now, it will radiate throughout your entire being
It is pure and magnificent light of love giving your life anew

Please, I wish to show you the garden's canopy high above
You will hear nature's diverse songs sung by birds of beauty
All about you, up in trees are rare and exotics, presumed lost
Displaying brilliant colors that radiated rich, treasured spirits

Fragrances are at every turn, perfumes never imagined, yet
Listen when the spirits sing, the garden becomes a symphony
Harmony and peace become a carpet of freshness to walk upon
Look around this garden, and know the peace felt within you

Welcoming those confused and somehow lost from within
If it is rest that you desire, all your worries will be no longer
Serenity and contentment play a magnificent role in the garden
Endless and always at peace in this garden for the in-between

Unseen are the caretakers that maintain the garden's majesty
All are welcome here to rest, making the journey a blessed one
Consoling their fears, comforting the sadness that souls may feel
Please, sit by my side in the magnificence of everlasting beauty...

Precious Were You

How precious your life truly was?

When you were given to us by our Heavenly Father

The miracle of life is truly an amazing gift

You brought much love and joy into our hearts

You brought light where there was darkness

My heart was filled with comfort and peace

How was I to know that your time was cut short

Never was a spirit so blessed

You were bright as the first star that appears in the Heavens

How unbelievably precious your life was to me

Yet in a blink of an eye, you and your mother were gone

The sadness clinched my soul for a long time

My special angels are gone forevermore

Before I ever got to lay eyes upon you, you were loved

I sang to you as your mother carried you for all those months

I know your heard me for you moved at my voice

I watched you come into this world

My heart was full, I now was a father

I held you, bonded with you, and cried at your beauty

You were daddy's little boy

How wonderful and lovely you're sent was

You were brand new, and my fear of breaking you was immense

I gazed at your mother's beautiful face, and she assured me all is well

I learned to become caring and so very gentle with you

My God, how precious your first breath was to me

Daddy held you close to his heart

The day I was informed that you and your mother were hit by a drunk driver

My heart exploded in my chest

It was Easter and yours and I's birthday

You and your mother went to church, and I stayed home

I wanted to surprise you with a cake and presents when you two returned

How precious your life was for five glorious years?

Memories of you Cody-Li, and your Mother Nikki-Lynn

Are all I have

I can still smell your heavenly scent to this very day

Precious you two will be forever in my heart

Until we meet again...

RAIN SINGS TO ME

Rain is life, rain governs emotions, rain is a reflection
The Poet can reveal all the depths of love in its trickle
Rain creates, rain conducts remarkable symphonies
Sometimes in torrents, crescendos of anger and rage

Rain upon your tongue is the forgotten taste of a kiss
Rain is when the heartstrings no longer vibrate in tune
Rain is memories no longer having the ability to tease
Destructive in its multitude, deadly when there's a lack of

Rain can paint a rainbow of colors within a veil of mist
Like a delicate dove that writes love across the blue sky
When you love it's like the feeling of rain on your face
I see beauty in the rain when a child jumps from puddle to puddle

There are times it helps to wash away, to forget one's past
I love the rain because it knows all the secrets of my pain
It caters not to distrust, no judging, it comes, and it goes
The rain sings to me in a language my heart understands

Raven Haired Beauty

{I was seduced at sixteen by an older woman twice my age}

Complete silence filled the country night. Cassie, the gypsy beauty stepped out of her wagon. She raised her hands, running her fingers through a full head of hair. Tossing it back and forth. Looking up at the evening sky. Flirting with the man-in-moon so that he would shine brightly down on her like a personal spotlight. Once again, she would do her seductive dance beneath the light of the **"Blood Moon".** Her long raven-black hair moved in slow motion around her body. It looked like a shadow in an eerie duet. In perfect harmony. There was more to her talent and beauty than form and movement. She was **"Seduction".** One could believe she was a **"Succubus".** The full Blood Moon was a certain promise that night would be intense. The crowd would be large, and the money would flow. Not a man's attention would falter from her dance of seduction. Before her turn to perform, Cassie would mingle through the crowd, teasing and flirting with the men. Always to give the night and herself purpose. During her dance, she would search for that one special man. Handsome, wide-eyed, and eager for attention. Once discovered she would face him with eyes that reflected the fire from the bonfire of the camp. Her eyes were a rare piercing amber. Seductively rolling her hips back and forth in a snake-like movement. Sending a message of unbelievable pleasure and so much more. What was not known by the handsome studs she selected, would lead them into her world of lustful evil. Once mesmerized and in her control, they would become an added fixture in a harem of studs. Cassie was attracted to handsome studly men in their mid-twenties and thirties. If you asked her what traits she desired in men, she would say, Chiseled *features, eyes that could melt ice, arms like Hercules, and legs as powerful as Samson. Overall, the most virile and handsome. Cassie had a hunger for exotic and erotic pleasures.*

*On this night her sister court of luxurious vixens had lured an incredible slew of young virile men. It was billed as a night of entertainment and a promise of wild imaginings. Throughout the neighboring countryside. Each performance starred, **"Cassie, The Raven-Haired Beauty"**. There were two weeks of adverting this special event. The Gypsies knew of the Blood Moon's scheduled event and worked hard to create a stage with curtains. A huge tent was erected. Cables ran from a generator to supply the theatrical lighting. Cassie peeked through a slit in the curtain from backstage. She could see that vixens had done their job enticing a hot selection of men. Cassie thought to herself, **"Well Done girls, well done!"** Just as she was closing the curtain slit, her eye caught the figure of a tall, dark, and extremely good-looking man. He certainly was the stallion amongst all the studs standing around. She was ready to robe in her prize stud. She took a second peek to be sure of what she had seen. As she watched him slowly make his way through the gathering crowd of men. Greeting some and shaking hands with others. He casually leaned against a wagon across from a roaring campfire. She watches intensely as the hunk opened a new pack of cigarettes. Retrieving one from the pack and placing it between his waiting lips. Cassie watched his every move. Something deep inside her was stirring with excitement. She hadn't felt a stirring like this for years. He struck a match, cupping the flame and raising it to his cigarette. The flickering flame accented his handsome features. Cassie thought, **"He was blessed. The genes in that family were far superior to most."** If Cassie was considered **"Evil to the core"** before this night, she certainly would give **"Evil"** a new purpose! The man tipped his hat down over his forehead. Looking coy, sly, and sexy as hell, as far as she was concerned. This night gave rise to her excitement. Conjuring a spell over the man that would become her lover.*

The lights dimmed under the huge tent. The men cheered and a few catcalls were amongst the applause. The men were excited that the evening had promised beautiful women and joyful merriment. No doubt erotic play. Drums began to thump out a rhythm. Stage lights slowly filled the stage to the beating of drums. The curtain opened. The men under the tent applauded with excitement as an orange fire with red flames from flash pots ignited on the stage. Within the flash pots, glitter and sparkle shot into the air and slowly fall to the stage. A half dozen outstanding scantly clothed young women danced to a jungle rhythm. No doubt their movements had turned the young men's hearts afire with a sexual charge. The men moved closer to the edge of the stage. Each with the hope a vixen would catch their eye. The dancers were spinning wildly to the faster pacing of the drums. A climax came to an end and the dancers fell to the floor. Now there was silence under the tent. All eyes were raised to the top of the stage as a rope slowly dropped to the sound of a flute. The audience was silent. Somewhat mesmerized like a cobra, swaying back and forth to the sound of the flute. The young women on stage formed a circle in the center of the stage. A shirtless gypsy man with a violin walked downstage from the up center out of the shadows. He resembled a masterpiece of a Pirate. Stunningly handsome with muscles that equaled any Adonis. He raised his bow and a column of white smoke from a flash pot ignited in front of the violinist.

He, the flutist, and the drums created an atmosphere for what was about to take place center stage. Rising out of the floor was a golden rope. Magically it rose higher and higher. Within a light change of green. Attached to the end of the rope with one hand was the star of the show. There was a sound of awl and disbelief at what they were seeing before their eyes. Cassie was dressed in a one-piece nude unitard that had the print of snakeskin painted that covered her breast and groin area. Giving her body the image of a serpent. Her movement was accented to every drumbeat. Her dance was erotic and sensual. From upstage came a nearly naked muscular male dancer. He wore a green rhinestone leaf jockstrap, covering a fully packed crotch. He oozed the mystic of an **"Adonis God".** *The few women that came to see what this show was all about. Squealed when the stud made his appearance on stage. Cassie was being raised in the air and the nearly naked stud grabbed the end of the rope as Cassie reached halfway up. The muscle man began to turn it to the beat of the drums. She began to spin in a circle around the rope with one arm holding on. The faster the drums went, the faster the stud would turn the rope. The audience was simply amazed watching her spinning and changing positions in the air. With her free arm, she took her hand and grabbed her ankle, going into a full straddle-split. The audience applauded wildly. The applause continued throughout her routine. At the conclusion of her act, the muscled stud controlled the rope's speed. Bringing it to a full stop. He pulled it taut, and Cassie slowly snaked her way headfirst down the rope landing on the broad shoulders of her performance partner. He lifted her over his head walking the star downstage toward the audience. He brought her down onto his shoulder once again. Like a snake, she circled around his body, down to the waist and through his muscular thighs, and slide onto the floor as if she hadn't a bone in her body. The men went crazy with applause and whistles. The lights went out and they took their curtain call. Curtain closed.*

Part Two

{to be Continued}

RAVEN'S BOG

Dark and dismal is the setting surrounding thee
Crooked and rotted now stand the dead Fir trees

Stale and stagnate hang Spanish Moss in decay
Fitted on broken branches wet in a slim-my array

Perched on a branch like sentinels in full guard
Are a Raven duet surveying in their courtyard,

Looking over a Bog Littered with grassy mounds
Reflected pools of rusty-colored water profound

A full moon shines brightly over the Bog-like glass
Silhouette gravestones made from mounds-of-grass

Evil caws echoing throughout a graveyard moor
Matched flight. Ruffled haste, disturbed to the core

Wicked are the shadows that arise from wings of black
Eyes dark as coal, inside screams, shutters, and flaps

One eye on heaven, circle around to hell and back
Toward barren trees, growing old yet holding on fast

In quiet seclusion, over the dark and dismal bog
Two Raven surveying their courtyard in the fog.

REALITY'S REFLECTION

Yesterday when I was in my youth
The world lay before my feet
There wasn't a dare not to be challenged
I was young, handsome, and strong

The idea of growing old was far off
Tomorrow was another day yet to come
For now, dreams were to be conquered
Living life to its fullest was the ticket

The wind was at my back pushing me forward
I searched for love among the stars
Something I longed for each day and night
Love became a cosmic adventure

I never gave a thought to being alone
My dreams came to life one by one
I laughed, and I cried in my abusive world
Life suddenly became a traffic jam

Commitment became a must to survive
My world slowed to a snail's crawl
The dream that kept me young and alive
The years began to fade into dusty memories

Aches and pains in life were true as reality
Looking into the mirror, life reflected the age
Yet behind those bright eyes was my yesterday
It was the aging process that contained my dreams

Memory allowed me a transformation to into a youth
There was a handsome young man, looking back at me
I smiled back, gave a wink and youth faded
Time is but a reality's reflection

RED WING SAYS FAREWELL

High upon an ancestral mountain that overlooks a sacred valley
A very old man sits on a blanket alone by a bright campfire
Smoke billows in a spiral fashion that braids up on high
The fire crackles and pops glowing embers high into the night sky

This old man sits in front of the fire and slowly rocks back and forth
He is becoming one with the spirits of the ancestors
From a distance, there is another fire that glows as bright
Where the drums of his people beat a rhythm of enchantment

The smoke swirls about from a light breeze that gives way to visions
Softly this brave chant the songs of greetings to the other world
"Come forth, come forth my brother and sisters who have crossed over
Greet me and help me to prepare for my travel to the other world"

"My past calls for one to guide me to where the buffalo run free
Where the thundering is heard, and the hunt is a good one for all
I, Red Wing now honor you, Oh Great Manitoba for all your blessings
I have throned the bones, it is time to travel to my Forefathers,

I grow weary and hard to keep up with those that love me dearly
Call to me as the wolf calls to the giant white moon above
Spirits of my Forefathers, Spirits of the Guardians do bless me
So that my spirit flies high on Eagle wings and my journey fairs"

He stands slowly, with all the pride he has felt for nearly two lifetimes
He then raises his arms to the Spirits and the drums seem to echo
And the fire bursts forth and the spiraling smoke creates stairsteps
That spiral up and up until there stands a Warrior mighty and strong

This warrior is in full Regalia, and on his shoulder is a Hawk with red wings
*The great warrior calls to Red Wing, **"Come to my brother, your traveling,***
Will not be a lonely one, come and walk by my side old man, together,
You will become as you were in your youth, we will hunt as once before."

The old man named Red Wing steps upon the smoke, and his body transforms
Into the smoke that swirls upward and beyond to the Great Warrior
Drums in the distance have faded as the spirit of Red Wing now has
The fire crackles no longer and slowly dies with the coming of dawn

The red sun rises with an orange glow across the horizon
When the sun touches the mountain where the old man sat by the fire
There lays a blanket that he placed to sit in front of the campfire
*Over the horizon, a hawk with red wings cries out as if to say **"farewell"***

RESTORATION OF MY SALVATION

This is what I want from thee, to fear not
Doth not be afraid to invite the devil
To sit in thy parlor is to have God by your side
To teach thee, thy heart will rise above all
Allow emotions the acceptance within the heart

I want thee to walk by my side always
Not to stroll blindly behind like so many others
Nor do I want you to walk in front of me
Do not put meters between us
Like a lesser, Nay! side by side as equals

Thy heart beats for me as mine does for thee?
I know so, for thee cannot hide thy emotions
Your eyes of ocean blue can't hide,
The waves crashing upon shores of enchantment
Thy love breakers for which I dive into

I wish for thee to sing sweet pleasantries
Harmonizing across a midnight Lagoon
Echoing love songs that are sung by the Loons
A love melody played upon still waters
A love song is sung to thee by one who loves you

We praise unto our Father in heaven above
Worry not, for we walk hand in hand as one
As we freely lift our voices in reference
In poetic poetry sung to thee like angels
In the total restoration of my salvation...

RONNIE BLUE EYES

Oh my God! Ronnie Blue Eyes, have you ever seen a pair of eyes that simply scream crystal blue? Such an amazingly blue that it pulled you in like a fish being reeled in on a line. That capture's your attention and you just must move in closer to see if they are real. Well, this truly happen to me in Baltimore, Maryland at the dance club called the "Hippo".

After an hour or so of staring at this beautiful man, he got the message that I was interested in him. He came over to me and started to speak. I ask him his name and he replied, "Ronnie." I pulled him over under the light and said I need to look at your eyes. After a line like that, what else could he do but walk into the light? Those eyes simply allow you to walk into their soul.

After a dance or two, we went to the other side of the club to sit down and talk about things. Ronnie was the nicest of guys, anyone would want to meet. For me, it was those eyes. I tell you without any reservations, it was his rich sapphire eyes and sweet soul that electrified my mind first. His amazing looks and body gave him the total package! I should have titled this poem, "Windows to His Soul!" ….

RONNIE BLUE EYES

Crystal blue persuasion, an ocean so deep
Pools of warmth within an amazing gaze
Blue as the bright of Sapphires do they shine.

How can one get so lost in two islands of crystal blues?
Twin lakes that own you at a single glance
Blue, deep blue, there's nothing to compare

They are like ribbons of blue satin rising and falling
Smooth and silky are their twinkles that flirt
Shards of blue light where duty does calls

One can investigate the depths of those blue pools
Hypnotized, mesmerized, and carried away
You find yourself taking a swan dive

Blue, the bluest of all shades imagined
He possesses the only "Crystal Blue Persuasions"
The indescribably gorgeous Ronnie Blue Eyes.

ROSES SWEET AND ORCHIDS RARE

With pen in hand my parchment thirsts for the words
A deep need within my soul compels me to compose
Aimlessly I sift through my emotions new and aged
*It seems like searching for **"The Lost City of Gold"***

Drifting so endlessly in a thicket of useless what-knots
Finding meaningful words to express how blessed I am
I pen this letter to someone who has captured my heart
We have bathed our love in roses sweet and orchids rare

Could my love be smiling that remarkable smile I adore?
Maybe reminiscing about the gentle caress of my touch?
Such sensitivity melts my heart when I see a tear appear
It's a great feeling in knowing I am missed as I do as well

No one ever touched my soul in such a passionate way
I always experience the warmth of passion within each kiss
With each thought of you, a fire ignites inside my heart
When in my arms, it is like roses sweet and orchids rare!

RUBY THE RED ROSE

There once were twelve sisters, fresh, long-legged, and beautiful
Clustered amongst baby's breath being featured on center stage
Day to day the attention needed waned in the settling dusty mire
Eleven sisters were lost in their glamoured celebration, all but one

Ruby in solo stands alone, surrounded by her sisters, dry, athirst
Arms lay at their sides lifeless while heads are lowered in prayer
Centered as if on point in a macabre ballet pose, Ruby is radiant
*Starring in a magical garden titled, **"A Mid-Summer's Nightmare"***

During the full moon, lunar rays spotlight her vessel-ed reservoir
The stillness is broken by a haunting breeze, stirring up the dust
Slowly trickling downward over Ruby like a mystical conjuring
Ruby is blushing in the electric glow of a blood-red magnificence

At last, the dawn comes blistering with dry heat in the stale room
Ruby's long stem shrivels from lack of moisture and arms wilt at the side
Gracefully she bows her head, joining her eleven sisters in prayer
Ruby's celebration of color, and fragrance, ends her final performance.

RUN CHILD RUN

Run Child Run...from your world of unforgiving horrors
Flee to that one place only you know and feel safe in
Far enough away, but close enough to maintain a hold,
Onto reality's jail, where the world turns without you

Dig further in under the roof of your mind-made shelter
Pull the leaves and dirt in around you and lie very quiet
Listen for the footsteps that you have grown terrified of
Cover your ears so as not to hear your name taken in vain

You have learned to lie in a cocoon of your own making
Praying that your hiding place will never be discovered
All the while praying your world suddenly disappeared
So, you'll safely emerge into a world of joyful imaginings

Where you can finally sleep peacefully and free of fear
Dream among starlight, rainbows, and musical carousels
For the first time in your tiny life, you rest amongst clouds
You've never known what peace of mind, body, and soul is

Daylight has risen as your fear has subsided to relax
You go about your day cautiously until the night arrives
Beware the monster will make his way back to his lair
At his first growl, Run Child Run to your secret place!

SACRED IS OUR FAMILY

Our Mother is the Earth
Aged she has become
We, her children have the duty to care for her
Where we walk upon her is sacred ground
She's the foundation of all life

Our Father is the Sun
His warmth sustains our lives
From sunrise to sunset, he lights Mother Earth
Enriching the Great Plains with endless bounties
Our Father has forever watched over us

Our Grandfather is the Sky
He is the giver of the air we breathe
It is his sacredness we draw upon with each breath
From the tallest peaks to the lowest valleys
Pray there is no end to his vastness

Our Grandmother is the Moon
Grandmother shall always be respected
Her sacred will creates the rise and fall of the tides
Her beauty is ageless
She is the light in the darkness

Our Sister is the water
We depend on her endless flow
She holds the salmon that forever return to her freshness
She is the one we must take care of to survive
Sacred is her spirit with every drink we take

Our Brother is the fire
He must be cared for, maintained, and contained
He is the giver of heat in our daily lives
We draw upon his greatness
He is beneficial or destructive if not controlled

We have many brothers
Blessed are their creations in animal spirits
Their gifts are valuable to our well-being
The birds are brothers who take to wing
Their flights are a mystery we marvel upon

Sacred is our sister's plenty
We are obligated to look after their beauty
All species of plants, trees, and flora
She is in abundance alongside our Mother Earth
Our sisters give life to animals and man alike

Our Mother, Father, Grandmother, and Grandfather
Created a world filled with amazing gifts and wonders
Their lessons teach us to take only what is needed
Cultivate the value needed to survive
Honor the sacred wisdom of our Elders...

For it is their wisdom
That will keep this wondrous and amazing
A world alive that we inhabit upon
RESPECT THY ELDERS
We are just children that need to be carefully taught to respect,
Our Sacred Mother Earth

SELF MADE PITCH

I have had my soul caught between two shades of darkness
For the longest of days
The times have been lonely
The loss of measuring time is like that of a careless whisper
Nearing an eternal sleep
Standing at the meeting of two walls
Creates a corner black and as deep as evil
Holds the secrets to vanishing souls
I know because I watch in secret
Here in this pitch dark as tar and smells as bad!
Where many hap-hapless souls fade into the endless darkness of nevermo
So many times, I would close my eyes
Walk into darkness, go weak throughout my body
Then feel the flushing in my soul
Tight in the corner, I would stand
Putting a hand and an elbow on each wall
Steady in what faith I might skim off the top
And decide to remain in this limbo
Blending into the darkness before
Shutting out all pain
Or trying to deal with it the best I can
After all, I am a master at it!
I have been at it for the longest time now
I open the door to this darkness
This pitch of black that has surrounded my miserable life
Where I witnessed horrors
Seen, done, created, plotted
And then cried after-wards
I cried so hard I couldn't breathe
Not a sound could anyone hear
I gathered myself up and ran like hell into the only place I felt safe
My Self-Made,
PANIC ROOM!

SENDING AN ANGEL TO YOU

I am sending you a very special messenger
She will arrive with open wings of a love divine
Her referent beauty radiates within her heart
She will arrive from heaven in a glorious light

It is so easy for me to send you an angel divine
In your hour of need for all reasons lost in time
To comfort you with my love so true that aches
She will whisper my special message in a sigh

Feel its warmth, feel love as her arms wrap you
Know her touch when your times long for me
When the world is filled with a lonely madness
Trust love is with you, that I believe to be true

My angel divine will bring the sunshine's light
She will protect and keep you safe from sorrow
When times seem dark and scary and full of fear
Your life will be brightened by the wave of her arm

I fell in love with you when we were children
I'm sending the angel divine with all my love
To help ease our loss of the one so very young
His bright spirit will forever be carried in love

I held our secret in my heart as you requested
My love's filled with hope that together we'll be
In the afterlife together as a family once again
I sleep with loneliness, no warmth in a memory

Angel divine holds our hearts with blessed love
I'll hold onto the memories of our beloved son
I'll turn to grieve into a celebration of his short life
My love for you still shines brighter than the sun

I miss you two with every beat of my heart...

SERENITY'S EMBRACE

Upon the breeze sweet as April's perfume, you came to me
No lovelier a fragrance had ever been bestowed before me
Knowingly I'm enchanted, I give way to serenity's embrace

A whisper sweet in new Lilac brushes soft against my cheek
Bathing my heart in the warmth of violins and a cello's kiss
I will dance to the passion of the lady who enchants the harp

Do tweet in my ear sweet lady, then experience a lover's sigh
I'm one who's enchanted by cupid's arrows of love's harmony
A melody etched upon my heart does breathe a contented sigh

Where mirth and frivolity play, love grows in a summer wind
I beckon to the hummingbird, come taste the Trumpet's Wine
I have tasted such a flower and found the nectar intoxicating

A lover's quencher, sensual in its flavor, a gift from the Gods
April's kiss captured my heart in a shower of Ambrosia Wine
Close your eyes and savor its warmth, and know a Hummingbird's Sin

Why do I laugh like a crazy Loon because I feel free and alive?
Plus, my thoughts are playfully wicked, for Cupid hit his mark
Take my hand, walk with me in Nature's Garden, if you dare.

SHADES OF REGRETS

"HIS"

Shout not unto the night, for the lonely dwell in the corners of this vast darkness
Somewhere in this dark sadness, loom unsaid emotions of those with wayward souls
Here the forgotten dreams lie, belonging to those left floating endlessly in the dark
So, whisper unto the night, for those of ill repute are hungry and wait to be released.

"HER"

The hope for light in my life has completely diminished
Only sadness permeates my mind endlessly
My dreams of a fulfilled life have ended far too soon my love
Only whispers of the past speak to me in my dreams

"HIS"

The darkness holds onto an excessive soul who dreams of his love still alive
His spirit aimlessly wonders through the darkness of haunts unyielding
Journeys that were unsure and trying to follow a path weak of uncertainty
It's I who whisper unto the night, a wanderer searching in vain for the light

"HER"

Heavenly Father, how could you have given so sweetly unto us
Such a wonderful promise and a blessed journey of love and life
To have me left alone in this darkened abyss with no exit to find
Holding only onto whispered memories of my love to remember

"HIS"

I whisper because the darkness chokes those who scream and shout
Softly these words that I speak are for the vision being held still in my heart
How I have dreamed of touching thee softly as a velvety baby's blanket
My lips tender, longing with a kiss for thee as sweet as nature's honey

"HER"

I just want to scream loud enough that the world shall know my pain
But alas I can only express my thoughts in a whisper when I want to scream
So, he can hear my call for his touch that is remembered, but I need him
My desperate need to feel his lips kiss mine is fading in my loneliness over time

"HIS"

Say that time hath not closed a chapter that was devoted to my love
So, whisper unto the night, softly the words my heart hath never stopped loving
The darkest corner of sadness will not keep me from hearing you whispering to me
Gently into my ear were words that taunted and teased, left me wanting more

"HER"

If only it were possible for me to turn back time for the love of my life
To tell him repeatedly in the softest of whispers
And the loudest of feelings, how much I love and adored him
To express to him that even death cannot diminish my love for him

"HIS"

Shout not unto the night for many a soul waits and listens upon the breeze
Why do you turn and walk away? Do not leave me drifting in this dark limbo
Wait, my love, STOP! Turn around and give me one more whisper upon my darkness
You must know that I looked beyond the darkness searching for your light

"HER"

As I stand here in pain at your final resting place
I try my best to walk away, but I feel you pulling me back
I always feel a deep need to turn back and stay every time
This time is different, this time your whispers are so clear

"HIS"

You have had your soul in the shadows with painful wounds of a gray yesterday
This I know my love, don't give up walking through pathways that vanish before you
Wait! Stop my love...my life...this is tearing me apart, don't walk away...
STOP! I'm shouting unto the night...come back and release me from this HELL!

"HER"

How can I walk away from my love, my heart, my everything?
How can I think of a tomorrow without you and the love we had?
How do I walk away from here and retain my sanity?
Why do I feel you pulling me every time I turn to leave?

"HIS"

My God! Please turn around and give hope a gentle embrace
If you could just see through the darkness, see the shades of regrets
NO, NO, COME BACK, I beg you, my love, I know I filled your life with false promises
PLEASE, just whisper softly to me in the dead of the night when a breeze blow

"HER"

Dear God, please let him hear my words and understand
These words I have in my heart, I must impart to him
My dearest love, please know I haven't one regret, not even one!
Loving you and sharing my life with you was my dream

"HIS"
What manner of man would I be in passion lonely breeze if I don't keep trying?
Long ago we found one another beneath the stars in a world of chaos
Our songs of love and romantic nights are no longer, shout not unto the night
For somewhere between passing shadows, here lies Shades of Regrets...

"HER"
My love, I must walk away from this place where you rest
Remembering our dreams and our songs of love will be with me forevermore
As I leave you here, I need you to know this one thing
There were no regrets in the love we shared!

"THE END"

Shadow Grim

The night crawls once more across the land

Who will be saved this night?

From the Shadow Grim

Hear her screams so loud they are silent the night

Watch her eyes form

Onto the shadow of a wall

Demon slant and cat-eyed

A putrid yellow green

No light filters onto the streets of despair

Where she haunts, it turns red to a near black

Children are wracked with fear

Their screams need to be silent

As the blood is forced from their throats

Where nothingness is released

The children know that

Darkness is a Shadow of Grim enormous

Her screams silence the Banshees

She is the frightener of the worst kind

Wherever you spy the shadow of darkness

Etched on the walls of an alleyway

An empty street or across a barren field

Watch for the slightest movement

One that gives you a reason to pause and gasp for air

Or question yourself with a second look

Somewhere in the shadows

It is she!

Creeping about to feed

On the light force of the innocent

Listen! Listen, children!

Can you hear the screams of the Shadow Grim?

I still due to this day

For I saw her face as a child

Once you have seen

The Shadow Grim

She will return to feed on your light force once again

Her hunger is only a Banshee scream

Away!

Shadows of My Past

Before this temple mild and meek, let the sunshine bright for my heart beats strong

Release the doves to soar high into the blue above, listen to their wings sing me a song

Vigorously I beat the tall grass to drive away the shadows of fear and shame

They follow me wherever I venture, I wait in my own shadow, it's my soul they claim

Twilight makes ware their presents I see, where evil lies double shadowed of my past

In the last few minutes of twilight, they rise in pursuit eagerly and gain my way fast

Native Americans echoed how the Shadows were painted across the mountain's face

Painted ponies were seen running frightened in and out of the Shadows at a frantic pace

At an early age, with no control of my own, in the dust of fear, I saw the Shadows cast

I would lie very still hidden in the tall grass so as not to be seen as they hauntingly did past

The Shadows are cruel and calculating, I close my eyes not to see, but they know my name

The Shadows that I've seen throughout the years, I'll never forget, nor ever be the same

SHADOWS REMAIN

I have walked a hundred miles or more through the pouring rain
Countless miles under the hot sun developing the greatest of thirst
I had to cover my mouth and eyes from the desert sands that blew
When the winds raged, I'd turn my back against its sharp biting

There were many nights so cold, below freezing, I'll never forget
My feet ached so, they were burnt, cut, and ravaged with blisters
Blisters or not, I was traveling onward to face my youth's horrors
Finally, there before me, the lane that was leading up to my demons

The moon was hauntingly bright, lighting my way to face the evil
Walking up to the top of the lane, there it stood in the moonlight
Crumbling ruins tell the tragic story of the lives lived as shadows
I stood in the moonlit dark, feeling the shadows pulling me back

*Dad christened it, **"Hell's Half Acre"** and it was in this farmhouse!*
A single light bulb was used to illuminate the tiny once window
I noticed the moon trickle upon the jagged edges of the broken panes
A ghostly shell left decaying memories of a run-downed farmhouse

I traveled back to face my memories head-on, I made my first step
Forward, stepping on the overgrown pathway escorted by shadows
Walking past a fallen barn that housed my sister's horse, "Apache"
Completely run over in thorns, thistles in a mountain of dead dreams

I took a breath and stepped up on the frame where the door uses to be
A door to Hell, a gateway housing abusive horrors on a young boy
Around me the icy cold mountain air blowing its haunting warnings
I heard silent tears that echoed from my mother, sister, and my own

I drifted back to reality and focused my eyes on the shattered window
That was our only early warning system telling us that he was home
A small piece of curtain weathered worn, dry rotted, hung by a nail
A tiny, embroidered bluebird that my mother had sown-ed still survived

Clearing my head, I listened to the silence that this house never knew
*I can't ever remember silence being heard up on, **"Hell's Half Acre"***
I returned to the house I clearly deemed as forbidden evil in my life
Mom's death released the chains that bound my reason for staying

I traveled far away, only to return to face the demons of my youth
Every mile I walked along the way, I was going to bury the demons
There were so many demons that shadowed our lives in this house
Here I stand in the center of my horrors, still, the shadows remain...

She In Black

She in black

I rest my head upon a mound of Lemon Grass

Hot is the day and time has stood still

As if in a dream state of my mind

I hear a name being called upon the wind

I open my eyes in confusion from my lazy slumber

I rub my eyes to focus

She in black

Shouts a name that isn't my name,

"THOMAS"!

*I say, **"You have made a mistake"***

*Looking around, **"I see no other here by that name"***

She looks at me with a stern and evil expression of hate in her eyes

*I say snapping back, **"My name is Loud Raven"**!*

She in black

Beckons me to come forward

I walk slowly, raising my head with each step I make

She speaks to me with haste in her voice

"Come Here, Thomas!"

I look amongst my kindred

Knowing what is about to take place in front of them

She in black

Taps her foot in a rhythmic beat

I look up at this woman with eyes, how dare you

*Demandingly, **"Put Out Your Hands!"***

This is something I have heard many times before

*Loudly she repeats, **" YOUR HANDS, THOMAS!"***

She in black

Repeating as she often does when upset,

"Your name is Thomas! Say it, Thomas, say it!"

She repeats the words that every Indian child has heard once or twice before

*She always says, **"This is going to hear me more than you"***

The stick is raised, then with all her might

WACK-WACK *and then a third* **CRACK!!!**

Her eyes showed such pleasure in this undertaking

I faced her eye to eye, I refused to shed a single tear as we stared at one another.

She in black

Could see a reflection of a mighty storm building

Raging deep in my Native American heart

I spoke for every Indian child in this room,

"No matter how hard the thunder will crack or how hard the wind will blow,

You, we call, "She in black"

Hear Me!

The white man has taken our land, our home, he has taken away our culture,

Taken away the life we have always known,

BUT!

The White man nor She in black will NEVER, EVER take away,

WHO I AM!

My name is "LOUD RAVEN!"

A proud Native American of the Blackfeet Nation!"

She in black

Took several steps backward for she saw all I said backed up in my eyes

I walked out of the classroom with bloody hands and with my pride.

Every Native child stood at their desk as I passed by,

And followed me out the door.

"WE ARE WHO WE ARE,

Not what you want us to be in your white eyes."

She in black

Couldn't say a Word.

SHINNING A LIGHT INTO THE DARKNESS

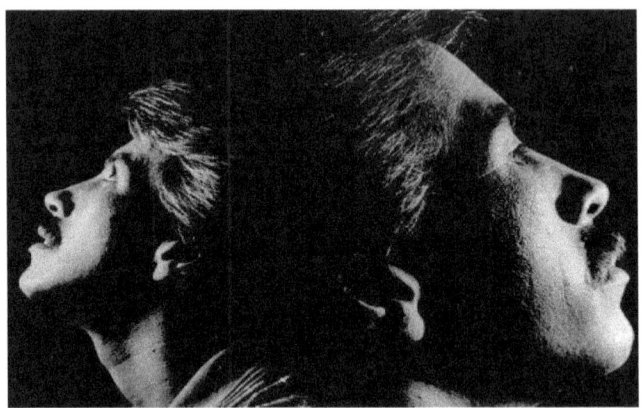

Several years have disappeared
A vacation by the mind's decree
Only recently my memory returned
Memories fresh as the morning dew

A flash before my eyes of you
Directly from the lost and beyond
Gently landing upon my blank heart
The time must have been just right

A bench sitting in the park that I love
It was just like a shot in the dark
The spirit of you found the lost me
Shinning a light into the darkness

I forgot how to live this life given
You were taken in a flash of lightning
Severe was the message that shocked
The seasons faded one after another

I will always remember that shock
A zombie's life became my breath
I lived in a snapshot portrait alone
Remembering tore my heart apart

I cried, I drowned in my own ocean
Your death wiped my mind clear
I discovered a whole new world
Shinning a light into the darkness...

SING OF SORROW

S.O.S.
Man, so often,
Sings of Sorrow
When the fires burn down
And the embers turn to gray ash

S.O.S.
It's so easy to
Sing of Sorrow
When the heart grows cold
And there's death in each tomorrow

S.O.S.
Ungodly pain
Sing of Sorrow
When there's no one lying beside you
And no gentle words to hold the tide back

S.O.S.
Listen to those
Singing of Sorrow
We journey on regardless of our troubles
For the sun will rise tomorrow

Sing of Sorrow

SLAPPED BY LIFE

For the longest time sorrow was my only companion
Days passed by followed by heartache and loneliness
I gave up thinking tomorrow will always be better
Solitude was my life and darkness became my lover

Memories of you seem to fade in the midst of despair
It was that day keeping you alive forever in my heart
Our eyes met and nothing would ever seem the same
At that first touch, my body trembled with anticipation

I felt alive once again, no longer silent, and muted
The world came alive, and music colored my world
You were heaven sent and life was well worth living
Once again purpose had given me a reason to believe

All is well, my guard was let down, and I felt like a child
I should have known better to do such a foolish thing
Life slapped me hard across the face of reality again
My heart stopped in mid-beat; all air escaped from me

For the longest time sorrow has been my companion
My days are cemented in heartbreak and loneliness
You were taken far too early from this world of mine
So young, so beautiful were you, my hope and reason

There has been a curse put upon my life forevermore
I am allowed bursts of magnificence and wonderment
I've only known grief, destined never to know happiness
Hello, solitude! My life, purpose, and lover in the dark...

Sleeping

Dreams come and dreams go

Floating, flying, and vertigo

Wonderland of wonders circles about time

Good things of hue, reason, and rhyme

Dreams up and dreams down

Dark flashes with falling stars all around

Nightmares of terror and hearts in pain

They're cold, and dark with enclosures and no flame

Dreams in and dreams out

In and over, twisting all about

Warmth, a family that faces a freeze

So many varieties, what is next do I see

Dreams dark and dreams in light

Grasping, holding on all so tight

Follow the light, follow your heart

Nothing can harm you here in the dark.

SO PRECIOUS WERE YOU

So precious were you in this thing we call life
Every day that you were here on this earth
Giving comfort and joy to my lonely strife
Happiness filled my young life with your birth

My heart burst with a father's love and joy
I held you in my arms, thanking the Lord above
For blessing my life with a beautiful baby boy
I was overly consumed with a new kind of love

You and your mother gave me a joyful reason to cry
Little did I know, I'd soon drown in my own tears
My tears turned to anger with questions of Why?
You lived and were loved an amazing five full years

A gifted spirit as precious as silver and gold
Then you vanished before the first rays of dawn
So precious were you, before a chance to grow old
In the blink of an eye, life's cruel curtain was drawn

With you in my arms, I'd rock steady in my chair
I would cradle you against my chest each night
Dreaming of a lifetime of dreams for us to share
I hear your giggle in the warmth of the morning light

Suddenly all I cherished vanished under the covers
The living horror and disbelief still haunt me
Killed by a drunk driver, both you and your mother
So precious were you and my love will always be...

SO, SAY THE RAVENS

This night is cradling a dark stillness within a blood moon painting
The red moon reflects his stare onto the mile-wide mirrored lake
A vast endless velvety black sky has frozen each star in its place

I watch the trees begin dancing to the macabre rhythmic breeze
The leaves seem to release a captive sigh between each stale wave
Nightly shadows dance readying for the unspoken haunted Sabbath

The blood moon now displays unrest within the twilight hours
The blood moon stares down onto the earth, lighting Death's path
Death's walk is certain, hung are the scarlet drapes of forevermore

"The taking of One's own life,"
So, say the Ravens of the night

Written with the understanding that some secrets should never be told, not ever to be told! As much as I know better than to open closet doors that we all share, sometimes it's a good thing to ask questions first. It's said, "The truth will set you free."

SOLITARY DARKNESS

My Father the Cube Master

Charles Lee Cook

I write about this solitary darkness that envelops me. This prison is deep in my mind. So deep that it's hard to find me anymore. I'm only eight years old! My name is Richard Lee, I have hazel color eyes, and my hair is blonde and wavy. I was born on April, the 23rd day, in the year 1951 of our Lord. I was led to believe my heritage was Native American Blackfoot Indian. You're thinking about my blonde hair and being Indian and all. It was something special amongst moms bloodline to see a child born with blonde hair. It's supposed to mean good luck will follow you or something like that. My sister Bonnie had blonde hair and my brother Mark did as well. Mark lived with my aunt on my father's sister. Mom always told us stories around and about our heritage. Just like the birth of a white buffalo. It means the rebirth of the Indian Nation and the coming of peace and harmony. She had a sixth sense about her. Mom said that Bonnie and I had the gift. That was a good thing, and she would help us channel the meanings as much as she could while we were still together. That was a strange thing to say, I thought to myself. I always knew when I felt dizzy or cold or even blackout at times, that something would enter my mind in bits and pieces. It would look like a scrapbook. From that point, I would tell her what I saw in my mind's eye. Sometimes I'd see what was going to happen, sometimes I felt as if it were a warning. Do you know what I mean? Then there were times when I felt like I wasn't in my body, yet my spirit moved about. I need to know, WHY? What happened to me that leaves me here alone and, in the darkness, feeling very cold? cold?

*I've been here in this cold dark chamber for the longest time. I don't know where everyone is. But I want something; I need to tell something to someone. Where is everyone? Am I alone here in the darkness? I wouldn't know what I'd do if I saw light once again. What did I do to be shut away and forgotten? This I have asked myself repeatedly. No matter, it's now a part of me. I can't seem to resist its touch or change the outcome. Sometimes it is very cold here. Most of the time I cradle myself and close my eyes and pray to Jesus, **WHY ME?** I have heard nothing from him, and I've stopped asking. Darkness is loneliness and loneliness are solitary, this I have learned.*

*Maybe I should tell the story of me? I can't write it down because I don't have a pencil or paper, but I can make believe I have pen and paper to tell my story of me that nobody knows. In hopes that maybe, someday I will be heard. Well, that's silly, isn't it? I will try to tell you what it's like to be in these black cubes I call home. My surroundings are tiny cubes stacked one against and on top of another. I feel entombed in these cubes that I now call my prison. It opens to reveal the childhood of abuse. Move these cubes around to see shadows and contours of a belt across the back, being slapped and chased by a hunter as if it's rabbit season. Yes, that's right, he would chase me with his twelve-gauge shotgun. Sometimes he would shoot over my head. Close enough for me to pee in my pants. That scared me beyond the slaps, kicks, and vulgar verbally abusive names. Then the mental pain of being told, **"Better things ran down my leg", or "you are a bastard" and "you're a worthless piece of shit."** He even went as far as laying this line on the three of us. Don't get me wrong, after a while you get used to certain things. Dad would say, **"You Indians, aren't nothing but a Niger turned the wrong side out!"** My God, I'm only a little boy! What in the hell was wrong with this frig-gen maniac?*

Change the cubes to view darkness at its best. A drunk grabbing you by the hair as you lay sleeping, screaming foul names at you, then dragging you down twenty-some steps, hurling you across the room, and landing on the couch just to show you who the boss is. You look into those eyes of a so-called human, a so-called man, yes, a so-called father. Then his eyes were red as a demon, staring into mine. Before I could blink, he would slap my face open-handed, then with his fist, driving me into the couch. Slap after slap, fist after fist. Then he would suddenly stop because he saw blood running from my nose and or mouth. He would then back up and stare at me. I think that was the worst of all. Him standing there and I wondered what in the hell will he do next. Is this fatherly love? Christ, let someone come to my aid. Someone, anyone, KILL the son-of-a-bitch. Please, please kill him. I remember how hard I would cry, I cried so hard it was silent. The lack of breath, the pain in the chest and gut. But my thoughts were in earnest. Have you ever cried that hard? It hurts like hell!!

*I wasn't the only one who received his **"love"** for my beautiful little sister Bonnie. My mother was beaten just about every other night, for reasons I could not understand, nor did she! Twenty-six years they were married, April sixth was their wedding anniversary and his gift to her was the worst beating she had ever Indore. She was beaten about the face and kicked in the stomach and then he'd grab her by the hair, jerking her back and forth, so hard that wads of her long beautiful black hair were seen in his hands. I remember it as if it were right now happening in front of me. That son-of-bitch ran my mother's head into the corner edge of the wall. She let out a horrible scream that shook me to the bone. I remember her falling to the floor. It was like she was in slow motion. She slowly sat up, after several kicks to the ribs. The blood ran down her face and onto the floor. It was in her eyes and rafting down her very long hair. I ran for a pan of water. I was suddenly halted by a backhand that made me fly into the wall. "Where are you going?*

*You little bastard." Crying, I got up and went downstairs anyway, to get a basin of water. My little heart was racing so hard that I began to vomit, and the weight of the basin was quite heavy for an eight-year-old. As I ran up the steps to Mom, I saw her there in a mass of blood, she was rocking back and forth. I went to her, and I held the basin under her face. Life was draining from her. The basin became red with blood, and it frightened the hell out of me. I called for Bonnie to come over and take care of mom. Wash her face a little bit. I told her I was going to run down to Hamilton's Restaurant and call the ambulance people to come and help mom. Dad was in his own little world now. Just like so many times before. It was the same old routine. Fight drank a little more and head for the bedroom. I whispered into Mom's ear, that I was going to call for help and that I loved her. I ran as fast as my little legs would carry me. The restaurant was about a mile down the hill and onto the highway. I know I fell a couple of times; it was dark outside. My arms and legs were cut up a bit. What the hell, I never felt the pain or burning. I ran into the restaurant, like a bat out of hell, and ran up to Mr. Hamilton and begged him to call for help. After a bit of trying to calm me down, he then realized it was about my mother being beaten. Mr. Hamilton knew all so well what it was like up on Blue Berry Hill. That's another story within itself. I then ran back up to the bottom of the hill. Taking a deep breath, I ran up the hill and onto our driveway of sorts and ran into the house. Mom was trying to get up from the couch to get to her chair. She was white as a ghost. So much blood ran out of her. I ask mom where Bonnie was. "Over there," mom pointed. My God, there little Bonnie was. She was blood from head to toe. Cowering in the corner leading down to the kitchen. She was shivering and crying. I ran over to her with her blue jean jacket that was lying on the floor and ask if she were, OK? She didn't say a word to me. I took her hand and went over to mom to tell mom that the ambulance was on its way. With Bonnie hand in hand and not watching where I was going, I tripped over the blood-filled basin that was still on the floor. I splashed blood on the walls and on myself as well. Thinking about it now, it looked like a blood bath had occurred. I grabbed the basin and went downstairs to get fresh water and a washcloth to wipe Bonnie and moms face a little bit. Just about that time, I heard the ambulance coming up the hill. I ran out the bottom floor door and ran out to the lane, to show them where to come. I began to cry again; it made me feel happy to see them coming. I knew mom was in bad shape. My dad had taught me how to dress rabbits. I knew what it looked like when they were dying. Mom had that look and when I touched her, she felt waxy and cold. They stopped in the lane and gathered what was needed. I took off running back into the house just in time to see dad doing his Houdini Act. Around this time, that drunken Bastard, got up from his chair, smelling of wine and beer as well as cigarettes. He had been sitting in his underwear not giving a damn who was around. Cigarette in one hand and a pint of Club 400 in the other one, he disappears into the bedroom. It was as if nothing had ever happened. The team walked up to the door, came in, they scanned the room in all directions. The first guy spoke out loud, **"What in the hell.!"** I would too if I walked in on a mess like this place was in. Blood up the walls, on furniture, on the floor, and in the corner where the sofa was, a pile of red clothes on three bodies. One pulled me to the side, another picked Bonnie up and the other two were taking care of mom. Then there were two police officers followed behind the medics. **"Who can tell me what happen here?",** said the tall lanky Officer. It was explained, however, it went in one ear and out the other. You could tell they weren't interested one bit. They got dad up and took him outside. When the medic finished with me, I got my way over to the door and walked outside. There in the dark, but I could see very well, even after the swollen face and eyes, were the two officers and dad lighting up cigarettes and laughing it up. I remember yelling over to them, but I don't recall what I said to this day. But everyone heard me very well, very well indeed.*

Mrs. Elizabeth Vernus Martinez Wetzel Lema Cook, forty-five years old, died in the Frederick Memorial Hospital, ten days after her twenty-sixth-year wedding anniversary due to compilations from a surgery taken earlier that year. Bonnie and I were by the bedside every day she spent there, until the day of her death. Here I am fifteen and Bonnie twelve, we both knew what death looked like and at what stage the last breaths were made. We grabbed onto each other crying so hard. I took moms hand into mine. I saw Mom's eyes roll back and her cold hand squeezed mine. It looked like she wanted to say something to me. I leaned over and with my ear to her lips, she whispered the words, **"Take care of Bonnie and get out of that house."** Then her hand released its grip. At that moment Bonnie and I went running out of the hospital. That day was the worst day of our lives.

We loved our mother more than life itself. The crying game for us was the knowledge of knowing we were going back home with this son-of-bitch at the end of the day. Scared to death of the unknown before us. Dad knew that we knew the truth about the beating she received from him. The beating was what ended her young life. He murdered her! Regardless of what anyone tells us, that animal KILLED our mother. She was cradled in my arms on the bloody living room floor. No charges were ever issued to Charlie Cook. I found out a week later that dad wasn't charged with anything. Wasn't that a kick in the ass? For twenty-six years, she was beaten nearly every day and or night. She once left him for two weeks. Bonnie and I were at home on a Saturday morning, when we saw a cab pull up outside. It was mom and dad. Dad was somewhat drunk again. They came in and of course, we ran to mom and hugged her tight. I whispered into Mom's ear, **"You know what he is going to do."** She whispered back, **"He's okay, he has promised he will never hit me again."** I started to cry in her ear, **"Mom, how damn stupid are you? He's going to do worse than before. All he did around here while you were gone, was to rant and rave like a mad man, he would say it repeatedly, I'm going to kill that fuckin whore! That Goddamn Whore! You just wait. You just wait. As sure as Christ has made little green apples, I'm going to kill the bitch!"**

To make an old story short, he would go out to the barn, where he hid his personal whiskey and drank the booze until it was gone. Telling us he is going out to the shed to feed the pigeons and rabbits. He would come back into the house and sit down for a while. Everything was fine. Then something would strike his fancy, so to speak. He'd start out with something like, **"Lib, What's for supper?"** She answered him and he would get quiet. Mom would go downstairs to fix supper. Ten minutes later, he'd say, **"What in the hell is taking so long?"** Mom raised her voice, **"Charles, I just got down here, give me some time to cook it, for Christ's sake."** Later, Mom would come upstairs for a break while things were cooking. Something she would always do. He would get mom upset after he would call her names. She'd jump up to go downstairs and when she would get to that first step, he would grab her by her hair and jerk her around until she would fall on the floor, then he'd go to work on her. This time mom started screaming, reminding him that he would never hit her again. Why in the hell does she still come back, knowing the lair he is? We asked her over and over, **"WHY?"** She'd replied, **"It's because of you kids. When you get older, then you will understand. I will leave forever. I don't want to see you kids end up in a foster home. I went through that, and I will never allow you kids to end up in something like that."** You see, my mother was around fifteen when she was placed in a foster home when her mother was struck and killed by a car. Her name was Minnie Jane Susanna Rebecca Cramer Wetzel.

I recall, even at five, that this so-called-man, would grab hold of mom and take her on the spot. He cared less that we were inches from him. Bonnie and I had an early education about Sex. Mom would fight and beg him to stop this in front of the kids. His response would be to turn his head around to where we were standing or sitting and dared us to move a muscle. He'd yelled at me to watch. **"Watch me you little bastard, this is how you fuck a woman. That's all they're worth. Cleaning the house, fixing dinners, and getting a good piece ass anywhere I want it!"** That's what he would say, and he wasn't nice about it at all. **I was "Mentally Raped of MY CHILDHOOD!"** His horrific actions right before me took what innocence was left in me.

So where do I go from here? Often, I would experience a recurring nightmare. It wasn't very long after mom was buried that they started and grew in intensity. I felt, no, I knew something was going to happen to Bonnie or me. It just so happens that one night he came home drunk as a stunk and I just happened to walk in front of him when he was in one of his corrosive moods. He grabbed me by my hair, pulled me towards him and he looked directly into my face with a strange look in those demon-green eyes. He growled, **"You look just like your fuckin mother."** Then the slapping began. One slap too many and the last one was hard as hell up against my head. He threw me up against the wall. I felt my little body slide down the wall. When I touched the floor, I could see Bonnie standing in the corner of the room. Terrified and screaming. Then everything went black. That was all I remember. Except for the feeling of calmness around me. No pain at all, then there was the coldness. darkness circled around my little body. I went into a deep sleep. A solitary sleep. I don't know how long I was out. I was in my solitary chamber of darkness.

It's my nightmare, the solitary darkness I am reminded of "Watt-knots". Each one has a meaning in someone's heart of hearts. They collect dust as I do in this black solitary capsule. Memories in brass, wood, and glass create a stationary menagerie of lifelessness. Yet, when I'm here in this cube of darkness, each seems to dance and move about at my request. Tears of dust that no one sees. Wishes never heard. Longing for a touch of another. Dreams that will never be. I ask, "Where does that come from?" It's just not fair. Not fair at all! I now focus on the empty darkness around my being. I lie down; my arms reach out as though I'm on a cross. I close my eyes and take a deep breath. Slowly let it out to relax me. Hearing only a humming deep in the core of my head. It takes me to a place where my spirit has exited the body and become one with the darkness. Quiet is the goal. Nothingness is achieved. So, I opened my eyes slowly and the dark seems to offer special effects on my mind. Diamonds begin to sparkle above my body. They begin to move in all directions, changing into tiny Angels beckoning me to join them. Without a second thought, one tiny Angel takes my right hand and another my left. The three of us float among bright stars that twinkle and explode into thousands of star lights. Lights that take you to a higher place, where dreams come true in an instant. These glorious sparkling Angels dressed in silver and gold, glide in and out of their sisters and brothers. Each wanted to grant me a dream come true. Any dark thoughts that I had, now sparkle like diamonds, which changed the blackness into daylight. It was full of warmth and comfort. It's memories of my mother covering me with a warm fuzzy blanket after getting out of the tub. I miss that touch, the touch of my mother's hand. Many memories surface in my mind. Every starlight that I passed, was an invitation to travel on. Tiny Angels circled about my head. Each called my name to follow them. Now I understand what was being said to me, follow the light. Go into the light. My eyes were filled with tears, as I walked into the light. There were family members standing in a row in full regalia. Then I saw Mom, she was beautiful, she looked like she did before the beatings. I was told to return to my cube of *solitary darkness. Soon, very soon things began to feel different. My head was light as a feather. I started to move in slow motion, then faster, I was moving backward, and I saw moments that I experienced once before. Things began to move so fast that all I was seeing were bright lights and a sinking feeling. Just sinking. All was calm in my solitary darkness. I no longer felt the cold or the confinement. I was free. I let go of the hurt, pain, and fear that was always before me. I'm going home. This eight-year-old boy returned to his cube of solitary darkness where he had laid these many years. No longer trapped in darkness, for he went into the light. Lee is now in the arms of those who love him. During the eight years that he walked upon the earth, wouldn't it have been nice to know that what he endured from his father, wasn't in vain? That, someone, heard his cries and his pain. Rest assured that Lee was heard loud and clear. No longer will he feel the pain and see the evil around him. If only I would die would this nightmare be ended?*

It was said many years later, that Lee's father leads a lonely, dark solitary life. Alone and with no one who gave a damn whether he live or died. Charles Cook paid for what he did to our mom, Bonnie, and me. Charlie Cook got his just dessert. What memories may linger about, fit the saying, ***"What goes around comes around." "And it Did"***

SOMETIMES

If I could take this day and put it in my pocket
Would I be able to relive its wonders?
This day was filled with happy-go-lucky feelings
What if it were possible to have dreams come true?
Sometimes I dream too much
Sometimes a dream will come true

Close your eyes and wish for anything the heart desires
Because sometimes we reach to damn high for happiness
Sometimes we lift our spirits to the heavens
Just to believe faith has a calling.
Sometimes my heart aches like hell
Sometimes too much is just too much

Putting all your love into one person is a risky adventure
Who likes to wake up one day and only have change left?
Sometimes the heart leads you astray
Sometimes the truth hurts a whole lot
I walk the streets as everyman
Darting in and out to save a penny or two

Sometimes feeling you are the only one there
Sometimes loneliness whittles you down to the bone
That's when you break out the Gin and give the Devil his due.
Sometimes everything works like clockwork
Sometimes that makes you mad as hell
And you just won't stand for it any longer!

Sometimes there is no answer for the loss of a loved one
Sometimes the thought of not wanting to live any longer
Is the answer to all your woes
Trusting yourself is a job that only you can handle
Sometimes you need to take a good look around
Sometimes that's a big mistake

For the day will be long and tempers run short
The dog barks, the cat scratches, and the damn bird won't sing
It's hot as hell and no air is blowing anywhere
Sometimes the day goes right
Sometimes it doesn't
It's a cat on a hot tin roof if you will

But sure, as the wind blows your faith grows stronger
Whistle a happy tune and find others will join in
Sometimes the crowd must sing, "Row, Row Your Boat"
Sometimes enough is enough.
Tomorrow is another day to put in your pocket
Or maybe not, for you have discovered a hole in your pocket

Sometimes you'll find that change in the cuff of your pants
Sometimes just letting it go is the best feeling around
Sometimes life is too short and sometimes that is scary
Stop, look, and listen to your world
Sometimes a whisper from mother earth is an important
Sometimes we get the message, sometimes not.

SONG OF THE DESERT SANDS

*There is a story called, **"The Song of the Desert Sands"***
You hear it when the wind blows across the hot sands
There is a clap of thunder as the hot sand turns cool overnight
The desert sings in volumes by creatures coming alive

Listen to the desert and sing her song to a shameless oasis
A sky that holds back the rains that could cool its fire
Many miles are wasted in thirst as the vulture circle above
Hear the eagles scream in flight over their barren land

I listen and I hear nothing but my own voice echoing
To the rhythmic beat of drums upon the desert's wind
There's the hot silent devil that shadows each footstep
As you cross the unforgiving lady to reach the mountains

When the sun is at its zenith, the sand is closest to Hell
Your tongue now swells with the thirst for refreshing water
Mirages playing tricks with your eyes begging to be true
It's a wicked haven for deadly poisonous unseen creatures

My horse has fallen, and the vultures are circling overhead
I grab my blanket, tomahawk, bow, and arrows, onward I go
My people depend on me, I carry the answers to visions
Important news of the White Eyes, two days ride behind

***"The Song of the Desert"** now sings loudly into my ears*
Her voice was enticing, longing, and seductive to play along
This She-Devil lures many brave men to a bed of embers
Her fiery red hair is in flames, naked body is made of lava

Walk onward with feet of fire that are blistered by her bed
Step by step I want to lie in her arms until I am consumed
Her seduction is contained by wave after wave of burning
The sun is going down, and I hear her song sweetly fading

The cool desert night air blankets my chills from her fire
My moccasins stick to my feet as I walk her seductive lava
Refreshing is the air upon my skin that danced in a fiery hell
The message I carry will get to my village, morning is near

*I say to all, the "**Song of the Desert Sands**" is a lovely tune*
Calm, cool at first, amazingly beautiful is her haunting voice
Be prepared with water to calm her naked flames dancing
Lay not in her bed of fire where there is no hope or easy exit

Cross her in two days, look at her beauty, and listen to her song
I live to tell this tale to my children about the desert's beauty
*Do learn to respect her, and listen well to her songs, but...**Beware!***
"Song of the Desert Sands"** is the **Goddess of Fire and Flame

r

SPIRIT OF REVENGE

During the darkest part of the black of night, evil reigns supreme. The spirit of the one who rises with a warrant for deadly revenge. On those who have no regard for the helpless and the less fortunate, he creates havoc on those who inflict physical and mental anguish. Beware you bullies that take the last peace of mind of the helpless. He's the Spirit of Revenge feeding on your taunts of verbal belittling. Endless is the hunger he has for those that take from the weak of heart, he'll find you where you dare to hide, redeeming your worthless souls. Hide if you think you can, it's a matter of time before he'll collect your soul. Imagine the worst of all horrors used in consuming your life's blood. There's no need to repent the evils you perpetrated upon the helpless, think about the pain put upon the innocent, the weak, and the frightened. No mercy has you ever shown to another when in need of compassion. He will come for you this night during the pitch of the unholy dark hour. He's known to gorge himself on your fright, and the weakness you display, you become one among many inmates in his torturous asylum of horrors. Consumed and digested in the dungeons amongst other criminals. Forever moans and horrific cries as you travel through his dark bowels. Then the time arrives for his redemption and revenge where death reigns. There isn't a damn thing you can do to change the outcome of your fate. You hateful bastards have finally met your own match with his wrath. The locking of doors, and pulling your shades down are hopeless causes. Revenge tears you apart, sucking the marrow from your worthless soul forever your actions will be eternal, a buffet that sustains his purpose. The time will come he'll introduce himself to you when fright swells. Your heart will become crushed by many hands that have accused you. You'll experience ungodly terrors as you face the faces of your accusers. Every pain you mentally and physically put upon them will greet you. Every soul that you bullied and tormented through the years will become razor blades in his hands as he shreds your worthless soul. Death is a luxury you will never know; you will beg for death repeatedly. It is your actions sealing your fate with

each victim you made to suffer. You will never know a tomorrow nor know a moment of peace again. He's the fuel that gives rise to fire and flames in the darkest of tempests, you will beg for the flames to consume your flesh, like a thirst for water. Know his revenge, for he will be your lover for all eternity and a day. Now, do you finally realize who I am, and see what your actions have created? You will be consumed by the agony you put me through, do know my love. I am **Revenge!** *created by you and the satisfaction of your digested taunting. I will never starve from lack of food, what you've sown, I'll reap in the bounty!*

I AM THE SPIRIT OF REVENGE!

SPRING'S ROSE DEVINE

I will know you as the Spring's Rose Divine, as lovely and pedals sweet
Befitting rightfully a name from an Angel, known as Lady Finger Pink

We sleep together on a heavenly carousel of many musical dreams
A floating garden as spring renews with awakening splendor of love

God must have sent a golden Chariot of Angels to whisper soft prayers
Lifting two hearts adorned in tiny Baby's Breath tears wrapped in love

Angels scented in Star lilies, Rose, Gardenia, and Lavender fragrances
Stroll endless pathways of true yearnings, written as only a Poet can

Thousands upon thousands of butterflies in an array of glorious colors
A fluttering symphony of darting to each blossom, helping to pollinate

Two surrounded by a multitude of Angels, butterflies down God's paths
The journey may have been long to get where they have ended in beauty

Their secret garden once barren now flourishes with the glorious news
Spring's love is always being blessed, renewed with an Angel's whisper

You awake as nature awakes on the first day of spring bright as the sun
Your kiss is soft as a warm breeze blew from the hand of God himself

I will know you as the Spring's Rose Divine, as lovely and pedals sweet
Befitting rightfully a name from an Angel, known as Lady Finger Pink

A generous gift from our Heavenly Father and Mother Nature...

STAIRWAY TO HEAVEN

How many countless times have I wished upon a star?
Without a doubt, I followed one elusive dream after another
I have built several steps to my stairways to heaven
And I have traveled across every known ocean and sea

The stars are endless, when wishing upon them is all there is
Dreams are made with hopes of being fulfilled in the future
Step after step, I've journeyed upward on endless staircases
Floating on an endless ocean of confusion with nothing to bare

Reach for one star at a time and find they can come true
Dreams can and do come true, laced with the drive to fulfill
Step one step at a time and discover your goals, then strive
From sea to shining sea, you'll reach a shore of fulfillment

I have ridden on a white swan floating into fairytale land
Floating on a lake calm as glass that sparkles like crystal
Mirror reflections of days past in glorious splendor array
Crystals and diamonds light the way for questions galore

I have traveled from one star to another, then another I see
Satisfaction wants to hold me back instead of searching on
Strive onward, believe in yourself that an answer will be found
A stairway leads to doors with not a key on a chain to behold

Don't be afraid to walk into each door to search for answers
Be in the spirit, or the heart, or the soul for God is everywhere
Climb higher and further to a brighter light that shines the way
I have wished upon a star and reached for many elusive dreams

I have finally reached the last step in the,
"Stairway To Heaven"

Standing Naked Before You

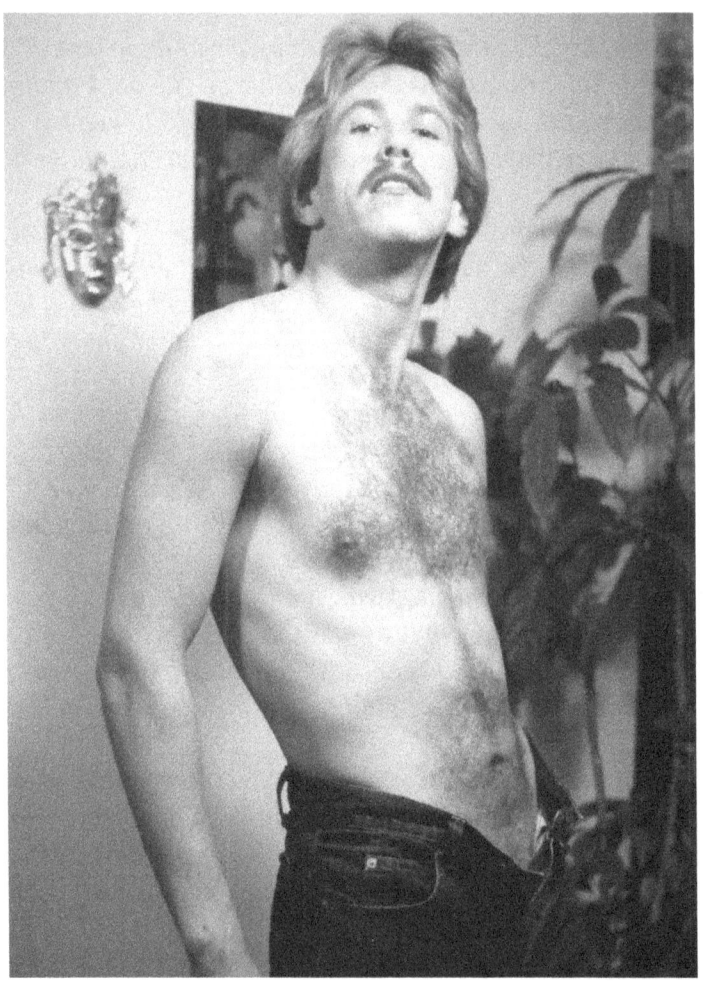

Covered in a dark cloak of misunderstanding. He stands before those who know him not. This young man has masked all his emotions from view. He stands strong with the feeling of being reborn. Without reservations, he drops the cloak to the floor. Now he stands totally naked before you, From across the dungeon-like room, a rush of cool air dances in a circle around his feet. It travels up his long muscular legs, around the firm buttocks to his tight washboard stomach. Up and around the chest and back. This causes him to suck in his stomach. Broadening the chest like the expanded head of a Cobra. Finally blown his long blond hair upward and about his handsome face. It all seemed to be somewhat of a dream to my eyes. Everything that just took place seemed to start in slow motion and then pick up in speed. I must admit, once the cloak had dropped to the floor, what happened next as I turned around, I took a deep breath in awl as another cloaked man entered. Standing in front of my eyes was an Adonis of rare beauty. He dropped the dark cloak. Face to face, flesh to flesh. The entire room was slowly returning to reality. I felt as if I were floating. It mattered not where the floating was taking me. My eyes never left this God of my every

dream come true. I'm sure how he felt standing there with all eyes upon his incredible naked physic. Tall, tanned about six-foot-four. Husky blue/white eyes and tousled blonde hair. He had the most outstanding sculptured lips I have ever seen on a man. We stood there for quite a while before staring into each other's eyes. Then I saw him slightly part his lips. The tip of his tongue appeared to moisten his lips. It rolled gently across those succulent lips. Glazing the top, then the bottom. My heart was pounding, my eyes froze at this small but erotic action. I moved my head slowly in a circle to ease the tension of the moment. That's when my eyes locked with his once again. Bedroom eyes that could melt anyone's heart. Hell, my heart reached my throat, and trying to swallow it back was hard to do. His stare was conducting my every thought. I was feeling as though I was becoming his slave, without any reservations. I could give in to his every whim. I tried to look away but couldn't or didn't want to. I could feel the power he had over me. I was mesmerized and lost within his eyes of pure desire. Feeling powerless felt exciting. This man was created by the Gods and kissed by Venus more than once. He leaned forward whispering his to me. **"My name is Marcus".** *As he leaned back, my eyes went from that face as beautiful as a blooming blush-colored rose. I enough. Broad shoulders exposing shield-like pecs tight and muscular. Arms like Spanish Canons. From there I went down to a washboard stomach. I counted eight strips of rolled tight muscles. His manhood was just as impressive, to say the least. One could say the family jewels handed down were the riches collection seldom seen in one's lifetime. Between those hard, tight massive thighs, Marcus was blessed with the most endearing and powerful piece of "Manhood". This stud horse was "Hung". His thighs were a sculpture's delight. I couldn't help myself as I slowly moved my hand gesturing for him to turn around. Without a second thought, he slowly turned. Oh my God, his ass was sculpted by Michelangelo's talented and divine hands. Firm, round, and just enough fuzz to accent their maleness. My private world was broken by several expressed loud sighs from the attendees'. Marcus shifted his weight giving those ass cheeks life. I bit my bottom lip and drew a drop of blood. As Marcus turned to face me, he noticed a drop of blood on my lip. Stepping as close as possible without pushing me, Marcus gently kissed my lips. He slowly parted his lips and with his tongue licked the drop of blood from my lip. His lips were soft. I started laughing inside my mind. I couldn't help myself I was in amber at the thought of the fantasies running through my mind. Standing there in the chamber with eyes that are waiting to be entertained. Hell, the price to be paid by the two of us was made clear. I knew between the two of us there would be a forest fire uncontrollable. I believe Marcus saw this in my eyes and body language. His blueish-white eyes turned to deep blue flames. Our surroundings began to change around us. This had to be Marcus's doing. He appeared out of nowhere after I dropped my cloak. He had to be from another world, another plain. He is just too perfect for words.*

From his center of focus, everything around us was fading into a bright white light. Everyone in the chambered dungeon was disappearing the brighter the light became. It was just the two of us surrounded by white light. I felt as if I were suspended in space. Face to face, now an arm's distance apart. What was about to happen next raced through my mind. Standing naked before me was a man I only thought was a sculpture in museums. Close enough to reach out and touch this God-like stud. Or was this a fantasy I conjured up? I watched every move Marcus was making. He *reached down for the cloak around his feet. Raising up he swung the cloak around like a matador over his head. The cloak and his massive arms were extended over me. He placed the black cape on my shoulders. Completely covering me. I wonder what this God-like creature was up to? Truthfully, I couldn't be careless at this point. My God, my dream, my fantasy was coming true. In the sexiest voice I had ever heard, he said, **"Open the cape and let it fall".** I did as he asked. I watched his eyes follow the dropping of the cape around my feet. With an expression of sheer bliss. Marcus let out a rumbling growl of sorts. Marcus lustfully said, **"I'm going to fill your every fantasy."** Inside I was burning with a fire of desire. Marcus cooed like a pigeon when he spoke again to me, **"I'm going to eat you alive."** I didn't know if I should be excited a hell at the thought of me on his menu or concerned. I looked down to see why his smile was like a Cheshire Cat. And I found out as we stood there face to face, alone. Our excitement for one another was in full glory. Let the games begin!*

STICKS AND STONES

There was a boy who had a natural talent for dance
A country boy watching television found a way of doing it
He would mimic every step by the,
"The June Taylor Dancers"
From the variety shows
His mind would recall chosen steps and combinations
But his dancing had to be carefully expressed, hidden within his heart
Boys, men are not supposed to dance around showing their asses off like women!
*So says the **"Master of the House!"***
*When the **"Red Skeleton Show"** came on the television*
The entire family would gather around to watch his show faithfully
To laugh, cry and hear Red's profound words of wisdom at the close of every show
*When **"The June Taylor Dancers"** were announced to perform a number*
My heart would beat furiously in my little chest from excitement and envy
I'd watch each step and dance intensely to the routine before my eyes
During the day when the master was at work
Up in my bedroom, I would put a record on the player and dance the day away
When the song was over, I would fall back onto the bed
Imagine the highest of hopes!
Often dozing off into a daydreaming state

I would replay the dance routine in my mind from the night before
The difference was that I was one of June Taylor's Dancers
Why were my dad and others so against my wanting to be a dancer?
When right there in front for all to see, were male dancers,
Guest stars like John Wayne, Fred Astaire, and Cary Grant, all men
They danced in the movies and on television, as well as on Broadway Stages of New York City
We were very poor and the idea of me wanting to take dance lessons,
Was certainly out of the question!
Hell, it would have caused a riot of vaguer language directed at me
Ending up with me receiving the belt across the back
I recall one evening when I thought dad had passed out,
The Red Skelton show was on.
I lay on my stomach with my legs in a straddled position.
I was very limber and felt very at ease.
When suddenly from behind me, there staggers dad.
The next thing I remembered was a flash of burning fire between my legs.
The master of the house had kicked me directly in the groin
It was days later when I woke up in my bed.
Mom managed to get a doctor to make a house call
Long story short,
Beyond the swelling, black and blue testicles
The doctor told mom that there very well be complications in the future.
The boss man never knew about the doctor's visit.
Time went on and he never changed his brutal assaults
He was going to make a man out of me one way or the other
His weapon of choice was often his fist or a backhand slap,
Up against the face and or the head!
Along with the added following comments,

"YOU WANNA BE KNOWN AS A FAGGOT, A GODDAMN QUEER?
DO YOU WANT PEOPLE TO CALL YOU A FUCKING QUEER?

By then I am crying so hard I can hardly breathe
Hurting all over, mind and body,
I questioned, ***"WHY!"*** *...*
Just because I wanted to become a dancer

Throughout my elementary, junior high, and high school years
I lived a rough life
Not to mention the beatings from the Master of the house
I took whatever he or the bullies at school wanted to dish out
Dance was going to be a part of who I am!
It was the only time in my life when I felt expressive, free, and alive!
It was joyful and God knows there was very little of that in my young life
My high school theater department became the world in which I was able to shine
And shine I did!
I became noticed as a dancer with a promise throughout the town

I was able to teach a variety of dance styles,
Even though I never had a dance lesson in my life
However, after a couple of years, the opportunity came about for me to leave my hometown
I was offered a job performing as an actor, singer, and dancer in musical theater
To hell with those that had a problem with me performing on stage
Ironic, isn't it?
It wasn't long before those that tried their damnedest to destroy the belief, I had in myself,
surprised, there sitting in the audience were the bullies, family members who shunned me,
Beat me and belittled me all those years.

Watching me performing dance on stage, they even had to pay admission to get in
The stage became my home, my escape, and my way of expression
My life and certainly my world had made a change
Leading me in the direction I knew I always wanted to travel...
I have now danced up and down the East coast
I accepted invitations to dance amongst stars on stage, screen, and on television
Each opportunity brought me closer to self-satisfaction
I felt blessed and always very lucky
I was fortunate to learn something unique from each celebrity I worked with
It has been a blissful romp for this country boy
Expressing himself in the 60s, 70s, 80s, 90s, and from 2000 to 2010
A dancer, singer, and actor in the Musical Theater
A dancing career only lasts for so long,
Before the body takes its toll by injury and or age

"Sticks and Stones may break my bones,
But words will never hurt me"

I learned at an early, early age that this quote of sorts is a damn lie
I felt the sticks and the stones upon my flesh, and they gave me pain
But I am here to assure you that
"WORDS"
Cut like razor blades and dull knives!

STILL ANOTHER DAY

{Writing this poem was like spreading soft butter on a slice of wheat bread. Laying all jokes aside, writing "Still Another Day" was all about grasping a moment of quiet peace in my head. For the first time in a very time, I had taught myself how to find my center. Once that was achieved, then I slowly pushed each negative thought out of my mind. Trust me when I say, confusion, belittlement, bullies, predictors, chaos, and abuse in many ways and manners, was more than enough to push me out of this mind. When I managed to achieve some manner of conformity. All that was left was a dull humming noise left behind. For me, that was a remarkable calmness. It was a good thing; it was a good day! It was possible for me to think about what I wanted for the future. The pain is to be remembered, but now I can hold it in my heart even if it should break once more. All I need do is repeat it in my head, that there's still another day!}

Still another day goes by
with those driving feelings and a tear in my eye.

How long, how long a day can seem
Just tons of feelings, memories, and those impossible dreams.

Reach for your goals and hold on tight
Straight from the heart with one goal, to fight.

I guess I'm as the story goes my friend
If you don't succeed, try, try again.

How hard to play this game this way?
We all know tomorrow is still another day!

SUFFER WE, THE WORLD

The core of humanity is dying in a mecca of suffering and pain. Mother Earth has had more than enough abuse from her children. Her actions speak extremely loud and clear. Earthquakes, Mega-Tsunamis, Historic Flooding, and Volcanoes erupting around the world. Mudslides, Hurricanes, Tornadoes, Droughts, Wildfires, and here comes the rain... "Man's Inhumanity to Man", "What a piece of work is a man." It's our inability to give a damn! Acting out like a "Loon-a-ticks" because of man's pent-up rage and raging egos. Compassion will help to reveal that which we hold in our weathered hands **"NOTHING!"** *Man believes he can and will control the rain. Well, my friend, Here come the rains. The most terrifying nightmare known to man is the one that you can't escape from,* **SELF-INDULGENCE AND GREED!** *There's a global epidemic of children being kidnapped. The loss of their innocence, mind, and body. The aftermath of a child raped and murdered or sold into sex slavery. It shows man's ultimate inhumanity to man! Still, the rain will pour... It's a fact that summer temperatures could reach a blistering 130 degrees in the shade. Cities open their fire-hydrogen, cooling the overheated urban unrest. Before it gets to a boiling point and is uncontrollable, children splash and play without a care in the world on their concrete beach without sand. The homeless will always find a puddle in which to quench their thirst. What will happen when there is a water shortage? You'll pray for the rains to come...The world's population is out of control! Any street in any town or city in any state or country. The homeless search for food, in filthy trash cans and dumpsters as well as dumpsites. There is* **NO EXCUSE** *as rich as this country is! Give the homeless a job with fair wages. Let them rebuild the vacant buildings across our country Give the people hope, there is wasted strength of know-how filled with faith and a dream. Here come the rains to wash hopelessness away... We live in the land of milk and honey, so, it is said! We love our senior citizens more than life. We're so busy in our lives that the old are too much of a burden. We put them away in an 8x10 room for their own good? Wake-up people, they are the teachers for the future of our children, it is they that have learned from their own mistakes. Their blood and sweat molded us for the future. Handed down pearls of wisdom. Look what you have done and still, the rain comes...*

The root of all evil is not money alone! It's the tidal wave of **"GREED!"** *That crashes upon the shores of man's reality. Man still kills rare and endangered species of animals for sport and for profit. At one time we hunted for food and clothing wasting is not a part of the animal. Every day one or more species disappear from the face of the earth. What animal breeds faster on this Planet RABBITS, RATS, MICE, no, my friends, it is* **M-A-N!** *We are supposed to be civilized and humane. Euthanasia is lurking around the corner as our last resort on this earth. Where's the rain when it's needed?... Man needs to consider* **"STERILIZATION".** *It's not that it should be mandatory, but one never knows what the future will hold for Man. God's eye is on the Sparrow. An emotional storm is developing around the world. Let your soul cry, somewhere a Mega-thrust Earthquake will rock the world. Creating a murderous Tsunami, washing across man's creative world that he believes is his! Everyone should kiss their assess goodbye! For this is something* **"No One"** *can prepare for. So, if life's anchor is too much weight to bear, Man must make a change quickly. Then my fellow man,* **LET THE RAINS COME!**

SUMMER BESIDE THE SINGING WATERS

"I dedicate this story-poem to my Native American Sister and magnificent Poet, Judith Johnson Krypto. I now tell a story about when Native Americans were at Peace. Young love filled the valleys and plains before the White Man" arrived.

Today, as it was nearly every day along the Singing Stream
The early morning meadow breeze was fresh across the water
Sweet is the music that's made by the water rolling over rocks
Birds sing their songs, and the music was soulful and referent

Truly this morning was filled with the sweetest of fragrances
Seated on a blanket in the tall lemon grass was **Morning Star**
This beautiful maiden was the daughter of **Chief Black Horn**
Her mother was **Running Fawn,** truly a beauty of nature too.

Her white buckskin dress was adorned with shells, feathers,
Freshwater Pearls and precious stones from Mother Earth.
A breeze as refreshing as a mountain stream blew about her
She could hear the wind softly sing through the lemongrass.

She began to comb her long Raven black hair blowing freely
So black that when she moved her head it glimmered purple
Her comb was crafted from the jawbone of the mountain Elk
Craved, jeweled, and polished by her mother, **Running Fawn.**

Morning Star could hear the women at work, washing clothes
The Singing stream held the laughter of happy children at play
The sounds of the clothes slapping across the rocks were one
Mixed with the songs of the birds created its own symphony.

Overhead a lazy hawk was heard as he glided upon the breeze
Morning Star raised her beautiful face to view the hawk gliding
She then opened her arms wide, throwing her long black hair back
She imagined soaring on the wings of the hawk through the clouds

It was moments like this when she felt alive and one with nature
The women were busy keeping that watchful eye on the children
A few of the women were making their way back to the village
This went on through the day, gathering berries or wood to fire.

The clouds were in slow motion today, creating pockets of sun
Morning Star then started to braid her long hair and adorn it
With sprigs of lemon grass, colorful beads, and strips of rawhide
She picked a few sweet-smelling blossoms to rub on her neck.

Such the vision, framed by the sunlight through the tall Oak tree
Glancing over to her left, as she was just finishing her last braid
She noticed three figures in the distance, one was coming her way
Her hands and face were on fire, she pretended not to notice him.

There stood **Strong Elk**, tall, dark, handsome with long raven hair
That caught a breeze blowing wildly across his bare muscular chest
The light seemed to frame him perfectly as he struck a regal pose
Cordially looking at this stud standing before her and nearly naked.

Strong Elk was now seventeen and very much a man, she fifteen
Strong Elk decides to play it coy and started to man strut around her
All the time her eyes were fixated on the beauty this man truly was
He had moccasins on his feet and lambskin chin leggings to the knees.

Her eyes slowly worked their way up to his muscular hard thighs
He stretched his arms out, looking like the mighty Oak he was under
His loincloth was tan, a material flap hung to the top of his knees
A breeze blew about his loincloth flapping to the side revealing a man

Both felt a desire in their hearts, he wanted her tightly in his arms
Strong Elk saw the beauty that the Great Spirit created just for him
Morning Star saw the man that will father their children in the future
In just two more cycles of the **"Blue Corn Moon,"** they will be wedded

Everyone in the village knew they were promised to one another
Yet they had to watch their actions amongst the Elders in the tribe
Chief Black Horn and **Running Fawn** saw their love growing closer
Strong Elk would be Chief one day and that was strong medicine.

When that day comes, each will be blessed in front of the entire tribe
Only walks by the Singing Stream will have to carry their love tunes
Dreams and hopes will carry the future of the tribe's next generation
Until then, the children are heard playing beside the Singing Stream

.

SUMMER'S STORM

Thunder is rolling in the distance across the darkening hills
It's the only symphony I will ever hear or know
The wind blows a silent song through the trees
I wait to hear the first drops of rain upon the rusty tin roof overhead
And on the dilapidated sheds lining the pathway leading to our old farmhouse
From my tiny bedroom window, I watch the sheets of rain slicing the air in the distance
The closer the storm gets,
My little body feels the bass rumbling of the approaching thunderstorm
During the summer storms, there is a cool mist that proceeds the rain
I love the coolness on my face and body
There is a sweet clover smell from their blossoms
That is blown in from the meadows and fields
I close my eyes to hear nature's symphony
Her music rides atop the breezes,
That rustle of the leaves high above in the tree's canopies
It's a gift she gives freely if one listens
My mother, a daughter of Blackfoot Heritage,
Taught me how to listen to nature, and hear the way she communicates
Listen to the messages she conveys
The secret is in everyone
The art is to silence your mind
Simply listen...listen...listen...
When you're a child of nature, living in poverty,
The world around you becomes your playground
Animals, trees, plants, and streams become nature's teacher
From age four until my teens,
From dawn to dusk I felt free and alive in my world of nature's
Until the blanket of the night covered the sun
That is if dad isn't home!
When he comes home from work the world seems to come to a halt
A blast of strong wind blew directly into my face
Brought me back from my imagination's seduction
The storm is rapidly moving across the meadows
Directly toward our small farmhouse
The sky is dark and filled with towering gray clouds
Then a loud crack of thunder rattled the windowpanes
I quickly slammed the window shut
It shook the entire house
A flash of white lightning struck the tall locust tree,
Not more than a thousand feet from the house
You could smell the burnt tree's smoke
That sound and its vibration were felt throughout my body
I curled up in the further-Est corner of the room away from the window

Sheets of rain pounded against the house
As it slices atop the tin roof over my head
The noise was overwhelming
It's like thousands of small stones being released from a dump truck
The thing about summer storms that strong is one of two things,
They are short-lived or increase in intensity and possibly develop into a tornado
The pinging had to be hail pounding on the tin roof
Sitting in the corner with my eyes closed
I heard the tempo changing often from harshness to calming
But a steady rhythm of binges, tapings, and plunks continued...
My mind's eye was relived yesterday
I hear my mother's voice outside
She is washing clothes
On those days she sometimes sings a song or two
Always when dad isn't home
We all seem to be in a good mood when he's not around
I would sit under the grape arbor that provided summer shade
We would keep each other company
There were times when mom told stories about her friend,
Patsy Cline *and how at family gathers and picnics*
Someone breaks out the guitar, and she and Pasty would sing together
*I was about four or five then, but I remember **Patsy Cline** very well.*
Dad would always spoil those happenings
Things became worse around the house and the abuse more frequent
After that, the singing was far and in-between
Mom was the youngest sibling in a family of ten
I can recall each of my aunts and uncles by name,
First her sisters,
***Pearl Augustus, Cora Cordelia, Esther, Florence Mae**, **Edith**, **Elizabeth Vernus Martinis,** and*
Myra.
One brother passed away at age eighteen,
Emery Elijah Benjamin Franklin John Henry Albert Wetzel
Yes, that was his full name!
*Then there was **Sterling John** and **Charles Harvey Ellsworth Wetzel***
*I knew him as **"Uncle Fuzzy"***
I started humming softly to myself
I could hear my heart beating to the rhythm of the last of the storm above my head
For that short moment,
I flew above the sounds of the rain
I got up and went to the tiny window
I opened it up
*My God, it was like Dorothy in the **"Wizard of Oz"***
The sun's ray was shining through the clouds upon the meadow
The air felt warmer and heavy
Across the meadow, light steam began to rise
From the heated moisture of the soaked earth

Every now and then a sparkle flashed from the raindrops on the leaves and flowers
Behind it, all was a brilliant sapphire sky
The birds emerged from their hiding spots singing their lovely songs
What an amazing sight to behold as a child
Poverty or not!
Summer's storm,
Bring the rains and memories of a long time ago...

SUMMERTREE
A Soldier's Prayer

"Summertree, A Soldier's Prayer", Has won three "Editor's Choice Awards" and was printed in a trio of Anthologies. This poem was written for the lonely and lost soldiers that became among those that are classified "Missing in Action" within a war, wherever, whatever era it may have been fought. My soldier represents, the every-man and the every-woman that are lost and never found. When I first wrote this poem, it was full of hate and anger. I found myself hating what I first put down on paper. So, I rewrote it in a softer frame of mind. The words and their meaning touched my heart. This soldier died from his wounds in the war between the states, known as the "Civil War." His body was discovered seating up against the tree trunk. It was summer when he was laid to rest under the tree, as unknown. A wooden cross marks his resting place. Carved into the wood was, "Summertree".

SUMMERTREE
A Soldier's Prayer

Beneath my Summer-tree, I now lie
Where is everyone, I hear not a cry
Help me Father for I fear the dark
It's cold, I hear not the Meadow Lark.

A mighty oak, this shading Summer-tree
Its branches now hover over me
Hear my cry, Oh Father up on high
Beneath this Summer-tree, I now lie.

The songs of my faith and laced white doves
I now sing a dream to Bonnie, my love
With waterfall eyes, I search far and near
Cold is the night, I'm lonely, death, I fear.

Beneath a Summer-tree, as willows do weep
I now lie here, memories I do keep
My heart is on fire, this I do know
All that is dear, it comes, and it goes.

Listen! Listen to the cricket's call
Summer is lost, leaves drop, it's fall
Winter's crisp, the branches are bare
Seasons do change, soon spring will be fair.

Cold is my room, stillness is at hand
A Soldier's Prayer, deep in the land
Forgotten he, when called to defend
This Summer-tree is my only friend...

Sweet Sanctuary

Staring unto the moon, on a clear lit night and when bright

Caught in its visitation, there is deliverance in the starlight

I'm shocked at what I see gazing up into the perfect mirror

I see the truth, within my nakedness, looking back at myself

Deceive me the first time without an excuse, I'm exposed

Through my recognition, haunted and chased by shadows

I walk unaware of my own motives, blinded by falsehoods

Sifting through dregs, shadows chasing the lights in my life

My emotions are like that of a comet, a vagabond ice storm

That echoes across a vast universe in the likes of a fiery stream

A birth in darkness, from an explosion of a dawning creation

A shot that catapulted the Golden Child through ages of time

Then there are those that are completely silent beyond belief

Quiet like a revolving planet on its axes hovering in blackness

The way things are in my life, it's just another day in my life for me

Another day smothered before it had a chance to take a breath

My dreams remind me of wild, untamed stallions in my mind

Rearing up and sprinting past me like a dark never-ending scream

Between my heart and what may be a battle of future conflicts

In the later years, Hell's Legions seem to control taking my mind

No longer will I allow my mind to waste away in loneliness

And for the fear of forgetting you, will no longer be a conflict

I can walk any road, drive to any destination my heart desires

*However, my heart seeks a **"Sweet Sanctuary"** for both of us.*

SWEET VAPERS

Today the wind whispered in my direction.

It came across wires that bring distance close.

The vapors are concerning and warm.

Mark it sweet in fragrance like April wine.

Sweet vapors make me high and overtake the loss in time.

The crystal waters were broken like the slow rise of an overflowing dam

The tears are like the twinkling of twilight's-glitter

To shrink small enough to travel with the wire

I would sing to your spirit and together yodel of our life.

Yet I sit in my own shadow trying to stand tall, afraid that I might fall.

Only dreams of fresh fallen soft snow cover the vapors all too quickly.

Today the whispers came sweet in my direction,

By way of vapors in the wires.

Ring...Ring...Ring

*To lose a child, your mind and heart scream how you both were cheated of time, time to grow, time to experience the world together. Time is a "Black book" that contains the world's sorrow of lost days, years, and regrets. I say enjoy every second the clock ticks. For when time runs out, so does the music in life. "rlc"

Take Your Time

When you take life too fast, you need to slow down.

As it is said from time to time, "Listen to the music"

As if you are about to slow dance with the one adored

Wrap those arms around someone you love dearly

Pull them close to you, feel the rhythm of making love

Take the time, to feel the butterfly's erratic flight inside

Slow down, and let the music carry you away to paradise

It's important to caress time as if it's a precious gem

When saying hello, do you take time to hear an answer?

When you lie in bed at night, close your eyes and listen

Does the entire day race through the mind at high speed?

Put the brakes on, slow down, and absorb the day's essence

Turn to music, select your favorite slow song, and listen to it

Allow the mind to slow dance to reflections of the day

Life is so damn short in this fast-paced world we live in

Have you ever said to your child, "We'll do it tomorrow"?

Stop! take the time to be a part of their growing years

To truly investigate the face of that child, you will realize

Time is so very short in this damn crazy world we live in

To miss those special moments in the life of your child

Will be gone in a flash, slow down and exit the racetrack!

Like the best of friendships that vanished over the years

Was it because you couldn't take the time to rekindle it

Stop for Christ's-sake, give yourself the time to slow down

Time is very, very short, take time to listen to the music!

Before the music is no longer...

TAPS

The evening sky has changed to red as the sun is setting from a long day of regrets. You can hear the faint sound of the lonely Bugler's call. In the far distance, signing off with his song of TAPS. As the sun is put to rest, the cloud's reflections are like Islands floating in the distance on a lake of cream, so calm and peaceful where our Pride is sleeping in the Forevermore...

*Mournfully, "**Taps**" are played o'er the graves. Loved ones bow their heads and weep. The flag is folded, and the casket is lowered. And our Hero is laid to endless sleep. This scene is played out far too many times with so much sadness and pain. As war-torn hearts ache from the loss, it happens time after time again and again. All people should attend a service to see the "**Honor Guard**" in formal attire. To hear the Bugler, play that sad tune, and feel a shockwave runs through your soul when the rifles fire. A small tribute to those that gave their lives. The true Patriots of our great land had to face the horrors of the battlefield. Where sometimes, "**Freedom**" makes its stand. **War** is the only thing we humans seem to know and wage. To take what we want or change what we don't like. It seems that peaceful times are always short-lived, and the conflict rears its ugly present, then there comes another military strike. **The Military Industrial Complex wins,** no matter if war is won, or if it is lost. A **New World Order** thirsts for power with its selfish goals no matter what the cost may be! Maybe one day we can live in harmony and learn to respect those with different cultures, ideas, dreams, and values before we destroy ourselves and the Earth. Ending the horrific price our young men and women as soldiers pay. But until that day finally comes, if ever it may. Our **Brave** no longer must die. We must honor their ultimate sacrifice even as we wait and wonder, "**WHY?**" Instead of just a day off work to enjoy the pleasures of our country, friends, and families. Just remember what this day is set aside for to "Honor those who gave the ultimate sacrifice for you and me!*

*As the very last note is held, then slowly fades as the sun itself. There is an old veteran standing in salute by the grave of one who has fallen. In the silence, after the Bugler has put his instrument to his side, the old soldier finishes his salute. That's when I witness him wiping the tears from his aged eyes. He turns slowly and walks away down the rows and rows of marbled white crosses. Each matches the other side by side. I called out to the old veteran to wait for a second. I explained I had watched him in salute. I asked if he didn't mind, who were you saluting? He told me it was his first grandson, he just turned nineteen today. He spoke in pride of those that fought and died. His father, his brothers, and two of his sons. Now here lies his first grandson who fought and died for this country they all loved. The tears returned to his eyes as he turned away into the evening walking away. But he turned and said to me, "**There's one more to put to rest**" as he saluted; "**That's Me!**" A lump the size of my fist formed in my throat. I watched him walk down the rows of crosses. Tears ran down my cheeks as I saluted, "**An American Hero**"!*

THANK YOU, LARRY WILLS

{I dedicate this acknowledgment
to a guy who made a difference in my life
and he never knew it!}

I have but one regret in my life I never told Larry what his kind demeanor meant to me during my rough years of abuse in my senior year at Thomas Johnson High School and after Graduation. I know he heard the harsh and vulgar comments being slung in my direction daily. Larry's acknowledgments, subtle nods, small conversations, and that amazing handsome face with a smile as bright as the sun was like having "Faith" tapping me on the shoulder to say, "You have my friendship!" I regret I never told him what his kindness had done for me. I should have had the nerve to tell him how much his friendship truly meant. Larry was one of a few in Frederick that I've held onto deep in my heart over all these years. His kindness and fellowship were needed factors among my peers. I hold my friends in high regard... Thank you, Larry Wills. Wherever you may be or beyond.

"There is no place like home" so it's told
Years away, I would love to return from time to time
It would be like traveling back to where time once halted
I always wanted there to be no place like home for me.

Patrick Street was filled with shops and cozy bistros
I would watch the townspeople walking by on the streets
The evenings were filled with music during the summer
Such a familiar and quaint feeling to experience

Rediscovering my youth, I wanted to make a difference
It still feels like it was just yesterday
Memories high and low linger within my crippled soul
But there was one, I still hold dear in my heart

I was afraid to express any feelings for fear of rejection
Larry the drummer in a very popular band
Tall, dark, and handsome, as the story is often told
Larry was kind to me, his voice assuring and sincere

We were in the same classes in high school
Wherever his band played, I'd watch him from the sidelines
If seen, he would always acknowledge me with a nod
His talent for drums held an envious place in my heart

One young man who was kind to another
It wasn't easy to shed the belittling names put upon me then
*Larry will always be the **"Milk and Honey"** loved by many*
In the hometown where I was born and raised

My wish then, all would have led by his example
Reaching out to others in friendship no matter their orientation
My hometown holds many good people that care less about such matters
My love for the stage put me into the limelight where I was excepted

Larry your kindness gave me a bit of faith when it was needed
Thanks to you and a few others like you
Helped in aiding a young man from taking his own life
Never lose that charming smile that nod of light,
Never my friend, never lose it!

THAT HAS BEEN TAKEN AS WELL

High on a sacred hill that's overlooking the holy valley below
The buffalo grass moves in slow-motion waves across the land
By the breath of fallen souls who fought and died for this land

Warriors, ponies, and the **White Eyes** *all fell on that same day*
The Spirits in the sky saw fit to paint the day a wicked gray
So many Braves came together and united in one great cause

Many nations came together to fight for their right to this land
As far as one could hear, there was such a cry never heard
The sun reflected the **Dog Soldier's** *swords belted to ridged blues*

Mighty were the Chiefs of the Apache, Cherokee, and the Kiowa
Comanche, Blackfoot, and Crow have sworn enemies rode side by side
The Shoshone, and Arapaho all were in war paint and in full Regalia

Famed Sitting Bull, the warrior Geronimo, and Chief Red Cloud
Along with Chief Joseph and Rain-in-the-face b became renowned
Signatures of a thousand painted Indians upon their ponies that day

These great leaders sat upon horses in command of their forces
The signals were given first to the east and then to the west end
Then the north and the band in the south moved in the gate to merge

The **White Eyes** *and* **Pony Soldiers** *galloped in army formation*
The bugler was giving the sign to blow the call for all to charge
From the four winds, the battle cry to commence was like thunder

Soldiers halted in their tracks and eyed attack from all directions
Wave after wave came out of the blue, advancing on the soldiers
For nearly half an hour the guns did roar, and the arrows did fly

Fathers, sons, and brothers on both sides laid quiet on the ground
From within a mighty cloud of dust, the Nations widen their stance
When the dust settled, there was an eerie silence it was deafening

Not a Calvary soldier was left standing on the battlefield that day
Just a lonely flag waved in the cloud of dust announcing the dead
A warrior on his dark pony swept the flag up in a victory scream

After many decades and generations that day a great story told often
The day Indian Nations united to fight the soldiers for the right to live
To hold onto their sacred lands, even now ***that has been taken as well!***

THE CRYING VIOLIN

***This is the story of a child that was found to be a prodigy at a very young age.
Tragedy always seems to come at a very high price in life. This story is of a
five-year-old boy and his father who believed in his son's God-given talent
for the violin. With the ability to reach the other side, namely his mother...***

*He walks across the stage in satin and silks of black
in his lapel a singular rosebud of white
The audience's applause is deafening to me as it echoes
throughout the Palace on opening night
Standing tall and handsome, his precious instrument
is poised ever so gently under his chin
The conductor's baton now taps his music stand twice
all is quiet, and slowly the house lights dim.*

*My heart, a kettle drum thump, I've waited for this night
since the very first time I heard him play
Serenading an audience in splendorous colored notes that
change before your eyes in a magical way
The cords hum in whispers, as if the greatest Violinists
in echo formations from the past are lifted
Creme-d-la-creme of high society in the world of music
will feel the blessing of one so very gifted.*

*The orchestra begins to play and right before the eyes
of the world, my little man begins to color
His bow seems to be guided by those that have come
before him, beyond his own rainbow cover
My heart beats with his, our souls are one, I'll always
protect him for he is my modern Voltaire
Number after number his professionalism waivers not,
even after we'd flown in on Hawaii Air*

*His concert has concluded, and a river of tears rolls from me
eyes as I watch roses adorn the floor
With his final bows, decorum intact, he walks off stage*

with the precious violin that he adores
Before he exits, he's handed two roses from a lady down
stage, he waves and to me, he does run
The house erupts in laughter and in thunderous applause,
a star at the age of five, that's my boy

Running he jumps into my arms saying, **"Thank you, daddy"**
with a big hug, then says, **"She gave me these?"**
He took a deep look into my eyes as two souls bonded
together in a united love newly felt and free
"Who was that that gave you two roses and kissed your cheek?"
She said **"One is for daddy and the other for me"**
A very pretty lady said, **"Mommy is very proud of you and**
I'll always watch over you and daddy"

She said to me, **"I should never forget this night.**
The red rose for me, never forget her love and devotion"
"The orange rose was for you daddy and to always remember
the orange sunset over the Hawaiian ocean"
My heart burst and then tears covered my cheeks, **"Why are**
you crying, daddy?" "I'm so very happy!"
I had given his mother an orange rose the night I purposed
and there was an orange sunset in Hawaii

The roses were from Nina, his mother, who died giving
birth to Ross, but before she passed away
She said to me, **"Thank you for asking me to marry you**
on an evening so beautiful and an amazing day
When we meet again, I'll give you an orange rose so you'll
know it's me saying, I will always love the two of you."
She kept her promise, I'll always remind Ross of that night
when each of us was given a rose of **"I love you"**

Somewhere along the way, I'll find words to tell him it was
his mother, as an angel came to see you and me
Then so like the twilight is to the last of the day, memories often
come to life to those that love and truly believe
At each concert he plays, I see a five-year-old boy reaching
across to the other side with his crying violin
Around the world at final bows,
there's his beautiful mother
handing him a red and orange rose, always first in line...

THE DANCE HAS ENDED

The last of the leaves are slowly dancing down to nature's dance floor
All has gone silent, for most dance cards have been beautifully fulfilled
The Goddess of Autumn has taken leave, colorfully loved, and adored
Her dance paints the season, a coat of many colors cheerfully revealed

There is but one-color remaining, the winter rose soon will be hidden
Forced to shed her pedals, hopelessly against an old man in winter's sky
It is he who lays destiny's blanket of winter white, fall is good ridden
He brings to the floor dancers that twirl in a flurry of ocean high tides

Now the earth is in a deep freeze, but under the snow sleeps a seed in care
Winter's chill seems to dance a macabre waltz that burns the dance floor
With spring's recital, there is the birth of a new rising in dance to repair
With each season that comes and goes, the dance has ended times four

THE DANCING DUST OF SORROW

*"The bare meaning stands out and this time we expressed sorrow,
can still be danced with because tomorrow won't have traces of
dust when we lift our yoke to the highest..."*

*I stand here barefooted dancing in the dust of sorrow
What's before me is beyond the thought of reason
Twenty-four pasts and another twenty-four makes way
Sun baked and a thirst rally, for the dust grows high*

*Shadows etched in the deepest core of the mind
Tear-jerking childhood days till the present time
Inheritance of the past, only traces of the dust
Dancing wildly in memory that never seems to last*

*The Gatherers have arrived with instruments made by
Enchantment is once written upon the sand with stories aged
I fear dry words won't be heard down this chain multiplied
My feet are hot, and the sun filters the dust of sorrow*

*Hear ye! With outstretched arm raised upon the sky
Surrendering completely, wailing, screaming out loud
The woes of long ago dancing to the beating of the drums
Yesteryear's sorrows and of tomorrow lifted unto God.*

The Death of Me

There's a deep thought everlasting in my mind

Drifting away, I fear the loss of its meaning

Will it lead to mourning, only to pass me by?

To what end will it leave me to ponder upon

My Lord, doesn't anybody love anymore?

Will I arrive on a promise, not eternal in Heaven?

This I say, Nay! I shout life has no meaning, why?

o many boundaries cause my complexity to waiver

Do not give me lengthy dialogue in uninspiring verses

God Jesus, doesn't anybody love anymore?

Complex-ed, unrewarding, and just plain weak

Weave me naught with words from other solos

Theorize in poetry and prose so deep one has in need.

In a dictionary to understand the word, "If"

My God, doesn't anybody love anymore?

Ponder if you will, of those that scratch and scrape

Deep thoughts are their hopelessness in dreamers' dreams

Hiding in the shadows of what a writer fears most,

The never-ending pit, the horror known as, "Writer's Block"

Doesn't anybody love anymore?

Must there be an endless pit of a mine, where all is useless

Fragments are dropped into this man-made darkened soul of mine

Mindless lovers jump into what they see as an expansion

Deep waters, which leave me to believe, I Thee drowned.

Christ, doesn't anybody realize that this is,

"THE DEATH OF ME"

THE DREAMER

The material covers the flesh
Only to hide what wants to open through time and space
Sunshine falls upon this chilled mortal
So that he can feel the burn and watch his flesh turn black
Feeling natural and healthy never again
Let me spread my arms out wide
Ever so wide that I might touch horizon to horizon
Feel the air about my face
Through my fingers, through my hair and eyelashes
Let me spin and jump wildly
As if to express an explosion of happiness in this lifetime
I want to hear the clammer and chatter of innocent children
Their joyful laughter rang loud and free
To be heard throughout this amazing universe
May my spin create the largest tornado man has ever eyed
May its encumbrance span and encircle the planet
Leaving behind the unscathed things of beauty,
Like freedom and love
Little wide-eyed boys and girls,
Puppies and kittens
Butterflies and birds of every color imaginable
Let their songs be heard around the world
Lyrics of songs reflect the music of love and a peace
Ribbons of amber and gold, with touches of red, orange, and yellow
The sweet aroma of wild roses, lilacs, orchids, and lilies
Let me find that land of the lost horizon
A paradise of harmony
But for now...
I must dig in for a possible survival
Against the explosive and senseless destruction of mankind
I hurry to life's
"Panic Room"
Where I can close my eyes and become
The Dreamer...

THE EAGLE TAKES TO WING

Let's begin with a reason why here...

Life itself is a metaphor for everything around us. This story is of a young man of eighteen years of age who goes to serve in a country filled with hatred, unrest, and evil. All the while his heart, "like so many" is locked in the mind and body of the home, and his grandfather of the amazing age of "One Hundred and Twelve" years old. His love and admiration for his grandson are beyond measure. These two are tighter than fleas on a mountain lion.

Back home are the usual family members praying for God to watch over him, with hopes of him returning home safe, sound, and with all body parts intact-ed. Picture this, a very old man sitting on a porch in an old rocking chair that happens to the creek when rocking backward every time. He is a grandfather, who has seen his share of war when he was a couple of years younger at sixteen. He fought for something or someone, well to him it matters no longer. As he dozes off in the chair, he falls into a deep sleep whereupon he begins to dream (or as his heritage believes, goes into a vision state) of his beloved grandson over in a country fighting for whatever or whoever? Here is my grandfather's vision...

I spy,
There is high on a mountain pine branch
He sits with his head drooped
For years I have watched him,
From hatchling to a regal king in his flock
Now it's time for the aged cock to take his last flight around this home
There was a time when he glistened in the midday sunshine
Feathers as dark as the black bear's fur
And his crowning glory of white
For miles, the eagle was heard singing
His shrill echoed deep in the forest's dark
But now the tune is gloomy, tattered, beaten, and a sore throat moan
Apparently, he no longer can sing a King's Tune
His song has faded deep into the forest,
Where the tongue slashers hunger
Often cursed and thought to be a mouthy free-loading crow
That my friend cuts like a knife straight through the heart
A world of wasted beauty on the fly-by fades to gray
However, the forest spirits sing of how glorious,
*The **"Ode to a Monarch"** is*
Beyond the tallest of all Ponderosa Pines
I remember following his flights
Those days are now gone, and they will never be replaced
Old buddy, Listen!
I hear the mighty eagle spirit calling out to you
The eagle sings,

"I must fly free as the wind sings across the land"
"Or Not at All!"
Now as the sun bows low,
As if in agreement, I see you in a glow of red
My heart knows it's your last as king
It is his spirit as Eagle King, that fades into the shadows of the setting minx
"I wish you field plentiful in corn to fatten you the winter long"
The mountain now chills
As the blanket of the night is drawn across the forest
But I will not leave you alone
I will stay by your side; your enemies are many
There in the thickest of moonlight, a face of shadows so familiar
Yet I cannot recall the name
Within the shadows of all my days yet to be night,
Do you think you've found fair game?
Well, not this night!
Sly you may be the foxy one,
There will be no dinner in your den of dens this night!
It's late and I am tired, this is where I say goodnight
As my heart hovers in mid-air
I need to rest my eyes...
I will keep vigil until the early morning light
I shook my head as time passes slowly!
What has changed?
Before my sight, what must be an act of wizard-trey
There in my mind, you were in an imaginative flight till the rising of the sun
It was as if you were placing footsteps upon billows of white cotton
As you walked across the evening sky,
Your wings were spread across a background of early-morning blessings
I, in amazement, stood in your great shadow
And I found it beautiful!
That's when you fell upon me...
Early morning was but a whisper away
Still, in the shadows of the moon, you fell from your branch
And there beyond my reach, yet before my eyes
I witnessed your very last breath
With the flapping of your mighty wings, your eyes slowly closed
Nature's King was no longer...
I now speak my words to an ungrateful nation
Take him home upon the mighty wings of the **"Thunderbird"**
Crossing over into paradise
He flew o'er the mountains, valleys, and the forests
That was his kingdom for so many years
My eyes began to swell as the moonlight fell upon your mighty wings
It's time the eagle takes to wing this is hidden forevermore...
Whose vision is this: The Grandfathers of his Grandson or the Grandsons of his Grandfather?

THE EARTH TREMBLED

How well I remember the earth trembling in earnest
The heavens above turned a dark charcoal gray
Another prophecy came to pass
Peace between **"The People"** and the **"White-eyes"** was no more
Indians fought for the right to exist on their own land
The others saw all Indians as a threat to expansion
Blood became the thirst among the two races
It was clear that treaty after treaty would never be honored by the **"White-eyes"**
Hatred blew across the plains like a raging fire
The Indian people were treated worse than barbaric dogs
The old, women, and children were butchered by raiding bands of **"Dog Soldiers"**
Villages were burnt to the ground in the early morning hours as the sun rose
It was impossible for the villagers to defend themselves
Chaos ensued as the attackers stormed through on their horses
Across the plains, valleys, and hills,
Smoke rose like thunderhead clouds before the deluge
As far as the eyes could see the grasslands were laid to rest
There was a stench that crept upon the western winds
Indians upon their ponies stood atop a knoll overlooking the land of plenty,
And saw a plaque of rotting and decaying flesh
The sacred buffalo had been slaughtered by hundreds of thousands
Bulls, cows, and calves had been skinned,
Leaving the meat to rot in the hot sun
The sound of drums echoed across this great land
The "White-eyes" heard the drums near and far
The white man saw many bonfires that ignited throughout the Tribal Nations
The Indians sang and danced
As the black sky was filled with glowing embers of revenge
Chanting in the night air along with the war cries in a multitude of anger
The creation of the red man's symphony of hatred toward the White man
There would not be a place to run and hide
"The People" the true natives of this land called **"America"**
Letting out a cry of **WAR** heard from coast to coast
Many on both sides now mourned their losses
Truly Death rides a black horse, counting the dead that lies on America's **"Killing Fields"**
Indians prayed to **"The Great Spirit"** in the heavens

"That you would blow the mighty winds from the four corners of the earth
To cleanse the stench of blood and death from the face of Our Mother Earth
Let your people know the bliss of victory against the White-eyes,
They have invaded the fertile lands like a plaque of Locust
It seems the last of our integrity was thrown to the Dust Devils,

That spin like their thirsty where no water exists
We have given our life's blood to enrich the lands put before us
We keep the waters running clean and clear,
We take only what is needed to survive from the land
It was foretold by our ancestors that the white man would come and cover this land,
Like the swarms of ravenous Locust
They will chew and defecate on our very existence,
Leaving the land covered in filth and laid barren for generations to come
Let the Great Chiefs and leaders of each Indian Nation band together for one great battle
The Lakota, Sioux, Apache, and Cheyenne come together to fight,
"The Yellow Haired Custer" and his Cavalry of Dog Soldiers
And gather at the "Little Big Horn."

It was foretold in dreams,
It was destiny that brought the Indian Nations together to fight for their existence,
The Great Chiefs circled Custer and his men
One by one the soldiers fell until only the "Yellow Hair" stood in defiance
The dust swirled in one great circle rising high in the air
Custer had fallen!
Fate and his brother Vengeance raged in anger,
Determination brought victory to all Indian people on that day
As the dust was clearing
There was a deafening silence throughout the **"Little Big Horn"**
No gunshots, no war cries, and no thundering hooves of horses were heard
Out of the lowering dust cloud
Rode one Indian on his painted pony came racing through the fallen soldiers
Letting loose a war cry of victory as he leaned sideways on his pony,
Grabbing the only thing standing, the flagstaff that stood silent amongst the dead soldiers
All the time sounding a war cry of victory!
Without missing a single beat,
The Indian on his pony flew through the dust cloud like an eagle catching its prey
Such a silence settled with dust as the light breeze blew across the grass,
Along with the fallen soldiers, Indians, and even the horses that lay beside their riders
History was made and written on that day
It wasn't long before the news traveled from one end of the country to the other
The glorious Indian Victory against General George Armstrong Custer became,
Legendary among All Native American Nations
What was foretold had come to pass
The prophecy came and went...
The soldiers and Custer himself were buried where they fell!
It wasn't long after that great battle that the Great White Father,
Ordered the Indian Nation to be rounded up and herded hundreds of miles to be placed,
"Reservations"
There were bands of angry warriors that resisted the **"White Man's Prisons"**
They were titled **"Renegades"**
This cattle drive of **"The People"** *were being driven from their homes*

The old and the sick were left to die where they dropped along the way
The dead and dying were left to the elements and the animals
They were offered no mercy, food, or water
Those that lived later called this inhumane cattle drive,

"THE TRAIL OF TEARS"

THE GREAT EAGLE SPIRIT

{It is said, from that very spot on the edge of the outcropping overlooking the canyon below, his story has been handed down through many generations. That the "Great Eagle Spirit" once landed on that spot directly from the heavens above, transforming into a living man of "The People" as the "Eagle Man." He walked among the Indian villages in search of a young maiden to wed.}

High above overlooking the canyon valley below
Stands a muscular and handsome Indian brave
Striking is his stature against the colorful western sky of the evening
A forceful wind always blows in earnest atop the bluff
I watched this powerful man holding his ground against the powerful wind
The lazy clouds change the formation high above
This magnificent bluff is known to be quite mystical and holy among my Indian People
I watched the clouds form the face of a beautiful long-haired maiden
She seemed to be looking down at the man standing on the holy plateau
as if to blow the handsome brave off the out-cropping
He raises his arms,
Singing a blessing to thank the Great Spirit for his family's bounties
In the picturesque setting of a magnificent red sunset
My heart raced and tears appeared at the beauty of it all
This truly was nature's cathedral
*He began his ritual by singing to the **"Spirits of Our Forefathers"***
His powerful baritone voice echoed against and throughout the canyon walls
His beautiful voice chanted blessings to the four winds
Once this was achieved there was total silence throughout the canyon below
This is when the handsome brave removed all his jewelry,
Breastplate, armbands, buckskin leggings and finally his loin cloth
Leaving him totally naked before his maker
I watched from my perfect hiding spot
I watched him as he retrieved a small clay jar
Taking the top off he then poured a small amount of its content into one hand
Putting the vessel down with the other,
He rubbed his hands together
A slight breeze blew in my direction
I could smell the scent of a powerful Cedar Oil
Rubbing his hands together was warming the magical and intoxicating oil
I observed this muscular brave begin to apply the oil to his manly body
First to his outstanding arms and across his chest and over his ripped stomach
He picked up the small jar once again, pouring the last of the Cedar Oil into his hand
First on one thigh then down to the calf and then to the other thigh
The brave rubbed the oil onto his buttocks, neck, face, and finally to his groin

The fragrance of the Cedar Oil permeated the air
It was intoxicating, to say the least
He walked over to the edge of the holy spot
There stood my idol glistening from head to toe in the red-setting sun
Every muscle on that magnificent man was accented by that incredible oil
This living work of art stood at the edge of the out-cropping
Giving of himself totally free of all earthly possessions,
In order to be judged for his contributions to both family and tribe
The powerfully built Indian then proceeded to undo his long-adorned braids
Once he achieved undoing both braids,
He ran his fingers through the long raven-black hair
Setting it free in the continuous flowing winds
This is where I witnessed the most amazing moment in my life!
The sunset was glowing as red as hot coals
The last of the dying sun was painted gloriously across the horizon
A huge thunderhead in the distance seemed to reach the heavens
I watched my admiration raise his massive arms stretching them out to each side
He then leaned forward into the constant and force-able wind
The world around me had come to a complete stop!
Freezing time if you will?
His magnificent head of long hair continued to move in slow motion about his tall muscular
frame
The hair's movement resembled the rise and fall action like that of dandelion seeds,
That got captured in a warm summer breeze
The sun took its last breath as the veil of darkness was taking over
Even after the setting of the sun,
There was enough light from the rising full moon to illuminate the canyon from top to bottom
Far in the distance was the rhythmic sound of a beating drum by a medicine man
The sound echoed back and forth against the canyon's interior
My heart raced as I was mystified at the miracle scene taking place before my eyes
Tears welled up in my eyes, for the beauty of it all, touched my very soul
It was Mother Earth's theater giving another grand performance
This was just the beginning of what I would be privy too
The action had stopped for a split second or two
At the time it felt as though it were minutes
All returned as it were before
I wiped my eyes and took a deep breath
Melding with my surroundings once again
There stood my God-like figure in silhouette against the now blueish night sky
I couldn't take my eyes off this man even if I wanted to
What I was witnessing was a miracle
Transforming himself before my now widening eyes,
A huge Golden Eagle!
I fell backward among the rocks within my hidden place
I was in a shocking awl of amazement
I just witnessed the admiration of my young life,

Spreading his muscular arms outward, changing them into spectacular wings
From my hidden spot,
I felt gush after gush of air from each flap of his now enormous wings
I lay there looking up into the heavens
Watching him glide upon the wind with ease
That thunderhead I had described earlier had kept its promise for action to come was,
Flashes of heat and lightning in the far distance
It seemed to outline every part of this unbelievable spiritual and godly creature
I observed him making several circles over the valley below
The flashes of silent lightning in the distance
Showed the Eagle flew higher and higher disappearing into the star-filled heavens
I searched the moonlit sky for nearly an hour,
When a shooting star caught my eye coming out of the clouds
The Great Eagle was returning to the out-cropping he had taken off from
I returned to my hidden spot between the rocks
He was coming in for a landing
Spreading those magnificent, outstretched wings at least a twelve-foot span
Just as he touched the surface with his massive, outstretched legs
He began to transform back into the tall and handsome warrior I admired
I watched intently for his next move against the blue and starry night sky
I watched the amazing Indian brave complete his reversal transformation as the Eagle God
In a swirling confection of wind and stardust!
There stood the six-foot-four handsome and muscular man naked and proud
I watched him redress, first into his lion cloth
Next, he put on his moccasins, leggings, breastplate, armbands, and jewelry
His raven black hair was thrown over the back of his wide and muscular shoulders
I knew it was time for me to leave my hiding place
Getting back to the village before he did would be the best thing for me to do
Just as I turned to make my hasty exit,
I heard that powerful baritone voice I knew all too well

"Little Eagle, I know it's you behind the boulders!
In fact, I was aware of you tracking me from the moment I left the village."

I slowly stepped out from behind the rocks
Looking like a sad-eyed puppy, asking,

"Am I in trouble"

The admiration of all my life replied,

"No, not with me, but I'm not so sure about your mother?"

His stern look turned to that handsome smile of fatherly love
I took off running into his open arms
A place where I feel safe and secure all the time
I watched him pull his long hair to one side giving me the cue to get ready

In one amazing swoop,
He hoisted me up in the air sitting me on his right shoulder
"Ready?" *he asked, and I answered,* **"Yes!"**
As we headed back toward the village,
I could not help myself from asking,

"Father, I have a lot of questions about what I saw before my eyes"
He let out a short laugh, then answered looking up at me with a smile,

"There is no doubt in my mind, "Little Eagle, No doubt!
Why don't we save the questions for another time?
Because your mother will have more than enough for the both of us."

We both laughed as we made our way through the trail leading back to the village, we call home...

THE LARK AND THE WISTERIA

Sweet memories in thou hast to touch my spirit
In these eyes, I carry a rage of unspoken miseries
Days hast to quicken and still give wake to thee
My heart soars like the Lark in search of another

The days of wine and roses still linger in my mind
Carry not thee my woes, instead, I hold your wings
Walk in summer's symphony amongst the willows
Feel the breeze that spins golden dreams for thee

How will the days mark my loss in its shackles?
I need to break free of the heartbreak consuming me
My ever-flowing rivers wander free will mark dear
It will take thee to Heaven's Gate for my beloved

Thus take thy gray skies and know sunshine dwells
Find thy way through tunnels marked in ambrosia
Thus, its sweet wine lightens thy heavy load again
I rest this heavy heart on scarlet silk and cream lace

God will lighten thy veil of burdens so you can see
Thy favorite blossoms, sweet flora of Wisteria Vines
Heavy in fragrance divine where the Lark gives the song
For thee to gather and lie upon thy midnight marble

THE MOST-QUIET NEED

I struggle for every day's most quiet need
I travel on wings with my heart in hand
I hold myself accountable for my lonely deeds

I dream of halos-glow and fiery eyes of passionate love
I hold tight to clinging shadows etched on a wall
I fly high on the wings of a snow-white seductive dove

I feel the need, I know my heart rests in the land of desire
I give to my partner all I am and ask for nothing more than truth
I want our lovemaking to explode into exploratory wildfires

I close my eyes, memories come easily laying before me
I know who I am and strive for the knowledge of the "Casanova"
He is lying before me, a wonder created by God it's Adam I see

I will give my heart and my flesh all the needed room to explore
I'll cry with this beauty, for we both climb the highest of mountains
I would gather him in my arms, and whisper that he is meant to be adored

I will know peace within the walls that circle his secret garden
I will fly over its walls to see the living beauty growing within
I call out his name in love, if I am too loud, I beg pardon...

The Moth Falls Clear of Emotions, But Not a Burning Candle

When the Moth flies drained of all her feelings

Flight weakens her wings, all that is cherished

Wings dry like powder, caught in a stale breeze

Powder falls up and out, tender this does make

When wings carry the weight of the world

Flight makes heavy the silken frame of love

Then a heart is weakened from yesterday's flight

A Moth has been burnt by the fire of the lovelorn

When the Moth takes a once-in-a-lifetime flight

There are no strings to this puppet of thought

Heat rises, but where there's a cold heart viewed

One falls clear of emotions, but not a burning candle

When slow sinking takes one to the depths of feelings

Strike a match and give life to the candle with flame

Offer roses of twenty for thirty seconds of wild and red

The Moth lands on a bud, yet to glory praising its luck

When a Moth flies high and touches the lunar edge

Kissed in morning dewdrops, mother taught to flutter

The powder dries quick, bide your time upon the rocks

Don't fly low to this candle's flame, burnt you shall be

The Phoenix Lies Dormant

"Our world to this very date has vented against the man for not respecting Mother Earth. The destruction and loss of life are staggering. Floods, fires, tornadoes, hurricanes, war, cutting of the forests, melting ice caps and heat has gone hey-wire in degrees. It is because of man. We need to start taking an active role in helping our world or else we can say goodbye to the best thing man has ever had!" rlc

****

MAN,

An animal that conducts his selfishness

And filth upon a wounded Earth

The probability of one holds the certainty

That destruction and death

Will prevail

How blinded is blind

That weaves a web of self-destruction

In his hallowed twilight

Mother Earth is crying out to God

For her spirit is broken

Beyond unshed tears

Once a breath of fresh clean air

Now stagnate at the door of darkness

Suffocating her heart.

A creature known as Man,

Created by the Heavenly Father

Holds no future

For it is ill-fated

In man's hour of everlasting shame

The Phoenix lies dormant

And hope is not spiritually attuned

This Earth is overpopulated

With complicated creatures

Steadfast in selfish temptations

A brisk turbulence

Releases the shadows of the past

In a mountain's mudslide of horrors

Scary revelations decorate the doors of darkness

That takes over the light of humanity

Blue ice represents

Compressed millions of years

Now flood the precious pages

Of the unmounting of the Good Book

Pages floating upon the muddy waters

Provoked by the injustice

Put upon by man

We are a family raised under the stars of Heaven

Where once upon a time

Sweet sunrises rose

And crying silent violins played a rhapsody of red sunsets

Then came the drowning

Of distressed dreams

The dew left its mark

Upon the soles of our shoes

And the wild spirit of born free

Lost its ovation of life's greatest mysteries

The light receded into the shadows

With a sigh, the sparrows had taken to flight

Stronger in its wrath

Escalating into burning wildfires

With the sounds of tortured winds

Stroking a death march

Strumming notes lead to a lifetime of sad songs

Tears crept from Mother Earth's wounded soul

Only she is left

To see the moon-lit mountains

That silhouette across

A horizon of a starless sky

Where once Man dreamt...

THE PRAYERS IN THE NIGHT

It is I who hear the prayers in the night
Prayers of long ago and just seconds past
Many times, my heart is broken by the innocent
Babes in need of comfort, begging for food, warmth, and love
I hear the ones that need to lighten their load
Many ask for forgiveness for a selfish deed
The prayers in the night sometimes strangle me
The need for a lighter heart to be more caring
So many in turmoil and filled with regret throughout their lives
I encounter so many souls wandering in complete darkness
These are unforgivable that have created evil
It is I who say a prayer for these misguided perpetrators
Many prayers are whispered upon wayward breezes
Then there are those that are screaming in a raging storm
These are the prayers that tear my soul apart every night
For they are many, confused, hopeless, and fear
Cursing the Almighty for being abandoned in their hour of need
I hear the prayers of the multitude in the night
Am I cursed?
Am I blessed?
For it is I who hear the prayers in the night...

THE QUIETEST NEED

I struggle with every day's most quiet need
I travel on wings with heart in hand
I hold myself accountable for my lonely deeds

I dream of halos glow and fiery eyes of love
I float high on the wings of desire
I hold tight to my love, as tight as a glove

I feel the need, I know my heart's desire
I give all I can and ask for nothing in return
I want my love to fill full of wildfires

I close my eyes and memories come easily
I know who I am and strive for the calm
I see how bright the days may be.

I will give my heart room to explore
I know how many times it has stopped
I will never dream alone, and that's no lore.

I will find my peace in a lovely secret garden
I will fly over its walls and see the beauty within
I will call out your name, if too loud, I beg pardon.

THE RAPE OF MOTHER EARTH

An old Indian sat outside a Trading Post under a huge oak tree in the shade
Such an amazing-looking man
His face is marred with deep valleys and deep crevasses
His skin tone is a deep reddish brown
When I asked, "Sir, what is your age?"
The old Indian politely answered.

"I am Walking Bird; I have seen many suns rise that cross the face of our Mother Earth. Thus, there have been many moons that have followed the path of the sun. As a very young child of Mother Earth, I was taught how to; listen and to hear the songs of the fresh waters that sing as they ramble across the surface of the land. Where the waters run, there is life given to the grasses and the trees. I have witnessed the birth of many, many species. What a gift Mother has given to all of us. She feeds us and clothes us. When thirsty she gives us cool, clean, clear fresh water to drink. Washing our flesh as well as washing the face of Mother. She filled the rivers and the lakes with fish. Mother Earth covered the plains in wheat, oats, and barley abundance. I have seen so many varieties of four-legged creatures. The bear, deer, beaver, buffalo, elk and wolves, and coyotes hunt them for food. These, my friends, were the life force of "The True People". The mighty and great buffalo roamed this country as far as the eyes could see! Billowing clouds of dust rose from the thundering herds of millions that grassed through the north down into the mid-west freely. As time walks onward, so have I. Growing up as a young Braves of the Cheyenne Nation, I studied my people and their struggles for survival was learned. Taught by the Elders who are brave and certainly wise. Learning amazing things upon the earth. She is like a forever blooming flower; we hold her within our hands."

The old Indian lowered his hands and shook his head white.
Once again, he raised his head and spoke as if in acknowledgment.
I took a quick look behind me
And I noticed a small crowd was now in attendance
To hear this amazing old man's words that he passionately speaks from his heart.
There was no doubt this man of age was filled with knowledge and sacrifice.
His face showed decades of wear and tear.
There were tears wrapped around each of his words spoken from that moment on.
We stood in silence to take in every word this elder had to say...

"Our beautiful Mother has been Raped! A sorrowful deed put upon by our very life force. Her forests are depleted! Vanished are the tall trees that reached the heavens, a loss forever. It seems that simple minds do simple things, leading to devastation. Wildlife has suffered the brunt of it all. The loss of their homes sheltered all living creatures apart from the circle of life itself. Once the surface of our mother's beautiful face was lush with green mosses and grasses that covered the forest floors. Her canopy is most, most important! The treetops act like umbrellas. When Father Sun becomes harsh and relentless, the canopy provides help to

cool the living creatures. Once there were thick canopies, no longer are they! Now flat and lifeless as the surface of our sister Moon. It is the forest and the grasses, and the trees that supply us with the air we breathe. All living creatures need the precious air that they supply for each one of us! The older I become, the more I can hear the moans and cries of our mother. We the Indians saw the beginning of discord many generations ago. Tribal medicine men had dreams, and visions and saw the omens of our demise coming. The land we were caring for was no longer free to us. Our Mother Earth has been repeatedly raped. Her rapist is well known to us! Man's "Blinded Greed!" Destroying without thinking. Taking more than needed, taking without remorse! Wildlife is vanishing by the hour, becoming ex-stint around the world! Man's population has "EXPLODED" into a critical phase around the world. More and more of Mother's sacred land is taken to build more homes, and sold as commercial businesses, all to "GREED!" The animal known as man will sooner or later destroy every living organism upon their only home, Earth. This includes himself. For once the land is paved over there will be no grasses, no trees, no water, and no life. There on "NO RESPECT!" No taking time to stop and acknowledge the life-giving gifts that are given to us all. It is all about "GREED! There's a very dark and evil entity that thrives on destruction for all. Digging deeper into the core of man's humanity and Mother. Man always wants more but is not willing to give back. Creating waste, creating hunger, and creating the living dead. All the signs are there, my sisters and brothers but no one sees them. Are we so blind as not to see what is right in front of our faces?"

The old Indian clenched his fists and teeth
Looking up at us, his eyes seemed to be on fire
Showed great pain and apathy I haven't ever experienced before
Here was an old Indian man who cherishes earth, the mother of All Creation
Being destroyed minute by minute, by the race of men in every nation around the world
Greed for land, greed for wealth, and the greed for MORE...
He spoke again in a manner that felt deflated to us all

"I do suspect the future of our Mother Earth will be sparse of any nature. Gone...Gone...will be not just the remaining "True People" but all of mankind. Barren will be our once beautiful world. The world is once known as "The Blue Planet." Now will be another frozen world floating through space. No longer the "Genius".

We all knew his words were truthful
A man of wisdom and truth
This old Indian caught our attention with every word and expression of gesture

"You had asked me my age. I am one hundred- and twenty-six years young! 126 years of suns have risen and traveled across the sky. 126 years the moons followed the very same path. I have seen, I have protested, and become a watcher among the race of men. "RAPE!" is the only word I can use for Earth's ongoing tragedy by the "MAN." Our Mother deserves our respect! Before it is too late to reverse our damages. I believe it is far too late... As a place in which to live, she should and needs to be respected by all. It is up to you now and your children and their children to make future amends. I have seen the future and our mother does NOT SURVIVE...

THE ROAD

{The Road, for me travels on and forward as far as the eyes can see. Not knowing where I am, not clear, or having faith in my decisions is like reading a road map upside down. Life is like a road you have never traveled on. The unknown can hold you back if you don't have the courage to make decisions. This Road is life. When you travel through time and space, stop along the way. Read the signs that are offered to you. It's like following the yellow brick road, you are off to see what's ahead in your life. Maybe a Wizard or two? The Road holds a message. Look inside your mind for the map that will take you to where you want to go.}

When the road never seems to end
Ride your soul into the horizon.

When signs reflect detours in your mind
Glance at them and forward you ride on.

When your road reflects the sun in your eyes
Blink twice and travel with a friend of mine.

Do not worry for the road is long
For there are many shops along the way

Pay whatever tolls there may be
Travel onward with faith at your side

The road is never straight
For there are twists and turns in abundance

Strap yourself in and move across the land
Knowing that tomorrow offers rest stops.

Never drive weary, focus on your faith
Then thank God, your road never ends.

THE SHADOWS SPEAK TO ME

Mountain streams, fresh and sparkling run musically under the sun
Trout fatten on Mayflies along the banks, and color flora accents its run
Shading trees of all types, fruit-bearing and floras, a wondrous sight
The ground-covered grasses galore, shrubbery bloom under father's light

Before this temple, as the sun shines bright, my heart beats strongly
Release the doves into the blue dawn where their wings sing a song
I beat the tall grasses to drive away the shadows of fear and shame
They move like the snake through the grass, hunting a soul to claim

Twilight makes me aware; Sister Moon creates a world for evil to play
Within the last of twilight, I see a lone rider on a horse racing my way
In a cloud of dust, he's before me, staring into my eyes with his fire
He moans, "I'm all shadows of your past people, know me as the crier"

The Indians echo their cries, seen painted across the mountain's face
Painted ponies dark wildly in and out of the shadows at a frantic pace
Lodges numbering in the thousands pitched beside the singing waters
Living off the land, peaceful people working as one unit, in total order

Within the cloud of dust, I am a witness to the shadows that they cast
It's clear to me, that hidden within the grass are shadows of a people's past
Shadows seen, are the echoes of souls etched across my people's heart
Forevermore they'll tell the story of my People's heritage, never to part

Stories of the American Indian, told by the shadows that history casts
Every time I turn around, wherever I go, there are shadows of the past
The Indian vanished in the dust, left are the shadows of their defeat
No longer do the tribes own the land of their forefathers, history repeats...

THE STORY OF HEAVEN'S KEEP

The grounds are holy at the Keep, the stones and shadows now sleep
It's he who comes not to fear shadows but to remember one in kind
In his weary hand, a wilted rose once fresh now twice does it but weep
Between the highs and lows, the strings of her harp play melodies fine

The walk is long through Heaven's Keep, shaded by Willow Weepers
A long time requested; a promise made to one held close to a heart's oath
He now stands where the beauty was a place named, "Love's Leapers"
Pleasant is the breezes as summer nears its own shadow to again toast

Sometimes he wishes for falling stars, do the eyes see the heart as wise?
Here is where his dreams were to come true, making their way in a dare
Their light shined as bright as the heavens above, torch deep in his eyes
He laid with the welted rose of white, kissed with dew from the tears of care

Walking over to the edge of yesterday, he overlooks the amazing valley
Wayward thoughts in forever rolling green, he saw heaven in her glory-be
He fought for this country bravely and for his valley, you can see in the rally
Post blame he cannot, this was his choice, his duty for all to stand free

The leaves have blown free from their season housing due to the change in time
Listen to the wind for words of unheard misbegotten, for she does not sleep
Time to make the long walk back, in a breeze he heard her whispering fine
"I'm always with you"** now his walk isn't lonely out of **"Heaven's Keep."

THE TOUCH BEHIND

"Picture total darkness...There is an amber spotlight in the center of the darkness. I am seated on a chair staring forward in total silence! a faint underscore of tense music is playing to set the mood."

I stare forward, never straight
A deep hollow ridge of nothingness
Calloused thoughts of days not yet!

I sit immune to my surroundings
Only a golden haze about my being
Its warmth covers my body with a designer's artistic ability

It makes my hair of blond shine like that of a golden lily
My hair lies layered like the mane of an African Lion into the wind
My features rise sharp and extend and accent the golden haze

From behind, a touch, cool and alive, I do not move a muscle
Slender fingers from a lady of leisure begin to dance about my face
Dancing with a rippled movement that makes me nervous

Creating insecurity in my corrosive mood
The music begins to build, louder and louder, roaring with a thunderous beat
A fit of excessive anger weaves in and out of my being

Twisting around my thoughts until they over-rides all other feelings
Tension, tightness in my jaw, and a pathogenic thought
"I SCREAM OUT IN A DEAFENING ROAR!"

Rough and with a vice-like grit in my teeth
I'm no longer immune, with the speed of an attacking Cheetah
I turn with a force uncontrollable

The calloused thoughts are released!
*The golden haze has turned **BLOOD RED!***
FIRE HOT** and with a Demon's Eye, the intent is to **KILL!

A lust for blood comes over me, the sweet flow of life itself,
I now crave the nectar like a starving Vampire...
All feelings are gone but the pounding beat of my heart

There's a rhythmic pounding in my stomach and in my temples
In a flash with unbelievable speed, I strike out!
Drawback my lips and find my mark with skill

SHE SCREAMS IN HORROR AS THE BLOOD SPLATTERS INTO THE AIR!
PAINFULLY MY FANGS TEAR AT HER THROAT
LUSTING AS THE BLOOD HEIGHTENS MY MORBID DESIRES

MY HUNGER
LINGERED IN THE SHADOWS FOR THE LONGEST OF TIME
TEARING INTO THE UNEXPECTING IS THRILLING!

Then...
The silence begins to swell
The bountiful stench of the hot coppery blood lies at my feet like a red tide
The liquid crimson drips from my lizard tongue to my chin

I am covered from head to toe with the river of life,
Back, back I transform to the stare forward, never straight of once before
Nothingness and calloused thoughts subside short

Fire turns from red into the golden haze of earlier
The only thing that has changed is the footing I place
And the sound of my stomach growling for more.

It is I who wait for another
to
"TOUCH BEHIND"

The Truth Lies Before Your Eyes

"Picture yourself walking through the thickest of fog. Smell the fumes from fuel and fire and burning flesh if you will. Listen to the silence as you step onto gravel and stone. The fog clears in front of you atop a hill mount overlooking a battlefield. Before you lie the Horrors of War!"

We're walking through the battlefield that was just bombed.

We are picking ourselves up and dusting the dirt and grime from our eyes.

We were on the right flank when we heard the whistling sound of a bomb approaching.

Someone yelled, "Run for cover" and that's what everyone did.

I guess you could say we were the lucky ones.

We stood there in the smoke, dirt, and dust.

Falling from the sky were particles of ash, clothing, pebbles, and sludge.

That's when we noticed the silence about us.

For a short period of time, the silence was deafening and horrifying.

Falling about us were pieces of burnt flesh.

The body parts of the men and women we fought beside were falling from above.

Wherever we stepped, the earth below our feet was a blood bath.

After a time, the air cleared.

Our eyes were met with our comrades laying on the battlefield before us.

Once my head had cleared from the ringing and pound of the blast Cries were being heard.

Soldiers calling out for help amongst the sound of gunfire in the distance.

Mounting around us was screaming, crying, and begging for assistance.

I pulled my hanky out and placed it on my nose and mouth.

The smell of burning flesh, gunpowder, and warm blood were sickening.

It's a stench you can never, ever get over in your life.

Damn it filled the air throughout the battlefield

It filled the air most days.

There were soldiers cursing God as the river of life ran from the destroyed bodies.

"Jesus Christ!!! What in the fuck was this for? Damn You, Damn You..."

You know, even after a man takes his last breath,

You can still see the blood oozing from the body.

It looks like slow-moving lava erupting from wounds.

As life ebbs away,

So does the flow of blood as it bubbles it's last and finally ceases.

We work through the night helping the wounded and gathering the dead.

Always searching for the Dog-Tags that help to identify the dead.

War is proof of man's unwarranted evils,

"The Truth Lies Before Your Eyes"

THE VISION

I dreamed of gray clouds, immense in their size
They never produce a single drop of precious rain
I watched the great mountain ranges crumble one after the other
All this right before my unbelieving eyes
I saw the great rivers shrink to trickles
Never again enrich the flood plains with vital nutrients
I witnessed the pure water that all drink turns to sludge
I watched the oldest of the great Red Sequoias fall upon the face of Mother Earth
And she cried!
One by one where they stood as kings, long before "The People" settled upon the land
Where once grass was plush and rich like a blanket across the plains
My heart beats like a drum at the sight as they became deserts of sand overnight
I stood on the cliffs that overlooked the fertile plains of my forefather
I saw not a living creature grazing,
There were no bees to pollinate the flowers and blossoms
This created wastelands of dust and death as far as the eyes could see
My heart weakens with each, and every tear being shed
The prayers of my people are no longer being heard by our glorious Father
High above us, there are no stars to be seen in the heavens
I dreamed of a world totally absent and void of all life
Our blessed Mother Earth has been declared forever barren
Her Sister Moon has disappeared from the sight of man
Father Sun has weakened, finally burning out, then the darkening of the sky
No longer will he warm Mother Earth nor flicker life's energy
Our planet, life's beating heart, our home in the universe,
Stupidly wasn't taken care of
It will be forevermore plunged into darkness
I witnessed Earth becoming a ball of ice...
Forever floating in oblivion
Man no longer exists on this planet called Earth!
We saw the warning signs multiply day after day,
We did nothing, we ignored nature's cries!
I know I am not the only one who has been given this message
*This is Man's...**FINAL**...Wake-up call!*
This I saw in a vision...

THE WHISPER OF LOVE

Tenderly you spoke to me in a whisper of love
The volume is one degree above heaven's soul

From the window, my lost horizon now dances
With the back of my fingers, I brush your cheek

Clearing a path of joy before it you can witness
Sighing softly, mingling with the ocean breezes

I ride upon its warm aroma of tantalizing spices
Feeling this island's magic in each other's arms

As the sunset slowly slips over the distant islands
Orange bursting into brilliant reds fading outward

To deep burgundy, painting our villa like a Picasso
The island sun-God romances us "Goodnight" to all

That great big ball of sunshine is sinking so slowly
Down behind the ocean's horizon, lower and lower

The blowing out of a candle silhouette is created
At that very moment, we could feel a push of air

Ancient island elders called it "The Wind of Change"
She stirs like a kitten, slippery in her chocolate teddy

Arms stretched over her head, eyes inviting wickedly
I join her joyful play; she rolls atop pinning my arms

Her beautiful long hair lies across my chest and face
Orchids permeate her hair and flesh, driving me crazy

She throws her locks back, and leans forward, tenderly she
Kisses my lips teasingly saying "We have reservations"

All right love but we eat island dessert here in the villa!
I watch her getting ready and I know my love is endless

What we had and what we've got, time can't take away
My heart sings body dances, touching her is loving her

While you were sleeping, I talked to our Heavenly Father
He told me you're one in a million, I am to hang onto you

I will love you for all time and on that alone, you can depend
You whisper love so tenderly to me; it makes me cry inside...

THE WILLOW'S WEEP

By the dull reddish moonlight, there is a mass of stale air being consumed
Shadows grow and cross each other in a dance of never-ending woes
Bare Willow's Weep stands chilled by a wind that wraps a hello
Harsh sharp tiny grains of quarry stones speak not of the sands of time

In a foggy wake of earthy morn raise the flag half-mast for a mother cry
She witnessed flashes high and low, to and frow a firefly's signature sow
Weep not for the season's gather no moss for the loss of a timely flight
March Tempest, another eye that sees God to a twenty-one-gun salute!

Night winds ripple and weave a coat of dark despair with a needle's eye
Weary shadows mark the stage for actors such as we lost in the woods
Clouds dance to a haunting reframe across a moon now turned blood red
Moving fast, such is the life of leaves dropping to the widow's command

Wind freakiest and hateful blow through the soul in living colors, not so!
The moon, though he may smile, cast reflections only to be mirrored by cold
Our sunset seems to be laden in the past just circling in yesteryear's cradle
Life in all its wisdom cannot keep us from taking our very last breath due

The thought that drifts endlessly across life's silvery moon lacks respect
The night darkens and the wind blows with a tightening grip that chokes
Sadden to see Willow's Weep in her wake to cracking limbs severed
Death gathers the ashes of young men and women, blowing into infinity

The World Turns

What is the Mystery of Life?

There is not a secret here, nor an enigma

No mystery as to why the Earth turns.

Our good times do come, and they do go

Hardships are many in our growing years

There is the cold breath known as Winter

A blanket of white soon melts into spring

Birds chirp and sing to natures greetings

The wind blows over, under, across, and into

Days are somber in the warmth of the sun

In the dark night, lonesome tears are heard

The silence is broken, a newborn now cries

Days come and the days go without a skip

The direction of the winds can change at will

Favor the night winds that conduct summer

Smelling the fresh-cut green grass of today

Before a story of Fall begins to speak in colors

The world turns

And the seasons tell the story.

This Is My Home

This is my home.

My father, his father, and his father before him as far back,

When this country cried like a baby. We never cared about the pain of mind and body,

When it was time to fight for our land. The danger was always around the corner

You fought for what was yours and what was right.

This is my home.

When sitting around the fire under the stars,

We talked about how hard it was for those that came before us.

We would talk about those we left behind. How our families stayed strong for one another.

That strength in the past has forged today's patriots handed down over generations

Regardless of the cause put forward, the family stands together.

This is my home.

We fought and still fight for the stars and stripes of this nation.

Because we believe in Freedom above all that is holy, I fight for the children of children.

We fight for those that return home to welcome and wait for the arms of loved ones.

Many of our family members have fought and died to maintain freedom,

Heroes everyone in the pursuit of freedom for All.

This is my home.

Now that death knocks at my door, I look back on my life,

I can say with truth in my heart and soul, my strength may falter, but never my courage.

When I speak about the love of family, love of friends, and my country,

It's for those that stood beside one another,

*Declaring, **"This is my home!"***

This is my home.

This is where I was born and raised. She may have many faults,

Along with mis comings within her government. We the voters elect the wrong people.

I have learned over the years to never trust our representatives

Most make promises just to get elected to office

Most are liars, cheats, and snake-oil cons!

This is my home.

I now say on my death bed, with my last breath,

America you're my beloved home, but you destroyers of humanity,

*Native Americans were marked for extinction for fighting for **"THEIR"** country.*

They once lived free and respected the land and nature

Can we truly not say, we are an evil species?

This is our home.

One that our government has tied a rope around the neck of this country's "True People". Twisting and tightening the rope that no longer could the Indian Nations breathe. Their memory and the horrific bloodshed put upon them by our forefathers who came and took and now are destroying the planet Earth and themselves to boot! It's a matter of time, but a matter of when we will be known as the vanishing Americans. What goes around, comes around!

Wake up you stupid Sons-of Bitches,

WAKE UP!

{IT IS WE WHO ARE TRESPASSING ON THEIR LAND}

THIS VESSEL
NEEDS AN OCEAN TO SAIL UPON

PASSION

When your heart conducts a love symphony,
It takes very little imagination
A touch of love here and a whisper there
Whatever your heart desires
Strolling hand in hand on a white sandy ocean shore
Listen to the waves in the distance
Feel the night breeze blow across your flesh
Where whispers echo upon moonbeams filtering across waves
Softly they sing their own songs,
Of love's eternal passion
Stand waist-deep in the rolling waves
Together your bodies dance to the rhythm of the ocean's passion
In the moonlight two shadows,
Seemly etched across the water
Kiss to the sound of the waves crashing at your feet
Where lovers have walked for ions
Listen to the songs,
That will seduce and captivate your senses with its symphonies
It's so easy,
Just close your eyes and dance across the night sky
Let your twirl amongst the stars
It's passion that takes the lead
You're just a whisper away from a heavenly delight
Kiss within the light of each star
Let passion sweep you off your feet
Into a fairytale dream world
A place you may have visited once or twice as a child
Look deep into my eyes,
I'm a vessel of love that desires an ocean to sail upon
I'm like the hummingbird,
Always in search of sweet nectar
Together we will gather the last drops from the rarest of flora
In the garden of everlasting and enchanted

Passion...

THOUGHT WALK

Thought Walk was written a couple of days before I was to Frederick, to attend the "American Academy of Dramatic Arts" in New York City. I wrote what my heart was feeling at that moment in time. I pictured myself outside of my body and made my way through my hometown of Frederick, Md. I didn't get to write the four lines of this poem for nearly a year later. On Thanksgiving break from "The American Academy of Dramatic Arts", I came home to see friends and Mrs. Anna May Hughes. My benefactor and former Theatric teacher. Before I went back to NYC and the Academy, I made another trek to downtown Frederick and got the inspiration to finish my poem. Don't get me wrong when I'm saying things that are unpleasant about my hometown. I was angry over comments that attacked my every move from childhood and through my teenage years. I was from the wrong side of the tracks. Frederick was born and raised in my hometown. I'm tired of every negative thing thrown my way. Who I am, Where I lived, What I do, and What I become in a fight for survival? After years of proving myself and desiring acceptance through Singing, dancing, and acting. It wasn't long before I got noticed by those who promote young and new talent. All the hurt and pain in my life were put aside when great and wonderful things were being offered to me. In the days before I left Frederick to work professionally in the Arts. I took a walk around my hometown for the last time. Thinking, remembering the good and bad and the horrific darkness in my life.

Thought Walk

I walk upon this lonely and cold street
My hands in my pockets, eyes at my feet
The mind travels to the far and wide
Where no other wants to walk by my side.

At the rise of my head, streetlights I do see
City shops tell the stories of you and me
Traffic sounds I do hear, take me back
Where I walked alone on these Trussell tracks.

City lights twinkle in the starry-starry night
Travel down my thought walk makes it all right
The past will be remembered, for today is today
What will the future bring, who can really say?

THOUGHTS

*I had written my **thoughts** down for many years after a car accident that we had in 1959. In the car were eight of us headed down the turnpike on a Sunday morning to buy some homemade wine.*

*Dad got to the turn-off and started across the highway when Mom screamed, **"Charles look out".** Right at that moment, we were hit broadside by a car clocked at 100 mph. We were told later by the officers on the site that nothing happens to the driver, however, he was drunk.*

In the front seat of our Pontiac were Dad, Mom with Bonnie on her lap, and Aunt Edith riding shotgun. That portion of the car was twenty-five feet from the back half. The car was split in two. The back half of the car had Uncle Fuzzy with me on his lap, Dick Flook, a friend, and Uncle Boots. All lived with different degrees of cuts, bruises, and broken bones in the crash of 59. Many different things happen to each one of us that day. I was thrown from the car and found knocked out in a ditch. They found my little sister Bonnie walking around in a daze, an artery under her arm was cut and she was bloody from head to toe. I was eight and Bonnie four. Mom suffered the worst. Nearly every bone in her body was broken. Aunt Edith had suffered as much as mom did. The others suffered broken bones and cuts. Dad didn't receive one serious injury. Although I would like to think he had some sense of concern for the passengers in Pontiac. All the adults had been drinking that day before heading out to buy homemade wine. That is when Dad lost his license to drive that day.

After several years of talking about the accident whenever the family got together to have their "Sunday drinking picnic parties". That's what it was called. I would sit down and run the accident through my mind over and over. Each time I remembered something new. You see from being knocked out and thrown from the car, I developed blackouts for nearly a year. Concentration was hard to maintain in school.

*I wrote **Thoughts** after I remembered what was in my head from being blacked out that day. I truly believe I died that morning. What you will read, is exactly how I remembered it, piece by piece. I was found by an officer of the law, in a ditch where I was thrown from the impact. The man carried me up to the accident site to be looked over. I came as he carried me to the highway. So, I was told over time.*

THOUGHTS

My mind is dwelling in the dark now
Alone and feeling as though all hope is gone
Encircled by dark dreams in a reality of confusion
Who, what, when, where, and how's?
Filtering the sands of all my life
Where do I go?
Follow the heart?
A heart that bleeds from arrows of pain
Driving on a hi-way of loneliness and torture
No exits, no rest stops on an endless black ribbon, even to walk upon
Distance is never ending and unknowing flight of reality
My heart is full of love that has dried like the sands in an hourglass
Forever draining out into the void of emptiness
Suddenly, a CRASH!
A crash into the wall of uncertainty
Signs, signs all around there are signs!
Do this--Don't do that!
Flashes of light in the corners of my sight
Eyes wide shut and staring into the face of the decision
As time goes by, reflections seem to die
I sit alone staring forward down at that ribbon of black
Rock steady is the day, family is grown
They said their good-byes
She gave what was true, and wisdom fair through those eyes of blue
Her soul warm beyond compare
Hair now white and aged hands
Rock steady in her wicker of white with an apron of gold
Behind those eyes of blue, I see wisdom ageless.
Down the road, I feel a breeze coming my way as I rock steady
A summer breeze, she walks down the lane like so many times before
Closer she comes reaching forward,
Her aged hands I know so well
A flash of light in my mind's eye.
The pain I feel is as bright as the light becomes
Grandmama speaks with such tenderness as I take her hand.
Suddenly as once before, things are racing down the ribbon of black
We are in slow motion as our steps match the hast around us
Suddenly the uncertainty melts into understanding
Blur to my sides and me in the gate of slow motion,
moving toward arms that reach for me to come closer.
Through this calm bright tunnel of light
Memories from my past, people I loved greeting me

All the pain, uncertainty, and chaos of decisions to make haunt me no more
The road I'm on takes me higher and higher from a mental pain
I turn and look back and down the ribbon of black
I see myself being carried away no longer in pain
No darkness in my haunted dreams of before
The light gets brighter and brighter
Fading more and more into calmness and peace.
Thoughts are no more for me.
Did I crash.?

Thy Hands

Through the glass window of a quaint shop, these eyes watched a very old man hard at work. He sat alone in the corner of the little shop. It has very little light and what light there be, comes from a small circular window atop his rustic station. Rays of sunlight filter down across the top of his desk through the windowpane that hasn't been washed since the day it was put there. The bright light shines almost reverently down his very old hands. The dust in the air creates a smoky effect that's very picturesque, that bears a tear to my eye. He wears a long dark duster-style coat. It's buttoned to the collar over a dingy white shirt. His hair is a yellowish-gray color, but his very long beard is silvery gray and white. On his head, he wears a dark gray pillbox-styled cap. My eyes are drawn back to his aged hands. For now, he is rolling them in a circle as if to make them warm or loosen them because of stiffness. He raises his hands up into the light rays from the window, then places them side to side and stares at them. You can almost imagine what he is thinking about his hands; "Thy hands are old and wrinkled, Dear Lord. It's hard not to give in to the pain." Over his many, many years of hard work in stitching leather and embossing designs onto a variety of leathered items. Thusly be it known that Arthritis has crippled and deformed both of his talented hands over the years. Where tools once made their mark in perfect harmony, his livelihood ceased and now he writes out the translation for transactions and invoices. Though I have noticed that he has had to tape the writing implements to his crippled fingers. It's heartbreaking... I can't count the endless days that I would sit outside the old man's workplace and walk up to the plate glass window where the public can see the shoes for sale and watch the cobblers make their fantastic wearables. Of course, my only interest was observing the old man, for he was my grandfather.

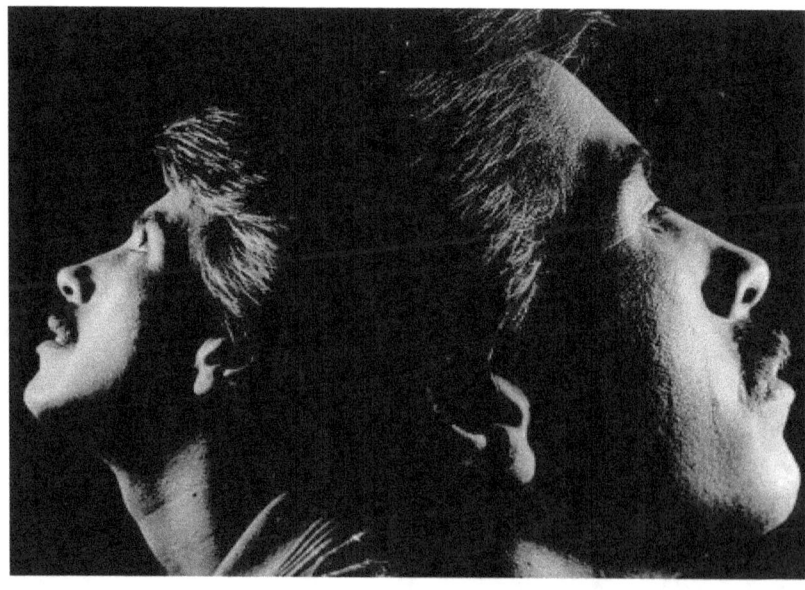

Thy Hands

"Mother, grandfather isn't well, is he?

"No, he is tired and needs his rest."

"Can nothing be done to ease his pain?"

"Come here and let me tell you a story."

"One day the burning and stabbing pain will cease."

"The curled and twisted branches on the tree of life will slowly open to stretch forth in graceful abandonment. Reaching through the clouds, onward racing between the stars to reach Heaven. To touch the hands of God. Grandfathers' hands forged a living by weaving and embossing leather. At the end of the day, he would go to his knees at night. He would fold those hands gracefully into prayer asking, God to let his hands continue to write. Let my eyes read what my hands have created. The way a flower blooms, let Thy hands grasp pen and paper. With the pain and sorrow, a few blissful memories allow Thy hands to touch. These old wrinkled and swollen hands once caressed with such tenderness his newborn sons and daughters. These old ugly deformed hands cooked, cleaned, and scrubbed floors. They taught children to fold their hands into prayer. Thy hands trembled and shook when he buried his parents. He folded his hands in prayer when he had to bury his wife. Thy hands were crippled and wrinkled, still, he folded them into prayer every night asking God, to send an angel to this lonely soul. Thy hands old and clumsy have worn a symbol of love for forty years. These hands have held the hands of faked and true friendship. They caressed, one, two, or three times his grandchildren. His hand has worked to the bone. Keeping me alive, they fed and dressed me. Held me through my cuts and bruises. Thy hands are a blessing from God..."

*"You have been taught about the **"Circle of Life"**. My hands have shown you how to fold them into prayer. thy hands are old, filled with arthritis that makes them wrinkled and weak. But they are filled with precious memories of the past. Present and future times in my life as yours have just begun, my sweet. So, grandfather will soon soar to Heaven's up above, and **Thy hands will greet and touch Thy Hands of God...**"*

TIME ELOQUENTLY LAIN BEFORE US

This newly found heart and soul feel a desire of many before
It takes wing like the Phoenix on a fiery quest for truth and fire
Explosive in a time that makes the way of my essence and pride
A river's rage that's covered in blue Chantilly lace of yesteryear

The center and core of my heart and soul cry out for rebirth
As the eruption of a volcano spewing forth the molten earth
Resetting the life and love-worn paths I have so often trekked
Clearing away for a new and sensual walk of love connected

My eyes wander to see every hiding spot there might be
It's who we are, what we are, and where we come from my love
We're of Mother Earth and the fire has been laden within our souls
That can't ever be forgotten, shall we walk side by side or stroll?

We are an intricately woven fabric of such an array of people
Each one of us is a stitch in this oddly tatted pattern of lace
Alone we are just colorful dangling threads sitting in needles
Together our hearts and spirits comprise the most beautiful quilts

Here we sit on this sewing bench wondering how many are before us.
I'm somewhat reserved in judgment, of my very own surroundings
Listen to the singing of songbirds, glance at the lovers as they walk
Young and old walk through the park with not a care hand in hand

Come let us together take the same stroll walking hand in hand
For we as lovers and as friends can enjoy all the splendor offered
That Mother Earth has so freely and eloquently lain before us
Knowing this path, though age-old, is renewed like time in our hearts

TOGETHER FOREVERMORE

Many times, in life's adventures we are conducted by our emotions creating a box around ourselves. Dark and lingering shadows were given birth, they were and are very real to me. It is possible to be Haunted by the dark shadows of grief, sadness, loneliness, fear, and pain. The following is written in Metaphors. My world was without light for the longest time. In my childhood and into my tortured Teens I would escape from living in abuse and witnessing the horrors put upon my mother and sister and myself. Lending to the realization of a world filled with dark and evil shadows at my every Turn. The shadows are still with me to this very day. Once they controlled my every move, I have Now taught myself to move in and out of their realm of control. They tease and taunt me to walk in Their garden of good and evil... Together Forevermore...

Time has stopped for the light and dark of us
Benediction has given way to sin's retreat
Fortune is a strip of wafered paper in the wind
Thin like a waft walking a haunted runway
Evil, wicked like in a breeze bearing its fangs
Cold is my heart blanketed with frost above
It's the shadows rising as black as the night sky
Down deep in the catacombs, cold and damp
Vermin run rampant through coffins and tombs
Gorging on the decayed remains put to rest
The air is foul with toxic vapors of rotting dead
Gases like a creeping fog spilling from cracks
Of exposed coffins that encase decaying bodies
Crawling like a ravenous hunger that never ends
The atmosphere reeks of stale and deadly molds
Covering my tomb with laden deadly parasites
The bowels of hell have spoiled over its gates
Here I lie, encased in ancient marble and mortar
The catacomb is flooded with muck and slim
Floating with eyes open, engaging a dark nothing
My marble vault was sealed with locking fear
I've been cursed for nearly five hundred years
Prone in silence for all time in this damn purgatory
Where I'll never know the sweetness of true death
My thoughts are of that one night when the earth,
Will rock and shake the aged mortar to crumble
Releasing me, for I have waited centuries to plan
My revenge that hungers for the river of life
My unbelievable mounting hunger will give me
The strength to claw my way out of this hell
The shadows of the night will become my friends,
Once again, Together Forevermore...

TRAIL OF TEARS

Once the Indian Nations celebrated Pride and Freedom
Now they weep for all that has been lost and destroyed
The Great Spirit in the sky cries for what once was theirs
Lands were stolen; worthless treaties were broken repeatedly
We the remaining still weep for a lost dream

We were forced from our lands, a fact known around the world
Our heritage was stolen along with our way of life
This caused our hostility to grow and fester in every tribe
Our people were forced to walk the "Trail of Tears
We the remaining still weep for a lost dream

Our Great Chiefs fought against an increasing annihilation
Sitting Bull, Crazy Horse, and Geronimo stood strong
Their devotion immense against the White Eyes
The Great White Father ordered us to destroy our homes
We the remaining still weep for a lost dream

Walking a Death trail, many perished along the way
We walked past all that we cherished and honored for a lifetime
Driven like cattle, forced to walk the "Trail of Tears"
We were forced onto reservations, caged, and guarded
We the remaining still weep for a lost dream

The "Trail of Tears" was foretold in dreams and in visions
Medicine Men had visions of death and destruction,
Old men and women taking to the hills to greet Death
Their bones were found bleached and dried where they fell
We the remaining still weep for a lost dream

Emerging slowly many tribes added to the "Trail of Tears"
The Crow, Apache, Arapaho, Cheyenne, Blackfeet, Sioux,
Cherokee, Comanche, Navajo, Chippewa, Pueblo, Pawnee, etc.
Hundreds more found their Tribes on Reservations over the years

We the remaining still weep for a lost dream
We the remaining still weep
We the remaining still
We the remaining
We lost dream
We weep
We...

Twilight's Waterfall

{Strange what the mind tells you in your dreams after being beaten to near death}

*Night descends over the mountain range named **"The Seven Sisters"**. I'm lying in the middle of freshly scented lemon grass with Summer's flavoring. With arms over my head, I stare into the face of the forever moon. It's amazing how large the moon is this night; I swear reach out and touch it. I close my eyes; in the distance, I faintly hear the music that I love so well. My heart dances on gossamer wings played by Angels behind silver-laced clouds. Like a whisper in the wind, I have been swept away to a world of dreamers. Twilight reaches its zenith in a swirling illusion of sparkling silver dusting the scene. I am in my own dreamscape. Magical pictures lie before me in colored frames. Creating a gallery at the base of Twilight's Waterfall, in hance by angelic music from afar. I find myself standing at the base. Looking up to the cascading water from an opening in the silver-laced clouds. The magic extends up and up to Heaven's Gate. Flowing from where the Angels dwell.*

*The beauty I behold touches my heart. Dreaming of swirling winds carrying whispered messages in search of lost loved ones. I am drifting along and above the center of the Falls and the height is dizzying. There is a swirl of wind circling me. It's the whisper I have longed for. The power coming from the Waterfall creates swirling winds that capture the whispers, adding to the quick flow of water cascading downward. It was impossible to make hide-nor-tail of its content. Over the falls my message went. I take an Olympic swan dive in the hope to catch my personal whisper. The closer I get, the louder the music becomes. Yet the message is clear to my ears. "I love you and miss you so!" My face is wet from the diamond mist. I close my eyes as I touch the heavenly water. I come up for air and swim to the edge, pulling myself up onto the shore. I am soaked with joy. Getting to my feet, there he is. Seated on a golden stool with his Cello of gold. Encased in diamonds and rubies. My Angel is playing **"Green Sleaves"**. A favorite that we both shared. Our love was cut short. Even in paradise, dreams often come true in **"Twilight's Waterfall."***

UNTIL TOMORROW, GOODNIGHT

It's been a rough day all around
I am filled with sorrow and pain
Feels like a rainy day on Monday
Memories trickle down like rain

There's a void without you my love
I wonder why it's God's will is the law
His will has a reason for everything
We have no choice when he calls

My loss was immense, and heartaches too
Desire cherished, vanished in a few days
My world is very vacant without you
The life we shared got lost in the haze

Coming here is the only light in my life
I talk to you where you rest in peace
In exchange, I feel serenity, not strife
The world's chaos is silenced in sleep

I miss the laughter that fed my heart
A feast of love that destroyed by a car
Forever your memory will be engraved
Five loving years are etched in the stars

I reach out to memory never done
My love beats like the heart of a dove
Hear my whispers, I miss you, my son
You're my life, my reason, and my love

Son, it's time that I go, it's getting late
You know my heart is forever yours
I'll turn and wave at the garden's gate
Goodnight my son sleeps forevermore...

VAPOR TO DECAY AND FORGOTTEN

"I am but the vapor that has no beginning or end
Forever changing across the endless sky
Like the clouds, I too pass by unnoticed
The world is filled with unnoticed beauties"

I am a chartered member of hell's lost and never found
Let me be among the forgotten, why shouldn't I be anything but forgotten?
Always the feeling of arriving too late, finding a sign, **"Sorry we're closed!"**
It's clear, from the moment of birth, I have been a disciple of fate

Not a nary soul ever heard my childhood cries for help!
I'm totally convinced I was heard, but no one gave a damn!
There were many times when my horrified eyes spoke volumes to me
If you would listen with your eyes, blind you would not be!

"Children are to be seen and not heard", **I GET IT**!
I am but a single blade of grass withering in a garden rich
How many sins can be put upon a child of six before someone takes notice?
How many children are swallowed whole by nature's unstable wrath-es?

Watch my conversation with sanity as I play a solo game of marbles
I fall backward into the dirt as sanity kicks dust into my eyes again and again
For that's what bullies do, inflict a barrage of belittlement time after time
Forgotten soul of a child, I would have rather never been born

My world was filled with fowl consumption carried in a jar along with the darkness
My childhood parallels the death of innocence
I felt orphaned in the city of Pain, Abuse, and Hopelessness
I am being consumed in the land of the lost and forgotten

Would anyone give a good goddamn if I simply vanished in the mist?
Wanting to be truly noticed, someone to give a second thought about me
My soul is plagued by misery within the darkness of my very own linage
A mother cradled by death, a father with a demonic soul

Depression was my crayons, my coloring book was a life I'd never known
I was lost in each page, like **"Hansel and Gretel"** *in the dark forest*
I know evil in its many forms at an early age, look at my body and you will see
The lack of my resistance diminished with each scar and blow given

My forest is dark, occupied with horrors remembered and foreboding
I have been lost in the real world for the longest time
The futility is reserved for the forgotten and unwanted on this earth
A symphony of silent tears resonates from the cries of the lonely children

I can't remember if I ever heard the laughter at the ages of four, five, or six...
Being forgotten was my salvation, my early years simply turned to dust
I have a secret, hidden within my roots, covered over with moss and leaves
Any ties to Mother Earth lie in the fertilizer that I have become

*I never was lucky enough to experience the **"Zest for Life"***
It remains a question that a six-year-old will never understand
I presume my cries of terror that night was never meant to be heard
For in one blinding instant, his knife slit my young throat, silencing my screams

I am a charter member in the land of the lost and forgotten, another missing child
No one apparently ever realized I was a living, breathing child of darkness
My body was bent and broken to fit amongst the roots of this cypress tree
Mother nature cradles my decaying body, my soul became vapor and is simply forgotten...

Veil of Sheer Bliss

*Dearest, I ache to my core of pleasure. Forgive me for speaking the truth to you when I say, I can't help laying my hand upon my excitement. No gentleman am I; I suppose? It's not the first time either. Here I am lying in bed. It's hot lying here with not a breeze tonight. I have all these romantic overtones running through my mind. How well I remember the honey sweetness of your flesh. As it covered my lips. The taste upon my tongue was your desire. It is now my lover that I will take the time to express my fantasies. After our glorious spring picnic at the **"Crystal Ponds"** under that magnificent Willow tree. I will be so bold as to write my wicked ideas upon this fragranced parchment. Which just happens to be your favorite, that turns your senses on. My fantasy begins.*

The air is warm and filled with the amazing fragrance of newly bloomed spring flora. We both expressed how loud the birds were during the afternoon. But that was perfectly fine with both of us. In unison, we both mentioned how still and mirrored-like the ponds were. We watched as the swallows swooped down for a drink of water. Creating ripples upon the surface. I remember how the sun peeked through the long tresses of the Willow tree. I watched the sun flash across your beautiful face. We stopped laughing after a second or two of squinting our eyes from the sun's flashes. In the quiet moment, we stared into each other's eyes. You leaned down from your seated position where my head lay in your lap. Our lips met. In what was a short kiss. For we were in an awkward position. I stood and offered my hand to help you up.

*Just then a blast from a horn broke the wonder of the day. Echoing across the ponds was the bus driver, saying it was time to board the bus for home. We gathered up the picnic blanket and kissed each other for we were on different buses. We waved one another goodbye as we stepped onto the bus. I'm home as I'm sure you are. Here I am alone thinking of you constantly. So, I decided to write to you and tell you, my thoughts. I am feeling playful as all hell. This is truth or dare letter. From this point on my lover, my fantasy is going to be a bit more vivid in content. An expression at the least. Beware, for the **"Metaphors"** will be just that!*

Quill to parchment, I dip the sturdy quill in the well of sheer bliss. I hold my quill firmly in hand for the moment is reflective. Do you not agree my mate? Every little move you make drives my desires to a place where the center of all my attention gathers in perfect harmony. With each sigh, we drive each other crazy. Our hungry lips meet and with eyes closed, I am aware of every inch of your unbelievable body. You're my one and only. A Mink of snow white and Gardenias of white are arranged throughout the room. Your naked body upon the cradle made of fur, and hundreds of lit candles serve for romance and love. Soft erotic music fills the air. You softly let out a sigh, and I know you approve. In candlelight, I walk to you and offer my naked body to you. You take your hand and rub the fur in a gesture to lay beside you. The candlelight upon your body accents every curve of your flesh. My hand has found excitement in full attention. I've written so much in setting up the scene, I must dip the quill in the well of sheer bliss. The core of my excitement aches at the thought of you and the invitation to ease your desires. That suggestion heightens the pleasure of one's open mind to exploration. My flesh is on fire as you take command. Each move you make is a flare in new adventures in the world of erotic love-play. Our growing sighs add to the friction between our two naked bodies. I worship your lovemaking. My desire nears its peak. You whisper in my ear, "Slow down, I've just begun to drive you mad with my pleasure techniques." I close my eyes as you kiss my chest. I feel your tongue rolling around my nipples. You teasingly nibble. I am purring like a kitten. I roll you over and spread the eagle across your hips. I now make my way to your neck. I kiss and nipple on your neck. My talented tongue explores your fully firmed nipple. It hardens as I blow cool air from the ice cube I hold between my teeth. The heat from your magnificent body melts the ice quickly. I blow cool air atop your nipple, and it hardens to attention. I repeat the same to your other nipple. I fully explore the tight stomach with my tongue. Lower I travel in a teasing replay several times. Driving you to shiver with ecstasy and anticipation of how far I intend to travel over your hills and valleys. My tongue snakes its way up to your waiting succulent lips. I watch as you spread your soul upon this cradle of sensual fur. Nothing gives me more pleasure than to watch you invite me to enter your world of ecstasy. Giving each other erotic pleasure brings harmony to the maleness being offered. I reach for your hand guiding it to my own extremely hard excitement. You slowly caress my swollen quill. That is so pleasurable to my own maleness. Together we each dive into our own "Crystal Ponds". Together the intent is to reach the heights of several organisms. You take me into your arms and our sweat mingles in a dance of flesh. You whisper in my ear that I taste like a sweet Apricot. In exchange I tell you I'm like the Hummingbird, I never get enough of your nectar.

Write me not a letter. The talent you possess in writing will not compare to the **"Incredible Raw Talent"** you have in your oral delivery alone! Please, my lover, trust me when I say, **"You are simply amazing"**. The moonlight strolls we take in paradise also reflect on this heart of mine. I believe God allows me to show you a wonderful time as we walk beside the ocean of Hawaii. Under the stars, their twinkling was like a trillion winks for you and me that joyous evening. I thank you for the greatest of all evenings. I wish you were here this very minute. I guess you can imagine what is next. That's right my love, I'm going to paradise as I take care of some personal business.

I need not say more for my quill can no longer dip into the well of sheer bliss. After recalling a night of sheer enlightenment, my quill needs to cool down. That is until you make another appearance. In-person is the real deal!

Yours in love and respect,

ME

WAITING
FOR THE LAST TEARDROP TO FALL

"Sometimes love simply falls apart for various reasons, right or wrong it hurts"

"This is the last time I'm waiting on anyone
I've packed my bags; I've got a ticket for one
You are never here, you're always there, and you never call
I'm waiting for the last teardrop to fall

In the beginning, you were a hero to me
What you have put me through everyone sees
I guess you think I'm blind to it all
I'm waiting for the last teardrop to fall

I'm tired of being lonely night after night
When you are home all we do is fuss and fight
I'm holding onto something that will never stand tall
I'm waiting for the last teardrop to fall

Every night I watch you walk out that door
It's like clockwork, it's quarter till four
I know where you're going, you know I saw
I'm waiting for the last teardrop to fall

This is farewell, I've had enough, I'm leaving tonight
With all that has been said, you know it's right
I've cried so many tears, I've given it my all
I'm not waiting for the last teardrop to fall!

Walk Not the Moors

There is silent dusk that slowly covers the last of the day's lonesome light. The evening's scent is in the air and it's sure to bathe the waking of twilight. Before my eyes, a mysterious vision takes form within the twilight anew. A manifestation of evil. A beautiful evil with the body of a Greek God. An Adonis frame housing a sensuality that screams sex. His dark facial features rise and recede throughout the moonlight that's full. So, striking is he, every woman has a rush of warmth up her thighs. It's like the very time she felt waves of an unexplained flushing fever. Beckoning to relieve her of youthful, captive womanhood. He easily savors the sweet fragrances that dance within the breeze that flows across the Moors. Throughout the mist of the cool night, his piercing ruby eyes scan the thickets. Her heart thumped in her throat when she saw eyes of red within this Greek God. There is a wicked need to thirst by the full moon.

There are signs posted everywhere along the roads leading to town and from town. **"WALK NOT THE MOORS AFTER NIGHTFALL"** *In the distance before she stood the Adonis. Her heart was about to explode. Twilight frames his stance, a quiet rage of sorts. A wicked evil waiting patiently. She is his prey without question. Should she run like a fox or faint dropping to the ground she is still his. She stood sturdy facing this gorgeous hunk. Thought to herself,* **"I'm not going to scream like a schoolgirl."** *Her heart was screaming,* **"HELP!"** *The moonlight accented the right side of his handsome face. A strong jaw, and beautifully shaped lips. She thought about how thick and luscious. She got lost in the moonlight as she licked her lips in anticipation of a seductive interlude with a stranger sent by the Gods. Love Gods from the underworld directly to the Moors. She thought,* **"What in the hell am I thinking?"** *Her eyes went directly to his when she heard a snarl. His eyes were blazing like fireballs and from those succulent lips, a stream of salvia was dangling over weapons that now shine with his very own anticipation.* **"Dear God",** *she thought.* **"By all that is holy, this can't be real."** *Just then the clouds covered the full silvery moon. The Moors went jet black to her sight. he remained still, for where could she run that he couldn't catch her? It wasn't long before the moon returned. The Moors once again were lit and shadows enhanced every little stick.*

No longer did she see her Greek God. He had disappeared. She wondered where he could have gone. Silent engulfed the night. She took a couple of steps backward. Suddenly she froze in place because there was the hottest of breath on the back of her neck. She went to turn around but was halted by a voice begging her not to scream at all. "Please, for if you scream, I will have no control of my transformation to a hideous creature. The concern and seriousness of his deep voice were clear. he gasped quietly and felt a tear flow down her cheek as she answered, **"Whatever you say."** *Her heart was racing a mile a minute. Not from fright or horror. No longer did she feel his breath or presence behind her. he asked if she could turn around. There was no answer. she turned around slowly to find he was gone.*

The fog covered the Moors completely and the stillness was haunting. Only the very top of the trees and rolling hills shined in the full moon of silver. Standing alone in disbelief with arms folded in front of her, she felt a chill in the night air. In the far distance atop a hill, she thought she had caught the figure of a man running into the brush. Then she heard the painful blood-curdling howl that echoed through the fog-covered Moors. The coldest of chills ran down her spine. She felt that hot breath on her neck again. Racing back toward the main road along the Moors, she couldn't run fast enough. With each step back to where she felt safe, the Greek God of a Man flashed through her mind. **"How lucky was I?"** *From now on she would stay clear of the Moors. For the signs say,*

"WALK NOT THE MOORS AFTER NIGHTFALL!"

WALK UPON

Through my glass, a laser light so bright a white that it seems too unreal to believe. It touches my physical being but enters my sadden soul with a creeping effect that flows with the river of life. I feel it winding, twisting, and pushing onward, upward to my temples with a throb overwhelming. The glare from the panes closes the lids with sharpness as though it is meant to be rude. I'm not warm nor am I hyper. But alive in feelings and thoughts. It, the beam seems to give a message. I question, who am I? Why do I feel lost and alone? Feelings of the last to arrive. Wondering what have I missed?

Entries in the gold-laced brown book of my day's past and present hold iodized salt crystals that when read show how the grains can melt from tears and feelings. The brown lies still, yet the pages want to dance. The key to opening lies in my hand. This hand controls the pen of memory ink. A guideline of who, what, when, and where. Entries consist of word after word. People are close and not so tight. Dreams that drive confusion one step above and beyond. Matter through space forms ideas as well as secrets. Sitting near the crystal glaze with eyes that peer through racing chaos, from a bright blinding ray. My eyes open and look onward to find a stairway of light that invites the imagination. Like a fantasy, walk upon this beam to a heightened affair. Travel across to another place in the sun. Warm and alive, free, and exciting. It must be calm and at peace. Flowers of the rainbow, sweet smells everywhere, and never the same. Sounds like a Disney wildlife scene. Butterflies large and small are kisses from God. Full of love, beauty, and life. A remembrance of what can be. A wonderland of wonder in a kaleidoscope. Air, and wind in motion push me to walk behind and beyond that bright staircase until I think and question once more. Sometimes I wish it were real, but my imagination allows me to visit when I so choose....

WALTZ OF THE LONELY

I'm sitting here contemplating my life's past
Good times were few, others filled with strife
It's very clear my final dance has come at last
I sit here in my own reflection on a lonely life

At five, I was already the age of twenty-five
Education in life before my time, can't undo
No time for childhood fun, I worked fields late
I ask myself, "Is there more in this life to do?"

Regrets are many, it's what I've grown to know
Far too late to feel sorry for me, what the hell
Tears like a river in full rage, my bank's overflow
See me waltzing ¾ time in the heartbreak hotel

It has been said, "Live life to its fullest" I tried to
I lived each and every moment as if it were my last
I nearly tried everything at least once, what a ruse!
I don't regret a damn thing from my youthful past

In my life, I have loved women and I've loved men
Living life hard, loving hard, and even playing harder
Wasn't a dance challenge I couldn't rise to defend
A life of hard work prepared me for a full dance card

I remember the many times I was verbally put down
Society rendered my family misfits and mistakes
My heart hardens, and my soul filled with the tears of a clown
All labels addressed to me, the punishment I did take

Would I live my life over again, knowing what I know?
I'd see America and her wonders before it is my time
"Act well your part, for there all honors lie" *is my motto*
Thanks to those who helped to make my journey fine

All the world is a stage for the young but not the old
Create amazing beauty within your time, and make fancy
In life dance to the music with all your heart and soul
I love to dance, and it has made my feet and soul fancy

Tragedy imprisoned me, the waltz of the lonely I dance
The waltz of the lonely, selected by destiny for me to do
The times are changing, our lives learn life's new dances
Nothing mattered to me when there was music and you

Wasting Wasted Lives

Wasted, wasted time in segments of our lives

Wrong, wronged judgments throne out like liter

Suitcases filled with errors and wrong dealings

Throne in piles of decaying minutes and hours

Pies here and there smelling from rotting regrets

Created dark fowl garbage of sinful memories

All kept hidden from the world and mostly from me

Living in a world of wreckage, regrets, and gall

Bad connections and heaps of forsaken rotted lies

Sign in sewage and the stench of gangrened bowels

Yet for the strangest reason, we long for a taste

We do long for a roll in the textures and aromas

Hidden desires lie in the deep dark of our minds

Hiking forward in new directions and frame of mind

Self-imposed, walking the straight and narrow clean

Trying so hard not to hear the dark voices deep inside

Seeking dark vile images of lust and sins of the flesh

How strong the earthly flesh and hardcore passions

That tempt, tease, entice, drawl, desire, want, need

Some are strong-willed and can fight with all their might

Others are weak in mind and certainly weak in the flesh

You choose for you, and I will choose for me...

WE BOTH KISS THE RAIN

If your heart longs for my presents
And I am not there
Simply kiss the rain

If time doesn't seem to move fast enough
And the day seems empty
Just kiss the rain

If you reach beside yourself to touch my hand
And I am not there
Simply kiss the rain

If your lips, feel the hunger for desire
And the memories are painful
Just kiss the rain

If dark clouds gather producing tears from heaven
Know that we're both under the same sky
We both just kissed the rain...

WE RODE THE MUSHROOM HEIGHTS

*People carry around opinions as if they're shopping carts are bottomless.
But one thing is for certain. When the "Big Bomb" is dropped, those that
Survive will not need to sit under the "Mighty Mushroom" of burnt orange.
Prepare to be dusted through and through by your fellow man. All because
Two old men, maybe women could not make hide-nor-hair out about the
writings on the wall! Let's Thanks to those who declared "war" on each
other...*

*Together we all stand in life's valley of man's decisions
Over the horizon, there comes a hell 'a furious wind
Rise like the stallions standing on their hindquarters
Taken shape of the Four Horsemen of the Apocalypse*

*Marking the day to endless night in ugly, fowl, stench
Rising to what's left of your fool halfhearted thoughts
Take another deep breath, you will vomit true tragedy
Walk into your mother's new dream kitchen for today*

*The shadows of yesterday have finally risen to mingle
Sloth covets Envy as they fight Greed for the new Lust
Slapped him hard he did, in the ill-prepared act of demise
Catching him in the arms of Gluttony's Darkest Angel*

*They ran a perverse steeple chase for a prize never won
Who will be the first to gang rape the remaining world foes?
Man has long since become the wild beast of the forest
All living creatures rode the mushroom heights together*

*The sky's nothing more than a huge crematorium for flesh
No more "Good Morning Star-Shine the Earth Says Hello"
What remains resembles multimillion pieces of a puzzle
Wild animal mutants are ravenous for leftover table-scraps*

*There's no speaking of survivors during the Atomic Winter
For its death gathering, it's the bounty of souls crying out loud
Thanks, you, for a ride upon the Mushroom Heights to us*
Demise...

*"Old men who declare war on one another,
But it is our youth who must fight and die,
H. Hoover"*

WEEP NOT WITH ME

Please, weep not with me on such a warm spring day as this
Together the weight of our sadness
Would be too much to bear for both of us, my friend
Though we are kindred in many of nature's ways
Still, this is not the first time
I've rained under your waterfall of swaying tears
As a small child you cried with me so many, many times
You were and are my silent guardian friend
That I could always depend on, so
Weep is not with me

Through my awkward teens, you listened to the secrets
Of one love-struck individual
When my heart got bruised or broken from time to time
I would take refuge under the comfort of your hanging tears
Under your tresses that lightly touch the ground
Like the dancing of a thousand faeries
Brushing against my cheeks
Tickling me as the wind whispers in and out of your tresses
I'd daydream of a beautiful ballet
Each lady on point moving like the waves upon the ocean
They dance like sparkling golden angels
In a semblance of a spiritual grace
Your touch would bring me back from my daydream
I would sit for hours staring out over the landscape
So many times, as a child
I'd run through the meadow of wildflowers
Around the mirror-like pond
Giving my world a glorious reflection of peace and harmony
Your waterfall branches are so long that the tips touched the water
As if to take a sip of refreshment
Looking into the clear water
I would watch the bluegills in a game of chase
In and out the longest of tresses
I would laugh at their cat-and-mouse antics
Until tears filled my eyes
Weep not with me
For these tears were a joy

Still, I would watch your branches sway in the breezes
Leaving me mesmerized by your beauty
Offering me a world of imagination
As I ran through swaying fields of golden wheat
Like an ocean filled with waves
Generated by the strong breezes blowing over the rolling meadows
Please, speak to me of your sadness
My lonesome friend
I hear your whispers in a song
Sweetly to be sung
A visage bent, never to be broken, standing strong
Yet so very familiar are we
Your soul seems to be always at a slumbering peace
My unspoken words will reflect your strength that is steadfast
You sing, weep not for me
Often, I'd sit and listen to your words riding the wind
Whispers of better days to come
I would thank mother earth for your gift of wisdom
So, weep not with me

I am older and wiser now
It has been many years away from the house of pain I occupied
You have never been forgotten
And it is a blessing to see you once again my old friend
We all see the Weeping Willow in different lights
In meaning, in faith, and in spirit
She is the **"Mother of Wisdom"**
I found peace under her waterfall of tears
I imagined she was a forever carousel
Slowly turning to the music nature conducts
When I am part of this world
My spirit will become the breeze that turns the carousel
Together she and I will sing
"Weep Not with Me"

When The Mountain Cries

Dancing around the tips of the lush green trees and under a silver moon

The summer wind picks her partner to dance

High above the mountains

Clouds against a painted sky

A layer of sweet lilacs floats on the wind across our valley

Summer mornings quench with a wondrous mist that gives the drink

But summer lights are flashing high beyond the mountains

Turning dark and ready to cry

It can't be denied

Valleys will feel how hard they will tear

Dark becomes the valley

All take cover high, the river will swell

Harsh winds, thunder to frighten, either way, we shiver

From the mountains her pain is deep

The river triples in size

The river's rage over her banks

Covering the plains that were dry

The drinks its fair share

Slowly the rage begins waltzing a recede

Blessed is nature in all her glory

All did receive a taste of the majestic tears

There is a hint of summer sun through the twirling skirts of gray skies

More couples feel the brightness

there is dancing throughout the valley floor

"God's creations are beautiful"

The sky reveals heavenly rays of light

Spotlighting areas on the valley floor

Once again sweet lilac fragrances dance atop a summer breeze

Painted colors behold an array of new blossoms across the land

Warm is the earth between two mountains high

Enriching the lush tall green where brown once was

Songs by colorful birds were heard everywhere

Some took flights to and froe

Others were seen in wondrous flocks above the valley

Mother Earth creates what is needed when needed there be

Look to the sky

Glance over the land

Smell the wind and hear her song

She needs to be ready for the tempo that we all will be dancing to

Music or not, prepare ye to choose a partner

When the mountain cries!

WHEN THE WEEPING BEGINS

In the pale moonlight stirs restless memories
Endless and ageless tugging somewhere in the heart
Across the vast starlit heavens
Filled with dreams that are yet to be made aware of
That's when the weeping begins

In the twilight hours of golden myths
Whispered thoughts are carried high upon crippling wings
Of the Phoenix who weakens as if fallen from grace
This final judgment is a serious loss to all
That's when the weeping begins

Hear the chanting, **"We Have No Rights!"**
Walk amongst thousands of faceless women wearing black parkas
Resembling crows gathered side by side
Upon long fences across fields of scattered dreams
Squawking within a society of social repercussions
That's when the weeping begins

Unrest across all the lands known to man
The Phoenix nears the moment of her final death
A single tear she sheds
Life ends in a spectacular explosion of flames
From her ashes, she is reborn-ed anew
That's when the weeping begins

The pale moon turns a blushing rose
"Have faith", *is written across the dark velvet of night*
Within the shooting stars
An angel's kiss upon the wounded cheek of the man
Angel-Rose has healed her faith as the Phoenix anew
That's when the weeping begins...

WHEN YOUR HERO DIES

I do believe that we all have a hero in our lives. The first day I met Jimmy Allen Angleberger I was in awe. Tall, handsome, and a personality that screamed, "Here I am world". He just happened to be my cousin.

When you are young and growing up in the country, you have nothing to do but work from dawn till dusk. Unless you are young enough and only had to work half a day in some cases. Jimmy took me fishing and hunting as often as time would allow him to do so. After all, he was dating and working as well as finishing high school. Jimmy had graduated a year before I was in the tenth grade. Everyone liked Jimmy and it was easy to see why.

I received the news of Jimmy's suicide many years later. I was away attending "The American Academy of Dramatic Arts" in New York City. After I had returned to Frederick for a visit to reacquaint myself with family and friends on Thanksgiving weekend. I studied hard for two years. Then auditioned for a Musical in the Village. Got the show and had the time to go back home. My first stop was to see my cousin Richard, one of four brothers Jimmy had. I found Richard's address and stopped to say hello and ask where Jimmy was living. After a few awkward moments, Richard explained what had happened to Jimmy. I was devastated, to say the least. I went to Frederick that very day to see Jimmy after two years away at school. I found where he was buried and went to say a few words. My world was once again turned around and upside-down... It was a very, very, very long ride home...

I was hurt that no one went out of their way to inform me. I blame no one, but myself. "When Your Hero Dies" was written in honor of Jimmy Allen, the greatest hero in my life. He never knew how much he meant to me. Jimmy was my "Hero". Rest in Peace, with all my love. You will be missed by many.

WHEN YOUR HERO DIES

My hero left this world at the sound of a gunshot!
He was everything I wanted to be as I matured in life
Handsome, strong, and with a smile that lit the sky
He was the big brother I never had, standing by my side
Was that too much to ask for?
Then your hero dies.

Jimmy was his name.
He turned twenty-six on that fatal day.
Coal black hair styled like James Dean
Hurt and confused over a woman very sly
Who never took the time to ask what he wanted in life?
That's when your hero dies.

Jimmy took me fishing and taught me how to cast
Eleven I was, still in my baby fat
He called me Baby Hughie; it uses to make me mad
Still, I miss the man that I wanted to be
Was that too much to ask for?
Then your hero dies.

It was said on a November night, things fell apart
Feeling lost, confused and alone, He had had enough
An amazing man that I wanted to be, took his life
I wanted you to stay around to guide me
Was that too much to ask for?
Before your hero dies.

WHERE'S THE RESPECT

Ancient, fragile, and duty-bound are we to turn to dust
There are many lost memories stored in the loneliness of our mind
Tear not for me once I have laid me down
Waste not your precious time in tears for this old gray hair
Dry that misguided haze and rejoice in memories
It is we that feel your lack of patience throughout the seeds of youth
Family, friends, and the everyman walk about as if old age is a plaque
Well, my fast-paced friends' time waits for no man
Everyday tasks are sometimes carrying a silent plea for help
We are afraid to ask for assistance
Throw me my shawl for this rocker is my only friend
Look at these trembling hands that helped to mold your lives
These bones are filled with injuries and the scars are many
The women and men were many, but too little time to love them all
Life has left me confused, filled with hopeless anger that overwhelms my heart
I'm the only one sitting on a bench in the park
Simply forgotten by those I love
So many of my beloved memories are imprisoned by this weakening mind
Is it too much to ask for a little respect for who I was and achieved?
The sun rises on you and sets on this soul in the twilight years
Where is the love, where is the compassion?
Remember the love I freely expressed as you grew from child to adult
Family as a unit has faded far to the wayside
Our wisdom throughout our years no longer is handed down to the next generations
Here is a little hand-me-down wisdom for you all
"Dust to Dust, Ashes to Ashes, if the Devil doesn't get you",
Old Age Must!

Whisper, Thank You

My dreams ride like a whisper on the winds of everyday

I feel it pick me up and carry me to where all is believed

Where love floats and dreams fade if not held onto quick

Wish you may wish you might, have this whisper fulfilled

My spirit has ridden high often on a whisper upon the wind

Like the ashes of forgotten dreams so are my whispers

My message can ride upon the whispering winds once more

I now know your whispered words are but a dream away

This night my lips softly whisper my love to one so precious

You've wandered across the whirling winds in search of mine

Were they sweet words, were the words of comfort, I hope?

Whispered messages are but a dreamscape away to retrieve

In the end, did I play but the fool again who waits and waits?

Will they forever blow in the wind like blank sheets of paper?

Are they lost to wayward clouds having never touched a heart?

Do I feel a new breeze carrying whispers lost in my direction?

I hear my whispers upon this breeze blowing in my direction

I want to catch this wind, ride its whispers around the moon

Just touch a star and hold a dream, for it now will come true

On this breeze is a whisper long desired to hear, Thank you!

WHISPERING, "BE MINE"

Everyone loves to give and get a Valentine on a special day of love. Valentine's day was around the corner, and I was asked to write a poem about this day. I thought and thought, and I decided to write about that sweet little Cupid. So, with that special someone in my mind, I wrote **"Whispering, Be Mine".** *I swore I'd never ever write another VD card for as long as I live. Below is why?*

I had never given Valentine's Card to anyone before. In grade school, in the art department we would color and paint hearts on paper, cut them out and the teacher would write four or five statements on the caulk board and tell us to pick one and write it on the card. Then we had to put it in one of the envelopes taped to that person's desk. The teacher would take us out into the hall and let us one at a time into the room to put our Valentine Cards or Cards into the envelopes of our Secret Valentine. It was the very first Valentine I made and gave to someone. When I finally did, I didn't put my name on it. The teacher went around to each child and ask who had given them a Valentine. I gave mine to **Judith Krantz.** *Oh My! I forgot to put my name on it. The teacher asked Judith who it was from. She said there is no name.* **Mrs. Davis** *asked who forgot to sign their name. I raised my hand and said it was mine. I had to; all were accounted for. Anyway, most kids had at least one. The most popular boy and the girl got several. I was last to show my Valentine and who it was from. I reached in and I didn't even get one damn Valentine from any of them. That hurt so bad, I just got up from my desk and went up to the teacher and told her I was going home and not to stop me. And that is what I did.*

Whispering, "Be Mine" *was the last Valentine's Day card I have written since my third-grade year in elementary school. Sad to say, Judith seemed to care less...*

WHISPERING, "BE MINE"

She is small and tiny as a baby pea in a pod
It's at twilight time, she winks, and nods
She dreams of hearts trimmed in white lace
A sweet child of light, in God's good grace

She awakens with a yawn, stretches her wings
Wings flutter for love's flight and wilder things
Driven by her desire to be the best she can be
She flutters, she flies and she's busy as the bee

Her smile is angelic, and her dimples are rose
She carries love arrows to shoot from her bow
She spreads her tiny wings both day and night
Young and old lovers both know of her flight

Starlight, Star bright, Cupid twinkles tonight
She flies to the left, then she flies to her right
She sparkles dust here and sparkles dust there
Add white doves and there's magic in the air

Ribbons of white and pink and ribbons of red
A beautiful halo of white daisies upon her head
Colors of the rainbow, they do sparkle and shine
Her giggles and wiggles are well worth the time

Valentine's day is always for everyone you know
Cupid takes her aim, firing her trusty little bow
Straight for the heart, she knows when it is time
*When hearts are warm, whispering, **"Be Mine!"***

WHISPERS IN THE SPANISH MOSS

I often float like a whisper on the waters of the Louisiana swamps
Where the tropical gulf breezes,
Lazily dance amongst the dangling Spanish moss
Mysteries are known and songs are sung,
By the hand-me-down Cajun traditions
That are known to be mystical and hauntingly magical spirits throughout
Their voices can be light and airy, sometimes they're haunting and vicious
Carried upon wings of gossamer overhead in the canopies
Moisture plays a symphony
Dripping like nature's musical notes
Holding tightly onto the ends of the Spanish moss
Shinning like sparkling dewdrops under the sun's rays
Lightly touching the floor of these ancient waterways
The Cajuns tell you to listen for the spirits
Both good and mischievous as well as the evil
Take heed as they ride upon the breezes and wild winds
That is being pushed in from the Gulf
They circle amongst the hanging moss
Where serenity is hidden within the profound and sacred
I love the magical-like-waving of the dangling Spanish moss in unison
When it moves it's like a secret being whispered to one another.
Secrets whispered upon each moisture-ridden breeze
No secrets are ever given up freely or willingly in the Louisiana swamps
The moon often accents the huge thunderheads that loam overhead
Reflections of endless mazes,
Floating islands covered in roaming mists and ground fogs
Deceiving and confusing the novice adventurer
Need not to venture far into the swamps that harbor their lies and confusions of ill-doings
Since time began it is known that the great Mississippi River,
Flowed through Louisiana to the ocean
The old Cajuns and medicine men and Voodoo queens,
Created their own potions to heal, for love, and for revenge
Their magic was whispered upon the air
Conjuring the first of spirits so long ago through black magical-like
They danced within the fragrances of the sweet magnolias and cypress trees
I too ventured too far into the swamp on my own
It's so easy to get lost and confused in the waterways
My cries echoed throughout the bayous
I remained lost, never to be heard from again
My spirit often hovers atop the ageless Weeping Willows
I move in and out of the Spanish moss
Riding on the breezes or the tempests that rage from the ocean annually

I am a maypole dancer, a whispering spirit with ageless others
Throughout the moss that is forever weaving whispers in their carousel of tresses
Longing to grasp onto the brass ring of lady luck
I'll whisper softly in your ear,
The secrets contained in the lonely songs echoing throughout the swamps
I sometimes dangle in the netting of the Spanish moss
Where long ago Native Americans first created,
"Dream Catchers"
A whisper of caution
Beware not to cross the spirits,
That guard the swamplands throughout Louisiana
The old, abandoned cabins and houseboats often pepper the swamps
Danger lurks around every tree, up and down every waterway
Gators and snakes rule and the spiders say,
"Beware!"
The Spanish moss hangs heavy with many spirits clinging to it
Holding onto the mysterious songs that whisper through the Louisiana Bayous
Waving endlessly on the breezes that always whispered
Resembling wings of gossamer...

WHISPERS

There is a stillness
The comforting to the soul kind
Faint whispers slowly pass by one's ear
A gentle brushing of a fairy-like breeze
A fresh breeze from a cool babbling brook
Echoes lingering on...
A forever mist following another and another
Sweetly being heard as a soft blossoming dream
Deeply seeded in your plush garden divine
Peaceful dreams that linger on
Simply waiting to become a silver-laced memory
Placing a gentle kiss upon mirrored waters
Creating so light a ripple
Moving across the reflecting pool of eternal love
From days remembered when running was a fairyland distance
A whisper of an enchanting love calls by the Loons on the Lake-Forevermore
Carried on the winds
Across the golden pond of reality
Framed in sweet fragrances of lavender
Lilac and honeysuckle for the soul
You are a heartbeat quiet
So, to listen for a whisper, be mine
Like a craving for Heaven's Ambrosia
Or taking a breath in anticipation
Filtering a long-awaited breeze
For what it could carry in its continuous looping
Then your heart becomes a sigh
You hear the whispering of,
"I Love You!"
There is a stillness
So, comforting to the soul
Just like a whisper upon the wind...

WICKED CONSUMPTION

It is believed that birth is just the beginning of one's journey into life
I am here to tell you, for me that is
It's the beginning of self-hatred and the loathing of life itself
You are fed with the scraps that poverty has to offer
Abuse, shame, despair, and everybody's bullshit!
As you manage to survive day by day
One is consumed with apathy and anger
Your days are one continuous night,
Filled with fear, agony, anguish, guilt, and a variety of demons
It isn't long before the hunger of emptiness befriends you
Deep down inside you thirst for a glimmer of some essence of light in the dark
You are very aware that there is another world out there,
Other than this goddamn cesspool that surrounds your being
You must expect the unknown to survive
You often ask yourself, "Is it worth hoping for something better?"
"Trust", *is another word for **"Illusionist"***
"Trust", *has another definition, **"Liar"***
Trust gives the heart false security
After a while, you catch on,
Learning how not to trust anyone but yourself
No pretty face or handsome pirate will ever entrap my emotions ever again!
Learning by example and by your mistakes,
Is life's ultimate teacher
One needs to become a pro at self-mental stability
The fact is that death after death,
Washed over me like a tsunami of despair, hopelessness, and loneliness
I wasn't far from borderline madness
I felt chewed up as I watched the world fly by
Projectile vomiting in my every dream
My essence became worthless amongst the manure that surrounded my life
Hopelessness is being chained to the darkness,
With no possible way of escape or being paroled from the hell, you're in!
Wicked are the lies coveted within a circle of faceless smiles,
Concealed with hideous fangs imprinted within those that see
"Trust" *is a lifelong lesson in the destruction of one's character*
That is my invitation to study those living on dire straights
*There is no such thing as **"True Trust"***
You're just fooling yourself
Behind poverty's eyes,
You might find a wall of defense with blinking red lights,
"DISTRUST"
Fear not to wear the scarlet letter upon your person that states,

"BEWARE, I TRUST NO ONE!"

For there is only one thing to trust in life and that's

"DEATH"

My early education existed in the confines of a small farmhouse
By an uneducated teacher of brutal abuse, poverty, alcohol, and sex
It was simply a haven of

"WICKED CONSUMPTION"

Picture it, if you can
Try to wrap your mind around being metaphorically chained and consumed,
In a dark and filthy cage of pure evil
And the warden is life's Ultimate Bitch,

"MISERY!"

Window of Illusions

By the windowpane in every moonlit bay

Flying amidst the skies on the wings of chance

Out of depths within the echoes of my thoughts

The unfading vision of a man imprinted upon my soul

By the stars, there before me I see my lovely be fair

Draped in black silk, she lays inviting on white fur

A Tiffany doth shines on perfect curves above her

Mine own true love, I beg thee, toy not, this heart of mine

The passion that is defined bounded by my hunger for more

The reason that ye seek proven in this sweet dance of love

Shine forth from my eyes, with nowhere to hide

Thine lust undress my soul and bring me to paradise

If angel she be, my love is thine to cherish, I weep in joy

Goddess of love, touch thy hearts so we dance in the stars

Thy heart hath made me captured, a songbird burst forth to sing

Thou art my tender kisser in sweet paradise be what thou wilt

Whilst in a view, by the window, returned the light that glows

Time be thine! Thy Heaven is on Earth where imagination flows

Between valleys and meadows where passion flowers grow

This sweet velvet rose, to follow thy heart wherever it goes

Ask for melodies, I shalt contrive notes to melt thy heart

Raptured are we, content in each other's arms dancing free

Naked before thee, like lovers in paradise, thy utmost desire

I speak of our souls, for thou wilt lie upon the wings of night

Wilt thou reach stars because they shine on thee?

Thou shalt remain here,

reflecting...

In the windows of illusions

WINGED TAPESTRY

The sky above turned dark and filled with massive motionless clouds

*It's been spoken time after time, **"In the Autumn of Your Years"***

Beauty inside and outside truly fades becomes but days counted

A life force is given, then taken back, and this world ends in mourning

Your mind and body are whipped by the vicious winds of sorrow

Life is a quest for humanity, it's a journey short-lived in this world

No longer are we flight-free and full of fanciful whims of colorings

Shake the Winter Tree and the last of Fall will dance at your feet

The future is lost to a red sky, burnt earth, and stagnating oceans

Once this world was filled with magnificent wings of tapestries

Man constructed a congested web of dangerous sky highways

Raging of fire, hail, and brimstone was launched on Hi-way 666

There she lays, wings a fluttering their last of what was and is

A tapestry scorched, void of color, all life on Earth is vaporized

The signs of the times, screaming in our ears, a man so damn stupid

A winged tapestry so like a moth that flew too close to the flame!

Winter Dances a Macabre Vengeance
"The harshness of loving someone that could not even care"

Must I hibernate as nature dictates my sleep
Falling into a cold cavern unnoticed, unaware
Waking not, I dream deep as winter dances

Darken depths of winter's sky never seen
Frigid from raging passions of cool intents
In a world of dark grays and bitter whites

Mourning the icy glances of death renderings
Stillness in the gardens once radiant in beauty
Baren are the trees, branched in boney hands

Frosted shrouds upon the faces on the ground
Forget-Me-Knot weep in frozen winter's hell
Lie naked during blows of macabre vengeance

The snow dances a macabre wave after wave
Frozen demise, lasting long as a frozen breath
Lie naked alone in the grasp of winter's dance

Wisdom Is Her Gift

Watch closely as the ferns unfurl their fronds slowly

Twilight's veil slowly awakens nature's precious life

Sanctuaries are hidden throughout a natural solitude

Remarkable places which to feed one hungry soul

Step lightly upon an abundant carpet of spongy moss

Nature's perfect carpet, plush and rich in its comfort

Protects us from the harshness of our busy lives

An everyday cruel and battered life of struggling efforts

To be upon nature's trueness is to feel her stillness

With each step, inhale all of Mother's fragrances'

Listen to the sounds that hug and caress the senses

Feel blessed by her knowledge, her wise references

Nature's garden is full of life and cradles the dead

Mother gives birth anew, her life eternally abounds

All beginnings dictate the cycles of life and death

What once lived in beauty, no longer can be found

There are no secrets to reveal, we live, and we die

We are fed with the riches of her ever-renewing soul

Throughout our life, hopefully, we retain her knowledge

We're slated to follow our own destiny, nature's goal

Her gift is wisdom, forevermore in life to our death

Earth's riches are fueled by the decay filtered by rain

Birth is the result of the recycling of creative species

Be mindful of her precious gifts, it's wise to maintain them!

WISHFUL THINKING

Our lips pressed together within wisdom fair
Two hearts wanting and longing to be shared

Lonely eyes that embrace in tearful waterfalls
A friendship, nothing more than the hearts recall

Like a lover's whisper, a silent sigh hint at more
Tell me softly there's a chance to open the door

Our emotions are like a sudden raging waterfall
Forever am I mystified by a friendship's law

By all the powers taking one step at a time
At arms, distance friendship weaved in twine

It is hard to be realistic, tragic as it may seem
I'd rather believe in fairy tales with you in my dreams

With Every Stroke, I Paint Memories

Painted memories upon a canvas I created of my flesh and blood

Remembering brush strokes as far back as this child can fathom

To keep from crying I became a master in the art of imagination

Count the grains of sand in an hourglass, it equals tears I've shed

The world around me is painted in cuts, bruises, and absolute pain

Reality completes the background, and a raw canvas comes to life

Truth begs to be released and from the shadow's sanity seeks light

Somewhere underneath it all lingers a boy in terror of its darkness

Color my world on a canvas of skin and bone, but tell me no lies

Country children blinded in the darkness; their souls ripped apart

Blood-curdling screams were heard from behind the barn of education

Lesson one, there are no shades of gray between black and white

Do as you are told and if not, the punishment was swift and painful

At the tender age of five, I was expected to carry my weight in grain

My paintings no longer were in earth tones, but Blood Red and Evil

Slash! across the canvas, Slash! Paint Not a Lie, not a nary one!

I keep painting memories of my sister and mother, so as not to forget

A painted canvas of memories marks the dreams that never came true

In every brushstroke, the horror of "Seven Deadly Sins" peered through

Dear God, please rain, let me wash clean all sins and lies we endured

Words From a Misty-Eyed Mole

The "Misty Eyed Mole" is no other than me. It's about being young and seeing clearly for the first time in your life. It's also about having the wool pulled over your eyes. I'll call myself "Broken Wings", a "Johnny come lately" unknown. I feel like this when my eyes finally became clear. I saw the dangers below and above, to the back of me, and to the front of me.

Slowly but surely the veil was removed from my sight and everything in the world became clear. There are hidden dangers among the beautiful. Among the Peacocks of this new world. I was used by a Peacock that filled my head with promises. You develop an education really fast. One that is etched upon your soul. Either you accept the situation or escape by digging underground.

"Words From a Misty-Eyed Mole", was written when I needed to know right from wrong and both truth and lies. I believe in a Misty-Eyed Mole. The Mole feels his way when tunneling through his everyday darkness underground. All is not wondrous, but when you lift your head out of the darkness. Finally, you see the amazing things about you, your lessons are worth wiping your eyes clear and taking a chance in the light. Life is about taking chances.

Words From a Misty-Eyed Mole

Seeing is believing; for the first time, your world is as vast as your imagination. With your newly found sight, see the world as it should be and not as it is! My, my, my, Is it ever that clear? Will the fog ever be lifted? Will there be a clearing in this forest that harbors many? You will find trees of every species. You're tunneling through many detours along your way. For the forest has rooted itself everywhere, growing 24/7, roots braid themselves tightly. But some seedlings tunnel through, just like a "Misty Eyed Mole." Rest assured neither gives way to the other....

As you work, (these Eyes) will become stronger. Before long they will strengthen and the world about you becomes beautiful. But remember, all is not beautiful in this world of truths and lies. Enjoy your new sight to its fullest. Do accept the colorless, for they haven't blossomed yet. Paint a picture of your goals and desires in life. Use your imagination, and paint beyond what your mind's eye sees in front of you. You just might discover a world of imagination. Hold your head up high and let your eyes wash clean from the tears of fear, hate, loneliness, and pain. Make your eyes always see the truth. Create a collection of your life's works. The tears, memories, hard times, and every day's most quiet needs.

My thoughts are written down on pages of white. There will be happy times and many unhappy happenings. I reach deep into my feelings, such as honesty and truthfulness. May my imagination carry me through unseen adventures. Through miles and miles of empty spaces. I'll offer much, to regain some sanity of it all. I'll give just enough so as not to confuse myself. I need to be there now. When one hand greets another in knowledge, peace, love, admiration, and respect.

Please, take time to listen closely to someone's silence. A lonely, frightened person behind eyes in a world that is full of unkind misfortunes. However, there is darkness in this carnival of life. I need to regain my sanity and ride my magic carpet over the memories of all my life. Fly high above the clouds that pillar-like mountains. From above these monstrous cushions dare you to see. I land this carpet softly on a truth-and-dare platform. Even Aladdin couldn't land a carpet this soft. For there are no stars in my sight. Once again, this Misty-Eyed Mole tunnels blindly. Soft is the classic dig, adventurous is how deep one goes, and wipe the glaze that lies on top of the eyes. Filter your desire to see as much as you can. There before you are the horizon of clarity. Wipe them clean, wipe them carefully. Slowly absorb any knowledge that lies before you. They will never be completely clear. Still, you will be amazed at what works in your favor. Sight is a wondrous instrument. When your head and heart are in the clouds, remember that wind is nothing more than air in motion. Nothing seems to be real too, in "A Misty-Eyed Mole." One can only be careful in the tunnels one dig...

WORK OF ART

There before you stand an easel with a painting upon it
Look deep into the painting
Until you experience the feeling of the purest of love
It's highlighted in romantic overtones
Notice how the brushstrokes accent the contours of the canyons
Moments of sheer bliss are shaded
So, to accent every erotic zone visible to one's eye
Then I gave these two lovers a world of expressive freedom
An exploration between two creating one
The center of attention is made ware
By the rich highlighting of their sculptured lips
Notice the gentle and caring manner of the kiss
Upon beautifully formed orchid amongst a sweet flora garden
Creating an amazing array of explosive blooms,
One after another...
This one singular movement explodes throughout the canvas
I invite you to use your imagination within their throws of passion
Whether you be a painter, sculptor, writer and or poet
Bring your creation to life with the realness of your own experiences
Feel the brushstrokes come alive across the canvas
Pull back the instrument that is in your hand
Close your eyes, imagine your fingers exploring the canvas
Guide your mind's eye to areas never explored
What colors come to mind as you touch the highs and lows of your subject?
Step back from the painting, open your eyes
Imagine the world these two lovers have discovered
A world filled with new and exciting hidden colors
Something very special ensues...
Feel every emotion placed upon this canvas
Your experience in viewing this painting is now complete!
For every male and female body, I have ever painted
There is a special emotional tying,
Conceived between the artist, models, and the canvas
That magic touch explodes in a color of sensual emotions
Enabling you to read the artists,
"Work Of Art"

WRITTEN AMONGST THE STARS

Deep within the corner of darkness
Across the vast universe, time marches onward
It's the cosmic birth, born to this world
Delivered by the Gods of ancient times
Upon the last shooting star belonging to an eve anew
Its arrival surrounded by prayers of peace
For our world troubled with strife
Anticipation heightens to a fever pitch
Waiting for the countdown to be witnessed by all
Over the mountain range
Giving birth to the Seven Sisters
Seven in light and seven in darkness
Exploding into glorious flames
Bursting into the brightest of hopeful and goodwill fires
So, like that of the magnificent Phoenix
From her ashes of once before
Now reborn from a spark gone ablaze
Countdown, ten, nine, eight, seven
To the birth anew
Six, five, four, three, two, one
Is finally here!
Etched forever amongst the constellations across the universe
Father time vanishes into the abyss of what once was
Written amongst the stars
Are the resolution of man's hopes and dreams?
Weighing heavy on the shoulders
Of the baby New Year...
Written amongst the stars
He shall be named,

"Blaze"

You Are My Everything

I still remember the very first time you came into my life

That day and into the night, my world had changed forever

For the first time, I could look at the stars and see my future

Even the man in the moon invited me to challenge the stars

There were times when your voice was as loud as thunder

Thousands of Muses under your tutelage sang your praises

Nearly thirty-four years of service in the development of us

You were confusing, spell bounding, captivating and harsh

For me to stand in your sunshine was like your arms around me

When it rained on me, I had shelter from raging storms at home

Dedication, understanding, problem solver, and teacher rare

You took an underdog, gave him shelter, fed him, and praised him

I knew every time I'd turn around, you would be there to support

You and God rescued a troubled mind from an attempt at suicide

Your faith held me up, giving me the drive to strive for recognition

You taught me to trust, honesty, humanity, and the wealth of the spirit

I know you're beside me with every step I take in this crazy life

What a powerful woman you were to guide me to believe in myself

So close to not getting to know you and that would have been a sin

I need to say it for the world to hear, you were my everything!

I thank you forever for showing me that it's all right to be myself

"No matter what in the hell anyone thinks or says to you, to hell with them!"

Your words often rang loud and clear throughout my ups and downs

I became the professional actor, singer, and dancer you knew was inside.

Anna May Hughes aka Momma Drama

You will remain in my heart as Mentor, Guardian Angel, Teacher

and above all,

The only one who believed in me.

I love you Momma until we meet again on that great stage.

YOU CAPTURED MY HEART

Speak softly in my ear, for my love dost balloon
My heart is a well-crafted instrument finely tuned
Play it, sounds as smooth as the touch of fine silk
My lips, sweet as clover is to the bee, honey milk

You play my heart like the master violinist play
Music to my soul, shining bright as the sun's rays
I wrap my arms around you, whispering your name
We're swept-ed away into love's everlasting flame

Beside you, I hear your heart beating in your chest
Steadily relaxing from your love's passionate crest
You are my inspiration, filled with love in my soul
You are the one for whom together we'll grow old

You have captured my heart
This I know...

You Know Who You Are

I know who you are

Here in this world, I can see you in the far beyond

You wander from hill to mountain and to every dale

Always complete a circle from beginning to end

Quite demanding of yourself and there's no fault

It is your land, and you are steadfast and true

Your spirit is your soul, let it not be tortured

Bravery is a heart that battles the evil scorn

Memories can weaken you, filling you with regrets

I know your life was not what you dreamed it to be

mighty boulders blocked your way repeatedly

Bringing you down into the valley of no return

Within you is the spirit to battle through the dark

It shines brighter than Father Sun and Mother Moon

Ask me if I know whom you are reflecting the strength

You are Our Lady of Spirit of the Strong and Pure

Many times, your brethren dumped misery at your feet

It's important to know my friend, a stranger I am Not

The weight you carry may cause you to stumble and fall

It's faith that will be the light that shines in the dark

You must have faith not to stray now and then

You have shed many tears for those that may falter

You are like the heart of the Hummingbird

It beats fast, faster than the drums within your head

This newly found heart and soul feel a desire

It takes wing like the Phoenix on a fiery quest

It's truth and light that supports the core of you

Because deep inside you know who you are!

You Stand Before Our Eyes

You are in a garden of many, many flowers

You are like the Rose before it blooms

You stand before our eyes

Gently the Rose opens to bass in the sun

Her fragrance is sweet and beautiful, rare

You stand before our eyes

You are a sweet dream as precious as a whisper

In all your glory there is none to compare

You stand before our eyes

Beneath the Rose no thrones do you bare

Two peddles to cherish and skirt

You stand before our eyes

I shall call you a garden queen, Cassandra Rose

I color you a rich sunset fire

It's your beauty that stands before our eyes

Young And Country

A country boy living in the style of the old country way

Growing up strong and as innocent goes by the day

I'm raised by the word of God, but living in the wild

Many miles from the wicked city life, a curious child

The cock crows at the crack of dawn, my friends

I worked hard as a child of five, with no time for sins

Did my job quietly, sure all the chores were done

Sheltered, I went by lessons taught under the sun

My teen years were innocent until on a cousin's whim

On a trip to the city in a 59 Ford, the wheels did spin

He stopped at a bar, age mattered not, so enter we

Filled with dirty men, and women dancing I did see

I got my first taste of gin, hello to wicked city life

Played poker and 21, my winnings are taken at strife

Confused for my head was dancing and spinning

A Florence Nightingale took all of my winnings

I once again heard the cocks crow loud and clear

My head pounding, the work hard as hell I feared

Lord has mercy, my lesson learned a hard way

My country's way of living is all right by me, this I say!

YOU ARE MY ONE AND ONLY

Sitting here in my lounge chair resting after a day's work
Reading the local newspaper from beginning to end
I pull the newspaper down enough to look over the edge
I watch you in heavy thought, pen in hand, foot tapping

In two weeks, we celebrate sixteen wonderful years together
You're the only one who holds the key to my heart and soul
My best friend, my confidante, truly my one and only one
How do I put into words what he has meant from the beginning?

How your mind must be walking through a world of dreams
You raise your pen and eagerly put it on the parchment
Somewhere between a thought, an idea, or from your memory
You write your words on your page of loving proses

The beautiful memories we have made together over the years
So intense, yet the sweetest of ways that he reads his evening paper
All the while he secretly watches me as I do my work
I can feel his stare with those handsome blue eyes loving me

Folding my paper gingerly, I place it down on my side
I sink into my lounger and study your every move
I wonder why I'm so blessed in this life that we share
That our Heavenly Father would bless me with such riches as you

Dear God, I thank you so much for blessing me
With a man whose every action excites and stimulates my senses
It's amazing how lovingly and completely he captivates me
How he is the catalyst for every beat of my heart

It has been fourteen years since you and I first said hello
We were standing in line to buy tickets at a local carnival
We ended up having to share a seat on the tallest of Ferris-wheels
Such a night of poetic freedom between us, starting a fire that still glows

Just think, if I had not decided to go to that carnival, that night
I would have never received the gift of my truest love
That day will still stay embedded in my heart forevermore
Each day I wake up next to him, I thank the Lord for all his good gifts

I sit here in the home that you and I created in repose
Just the sight of you makes my heart dance to the song of love
My heart is full of love and devotion for you still
*Still, as the song goes, **"You take my breath away!"***

> *You, my love, have been the twine that bounds our needs*
> *Our hopes, dreams, happiness, and passion are all together in one*
> *Pure and honest is your love that has endured over the years*
> *Your passion leaves me breathless, yet wanting more of the same*

Sixteen years later, I still find you a rare and a precious gem
Physically beautiful, but it's the beauty contained within you that's stunning
You are an incredible human being with a beautiful and generous heart
With joy, I have often wondered why you love me so much.

> *You are handsome beyond all measures of beauty and light*
> *But the true essence of your beauty lies in the depth of your heart*
> *You continually love me past all flaws and any imperfections*
> *In my eyes, you can clearly see your reflection in my soul*

Where would I be if a laugh wouldn't bring us together?
What manner of man would I be without the warmth of your light?
Sixteen years together, you gave yourself willingly and free
I'd be lost, alone and I would have missed love's message

> *Just when I thought we had reached the highest of all plateaus*
> *You encouraged this heart to reach for the stars and beyond*
> *God blessed our union with love, trust, and a canvas painted of memories*
> *The blending of our two worlds created this future we now endure*

Like a candle, I want you to always light my way in the dark
If I was a river, I'd run into your ocean with my arms opened wide
What I'd do for you, I wouldn't think twice, I have no shame
After sixteen years you still take my breath away, and I sigh...

> *You are my stars at midnight, my sunlight through the dark*
> *You are my strength when I am weak, my spirit guide keeping me on course*
> *You are the other half of my soul and the beating of my heart*
> *It's the summer of our lives, for you are my one and only one!*

ODE TO ROCKY
A Chow-Chow, my first pet, and first friend

The years have been kind to us my friend
Yesteryear is remembered with love
Cute, soft, and cuddly kin
Hours of laughter and running wild
Free as the wind, days swirling by
You were there when the pain was about
Laying in my arms, I hug you tight
You're my friend, there is no doubt
Through the growing years, nothing could part us
We were tight, the closes of friends
Years have gone by, and buddies we remain
Here you lay with loving eyes
My heart is full, I see your pain
Remember one thing, we will be side-by-side
Close your eyes my dearest friend
Run as free as the wind does blow
I am forever at your side
You will always be my friend
Even when I die.

www.ingramcontent.com/pod-product-compliance
Lightning Source LLC
Chambersburg PA
CBHW080943120626
46546CB00010B/2820